MARVEL TWO-IN-ONE #60
WRITER: MARK GRUENWALD & RALPH MACCHIO
PENCILER: GEORGE PÉREZ
INKER: GENE DAY
COLORIST: ROGER SLIFER
LETTERER: JOHN COSTANZA
EDITOR: ROGER STERN
COVER ARTISTS: BOB BUDIANSKY & JOE RUBINSTEIN

FANASTIC FOUR ANNUAL #14
PLOTTERS: MARV WOLFMAN & GEORGE PÉREZ
SCRIPTER: MARV WOLFMAN
PENCILER: GEORGE PÉREZ
INKER: PABLO MARCOS
COLORIST: CARL GAFFORD
LETTERER: JIM NOVAK
EDITOR: MARV WOLFMAN
COVER ARTIST: JOE SINNOTT

"A GALLERY OF THE FANTASTIC FOUR'S MOST FAMOUS FOES!"
WRITER: PETER GILLIS
PENCILER: KEITH POLLARD
INKER: PABLO MARCOS

FANASTIC FOUR ANNUAL #15
WRITER: DOUG MOENCH
PENCILER: GEORGE PÉREZ
INKERS: CHIC STONE, JOHN D'AGOSTINO & MIKE ESPOSITO
COLORISTS: BEN SEAN & GEORGE ROUSSOS
LETTERER: JIM NOVAK
EDITOR: JIM SALICRUP
COVER ARTISTS: GEORGE PÉREZ & JOE SINNOTT

"THE POWER OF THE PEOPLE!"
WRITER: DOUG MOENCH
ARTIST: TOM SUTTON
COLORISTS: BEN SEAN
LETTERER: JIM NOVAK
EDITOR: JIM SALICRUP

ADVENTURES OF THE THING #3
WRITER: TONY MATIAS
ARTIST: GEORGE PÉREZ
COLORIST: FRED MENDEZ
LETTERER: DAVE THE BARBARIAN
EDITOR: HILDY MESNIK
ART RECONSTRUCTION: DALE CRAIN

COVER ART:
GEORGE PÉREZ

COLOR RECONSTRUCTION:
JERRON QUALITY COLOR & TOM SMITH

SENIOR EDITOR, SPECIAL PROJECTS:
JEFF YOUNGQUIST
ASSOCIATE EDITORS:
JENNIFER GRÜNWALD & MARK D. BEAZLEY
ASSISTANT EDITOR:
MICHAEL SHORT
VICE PRESIDENT OF SALES:
DAVID GABRIEL
PRODUCTION:
JERRON QUALITY COLOR
VICE PRESIDENT OF CREATIVE:
TOM MARVELLI
SPECIAL THANKS TO
TOM BREVOORT & RAY PELOSI

EDITOR IN CHIEF:
JOE QUESADA
PUBLISHER:
DAN BUCKLEY

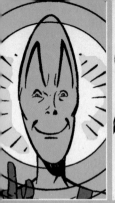

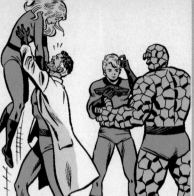

Fantastic Four

VISIONARIES: GEORGE PÉREZ VOL. 2

FANASTIC FOUR #187
WRITER: LEN WEIN
PENCILER: GEORGE PÉREZ
INKER: JOE SINNOTT
COLORIST: GLYNIS WEIN
LETTERER: JOE ROSEN
EDITOR: LEN WEIN
COVER ARTISTS: GEORGE PÉREZ & DAVE COCKRUM

FANASTIC FOUR #188
WRITER: LEN WEIN
PENCILER: GEORGE PÉREZ
INKER: JOE SINNOTT
COLORIST: GLYNIS WEIN
LETTERER: JOE ROSEN
EDITOR: LEN WEIN
COVER ARTISTS: GEORGE PÉREZ & JOE SINNOTT

FANASTIC FOUR #191
WRITER: LEN WEIN
PENCILER: GEORGE PÉREZ
INKER: JOE SINNOTT
COLORIST: GLYNIS WEIN
LETTERER: JOHN COSTANZA
EDITOR: LEN WEIN
COVER ARTISTS: GEORGE PÉREZ & JOE SINNOTT

FANASTIC FOUR #192
PLOTTER: LEN WEIN
SCRIPTER: ROGER SLIFER
PENCILER: GEORGE PÉREZ
INKER: JOE SINNOTT
COLORIST: GLYNIS WEIN
LETTERER: JOE ROSEN
EDITOR: MARV WOLFMAN
COVER ARTISTS: GEORGE PÉREZ & FRANK GIACOIA

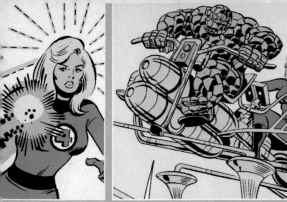

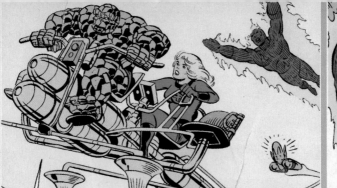

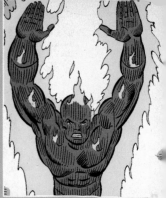

Fantastic Four

VISIONARIES:
GEORGE PÉREZ
VOL. 2

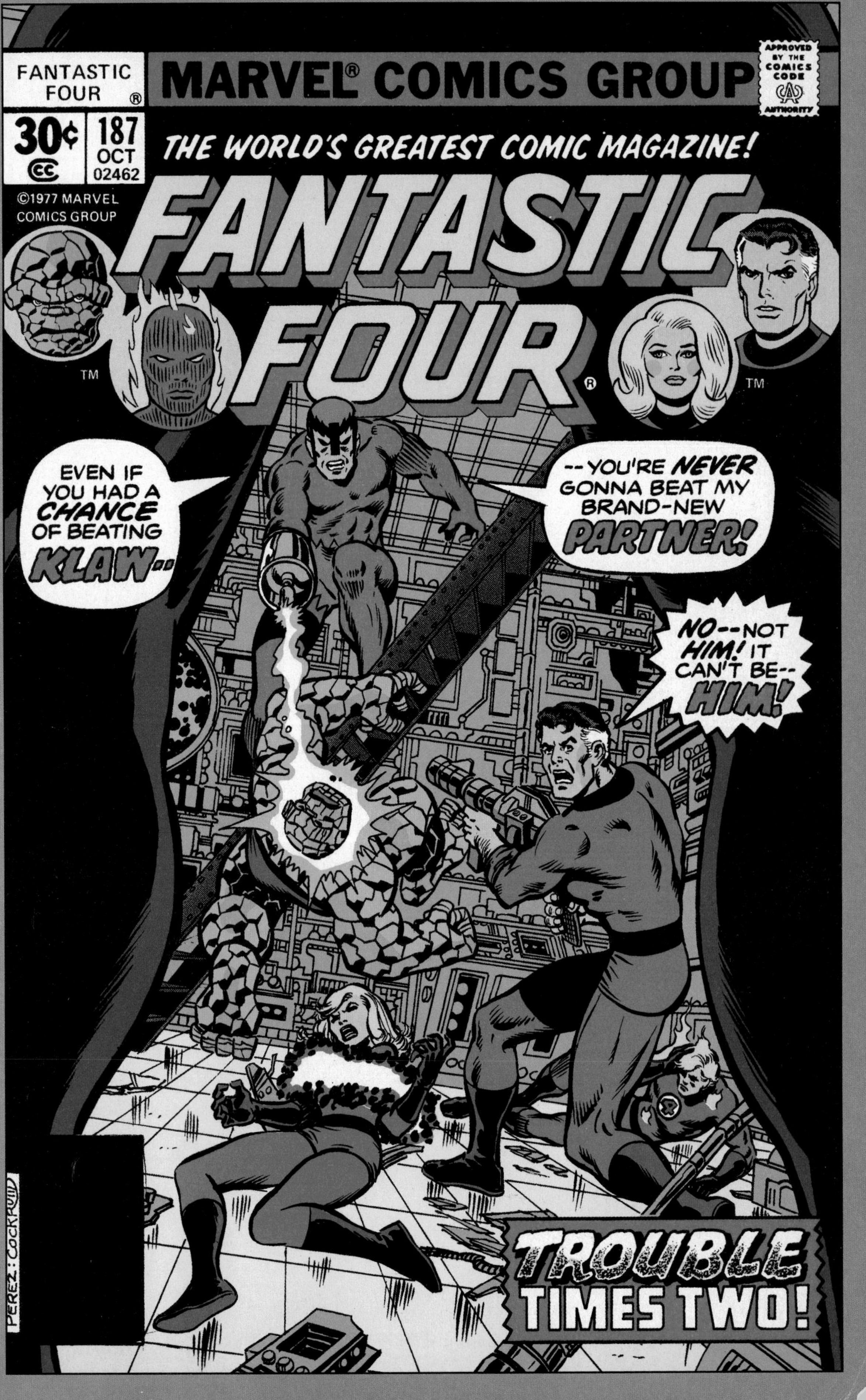

FANTASTIC FOUR ®
MARVEL® COMICS GROUP
APPROVED BY THE COMICS CODE AUTHORITY
30¢
187 OCT 02462
THE WORLD'S GREATEST COMIC MAGAZINE!
©1977 MARVEL COMICS GROUP
FANTASTIC FOUR®
TM
TM
EVEN IF YOU HAD A CHANCE OF BEATING KLAW--
--YOU'RE NEVER GONNA BEAT MY BRAND-NEW PARTNER!
NO--NOT HIM! IT CAN'T BE--HIM!
TROUBLE TIMES TWO!
PEREZ : COCKRUM

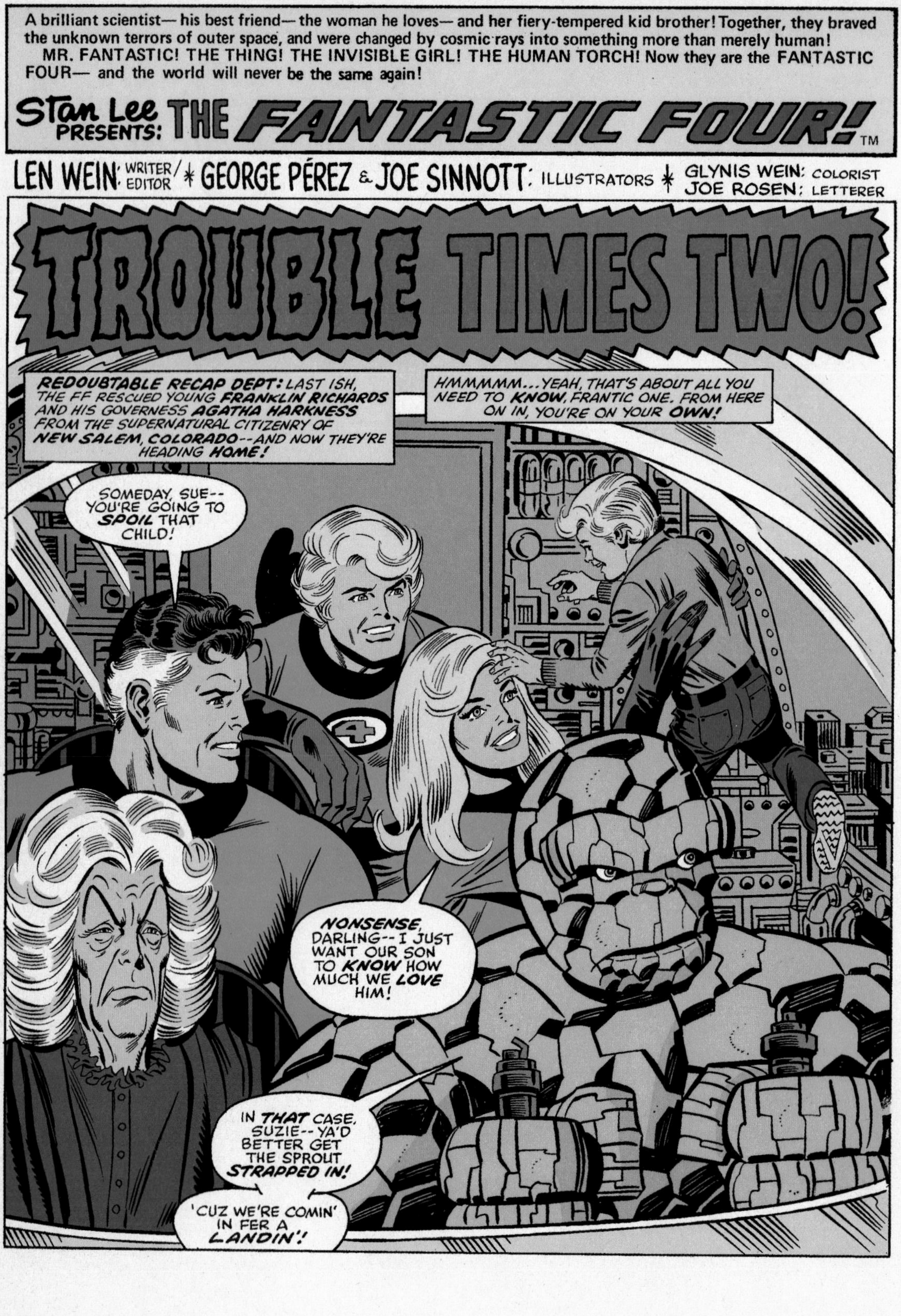
A brilliant scientist— his best friend— the woman he loves— and her fiery-tempered kid brother! Together, they braved the unknown terrors of outer space, and were changed by cosmic rays into something more than merely human!
MR. FANTASTIC! THE THING! THE INVISIBLE GIRL! THE HUMAN TORCH! Now they are the FANTASTIC FOUR— and the world will never be the same again!
Stan Lee PRESENTS: THE FANTASTIC FOUR! TM
LEN WEIN: WRITER/EDITOR * GEORGE PÉREZ & JOE SINNOTT: ILLUSTRATORS * GLYNIS WEIN: COLORIST JOE ROSEN: LETTERER
TROUBLE TIMES TWO!
REDOUBTABLE RECAP DEPT: LAST ISH, THE FF RESCUED YOUNG FRANKLIN RICHARDS AND HIS GOVERNESS AGATHA HARKNESS FROM THE SUPERNATURAL CITIZENRY OF NEW SALEM, COLORADO--AND NOW THEY'RE HEADING HOME!
HMMMMM...YEAH, THAT'S ABOUT ALL YOU NEED TO KNOW, FRANTIC ONE. FROM HERE ON IN, YOU'RE ON YOUR OWN!
SOMEDAY, SUE--YOU'RE GOING TO SPOIL THAT CHILD!
NONSENSE, DARLING-- I JUST WANT OUR SON TO KNOW HOW MUCH WE LOVE HIM!
IN THAT CASE, SUZIE-- YA'D BETTER GET THE SPROUT STRAPPED IN!
'CUZ WE'RE COMIN' IN FER A LANDIN'!

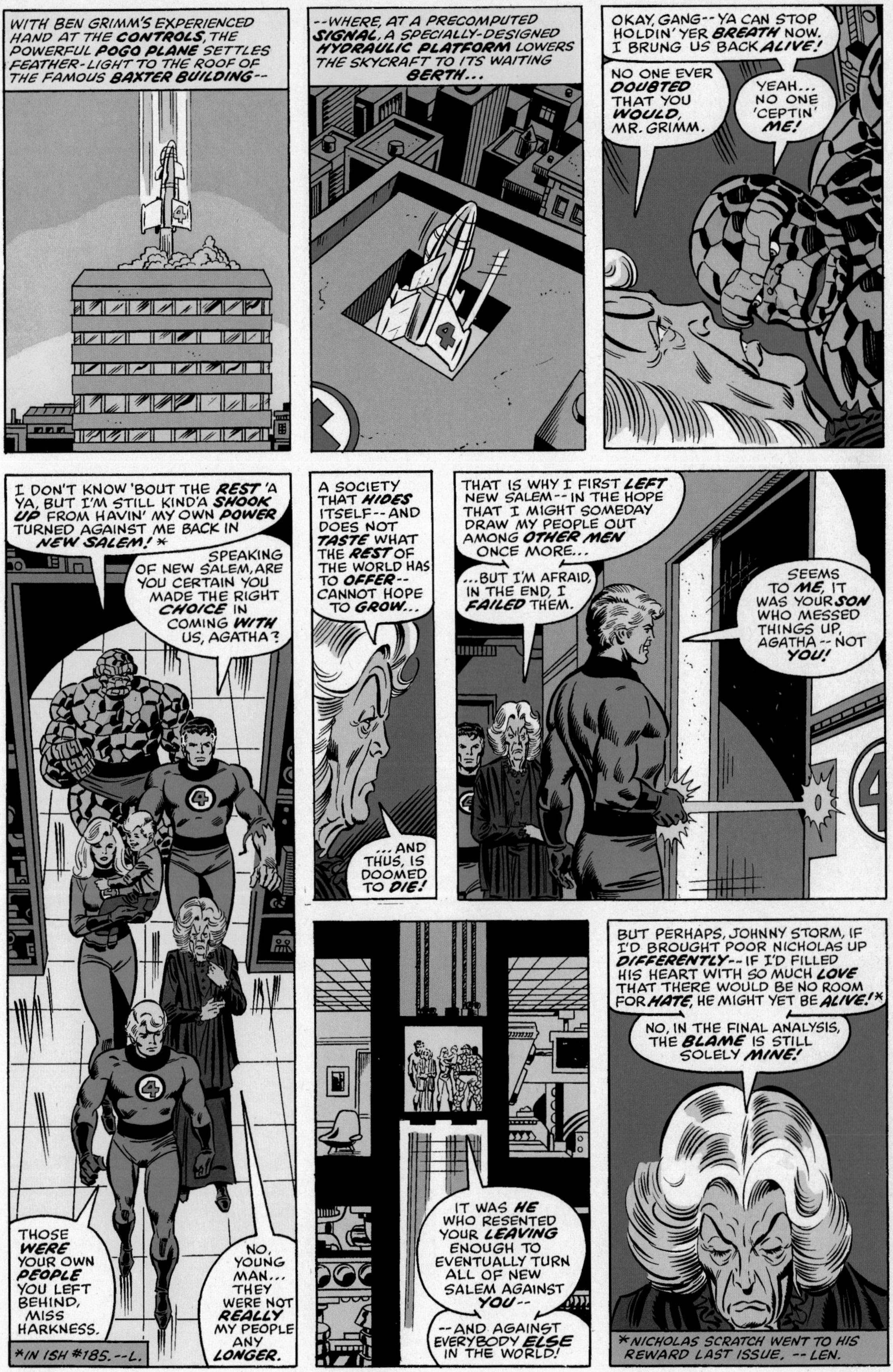

WITH BEN GRIMM'S EXPERIENCED HAND AT THE CONTROLS, THE POWERFUL POGO PLANE SETTLES FEATHER-LIGHT TO THE ROOF OF THE FAMOUS BAXTER BUILDING--
--WHERE, AT A PRECOMPUTED SIGNAL, A SPECIALLY-DESIGNED HYDRAULIC PLATFORM LOWERS THE SKYCRAFT TO ITS WAITING BERTH...
OKAY, GANG-- YA CAN STOP HOLDIN' YER BREATH NOW. I BRUNG US BACK ALIVE!
NO ONE EVER DOUBTED THAT YOU WOULD, MR. GRIMM.
YEAH... NO ONE 'CEPTIN' ME!
I DON'T KNOW 'BOUT THE REST 'A YA, BUT I'M STILL KIND'A SHOOK UP FROM HAVIN' MY OWN POWER TURNED AGAINST ME BACK IN NEW SALEM! *
SPEAKING OF NEW SALEM, ARE YOU CERTAIN YOU MADE THE RIGHT CHOICE IN COMING WITH US, AGATHA?
THOSE WERE YOUR OWN PEOPLE YOU LEFT BEHIND, MISS HARKNESS.
NO, YOUNG MAN... THEY WERE NOT REALLY MY PEOPLE ANY LONGER.
*IN ISH #185.--L.
A SOCIETY THAT HIDES ITSELF--AND DOES NOT TASTE WHAT THE REST OF THE WORLD HAS TO OFFER--CANNOT HOPE TO GROW...
...AND THUS, IS DOOMED TO DIE!
THAT IS WHY I FIRST LEFT NEW SALEM--IN THE HOPE THAT I MIGHT SOMEDAY DRAW MY PEOPLE OUT AMONG OTHER MEN ONCE MORE...
...BUT I'M AFRAID, IN THE END, I FAILED THEM.
SEEMS TO ME, IT WAS YOUR SON WHO MESSED THINGS UP, AGATHA--NOT YOU!
IT WAS HE WHO RESENTED YOUR LEAVING ENOUGH TO EVENTUALLY TURN ALL OF NEW SALEM AGAINST YOU--
--AND AGAINST EVERYBODY ELSE IN THE WORLD!
BUT PERHAPS, JOHNNY STORM, IF I'D BROUGHT POOR NICHOLAS UP DIFFERENTLY--IF I'D FILLED HIS HEART WITH SO MUCH LOVE THAT THERE WOULD BE NO ROOM FOR HATE, HE MIGHT YET BE ALIVE!*
NO, IN THE FINAL ANALYSIS, THE BLAME IS STILL SOLELY MINE!
*NICHOLAS SCRATCH WENT TO HIS REWARD LAST ISSUE. --LEN.

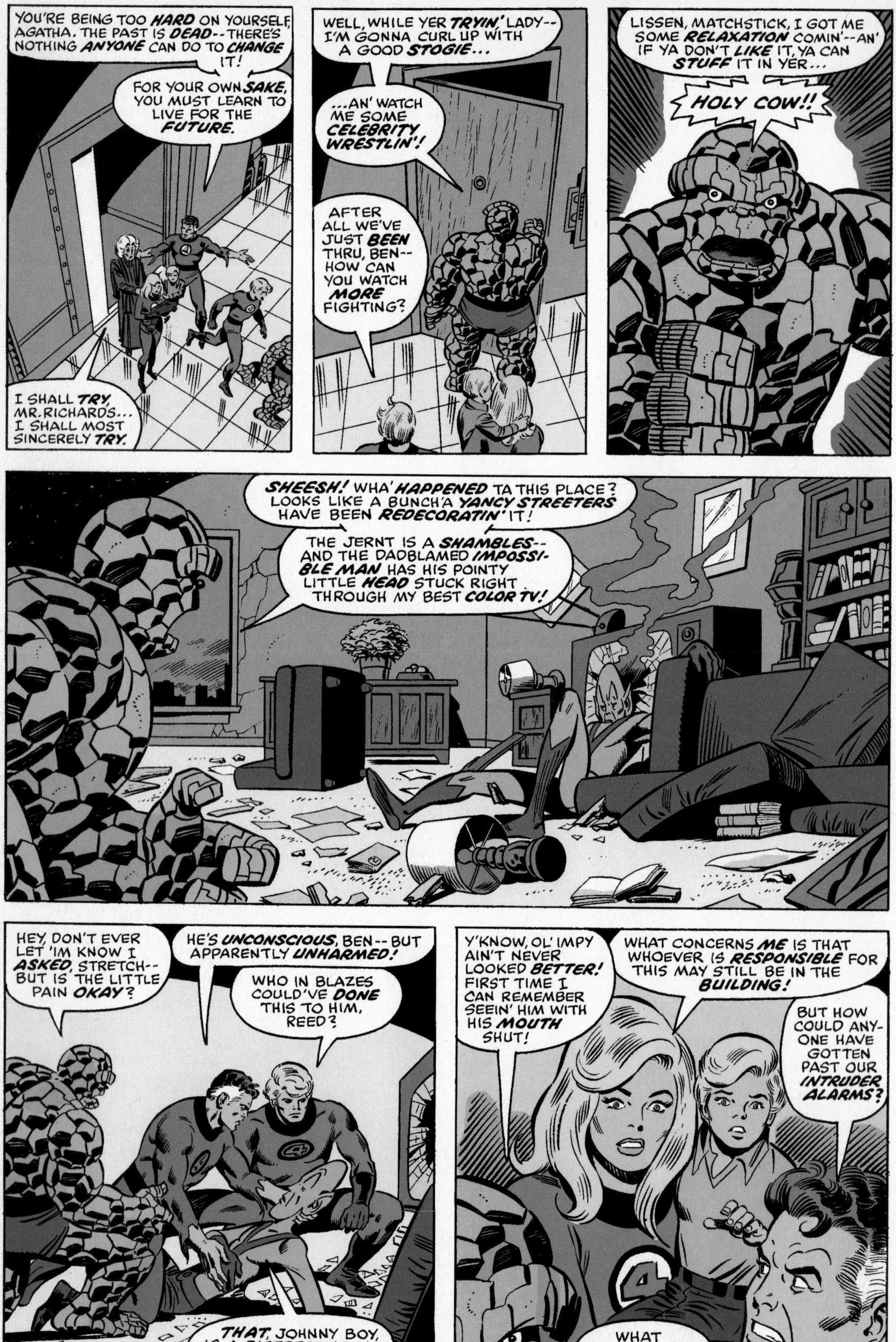
YOU'RE BEING TOO HARD ON YOURSELF, AGATHA. THE PAST IS DEAD-- THERE'S NOTHING ANYONE CAN DO TO CHANGE IT!
FOR YOUR OWN SAKE, YOU MUST LEARN TO LIVE FOR THE FUTURE.
I SHALL TRY, MR. RICHARDS... I SHALL MOST SINCERELY TRY.
WELL, WHILE YER TRYIN,' LADY-- I'M GONNA CURL UP WITH A GOOD STOGIE...
...AN' WATCH ME SOME CELEBRITY WRESTLIN'!
AFTER ALL WE'VE JUST BEEN THRU, BEN-- HOW CAN YOU WATCH MORE FIGHTING?
LISSEN, MATCHSTICK, I GOT ME SOME RELAXATION COMIN'--AN' IF YA DON'T LIKE IT, YA CAN STUFF IT IN YER...
HOLY COW!!
SHEESH! WHA' HAPPENED TA THIS PLACE? LOOKS LIKE A BUNCH'A YANCY STREETERS HAVE BEEN REDECORATIN' IT!
THE JERNT IS A SHAMBLES-- AND THE DADBLAMED IMPOSSI-BLE MAN HAS HIS POINTY LITTLE HEAD STUCK RIGHT THROUGH MY BEST COLOR TV!
HEY, DON'T EVER LET 'IM KNOW I ASKED, STRETCH-- BUT IS THE LITTLE PAIN OKAY?
HE'S UNCONSCIOUS, BEN-- BUT APPARENTLY UNHARMED!
WHO IN BLAZES COULD'VE DONE THIS TO HIM, REED?
THAT, JOHNNY BOY, IS A DISTRESSINGLY GOOD QUESTION!
Y'KNOW, OL' IMPY AIN'T NEVER LOOKED BETTER! FIRST TIME I CAN REMEMBER SEEIN' HIM WITH HIS MOUTH SHUT!
WHAT CONCERNS ME IS THAT WHOEVER IS RESPONSIBLE FOR THIS MAY STILL BE IN THE BUILDING!
BUT HOW COULD ANY-ONE HAVE GOTTEN PAST OUR INTRUDER ALARMS?
WHAT COULD THEY BE AFTER?

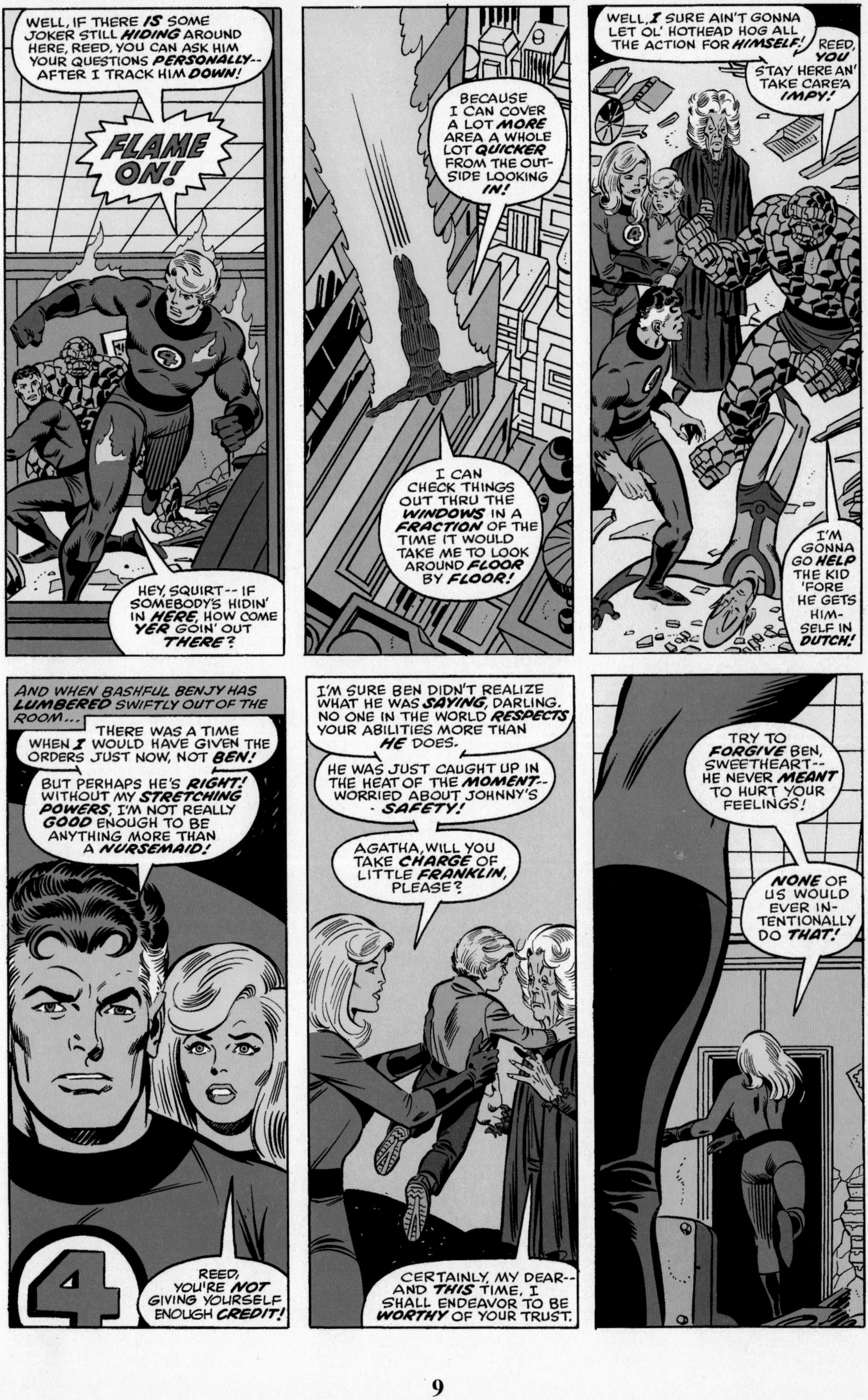
WELL, IF THERE IS SOME JOKER STILL HIDING AROUND HERE, REED, YOU CAN ASK HIM YOUR QUESTIONS PERSONALLY-- AFTER I TRACK HIM DOWN!
FLAME ON!
HEY, SQUIRT-- IF SOMEBODY'S HIDIN' IN HERE, HOW COME YER GOIN' OUT THERE?
BECAUSE I CAN COVER A LOT MORE AREA A WHOLE LOT QUICKER FROM THE OUT-SIDE LOOKING IN!
I CAN CHECK THINGS OUT THRU THE WINDOWS IN A FRACTION OF THE TIME IT WOULD TAKE ME TO LOOK AROUND FLOOR BY FLOOR!
WELL, I SURE AIN'T GONNA LET OL' HOTHEAD HOG ALL THE ACTION FOR HIMSELF!
REED, YOU STAY HERE AN' TAKE CARE'A IMPY!
I'M GONNA GO HELP THE KID 'FORE HE GETS HIM-SELF IN DUTCH!
AND WHEN BASHFUL BENJY HAS LUMBERED SWIFTLY OUT OF THE ROOM...
THERE WAS A TIME WHEN I WOULD HAVE GIVEN THE ORDERS JUST NOW, NOT BEN!
BUT PERHAPS HE'S RIGHT! WITHOUT MY STRETCHING POWERS, I'M NOT REALLY GOOD ENOUGH TO BE ANYTHING MORE THAN A NURSEMAID!
REED, YOU'RE NOT GIVING YOURSELF ENOUGH CREDIT!
I'M SURE BEN DIDN'T REALIZE WHAT HE WAS SAYING, DARLING. NO ONE IN THE WORLD RESPECTS YOUR ABILITIES MORE THAN HE DOES.
HE WAS JUST CAUGHT UP IN THE HEAT OF THE MOMENT-- WORRIED ABOUT JOHNNY'S SAFETY!
AGATHA, WILL YOU TAKE CHARGE OF LITTLE FRANKLIN, PLEASE?
CERTAINLY, MY DEAR-- AND THIS TIME, I SHALL ENDEAVOR TO BE WORTHY OF YOUR TRUST.
TRY TO FORGIVE BEN, SWEETHEART-- HE NEVER MEANT TO HURT YOUR FEELINGS!
NONE OF US WOULD EVER IN-TENTIONALLY DO THAT!

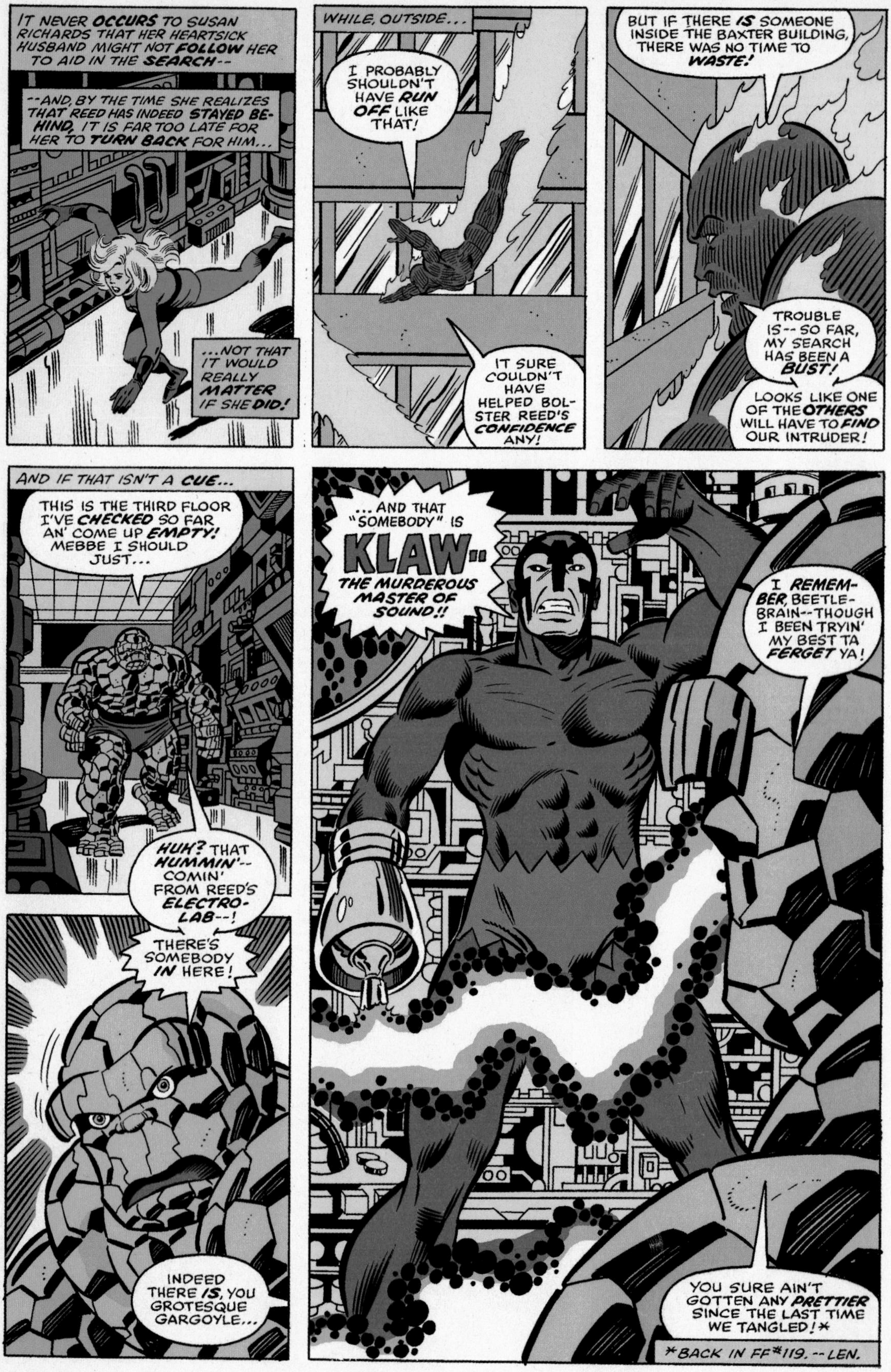
IT NEVER OCCURS TO SUSAN RICHARDS THAT HER HEARTSICK HUSBAND MIGHT NOT FOLLOW HER TO AID IN THE SEARCH--
--AND, BY THE TIME SHE REALIZES THAT REED HAS INDEED STAYED BEHIND, IT IS FAR TOO LATE FOR HER TO TURN BACK FOR HIM...
...NOT THAT IT WOULD REALLY MATTER IF SHE DID!
WHILE, OUTSIDE...
I PROBABLY SHOULDN'T HAVE RUN OFF LIKE THAT!
IT SURE COULDN'T HAVE HELPED BOLSTER REED'S CONFIDENCE ANY!
BUT IF THERE IS SOMEONE INSIDE THE BAXTER BUILDING, THERE WAS NO TIME TO WASTE!
TROUBLE IS-- SO FAR, MY SEARCH HAS BEEN A BUST!
LOOKS LIKE ONE OF THE OTHERS WILL HAVE TO FIND OUR INTRUDER!
AND IF THAT ISN'T A CUE...
THIS IS THE THIRD FLOOR I'VE CHECKED SO FAR AN' COME UP EMPTY! MEBBE I SHOULD JUST...
HUH? THAT HUMMIN'-- COMIN' FROM REED'S ELECTRO-LAB--!
THERE'S SOMEBODY IN HERE!
INDEED THERE IS, YOU GROTESQUE GARGOYLE...
...AND THAT "SOMEBODY" IS KLAW-- THE MURDEROUS MASTER OF SOUND!!
I REMEMBER, BEETLE-BRAIN--THOUGH I BEEN TRYIN' MY BEST TA FERGET YA!
YOU SURE AIN'T GOTTEN ANY PRETTIER SINCE THE LAST TIME WE TANGLED!*
*BACK IN FF#119. --LEN.

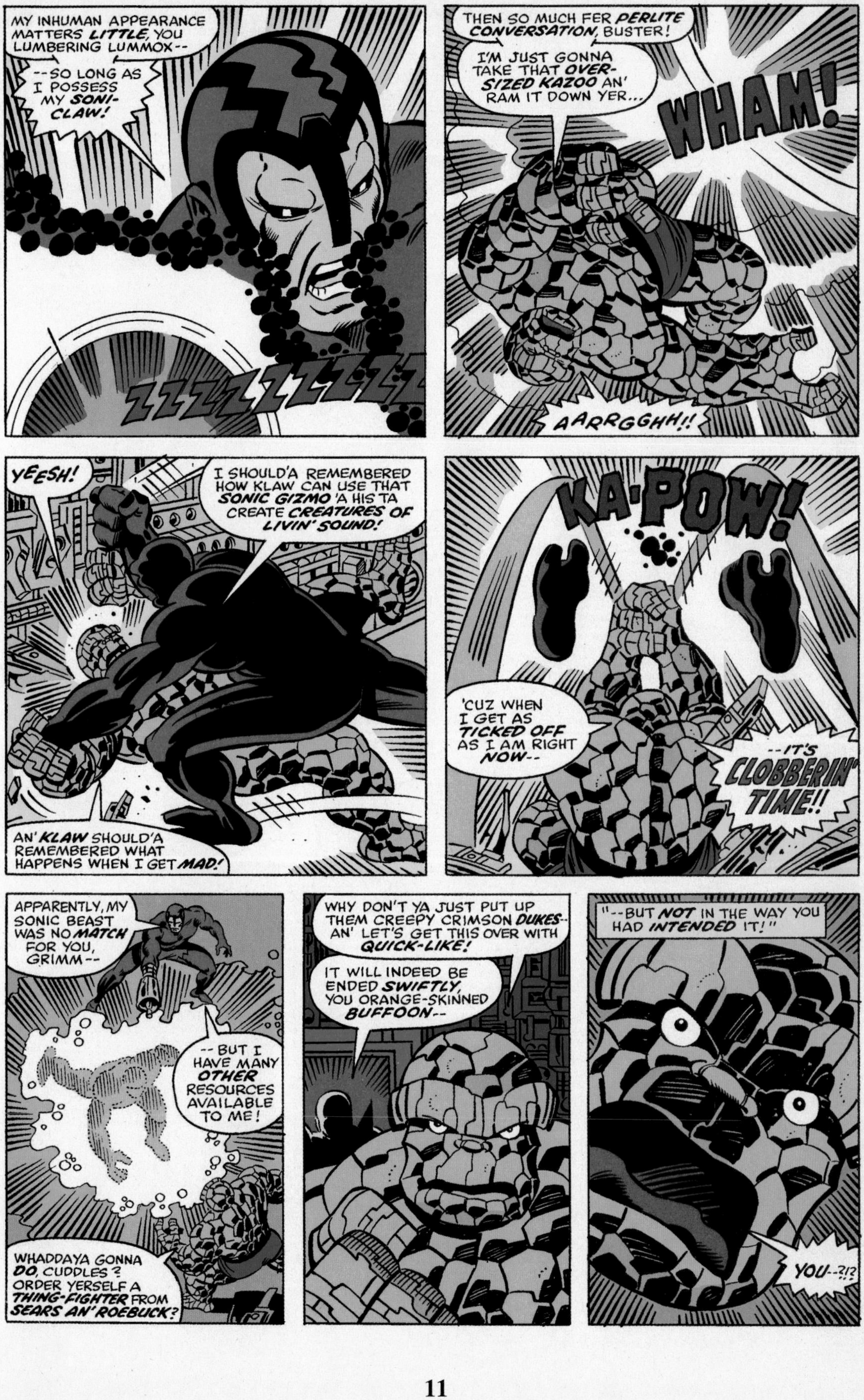
MY INHUMAN APPEARANCE MATTERS LITTLE, YOU LUMBERING LUMMOX--
--SO LONG AS I POSSESS MY SONI-CLAW!
ZZZZZZZZZ
THEN SO MUCH FER PERLITE CONVERSATION, BUSTER!
I'M JUST GONNA TAKE THAT OVER-SIZED KAZOO AN' RAM IT DOWN YER...
WHAM!
AARRGGHH!!
YEESH!
I SHOULD'A REMEMBERED HOW KLAW CAN USE THAT SONIC GIZMO 'A HIS TA CREATE CREATURES OF LIVIN' SOUND!
AN' KLAW SHOULD'A REMEMBERED WHAT HAPPENS WHEN I GET MAD!
KA-POW!
'CUZ WHEN I GET AS TICKED OFF AS I AM RIGHT NOW--
--IT'S CLOBBERIN' TIME!!
APPARENTLY, MY SONIC BEAST WAS NO MATCH FOR YOU, GRIMM--
--BUT I HAVE MANY OTHER RESOURCES AVAILABLE TO ME!
WHADDAYA GONNA DO, CUDDLES? ORDER YERSELF A THING-FIGHTER FROM SEARS AN' ROEBUCK?
WHY DON'T YA JUST PUT UP THEM CREEPY CRIMSON DUKES-- AN' LET'S GET THIS OVER WITH QUICK-LIKE!
IT WILL INDEED BE ENDED SWIFTLY, YOU ORANGE-SKINNED BUFFOON--
"--BUT NOT IN THE WAY YOU HAD INTENDED IT!"
YOU--?!?

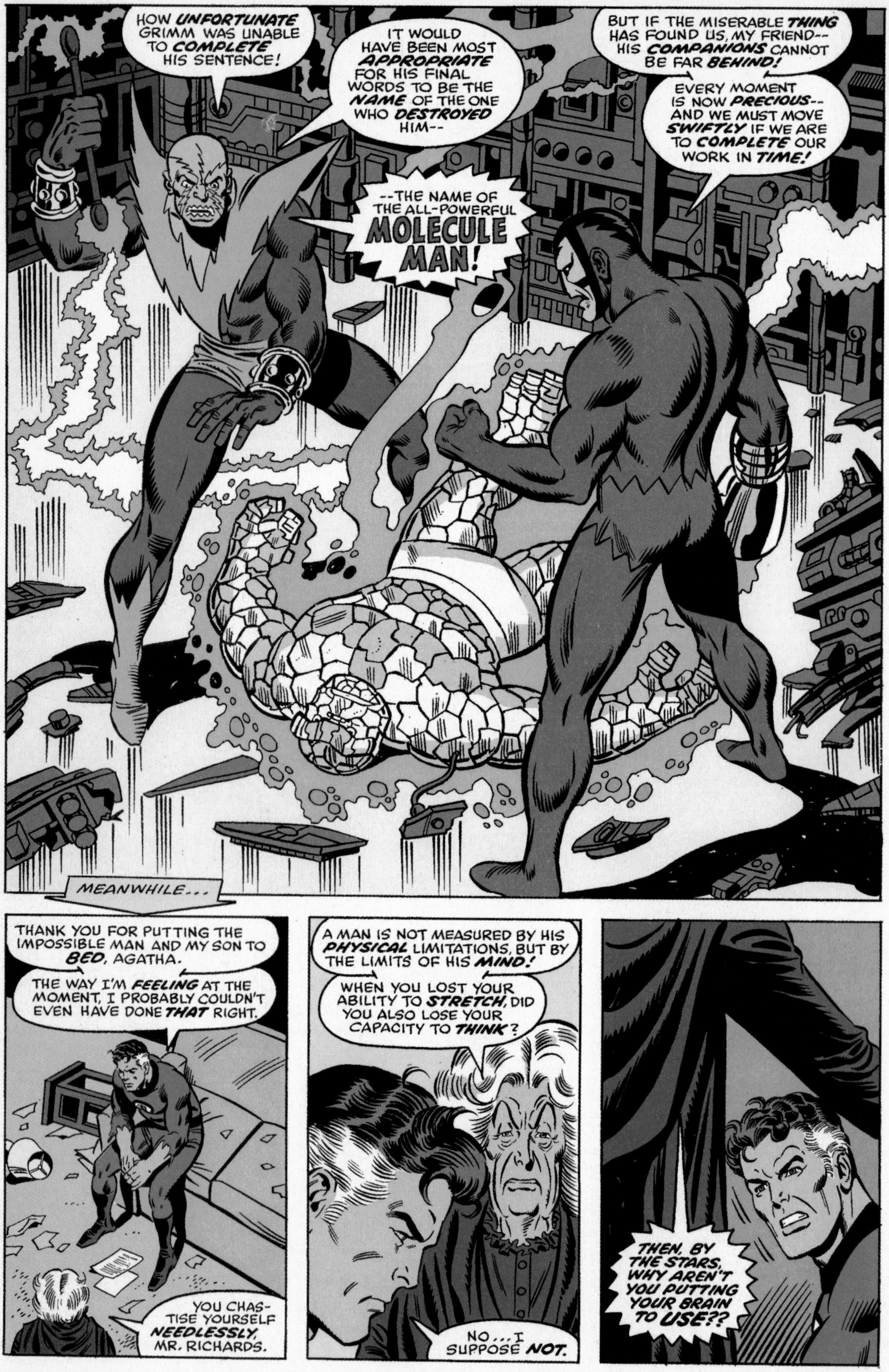
HOW UNFORTUNATE GRIMM WAS UNABLE TO COMPLETE HIS SENTENCE!
IT WOULD HAVE BEEN MOST APPROPRIATE FOR HIS FINAL WORDS TO BE THE NAME OF THE ONE WHO DESTROYED HIM--
--THE NAME OF THE ALL-POWERFUL MOLECULE MAN!
BUT IF THE MISERABLE THING HAS FOUND US, MY FRIEND-- HIS COMPANIONS CANNOT BE FAR BEHIND!
EVERY MOMENT IS NOW PRECIOUS-- AND WE MUST MOVE SWIFTLY IF WE ARE TO COMPLETE OUR WORK IN TIME!
MEANWHILE...
THANK YOU FOR PUTTING THE IMPOSSIBLE MAN AND MY SON TO BED, AGATHA.
THE WAY I'M FEELING AT THE MOMENT, I PROBABLY COULDN'T EVEN HAVE DONE THAT RIGHT.
YOU CHASTISE YOURSELF NEEDLESSLY, MR. RICHARDS.
A MAN IS NOT MEASURED BY HIS PHYSICAL LIMITATIONS, BUT BY THE LIMITS OF HIS MIND!
WHEN YOU LOST YOUR ABILITY TO STRETCH, DID YOU ALSO LOSE YOUR CAPACITY TO THINK?
NO... I SUPPOSE NOT.
THEN, BY THE STARS, WHY AREN'T YOU PUTTING YOUR BRAIN TO USE??

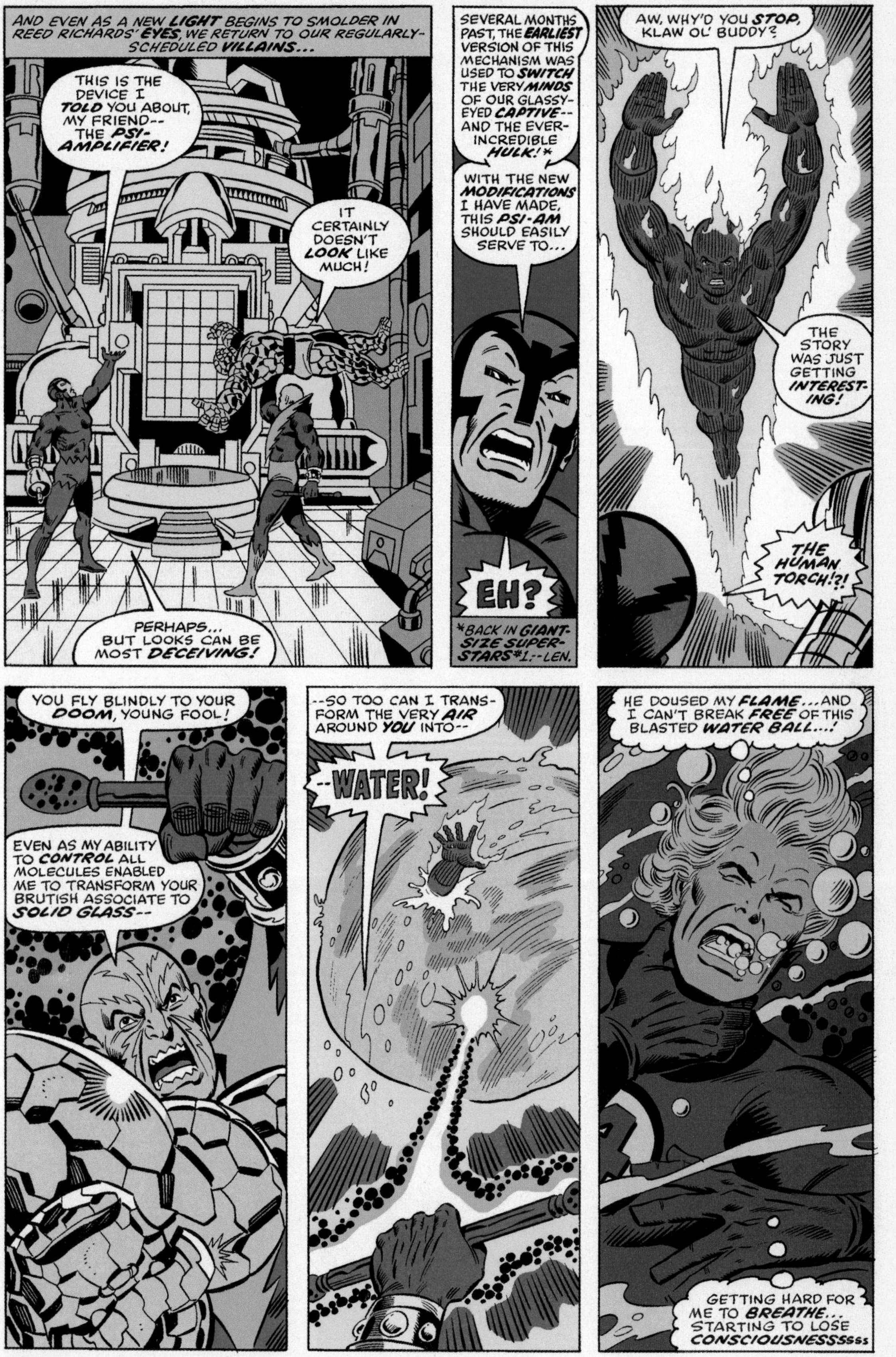
AND EVEN AS A NEW LIGHT BEGINS TO SMOLDER IN REED RICHARDS' EYES, WE RETURN TO OUR REGULARLY-SCHEDULED VILLAINS...
THIS IS THE DEVICE I TOLD YOU ABOUT, MY FRIEND-- THE PSI-AMPLIFIER!
IT CERTAINLY DOESN'T LOOK LIKE MUCH!
PERHAPS... BUT LOOKS CAN BE MOST DECEIVING!
SEVERAL MONTHS PAST, THE EARLIEST VERSION OF THIS MECHANISM WAS USED TO SWITCH THE VERY MINDS OF OUR GLASSY-EYED CAPTIVE--AND THE EVER-INCREDIBLE HULK!*
WITH THE NEW MODIFICATIONS I HAVE MADE, THIS PSI-AM SHOULD EASILY SERVE TO...
EH?
*BACK IN GIANT-SIZE SUPER-STARS #1.--LEN.
AW, WHY'D YOU STOP, KLAW OL' BUDDY?
THE STORY WAS JUST GETTING INTERESTING!
THE HUMAN TORCH!?!
YOU FLY BLINDLY TO YOUR DOOM, YOUNG FOOL!
EVEN AS MY ABILITY TO CONTROL ALL MOLECULES ENABLED ME TO TRANSFORM YOUR BRUTISH ASSOCIATE TO SOLID GLASS--
--SO TOO CAN I TRANSFORM THE VERY AIR AROUND YOU INTO--
--WATER!
HE DOUSED MY FLAME...AND I CAN'T BREAK FREE OF THIS BLASTED WATER BALL...!
GETTING HARD FOR ME TO BREATHE... STARTING TO LOSE CONSCIOUSNESSSsss

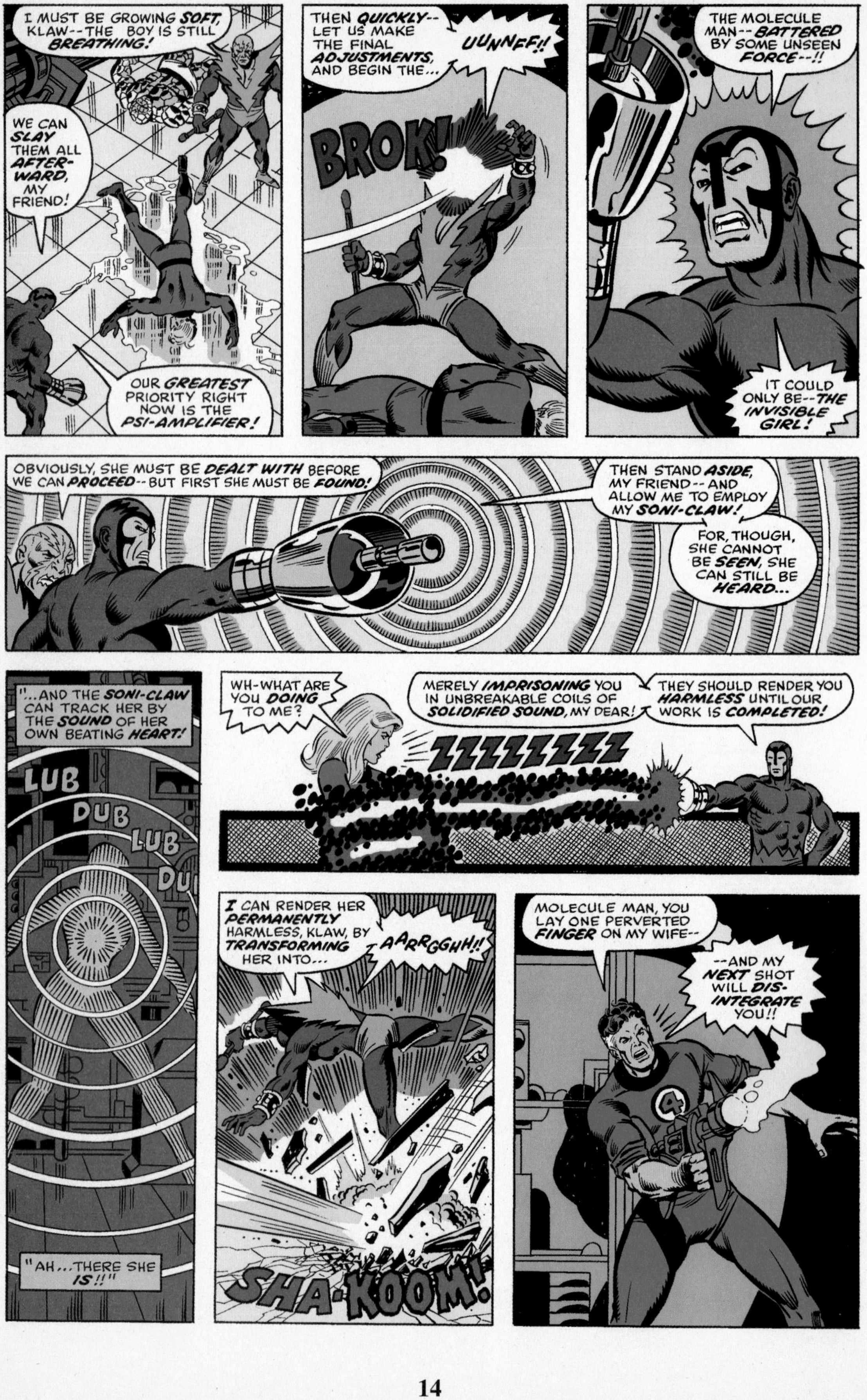

I MUST BE GROWING SOFT, KLAW--THE BOY IS STILL BREATHING!
WE CAN SLAY THEM ALL AFTER-WARD, MY FRIEND!
OUR GREATEST PRIORITY RIGHT NOW IS THE PSI-AMPLIFIER!
THEN QUICKLY--LET US MAKE THE FINAL ADJUSTMENTS, AND BEGIN THE...
UUNNFF!!
BROK!
THE MOLECULE MAN--BATTERED BY SOME UNSEEN FORCE--!!
IT COULD ONLY BE--THE INVISIBLE GIRL!
OBVIOUSLY, SHE MUST BE DEALT WITH BEFORE WE CAN PROCEED--BUT FIRST SHE MUST BE FOUND!
THEN STAND ASIDE, MY FRIEND--AND ALLOW ME TO EMPLOY MY SONI-CLAW!
FOR, THOUGH, SHE CANNOT BE SEEN, SHE CAN STILL BE HEARD...
"...AND THE SONI-CLAW CAN TRACK HER BY THE SOUND OF HER OWN BEATING HEART!"
LUB
DUB
LUB
"AH...THERE SHE IS!!"
WH-WHAT ARE YOU DOING TO ME?
MERELY IMPRISONING YOU IN UNBREAKABLE COILS OF SOLIDIFIED SOUND, MY DEAR!
THEY SHOULD RENDER YOU HARMLESS UNTIL OUR WORK IS COMPLETED!
ZZZZZZZZZ
I CAN RENDER HER PERMANENTLY HARMLESS, KLAW, BY TRANSFORMING HER INTO...
AARRGGHH!!
SHA-KOOM!
MOLECULE MAN, YOU LAY ONE PERVERTED FINGER ON MY WIFE--
--AND MY NEXT SHOT WILL DIS-INTEGRATE YOU!!

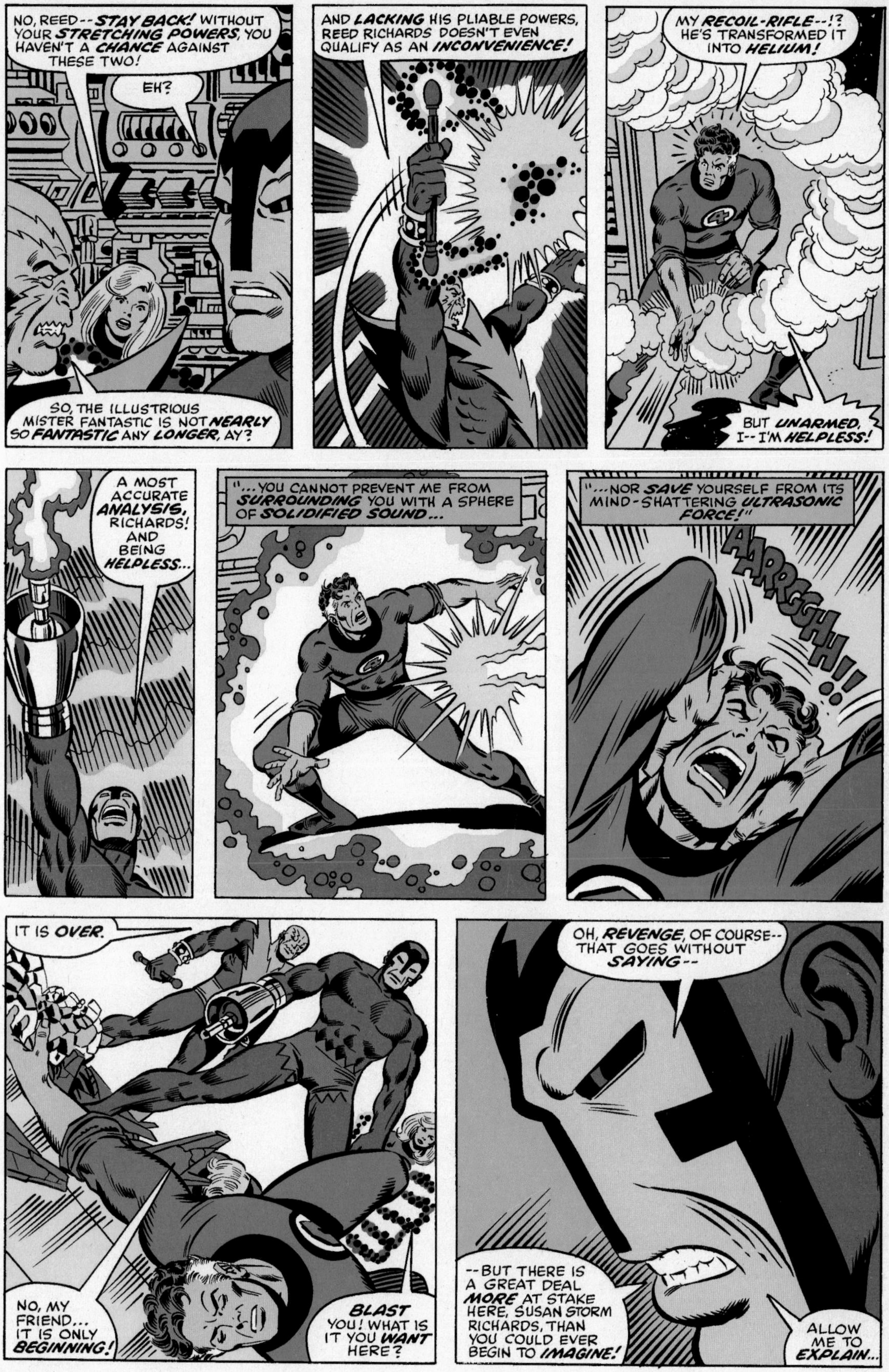
NO, REED--STAY BACK! WITHOUT YOUR STRETCHING POWERS, YOU HAVEN'T A CHANCE AGAINST THESE TWO!
EH?
SO, THE ILLUSTRIOUS MISTER FANTASTIC IS NOT NEARLY SO FANTASTIC ANY LONGER, AY?
AND LACKING HIS PLIABLE POWERS, REED RICHARDS DOESN'T EVEN QUALIFY AS AN INCONVENIENCE!
MY RECOIL-RIFLE--!? HE'S TRANSFORMED IT INTO HELIUM!
BUT UNARMED, I--I'M HELPLESS!
A MOST ACCURATE ANALYSIS, RICHARDS! AND BEING HELPLESS...
"...YOU CANNOT PREVENT ME FROM SURROUNDING YOU WITH A SPHERE OF SOLIDIFIED SOUND...
"...NOR SAVE YOURSELF FROM ITS MIND-SHATTERING ULTRASONIC FORCE!"
AARRGGHH!!
IT IS OVER.
NO, MY FRIEND... IT IS ONLY BEGINNING!
BLAST YOU! WHAT IS IT YOU WANT HERE?
OH, REVENGE, OF COURSE--THAT GOES WITHOUT SAYING--
--BUT THERE IS A GREAT DEAL MORE AT STAKE HERE, SUSAN STORM RICHARDS, THAN YOU COULD EVER BEGIN TO IMAGINE!
ALLOW ME TO EXPLAIN...

"IT BEGINS, YOU SEE, WITH MY *ESCAPE* FROM AN ALIEN *DIMENSION!* *

"A MALFUNCTION IN THE *SHUTTLE-CHAMBER* SENT ME HURTLING WILDLY THRU THE *VOID* BETWEEN WORLDS...

*AS DETAILED IN ISSUE #20 OF THE LATE, LAMENTED *KA-ZAR* MAG. --LEN.

"...AND WHEN AT LAST I *RE-MATERIALIZED,* IT WAS NOT IN THE HEART OF *NEW YORK CITY,* AS I HAD INTENDED...

"...BUT IN THE DISMAL DEPTHS OF THE PRIMITIVE *FLORIDA EVERGLADES!*

"A HEAVY *SHUFFLING* SOUND ATTRACTED MY *ATTENTION,* AND I TURNED TO SEE THE MISSHAPEN *MAN-THING* SHAMBLING BY...

"...A GLOWING CRIMSON *WAND* CLENCHED TIGHTLY IN HIS CLAW-LIKE *HAND!*

"MY CURIOSITY *PIQUED,* I FOLLOWED THE MINDLESS MURK-DWELLER UNTIL HE *DROPPED* THE PULSATING WAND INTO THE *MIRE...*

"...AS IF HE'D *FORGOTTEN* HE HAD EVER BEEN *HOLDING* IT!

"SWIFTLY, I *SNATCHED UP* THE SINKING SCEPTER--AND FOUND IT POSSESSED OF A *LIVING INTELLIGENCE,* WHICH SOUGHT TO TAKE *CONTROL* OF ME...

"...AND VERY WELL *MIGHT* HAVE, HAD MY BODY BEEN MADE OF FLESH-AND-BLOOD, INSTEAD OF *SOLIDIFIED SOUND!*

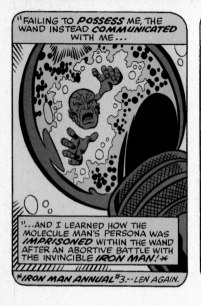

"FAILING TO *POSSESS* ME, THE WAND INSTEAD *COMMUNICATED* WITH ME...

"...AND I LEARNED HOW THE MOLECULE MAN'S PERSONA WAS *IMPRISONED* WITHIN THE WAND AFTER AN ABORTIVE BATTLE WITH THE INVINCIBLE *IRON MAN!* *

*IRON MAN ANNUAL #3.-- LEN AGAIN.

"AFTER SOME NEGOTIATION, MY MOLECULAR FRIEND AND I STRUCK A *BARGAIN...*

"...THEN RETURNED TO *MANHATTAN* AT THE SPEED OF...*SOUND!*

"FOR THE MOLECULE MAN STILL NEEDED A *BODY* TO POSSESS; ONE LACKING THE INTELLIGENCE TO *DEFY* HIS WILL...

DO NOT ENTER

"...YET *POWERFUL* ENOUGH TO SERVE HIS URGENT *NEEDS...*

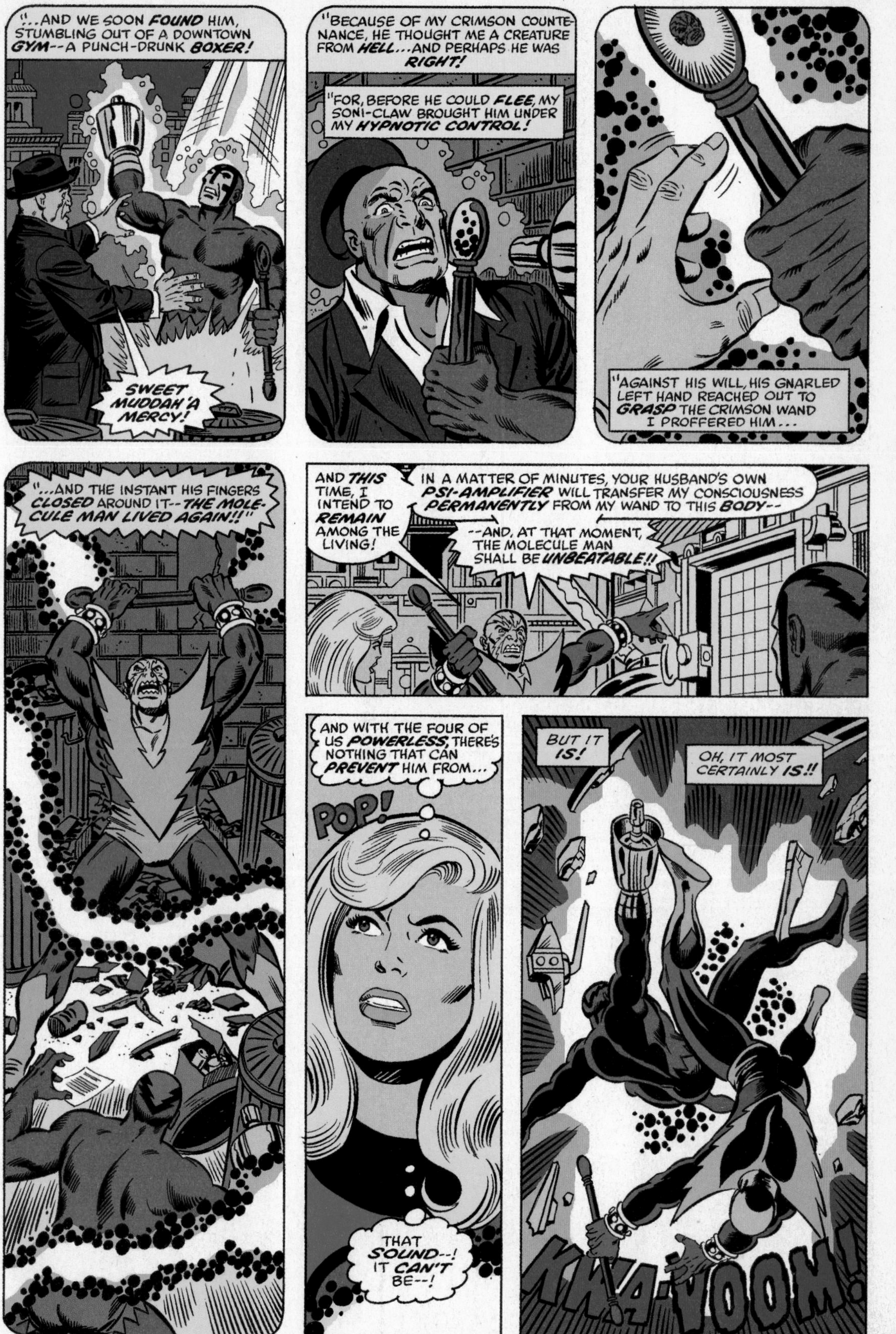
"...AND WE SOON FOUND HIM, STUMBLING OUT OF A DOWNTOWN GYM--A PUNCH-DRUNK BOXER!
SWEET MUDDAH 'A MERCY!
"BECAUSE OF MY CRIMSON COUNTENANCE, HE THOUGHT ME A CREATURE FROM HELL...AND PERHAPS HE WAS RIGHT!
"FOR, BEFORE HE COULD FLEE, MY SONI-CLAW BROUGHT HIM UNDER MY HYPNOTIC CONTROL!
"AGAINST HIS WILL, HIS GNARLED LEFT HAND REACHED OUT TO GRASP THE CRIMSON WAND I PROFFERED HIM...
"...AND THE INSTANT HIS FINGERS CLOSED AROUND IT--THE MOLECULE MAN LIVED AGAIN!!"
AND THIS TIME, I INTEND TO REMAIN AMONG THE LIVING!
IN A MATTER OF MINUTES, YOUR HUSBAND'S OWN PSI-AMPLIFIER WILL TRANSFER MY CONSCIOUSNESS PERMANENTLY FROM MY WAND TO THIS BODY--
--AND, AT THAT MOMENT, THE MOLECULE MAN SHALL BE UNBEATABLE!!
AND WITH THE FOUR OF US POWERLESS, THERE'S NOTHING THAT CAN PREVENT HIM FROM...
POP!
THAT SOUND--! IT CAN'T BE--!
BUT IT IS!
OH, IT MOST CERTAINLY IS!!
KWA-VOOM!

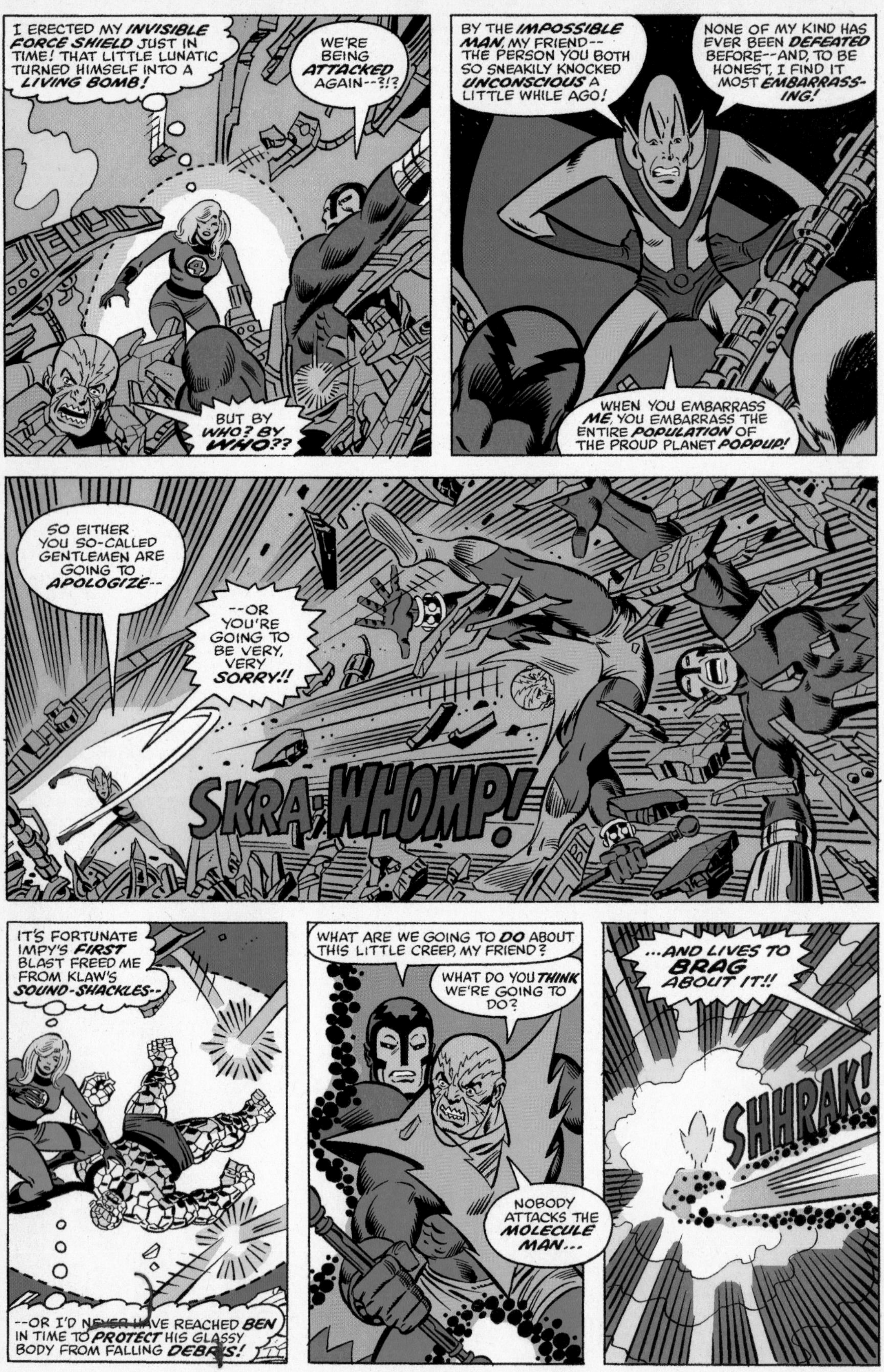

I ERECTED MY INVISIBLE FORCE SHIELD JUST IN TIME! THAT LITTLE LUNATIC TURNED HIMSELF INTO A LIVING BOMB!
WE'RE BEING ATTACKED AGAIN--?!?
BUT BY WHO? BY WHO??
BY THE IMPOSSIBLE MAN, MY FRIEND-- THE PERSON YOU BOTH SO SNEAKILY KNOCKED UNCONSCIOUS A LITTLE WHILE AGO!
NONE OF MY KIND HAS EVER BEEN DEFEATED BEFORE--AND, TO BE HONEST, I FIND IT MOST EMBARRASS-ING!
WHEN YOU EMBARRASS ME, YOU EMBARRASS THE ENTIRE POPULATION OF THE PROUD PLANET POPPUP!
SO EITHER YOU SO-CALLED GENTLEMEN ARE GOING TO APOLOGIZE--
--OR YOU'RE GOING TO BE VERY, VERY SORRY!!
SKRA-WHOMP!
IT'S FORTUNATE IMPY'S FIRST BLAST FREED ME FROM KLAW'S SOUND-SHACKLES--
--OR I'D NEVER HAVE REACHED BEN IN TIME TO PROTECT HIS GLASSY BODY FROM FALLING DEBRIS!
WHAT ARE WE GOING TO DO ABOUT THIS LITTLE CREEP, MY FRIEND?
WHAT DO YOU THINK WE'RE GOING TO DO?
NOBODY ATTACKS THE MOLECULE MAN...
...AND LIVES TO BRAG ABOUT IT!!
SHHRAK!

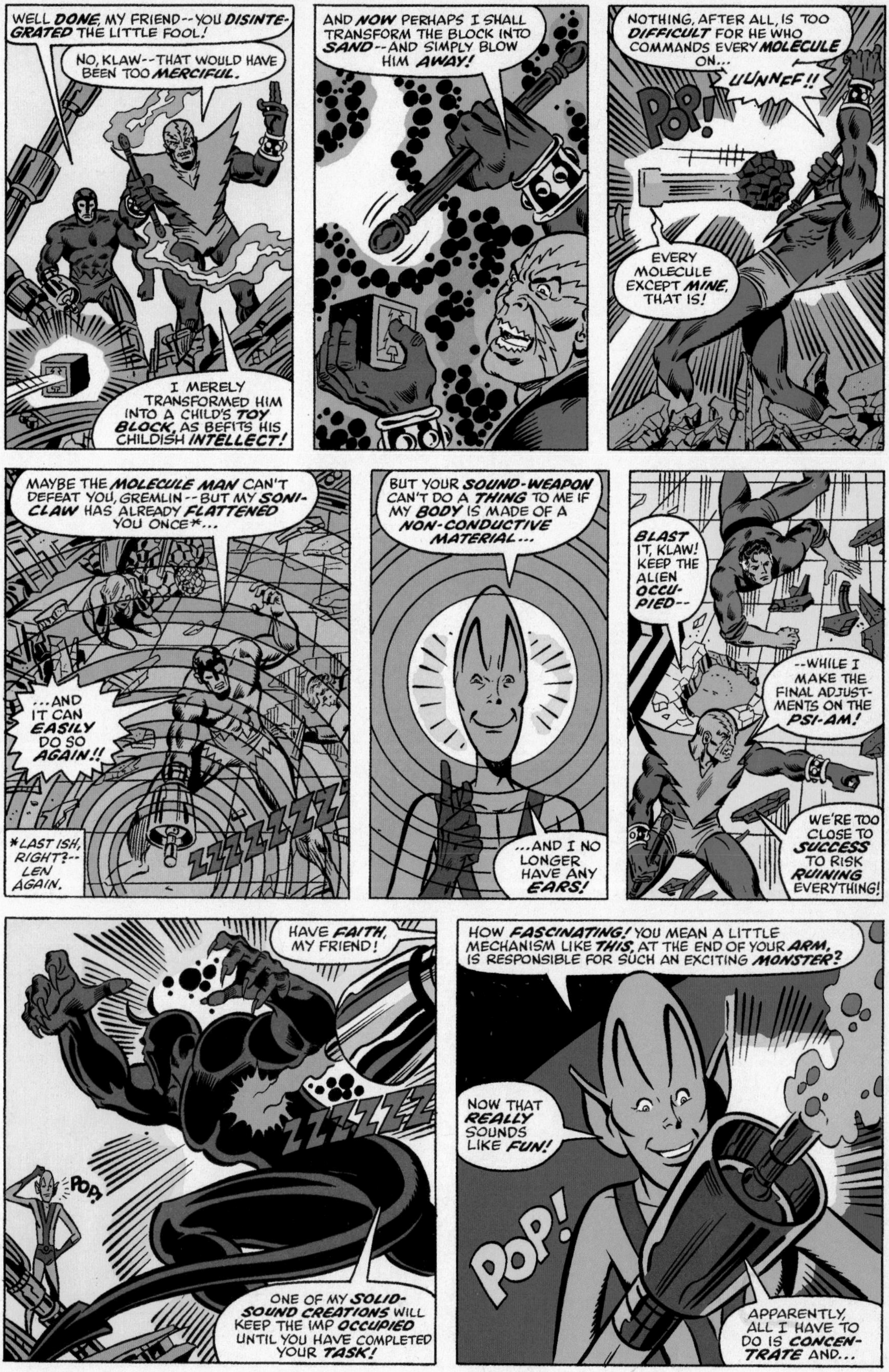

WELL DONE, MY FRIEND--YOU DISINTEGRATED THE LITTLE FOOL!
NO, KLAW--THAT WOULD HAVE BEEN TOO MERCIFUL.
I MERELY TRANSFORMED HIM INTO A CHILD'S TOY BLOCK, AS BEFITS HIS CHILDISH INTELLECT!
AND NOW PERHAPS I SHALL TRANSFORM THE BLOCK INTO SAND--AND SIMPLY BLOW HIM AWAY!
NOTHING, AFTER ALL, IS TOO DIFFICULT FOR HE WHO COMMANDS EVERY MOLECULE ON...
UUNNFF!!
POP!
EVERY MOLECULE EXCEPT MINE, THAT IS!
MAYBE THE MOLECULE MAN CAN'T DEFEAT YOU, GREMLIN--BUT MY SONI-CLAW HAS ALREADY FLATTENED YOU ONCE*...
...AND IT CAN EASILY DO SO AGAIN!!
*LAST ISH, RIGHT?--LEN AGAIN.
BUT YOUR SOUND-WEAPON CAN'T DO A THING TO ME IF MY BODY IS MADE OF A NON-CONDUCTIVE MATERIAL...
...AND I NO LONGER HAVE ANY EARS!
BLAST IT, KLAW! KEEP THE ALIEN OCCUPIED--
--WHILE I MAKE THE FINAL ADJUSTMENTS ON THE PSI-AM!
WE'RE TOO CLOSE TO SUCCESS TO RISK RUINING EVERYTHING!
HAVE FAITH, MY FRIEND!
POP!
ONE OF MY SOLID-SOUND CREATIONS WILL KEEP THE IMP OCCUPIED UNTIL YOU HAVE COMPLETED YOUR TASK!
HOW FASCINATING! YOU MEAN A LITTLE MECHANISM LIKE THIS, AT THE END OF YOUR ARM, IS RESPONSIBLE FOR SUCH AN EXCITING MONSTER?
NOW THAT REALLY SOUNDS LIKE FUN!
POP!
APPARENTLY, ALL I HAVE TO DO IS CONCENTRATE AND...

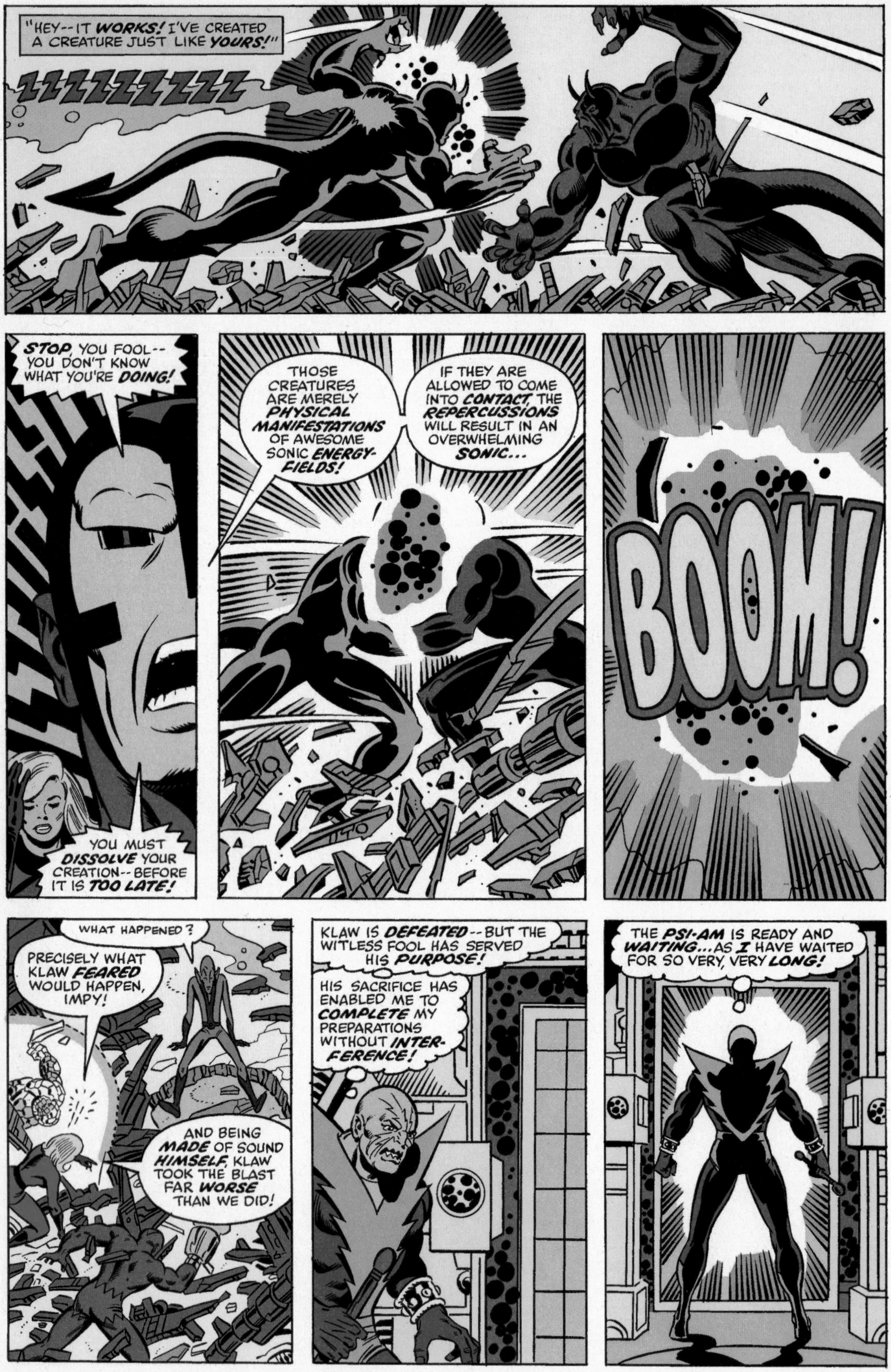

"HEY--IT WORKS! I'VE CREATED A CREATURE JUST LIKE YOURS!"
ZZZZZZZZZZ
STOP, YOU FOOL--YOU DON'T KNOW WHAT YOU'RE DOING!
YOU MUST DISSOLVE YOUR CREATION--BEFORE IT IS TOO LATE!
THOSE CREATURES ARE MERELY PHYSICAL MANIFESTATIONS OF AWESOME SONIC ENERGY-FIELDS!
IF THEY ARE ALLOWED TO COME INTO CONTACT, THE REPERCUSSIONS WILL RESULT IN AN OVERWHELMING SONIC...
BOOM!
WHAT HAPPENED?
PRECISELY WHAT KLAW FEARED WOULD HAPPEN, IMPY!
AND BEING MADE OF SOUND HIMSELF, KLAW TOOK THE BLAST FAR WORSE THAN WE DID!
KLAW IS DEFEATED--BUT THE WITLESS FOOL HAS SERVED HIS PURPOSE!
HIS SACRIFICE HAS ENABLED ME TO COMPLETE MY PREPARATIONS WITHOUT INTER-FERENCE!
THE PSI-AM IS READY AND WAITING...AS I HAVE WAITED FOR SO VERY, VERY LONG!

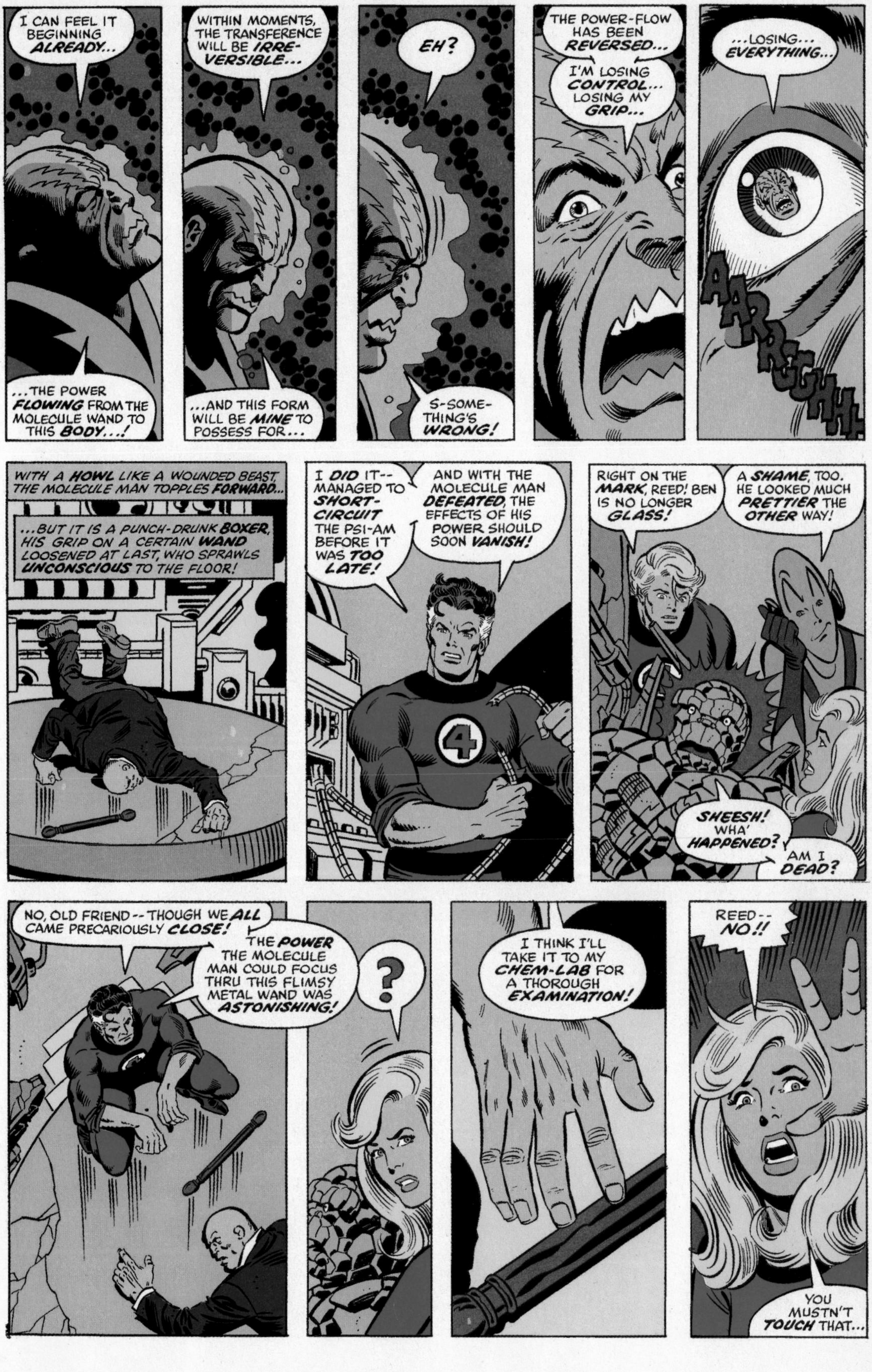

I CAN FEEL IT BEGINNING ALREADY...
...THE POWER FLOWING FROM THE MOLECULE WAND TO THIS BODY...!
WITHIN MOMENTS, THE TRANSFERENCE WILL BE IRRE-VERSIBLE...
...AND THIS FORM WILL BE MINE TO POSSESS FOR...
EH?
S-SOME-THING'S WRONG!
THE POWER-FLOW HAS BEEN REVERSED...
I'M LOSING CONTROL... LOSING MY GRIP...
...LOSING... EVERYTHING...
AARRGGHHH
WITH A HOWL LIKE A WOUNDED BEAST, THE MOLECULE MAN TOPPLES FORWARD...
...BUT IT IS A PUNCH-DRUNK BOXER, HIS GRIP ON A CERTAIN WAND LOOSENED AT LAST, WHO SPRAWLS UNCONSCIOUS TO THE FLOOR!
I DID IT-- MANAGED TO SHORT-CIRCUIT THE PSI-AM BEFORE IT WAS TOO LATE!
AND WITH THE MOLECULE MAN DEFEATED, THE EFFECTS OF HIS POWER SHOULD SOON VANISH!
RIGHT ON THE MARK, REED! BEN IS NO LONGER GLASS!
A SHAME, TOO. HE LOOKED MUCH PRETTIER THE OTHER WAY!
SHEESH! WHA' HAPPENED?
AM I DEAD?
NO, OLD FRIEND -- THOUGH WE ALL CAME PRECARIOUSLY CLOSE!
THE POWER THE MOLECULE MAN COULD FOCUS THRU THIS FLIMSY METAL WAND WAS ASTONISHING!
?
I THINK I'LL TAKE IT TO MY CHEM-LAB FOR A THOROUGH EXAMINATION!
REED-- NO!!
YOU MUSTN'T TOUCH THAT...

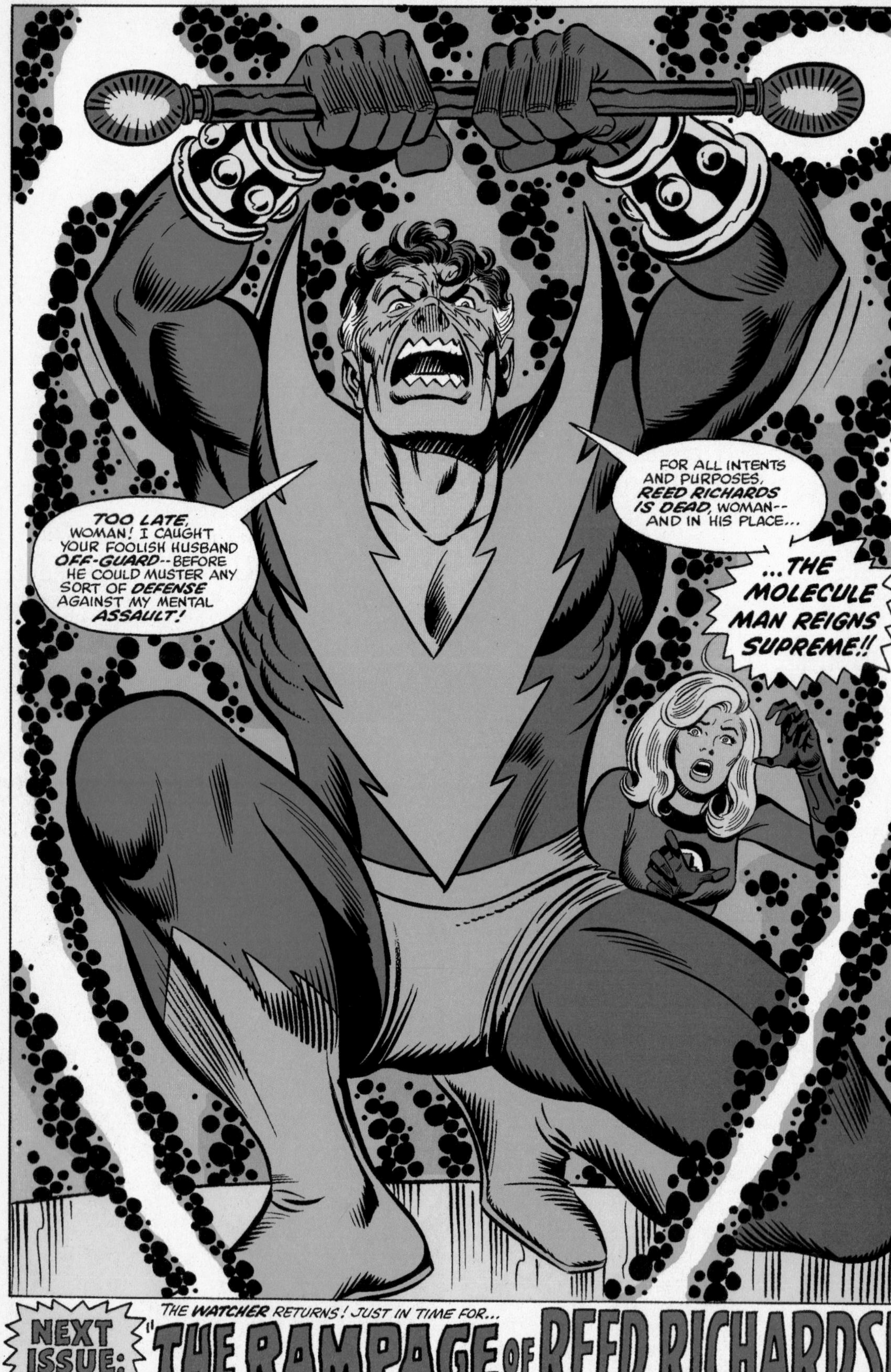
TOO LATE, WOMAN! I CAUGHT YOUR FOOLISH HUSBAND OFF-GUARD--BEFORE HE COULD MUSTER ANY SORT OF DEFENSE AGAINST MY MENTAL ASSAULT!
FOR ALL INTENTS AND PURPOSES, REED RICHARDS IS DEAD, WOMAN--AND IN HIS PLACE...
...THE MOLECULE MAN REIGNS SUPREME!!
NEXT ISSUE:
THE WATCHER RETURNS! JUST IN TIME FOR...
"THE RAMPAGE OF REED RICHARDS!"
BE HERE!

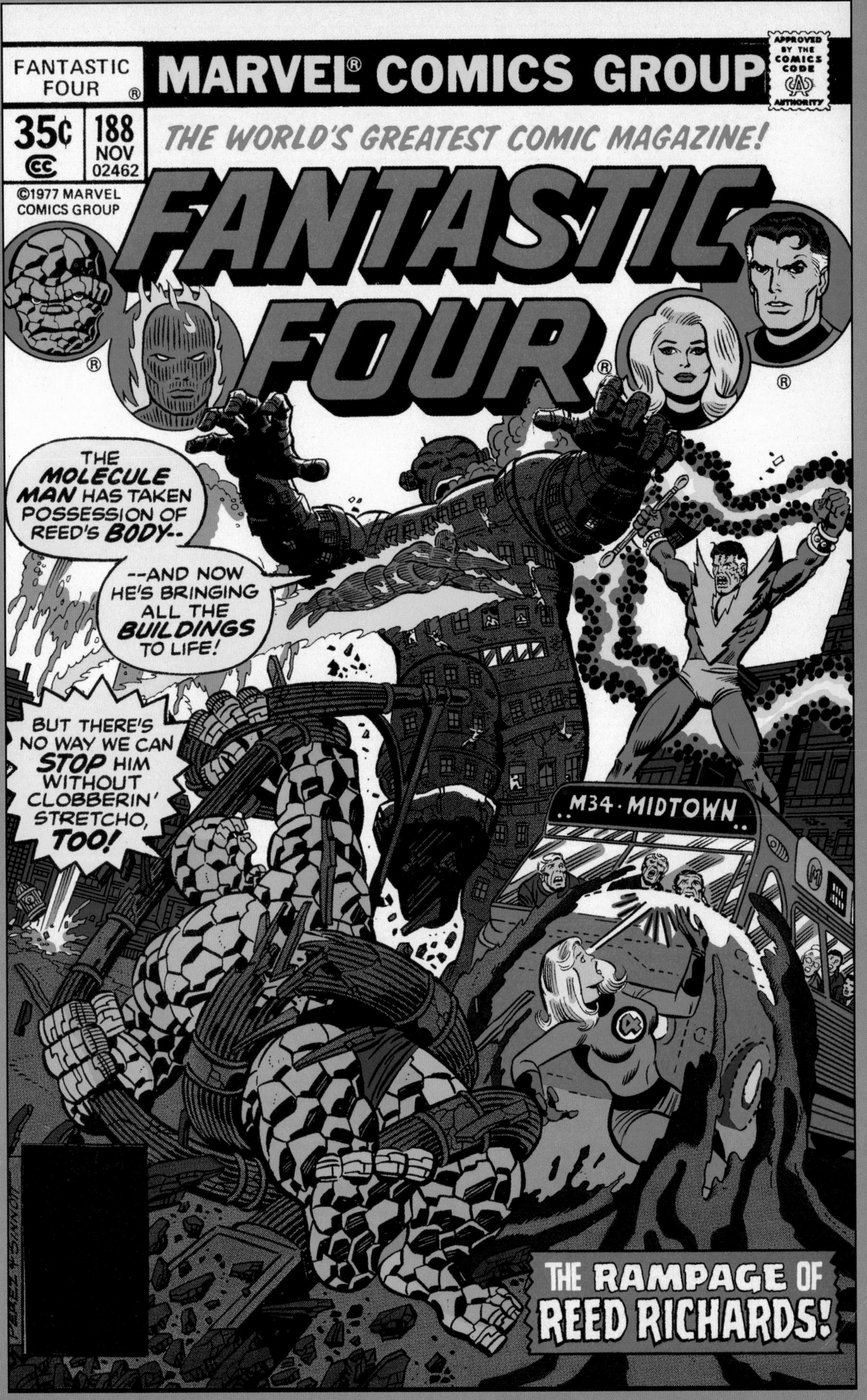

FANTASTIC FOUR ®
MARVEL® COMICS GROUP
APPROVED BY THE COMICS CODE AUTHORITY
35¢
188 NOV 02462
©1977 MARVEL COMICS GROUP
THE WORLD'S GREATEST COMIC MAGAZINE!
FANTASTIC FOUR®
THE MOLECULE MAN HAS TAKEN POSSESSION OF REED'S BODY--
--AND NOW HE'S BRINGING ALL THE BUILDINGS TO LIFE!
BUT THERE'S NO WAY WE CAN STOP HIM WITHOUT CLOBBERIN' STRETCHO, TOO!
M34 · MIDTOWN
THE RAMPAGE OF REED RICHARDS!

A brilliant scientist— his best friend— the woman he loves— and her fiery-tempered kid brother! Together, they braved the unknown terrors of outer space, and were changed by cosmic rays into something more than merely human!
MR. FANTASTIC! THE THING! THE INVISIBLE GIRL! THE HUMAN TORCH! Now they are the FANTASTIC FOUR— and the world will never be the same again!

Stan Lee PRESENTS: THE FANTASTIC FOUR!™

LEN WEIN, WRITER / EDITOR ✶ GEORGE PÉREZ & JOE SINNOTT, ARTISTS / STORYTELLERS ✶ GLYNIS WEIN, COLORIST ✶ JOE ROSEN, LETTERER

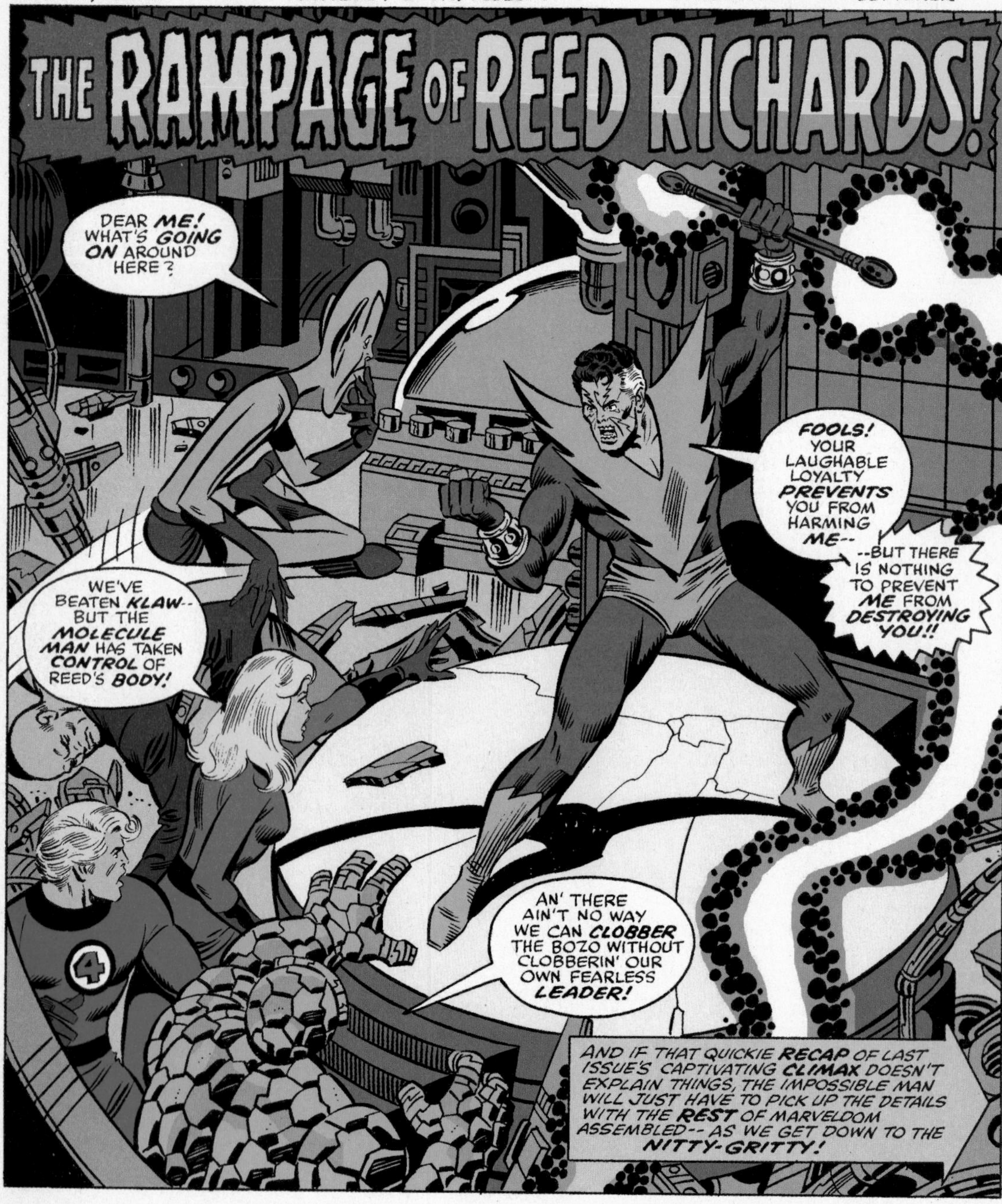
THE RAMPAGE OF REED RICHARDS!
DEAR ME! WHAT'S GOING ON AROUND HERE?
FOOLS! YOUR LAUGHABLE LOYALTY PREVENTS YOU FROM HARMING ME--
--BUT THERE IS NOTHING TO PREVENT ME FROM DESTROYING YOU!!
WE'VE BEATEN KLAW-- BUT THE MOLECULE MAN HAS TAKEN CONTROL OF REED'S BODY!
AN' THERE AIN'T NO WAY WE CAN CLOBBER THE BOZO WITHOUT CLOBBERIN' OUR OWN FEARLESS LEADER!
AND IF THAT QUICKIE RECAP OF LAST ISSUE'S CAPTIVATING CLIMAX DOESN'T EXPLAIN THINGS, THE IMPOSSIBLE MAN WILL JUST HAVE TO PICK UP THE DETAILS WITH THE REST OF MARVELDOM ASSEMBLED-- AS WE GET DOWN TO THE NITTY-GRITTY!

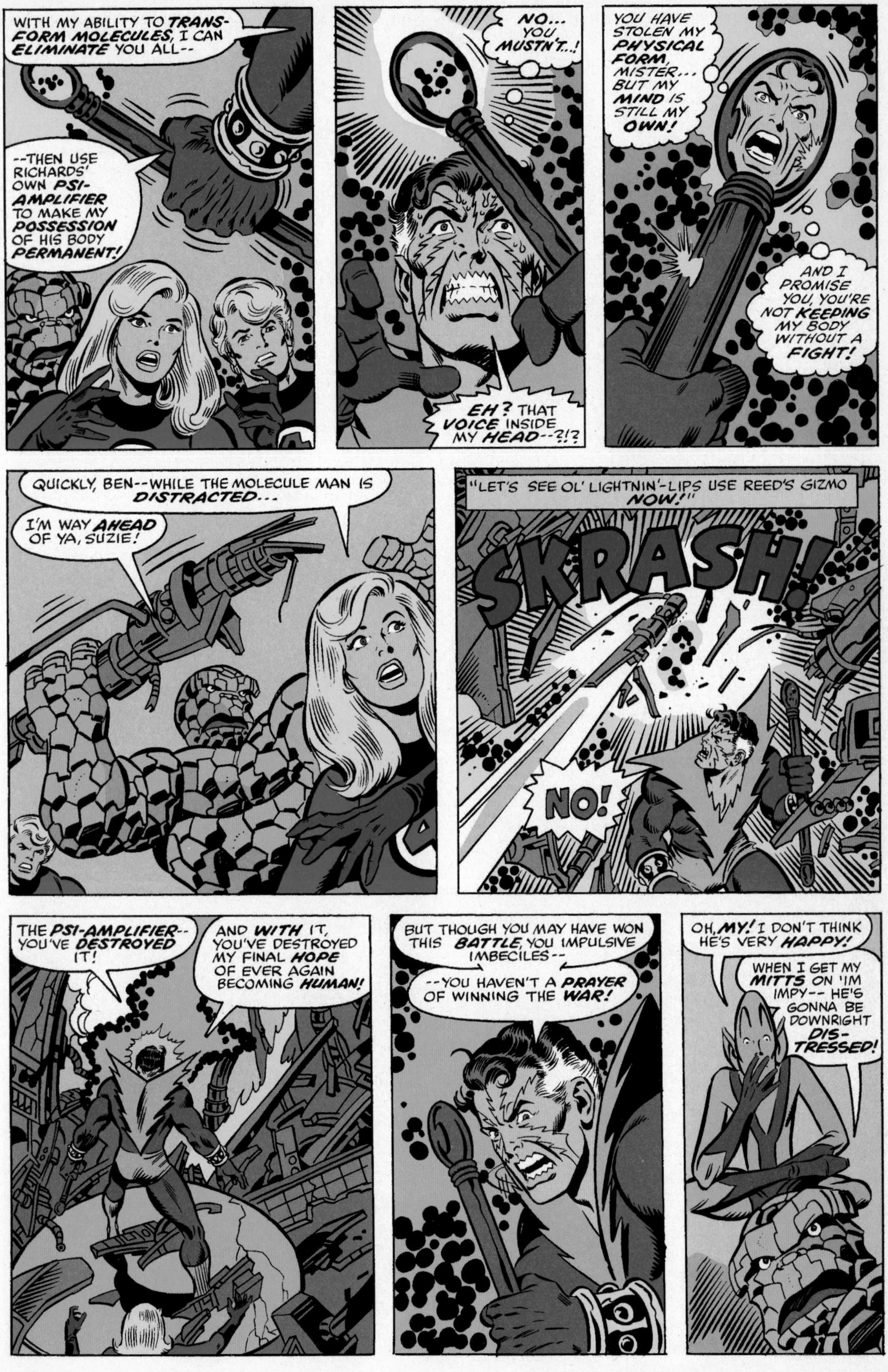
WITH MY ABILITY TO TRANSFORM MOLECULES, I CAN ELIMINATE YOU ALL--
--THEN USE RICHARDS' OWN PSI-AMPLIFIER TO MAKE MY POSSESSION OF HIS BODY PERMANENT!
NO... YOU MUSTN'T...!
EH? THAT VOICE INSIDE MY HEAD--?!?
YOU HAVE STOLEN MY PHYSICAL FORM, MISTER... BUT MY MIND IS STILL MY OWN!
AND I PROMISE YOU, YOU'RE NOT KEEPING MY BODY WITHOUT A FIGHT!
QUICKLY, BEN--WHILE THE MOLECULE MAN IS DISTRACTED...
I'M WAY AHEAD OF YA, SUZIE!
"LET'S SEE OL' LIGHTNIN'-LIPS USE REED'S GIZMO NOW!"
SKRASH!
NO!
THE PSI-AMPLIFIER--YOU'VE DESTROYED IT!
AND WITH IT, YOU'VE DESTROYED MY FINAL HOPE OF EVER AGAIN BECOMING HUMAN!
BUT THOUGH YOU MAY HAVE WON THIS BATTLE, YOU IMPULSIVE IMBECILES--
--YOU HAVEN'T A PRAYER OF WINNING THE WAR!
OH, MY! I DON'T THINK HE'S VERY HAPPY!
WHEN I GET MY MITTS ON 'IM IMPY-- HE'S GONNA BE DOWNRIGHT DIS-TRESSED!

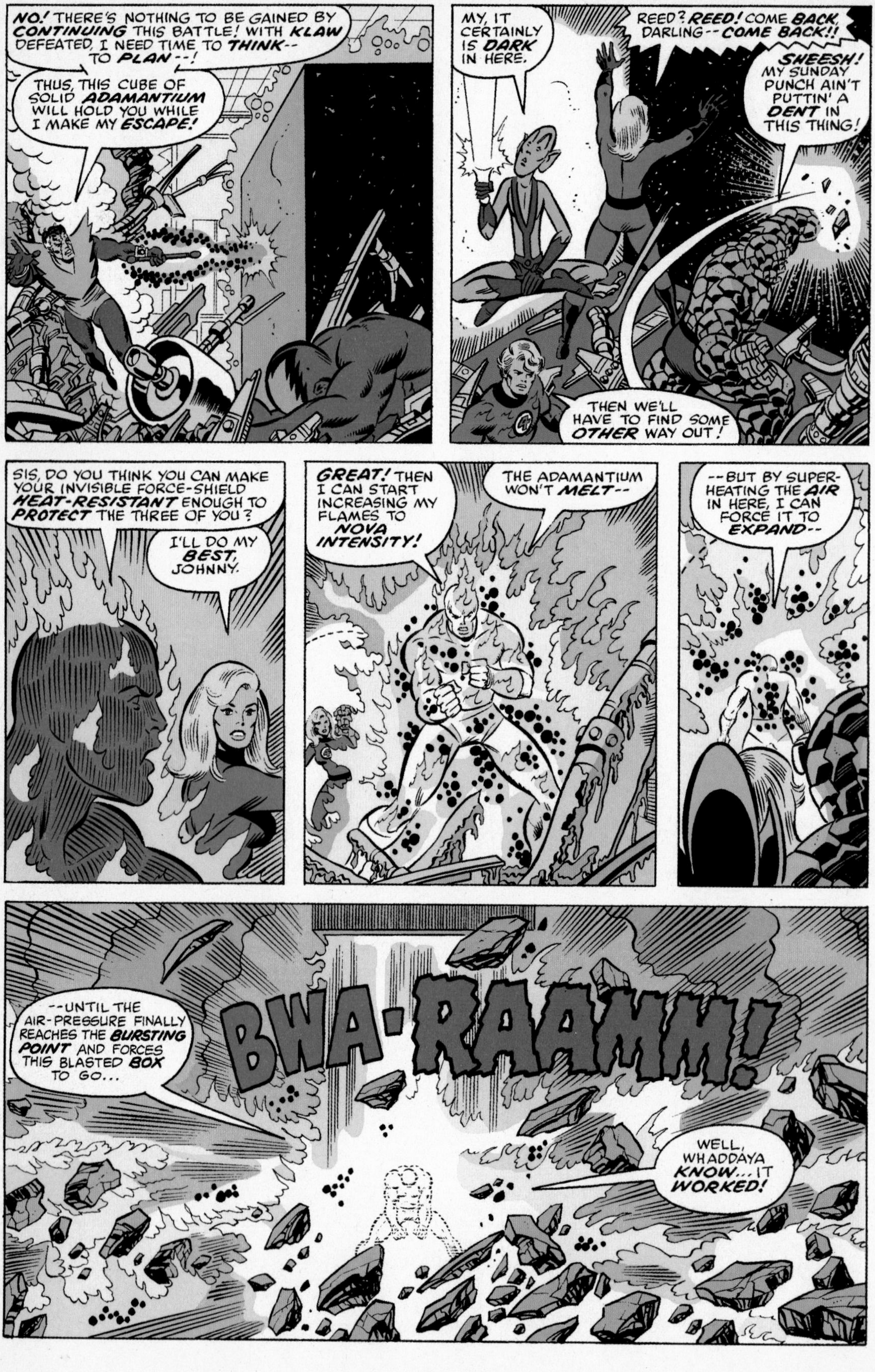

NO! THERE'S NOTHING TO BE GAINED BY CONTINUING THIS BATTLE! WITH KLAW DEFEATED, I NEED TIME TO THINK-- TO PLAN--!
THUS, THIS CUBE OF SOLID ADAMANTIUM WILL HOLD YOU WHILE I MAKE MY ESCAPE!
MY, IT CERTAINLY IS DARK IN HERE.
REED? REED! COME BACK, DARLING-- COME BACK!!
SHEESH! MY SUNDAY PUNCH AIN'T PUTTIN' A DENT IN THIS THING!
THEN WE'LL HAVE TO FIND SOME OTHER WAY OUT!
SIS, DO YOU THINK YOU CAN MAKE YOUR INVISIBLE FORCE-SHIELD HEAT-RESISTANT ENOUGH TO PROTECT THE THREE OF YOU?
I'LL DO MY BEST, JOHNNY.
GREAT! THEN I CAN START INCREASING MY FLAMES TO NOVA INTENSITY!
THE ADAMANTIUM WON'T MELT--
--BUT BY SUPER-HEATING THE AIR IN HERE, I CAN FORCE IT TO EXPAND--
--UNTIL THE AIR-PRESSURE FINALLY REACHES THE BURSTING POINT AND FORCES THIS BLASTED BOX TO GO...
BWA-RAAMM!
WELL, WHADDAYA KNOW... IT WORKED!

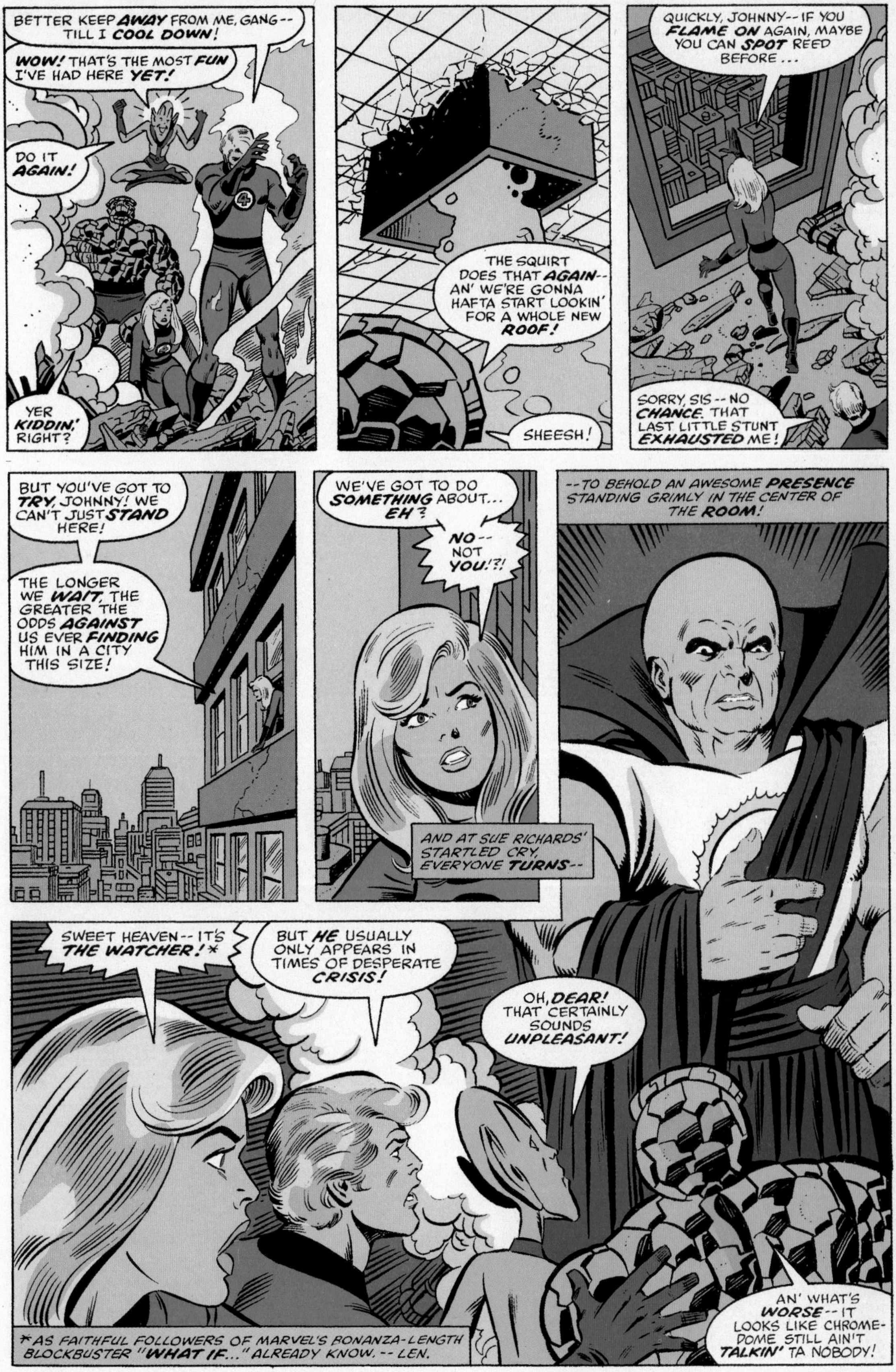

BETTER KEEP AWAY FROM ME, GANG-- TILL I COOL DOWN!
WOW! THAT'S THE MOST FUN I'VE HAD HERE YET!
DO IT AGAIN!
YER KIDDIN,' RIGHT?
THE SQUIRT DOES THAT AGAIN-- AN' WE'RE GONNA HAFTA START LOOKIN' FOR A WHOLE NEW ROOF!
SHEESH!
QUICKLY, JOHNNY-- IF YOU FLAME ON AGAIN, MAYBE YOU CAN SPOT REED BEFORE...
SORRY, SIS-- NO CHANCE. THAT LAST LITTLE STUNT EXHAUSTED ME!
BUT YOU'VE GOT TO TRY, JOHNNY! WE CAN'T JUST STAND HERE!
THE LONGER WE WAIT, THE GREATER THE ODDS AGAINST US EVER FINDING HIM IN A CITY THIS SIZE!
WE'VE GOT TO DO SOMETHING ABOUT... EH?
NO-- NOT YOU!?!
AND AT SUE RICHARDS' STARTLED CRY, EVERYONE TURNS--
--TO BEHOLD AN AWESOME PRESENCE STANDING GRIMLY IN THE CENTER OF THE ROOM!
SWEET HEAVEN-- IT'S THE WATCHER!*
BUT HE USUALLY ONLY APPEARS IN TIMES OF DESPERATE CRISIS!
OH, DEAR! THAT CERTAINLY SOUNDS UNPLEASANT!
AN' WHAT'S WORSE-- IT LOOKS LIKE CHROME-DOME STILL AIN'T TALKIN' TA NOBODY!
*AS FAITHFUL FOLLOWERS OF MARVEL'S BONANZA-LENGTH BLOCKBUSTER "WHAT IF..." ALREADY KNOW. -- LEN.

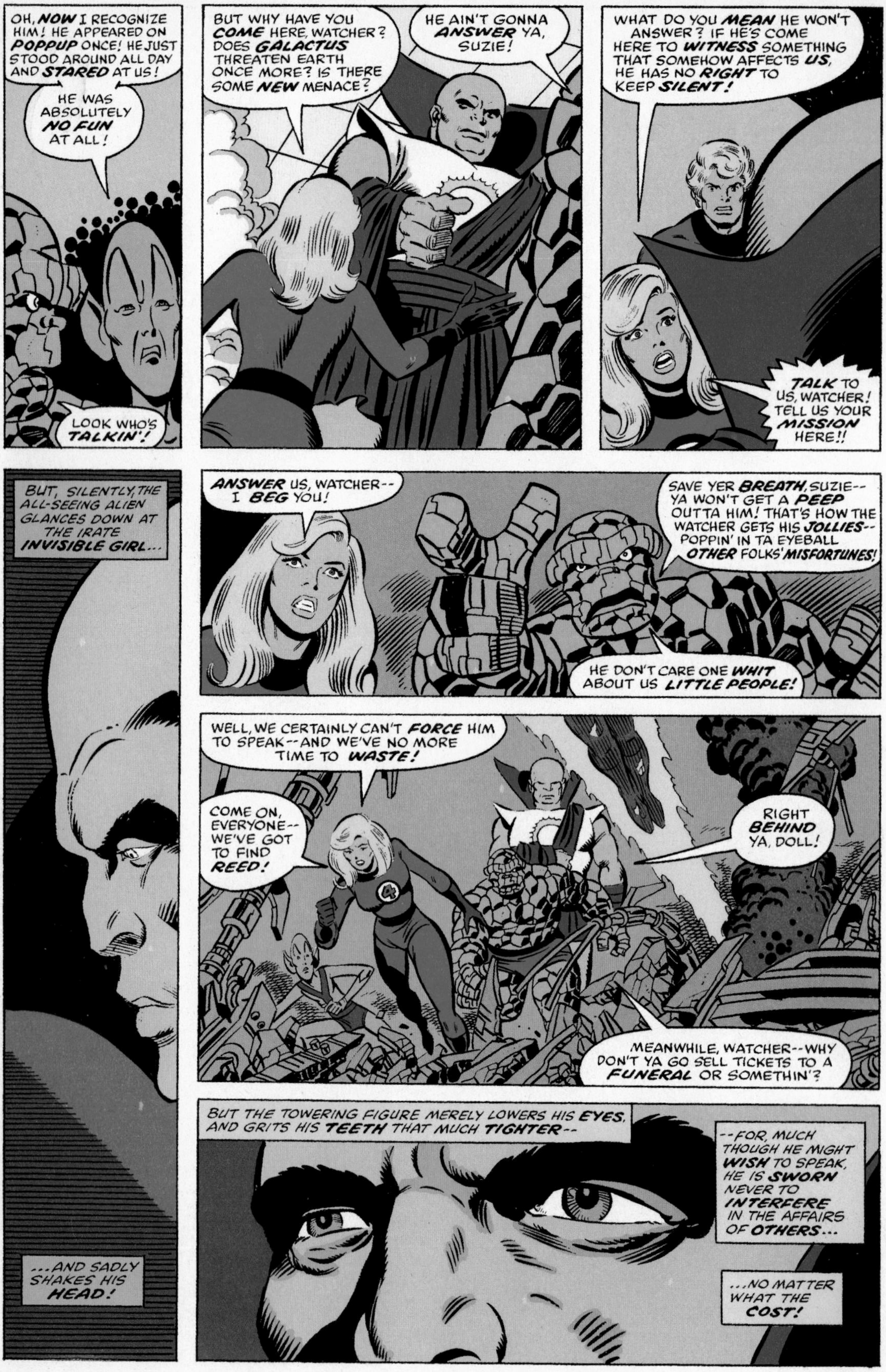

OH, NOW I RECOGNIZE HIM! HE APPEARED ON POPPUP ONCE! HE JUST STOOD AROUND ALL DAY AND STARED AT US!
HE WAS ABSOLUTELY NO FUN AT ALL!
LOOK WHO'S TALKIN'!
BUT WHY HAVE YOU COME HERE, WATCHER? DOES GALACTUS THREATEN EARTH ONCE MORE? IS THERE SOME NEW MENACE?
HE AIN'T GONNA ANSWER YA, SUZIE!
WHAT DO YOU MEAN HE WON'T ANSWER? IF HE'S COME HERE TO WITNESS SOMETHING THAT SOMEHOW AFFECTS US, HE HAS NO RIGHT TO KEEP SILENT!
TALK TO US, WATCHER! TELL US YOUR MISSION HERE!!
BUT, SILENTLY, THE ALL-SEEING ALIEN GLANCES DOWN AT THE IRATE INVISIBLE GIRL...
...AND SADLY SHAKES HIS HEAD!
ANSWER US, WATCHER-- I BEG YOU!
SAVE YER BREATH, SUZIE-- YA WON'T GET A PEEP OUTTA HIM! THAT'S HOW THE WATCHER GETS HIS JOLLIES-- POPPIN' IN TA EYEBALL OTHER FOLKS' MISFORTUNES!
HE DON'T CARE ONE WHIT ABOUT US LITTLE PEOPLE!
WELL, WE CERTAINLY CAN'T FORCE HIM TO SPEAK--AND WE'VE NO MORE TIME TO WASTE!
COME ON, EVERYONE-- WE'VE GOT TO FIND REED!
RIGHT BEHIND YA, DOLL!
MEANWHILE, WATCHER--WHY DON'T YA GO SELL TICKETS TO A FUNERAL OR SOMETHIN'?
BUT THE TOWERING FIGURE MERELY LOWERS HIS EYES, AND GRITS HIS TEETH THAT MUCH TIGHTER--
--FOR, MUCH THOUGH HE MIGHT WISH TO SPEAK, HE IS SWORN NEVER TO INTERFERE IN THE AFFAIRS OF OTHERS...
...NO MATTER WHAT THE COST!

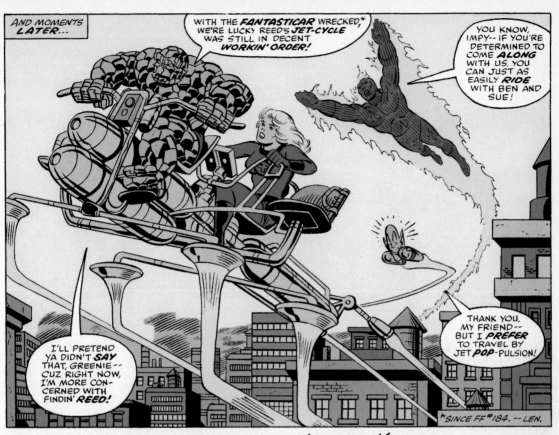

AND MOMENTS *LATER*...

WITH THE *FANTASTICAR* WRECKED,* WE'RE LUCKY REED'S *JET-CYCLE* WAS STILL IN DECENT *WORKIN' ORDER!*

YOU KNOW, IMPY-- IF YOU'RE DETERMINED TO COME *ALONG* WITH US, YOU CAN JUST AS EASILY *RIDE* WITH BEN AND SUE!

I'LL PRETEND YA DIDN'T *SAY* THAT, GREENIE-- CUZ RIGHT NOW, I'M MORE CONCERNED WITH FINDIN' *REED!*

THANK YOU, MY FRIEND-- BUT I *PREFER* TO TRAVEL BY JET *POP*-PULSION!

*SINCE FF #184. --LEN.

WHILE, HALFWAY ACROSS *TOWN*...

HEY, WHAT'S *WRONG* WITH THAT GUY? WHY'S HE FOULIN' UP *TRAFFIC* LIKE THIS?

I DON'T *KNOW*, PAL! HE JUST KEEPS STANDIN' THERE WIT' THAT SCREWY *GLOW* AROUND HIM-- *SHOUTIN'* AT HIMSELF!

GIVE UP, RICHARDS-- YOU CANNOT HOPE TO *WIN!* YOUR BODY IS *MINE* NOW--

--AND IT SHALL *REMAIN* MINE... *FOREVER!*

NO *CHANCE*, MISTER! SO LONG AS I RETAIN MY *CONSCIOUS-NESS*, I'LL *FIGHT* YOU--

--AND I'LL *KEEP* FIGHT-ING... TILL THE BITTER *END!!*

THEN I WILL HAVE TO *FORCE* THE ISSUE! *SURRENDER* YOURSELF TO ME, RICHARDS--

-- OR I WILL REDUCE THIS CITY TO *RUBBLE!!*

29

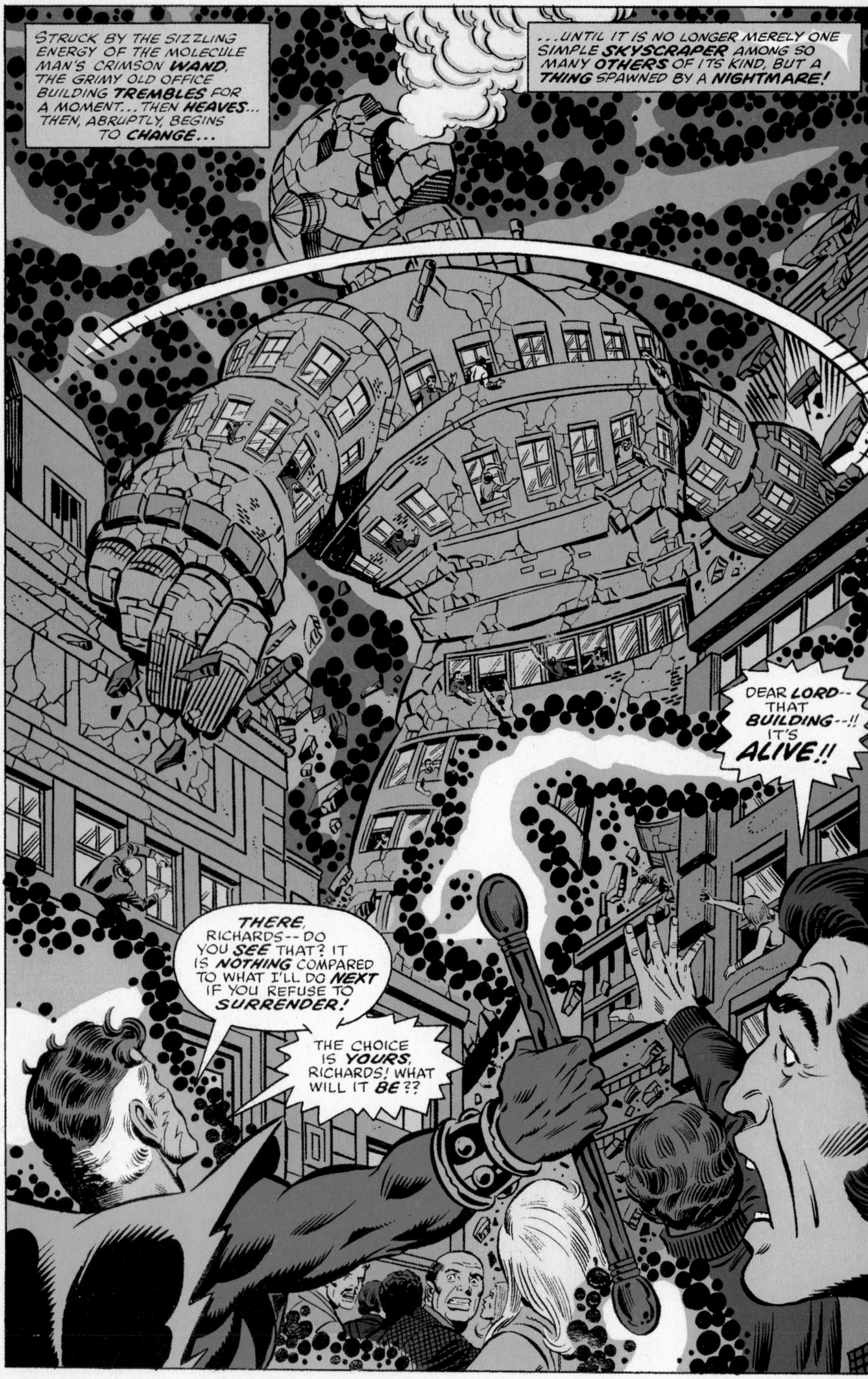
STRUCK BY THE SIZZLING ENERGY OF THE MOLECULE MAN'S CRIMSON WAND, THE GRIMY OLD OFFICE BUILDING TREMBLES FOR A MOMENT... THEN HEAVES... THEN, ABRUPTLY, BEGINS TO CHANGE...
...UNTIL IT IS NO LONGER MERELY ONE SIMPLE SKYSCRAPER AMONG SO MANY OTHERS OF ITS KIND, BUT A THING SPAWNED BY A NIGHTMARE!
DEAR LORD-- THAT BUILDING--!! IT'S ALIVE!!
THERE, RICHARDS-- DO YOU SEE THAT? IT IS NOTHING COMPARED TO WHAT I'LL DO NEXT IF YOU REFUSE TO SURRENDER!
THE CHOICE IS YOURS, RICHARDS! WHAT WILL IT BE??

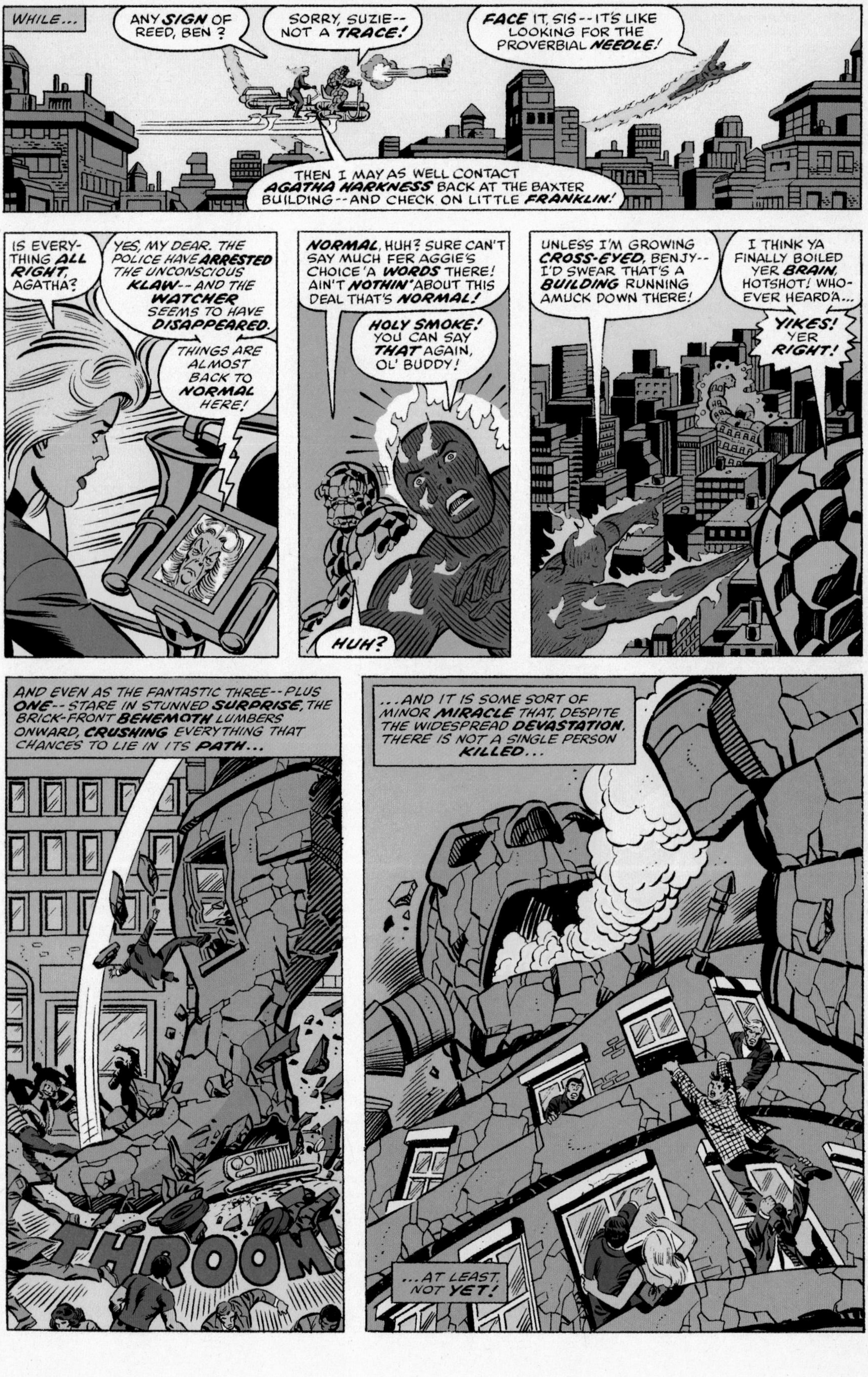
WHILE...
ANY SIGN OF REED, BEN ?
SORRY, SUZIE-- NOT A TRACE!
FACE IT, SIS--IT'S LIKE LOOKING FOR THE PROVERBIAL NEEDLE!
THEN I MAY AS WELL CONTACT AGATHA HARKNESS BACK AT THE BAXTER BUILDING--AND CHECK ON LITTLE FRANKLIN!
IS EVERY-THING ALL RIGHT, AGATHA?
YES, MY DEAR. THE POLICE HAVE ARRESTED THE UNCONSCIOUS KLAW--AND THE WATCHER SEEMS TO HAVE DISAPPEARED.
THINGS ARE ALMOST BACK TO NORMAL HERE!
NORMAL, HUH? SURE CAN'T SAY MUCH FER AGGIE'S CHOICE 'A WORDS THERE! AIN'T NOTHIN' ABOUT THIS DEAL THAT'S NORMAL!
HOLY SMOKE! YOU CAN SAY THAT AGAIN, OL' BUDDY!
HUH?
UNLESS I'M GROWING CROSS-EYED, BENJY--I'D SWEAR THAT'S A BUILDING RUNNING AMUCK DOWN THERE!
I THINK YA FINALLY BOILED YER BRAIN, HOTSHOT! WHO-EVER HEARD'A...
YIKES! YER RIGHT!
AND EVEN AS THE FANTASTIC THREE--PLUS ONE--STARE IN STUNNED SURPRISE, THE BRICK-FRONT BEHEMOTH LUMBERS ONWARD, CRUSHING EVERYTHING THAT CHANCES TO LIE IN ITS PATH...
THROOM!
...AND IT IS SOME SORT OF MINOR MIRACLE THAT, DESPITE THE WIDESPREAD DEVASTATION, THERE IS NOT A SINGLE PERSON KILLED...
...AT LEAST, NOT YET!

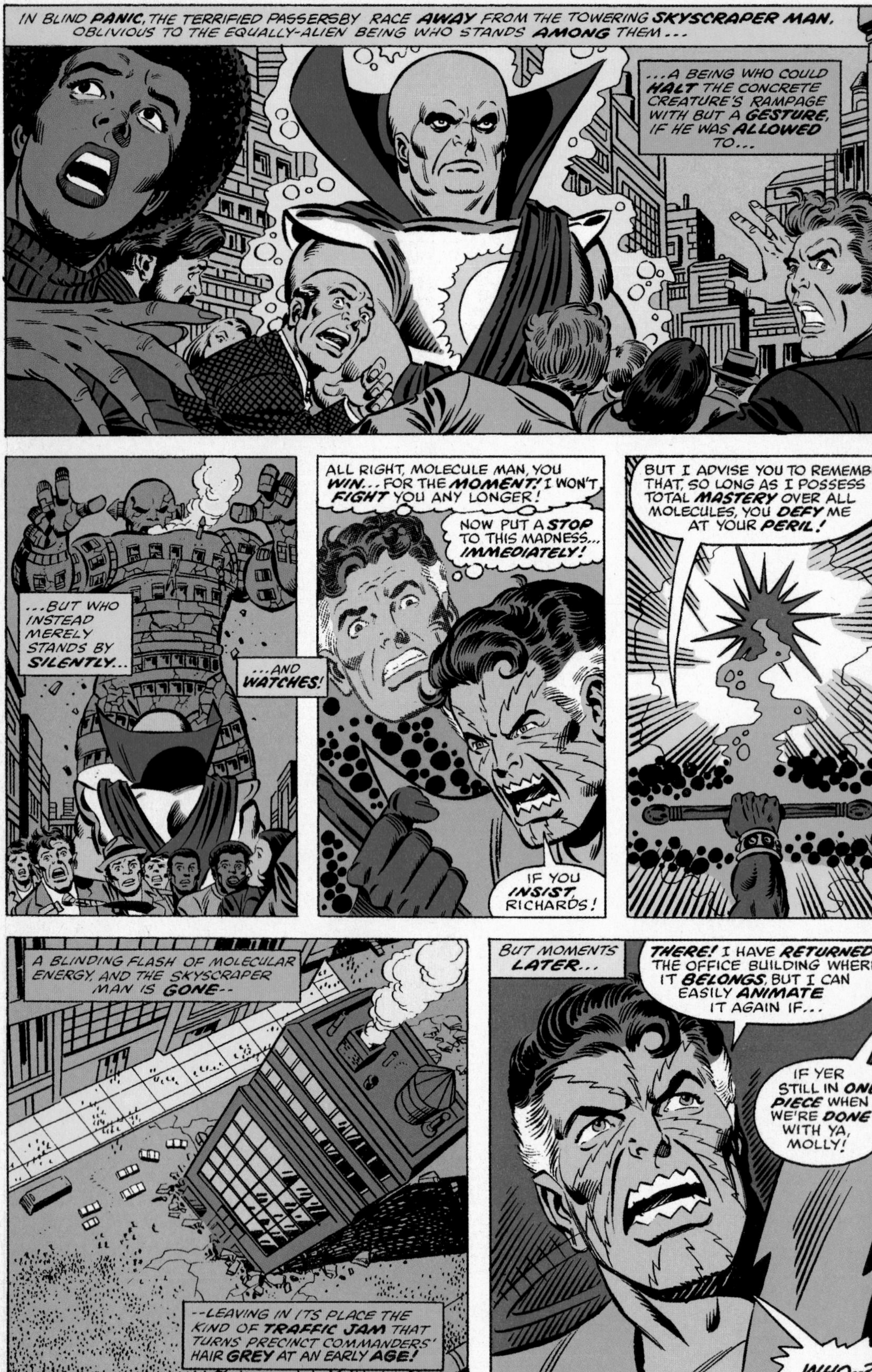
IN BLIND PANIC, THE TERRIFIED PASSERSBY RACE AWAY FROM THE TOWERING SKYSCRAPER MAN, OBLIVIOUS TO THE EQUALLY-ALIEN BEING WHO STANDS AMONG THEM...
...A BEING WHO COULD HALT THE CONCRETE CREATURE'S RAMPAGE WITH BUT A GESTURE, IF HE WAS ALLOWED TO...
...BUT WHO INSTEAD MERELY STANDS BY SILENTLY...
...AND WATCHES!
ALL RIGHT, MOLECULE MAN, YOU WIN... FOR THE MOMENT! I WON'T FIGHT YOU ANY LONGER!
NOW PUT A STOP TO THIS MADNESS... IMMEDIATELY!
IF YOU INSIST, RICHARDS!
BUT I ADVISE YOU TO REMEMBER THAT, SO LONG AS I POSSESS TOTAL MASTERY OVER ALL MOLECULES, YOU DEFY ME AT YOUR PERIL!
A BLINDING FLASH OF MOLECULAR ENERGY, AND THE SKYSCRAPER MAN IS GONE--
--LEAVING IN ITS PLACE THE KIND OF TRAFFIC JAM THAT TURNS PRECINCT COMMANDERS' HAIR GREY AT AN EARLY AGE!
BUT MOMENTS LATER...
THERE! I HAVE RETURNED THE OFFICE BUILDING WHERE IT BELONGS, BUT I CAN EASILY ANIMATE IT AGAIN IF...
IF YER STILL IN ONE PIECE WHEN WE'RE DONE WITH YA, MOLLY!
WHO--?!?

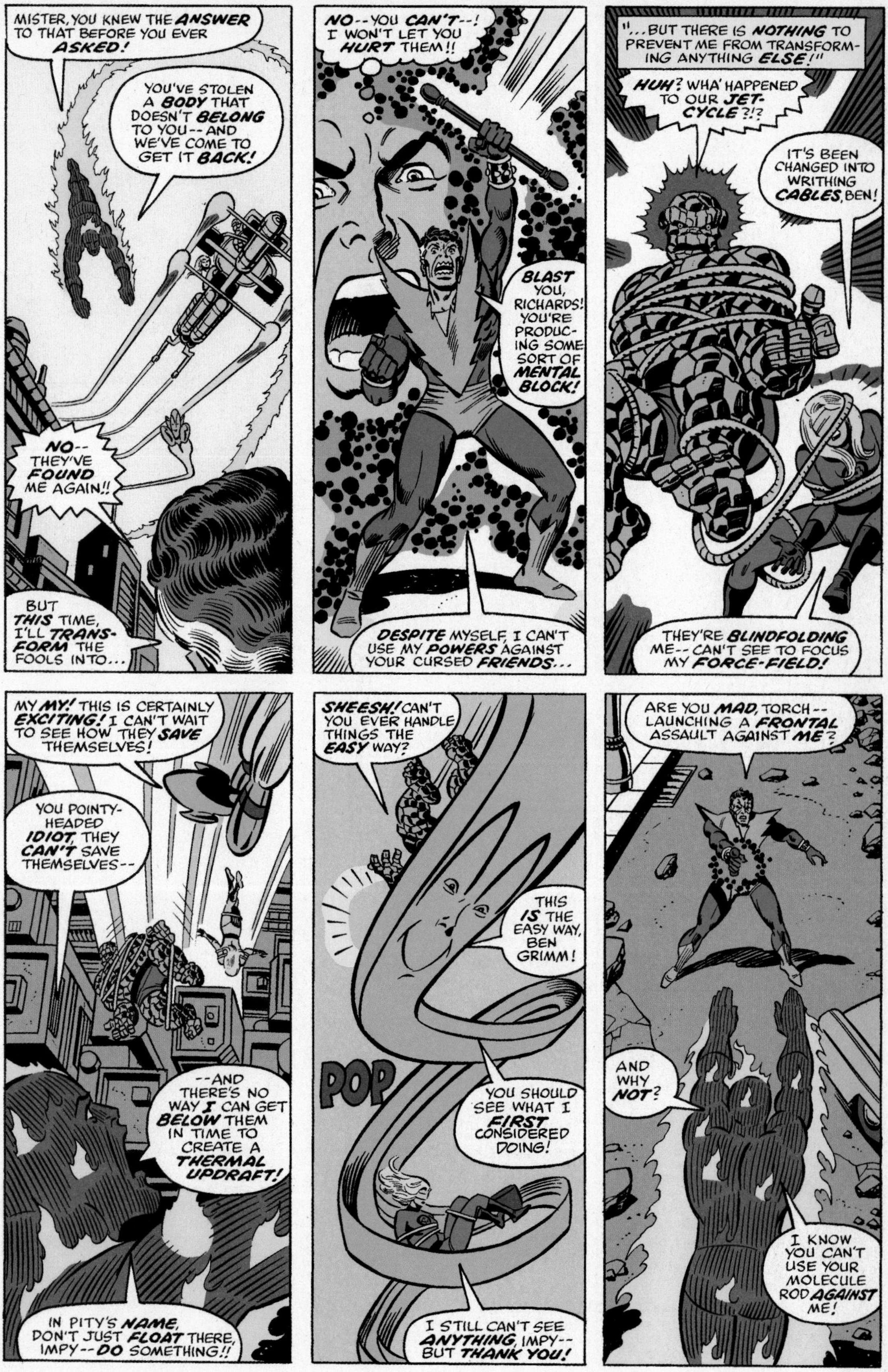
MISTER, YOU KNEW THE ANSWER TO THAT BEFORE YOU EVER ASKED!
YOU'VE STOLEN A BODY THAT DOESN'T BELONG TO YOU--AND WE'VE COME TO GET IT BACK!
NO-- THEY'VE FOUND ME AGAIN!!
BUT THIS TIME, I'LL TRANSFORM THE FOOLS INTO...
NO--YOU CAN'T--! I WON'T LET YOU HURT THEM!!
BLAST YOU, RICHARDS! YOU'RE PRODUCING SOME SORT OF MENTAL BLOCK!
DESPITE MYSELF, I CAN'T USE MY POWERS AGAINST YOUR CURSED FRIENDS...
"...BUT THERE IS NOTHING TO PREVENT ME FROM TRANSFORMING ANYTHING ELSE!"
HUH? WHA' HAPPENED TO OUR JET-CYCLE?!?
IT'S BEEN CHANGED INTO WRITHING CABLES, BEN!
THEY'RE BLINDFOLDING ME-- CAN'T SEE TO FOCUS MY FORCE-FIELD!
MY MY! THIS IS CERTAINLY EXCITING! I CAN'T WAIT TO SEE HOW THEY SAVE THEMSELVES!
YOU POINTY-HEADED IDIOT, THEY CAN'T SAVE THEMSELVES--
--AND THERE'S NO WAY I CAN GET BELOW THEM IN TIME TO CREATE A THERMAL UPDRAFT!
IN PITY'S NAME, DON'T JUST FLOAT THERE, IMPY--DO SOMETHING!!
SHEESH! CAN'T YOU EVER HANDLE THINGS THE EASY WAY?
THIS IS THE EASY WAY, BEN GRIMM!
POP
YOU SHOULD SEE WHAT I FIRST CONSIDERED DOING!
I STILL CAN'T SEE ANYTHING, IMPY-- BUT THANK YOU!
ARE YOU MAD, TORCH-- LAUNCHING A FRONTAL ASSAULT AGAINST ME?
AND WHY NOT?
I KNOW YOU CAN'T USE YOUR MOLECULE ROD AGAINST ME!

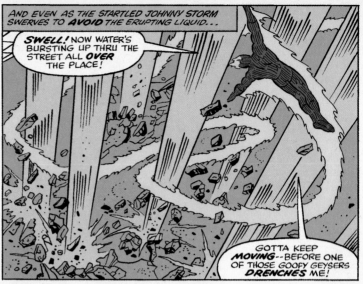

BUT I NEEDN'T AFFECT YOU *PERSONALLY*, DOLT, IN ORDER TO *DESTROY* YOU!!

HOLY SMOKE!

HE'S BURST AN UNDERGROUND *WATER* MAIN!

AND EVEN AS THE STARTLED JOHNNY STORM SWERVES TO *AVOID* THE ERUPTING LIQUID...

SWELL! NOW WATER'S BURSTING UP THRU THE STREET ALL *OVER* THE PLACE!

GOTTA KEEP *MOVING*--BEFORE ONE OF THOSE GOOFY GEYSERS *DRENCHES* ME!

STOP--YOU *MUSTN'T*--!

GET OUT OF MY *HEAD*, RICHARDS--

--OR YOU'RE GOING TO *REGRET* IT!!

WHILE, ACROSS THE *STREET*, ALL BUT *UN-NOTICED*, THE WATCHER *SURVEYS* THE SCENE OF BATTLE...

...AND SILENTLY *SCOWLS*.

MAN, I BEEN ON SOME *ROLLER-COASTERS* IN MY TIME-- BUT *THIS* ONE TAKES THE *CAKE!*

YOU *OKAY*, SUZIE?

FINE, BEN.

MY *FORCE FIELD* IS SHATTERING MY *BONDS!*

YER REALLY GETTIN' *FANCY* WIT' YER INVISIBLE POWERS LATELY SUZIE DOLL, BUT *YERS* TRULY...

SKRAKKT!

WELL, I *STILL* PREFER THE OL'-FASHIONED *SIMPLE* WAY!!

NOW THIS IS MORE *LIKE* IT! THIS IS THE SORT OF FUN I *EX-PECTED* TO HAVE WITH YOU FOLKS!

STAND *BACK*, EVERYONE-- IT'S *MY* TURN NOW!

HUH?

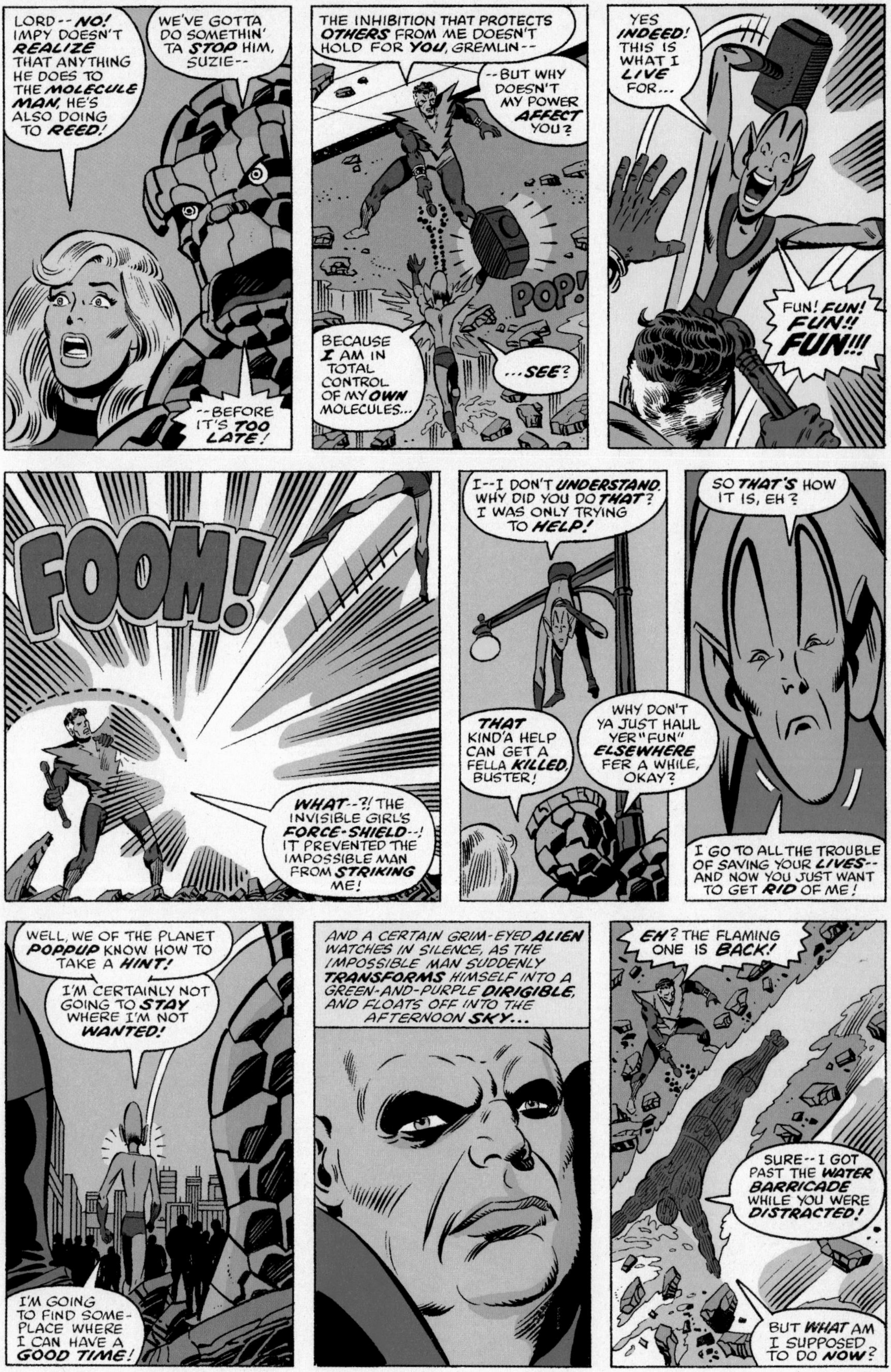
LORD--NO! IMPY DOESN'T REALIZE THAT ANYTHING HE DOES TO THE MOLECULE MAN, HE'S ALSO DOING TO REED!
WE'VE GOTTA DO SOMETHIN' TA STOP HIM, SUZIE--
--BEFORE IT'S TOO LATE!
THE INHIBITION THAT PROTECTS OTHERS FROM ME DOESN'T HOLD FOR YOU, GREMLIN--
--BUT WHY DOESN'T MY POWER AFFECT YOU?
POP!
BECAUSE I AM IN TOTAL CONTROL OF MY OWN MOLECULES...
...SEE?
YES INDEED! THIS IS WHAT I LIVE FOR...
FUN! FUN! FUN!! FUN!!!
FOOM!
WHAT--?! THE INVISIBLE GIRL'S FORCE-SHIELD--! IT PREVENTED THE IMPOSSIBLE MAN FROM STRIKING ME!
I--I DON'T UNDERSTAND. WHY DID YOU DO THAT? I WAS ONLY TRYING TO HELP!
THAT KIND'A HELP CAN GET A FELLA KILLED, BUSTER!
WHY DON'T YA JUST HAUL YER "FUN" ELSEWHERE FER A WHILE, OKAY?
SO THAT'S HOW IT IS, EH?
I GO TO ALL THE TROUBLE OF SAVING YOUR LIVES--AND NOW YOU JUST WANT TO GET RID OF ME!
WELL, WE OF THE PLANET POPPUP KNOW HOW TO TAKE A HINT!
I'M CERTAINLY NOT GOING TO STAY WHERE I'M NOT WANTED!
I'M GOING TO FIND SOME-PLACE WHERE I CAN HAVE A GOOD TIME!
AND A CERTAIN GRIM-EYED ALIEN WATCHES IN SILENCE, AS THE IMPOSSIBLE MAN SUDDENLY TRANSFORMS HIMSELF INTO A GREEN-AND-PURPLE DIRIGIBLE, AND FLOATS OFF INTO THE AFTERNOON SKY...
EH? THE FLAMING ONE IS BACK!
SURE--I GOT PAST THE WATER BARRICADE WHILE YOU WERE DISTRACTED!
BUT WHAT AM I SUPPOSED TO DO NOW?

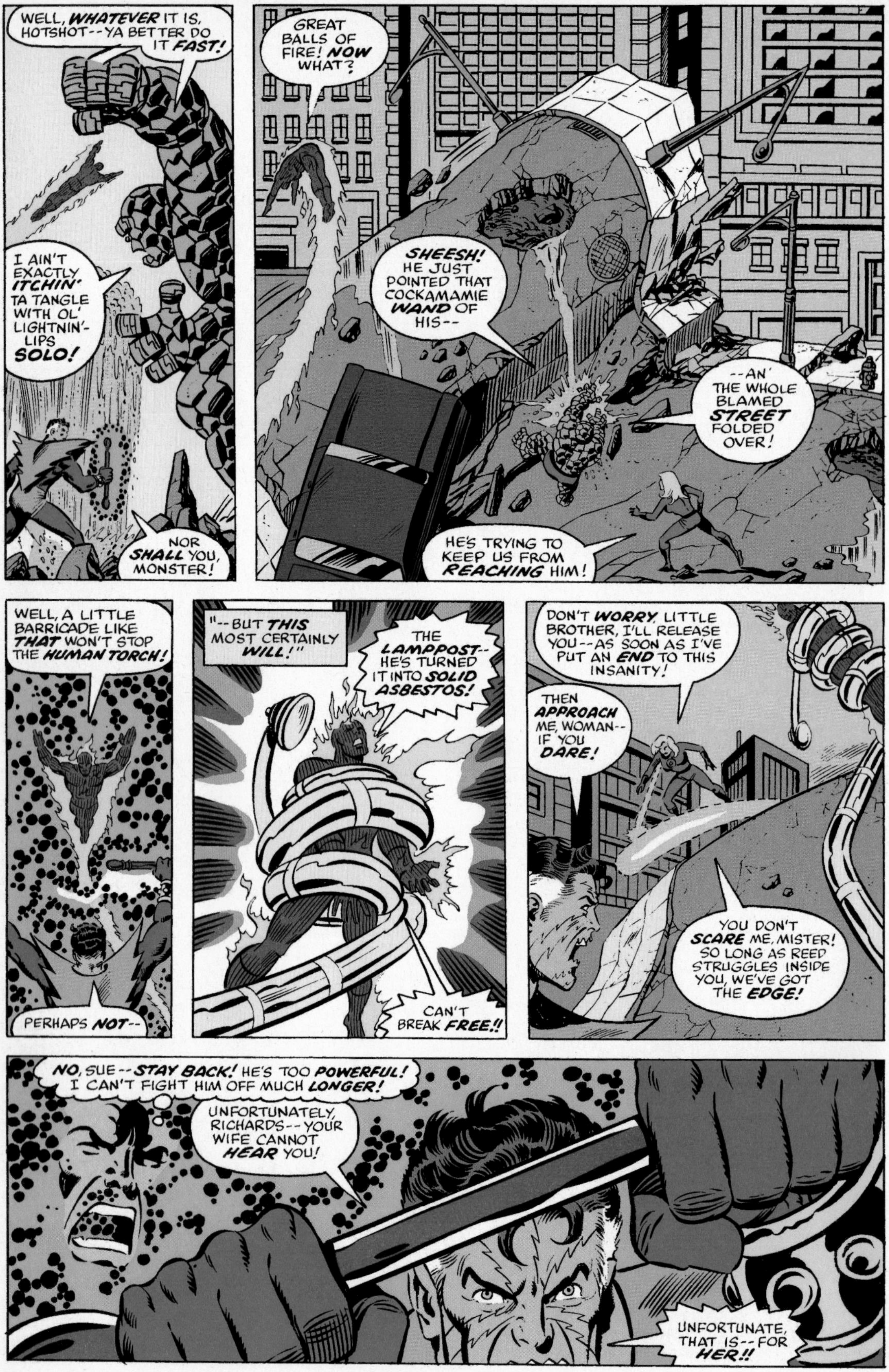
WELL, WHATEVER IT IS, HOTSHOT--YA BETTER DO IT FAST!
I AIN'T EXACTLY ITCHIN' TA TANGLE WITH OL' LIGHTNIN'-LIPS SOLO!
NOR SHALL YOU, MONSTER!
GREAT BALLS OF FIRE! NOW WHAT?
SHEESH! HE JUST POINTED THAT COCKAMAMIE WAND OF HIS--
--AN' THE WHOLE BLAMED STREET FOLDED OVER!
HE'S TRYING TO KEEP US FROM REACHING HIM!
WELL, A LITTLE BARRICADE LIKE THAT WON'T STOP THE HUMAN TORCH!
PERHAPS NOT--
"--BUT THIS MOST CERTAINLY WILL!"
THE LAMPPOST--HE'S TURNED IT INTO SOLID ASBESTOS!
CAN'T BREAK FREE!!
DON'T WORRY, LITTLE BROTHER, I'LL RELEASE YOU--AS SOON AS I'VE PUT AN END TO THIS INSANITY!
THEN APPROACH ME, WOMAN--IF YOU DARE!
YOU DON'T SCARE ME, MISTER! SO LONG AS REED STRUGGLES INSIDE YOU, WE'VE GOT THE EDGE!
NO, SUE--STAY BACK! HE'S TOO POWERFUL! I CAN'T FIGHT HIM OFF MUCH LONGER!
UNFORTUNATELY, RICHARDS--YOUR WIFE CANNOT HEAR YOU!
UNFORTUNATE, THAT IS--FOR HER!!

I'VE ALREADY TOLD YOU **ONCE**, MISTER -- YOU DON'T **FRIGHTEN** ME!

REMARKABLE! HER FORCE-SHIELD HAS NO TRUE **MOLECULAR** STRUCTURE! I CAN'T **AFFECT** IT!

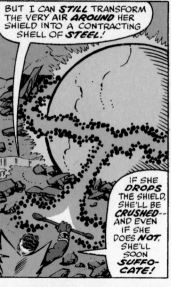

BUT I CAN **STILL** TRANSFORM THE VERY AIR HER SHIELD INTO A CONTRACTING SHELL OF **STEEL**!

IF SHE **DROPS** THE SHIELD, SHE'LL BE **CRUSHED** -- AND EVEN IF SHE DOES **NOT**, SHE'LL SOON **SUFFOCATE**!

TAKE A GOOD **LOOK**, RICHARDS -- YOUR OWN **WIFE** -- AND THERE'S NOTHING YOU CAN DO TO **SAVE** HER!

NO! GOT TO **CONCENTRATE** -- FORCE HIM TO **RELEASE** HER --!

BUT AT THAT SELFSAME **MOMENT**...

OKAY, **BUSTER** -- RECESS IS **OVER**! AS OF RIGHT **NOW**...

IT'S CLOBBERIN' TIME!!

THWOOM!

SAVAGELY, THE JAGGED **FRAGMENTS** OF THE SHATTERED STREET **SPRAY** THRU THE AIR...

UUNNHH!!

BROK!

...WHERE **ONE** OF THEM ACCIDENTLY STRIKES AN UNINTENDED **TARGET**!

HOLY COW!

I CLOBBERED **REED**!

DO WHAT YOU **CAN** FOR HIM, BENJY! I'M GOING TO RESCUE **SUE**!

GOT TO HANDLE THIS **CAREFULLY**! SUE'S FORCE-SHIELD -- AND THE UNSTABLE MOLECULES OF HER **COSTUME** -- WILL PROTECT HER TO **SOME** DEGREE...

...BUT THE **HEAT** I'M GENERATING TO **MELT** HER STEEL COFFIN CAN STILL **INCINERATE** HER UNLESS...

THANK HEAVEN -- I **DID** IT!

REED? ARE YA **OKAY**, PAL? I'M SORRY 'BOUT **FLATTENIN'** YA!

HERE, LEMME GIVE YA A HAND **UP**!

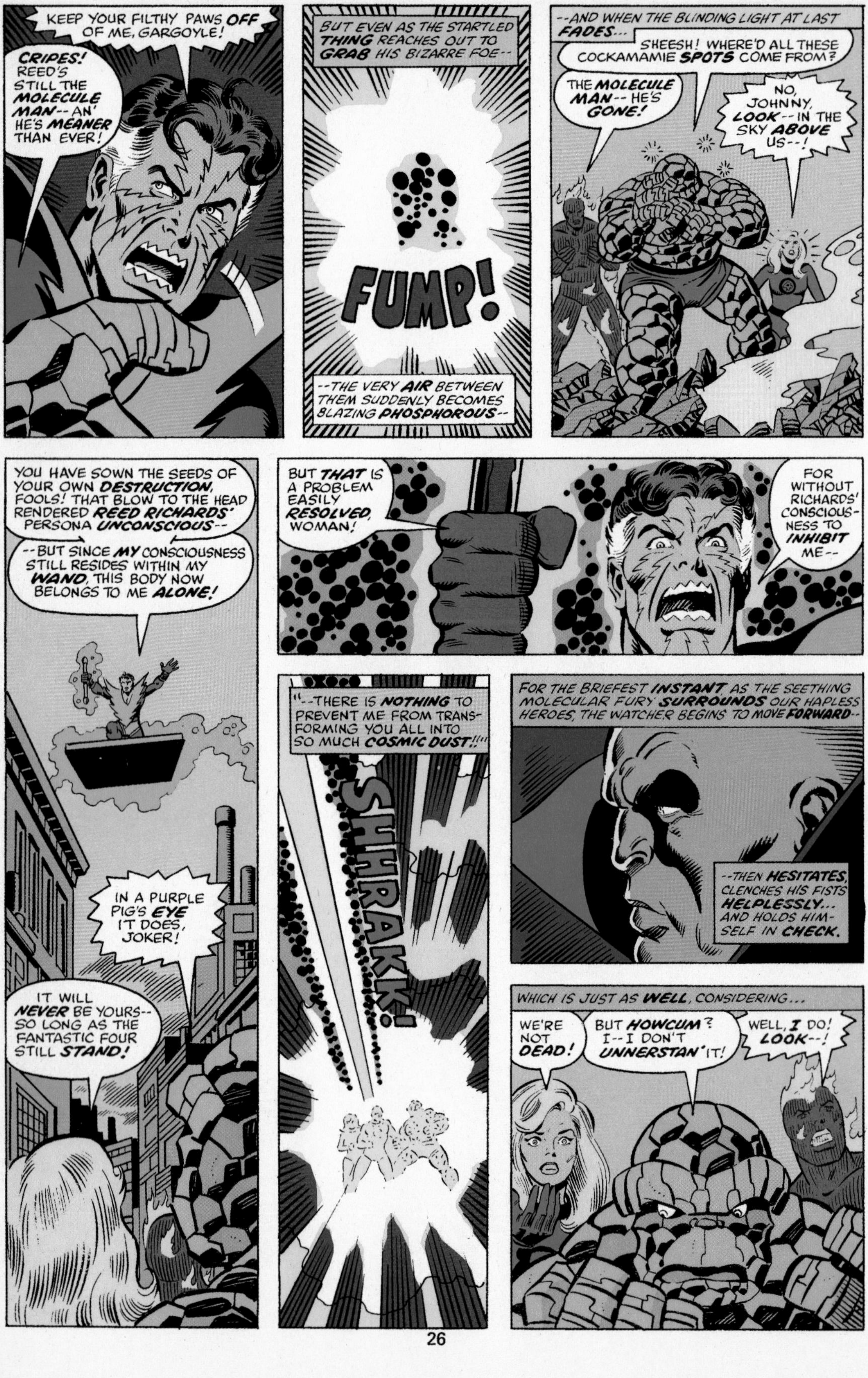
KEEP YOUR FILTHY PAWS OFF OF ME, GARGOYLE!
CRIPES! REED'S STILL THE MOLECULE MAN-- AN' HE'S MEANER THAN EVER!
BUT EVEN AS THE STARTLED THING REACHES OUT TO GRAB HIS BIZARRE FOE--
FUMP!
--THE VERY AIR BETWEEN THEM SUDDENLY BECOMES BLAZING PHOSPHOROUS--
--AND WHEN THE BLINDING LIGHT AT LAST FADES...
SHEESH! WHERE'D ALL THESE COCKAMAMIE SPOTS COME FROM?
THE MOLECULE MAN-- HE'S GONE!
NO, JOHNNY, LOOK-- IN THE SKY ABOVE US--!
YOU HAVE SOWN THE SEEDS OF YOUR OWN DESTRUCTION, FOOLS! THAT BLOW TO THE HEAD RENDERED REED RICHARDS' PERSONA UNCONSCIOUS--
--BUT SINCE MY CONSCIOUSNESS STILL RESIDES WITHIN MY WAND, THIS BODY NOW BELONGS TO ME ALONE!
IN A PURPLE PIG'S EYE IT DOES, JOKER!
IT WILL NEVER BE YOURS-- SO LONG AS THE FANTASTIC FOUR STILL STAND!
BUT THAT IS A PROBLEM EASILY RESOLVED, WOMAN!
FOR WITHOUT RICHARDS' CONSCIOUSNESS TO INHIBIT ME--
"--THERE IS NOTHING TO PREVENT ME FROM TRANSFORMING YOU ALL INTO SO MUCH COSMIC DUST!!"
SHHRAKK!
FOR THE BRIEFEST INSTANT, AS THE SEETHING MOLECULAR FURY SURROUNDS OUR HAPLESS HEROES, THE WATCHER BEGINS TO MOVE FORWARD--
--THEN HESITATES, CLENCHES HIS FISTS HELPLESSLY... AND HOLDS HIMSELF IN CHECK.
WHICH IS JUST AS WELL, CONSIDERING...
WE'RE NOT DEAD!
BUT HOWCUM? I-- I DON'T UNNERSTAN' IT!
WELL, I DO! LOOK--!

26

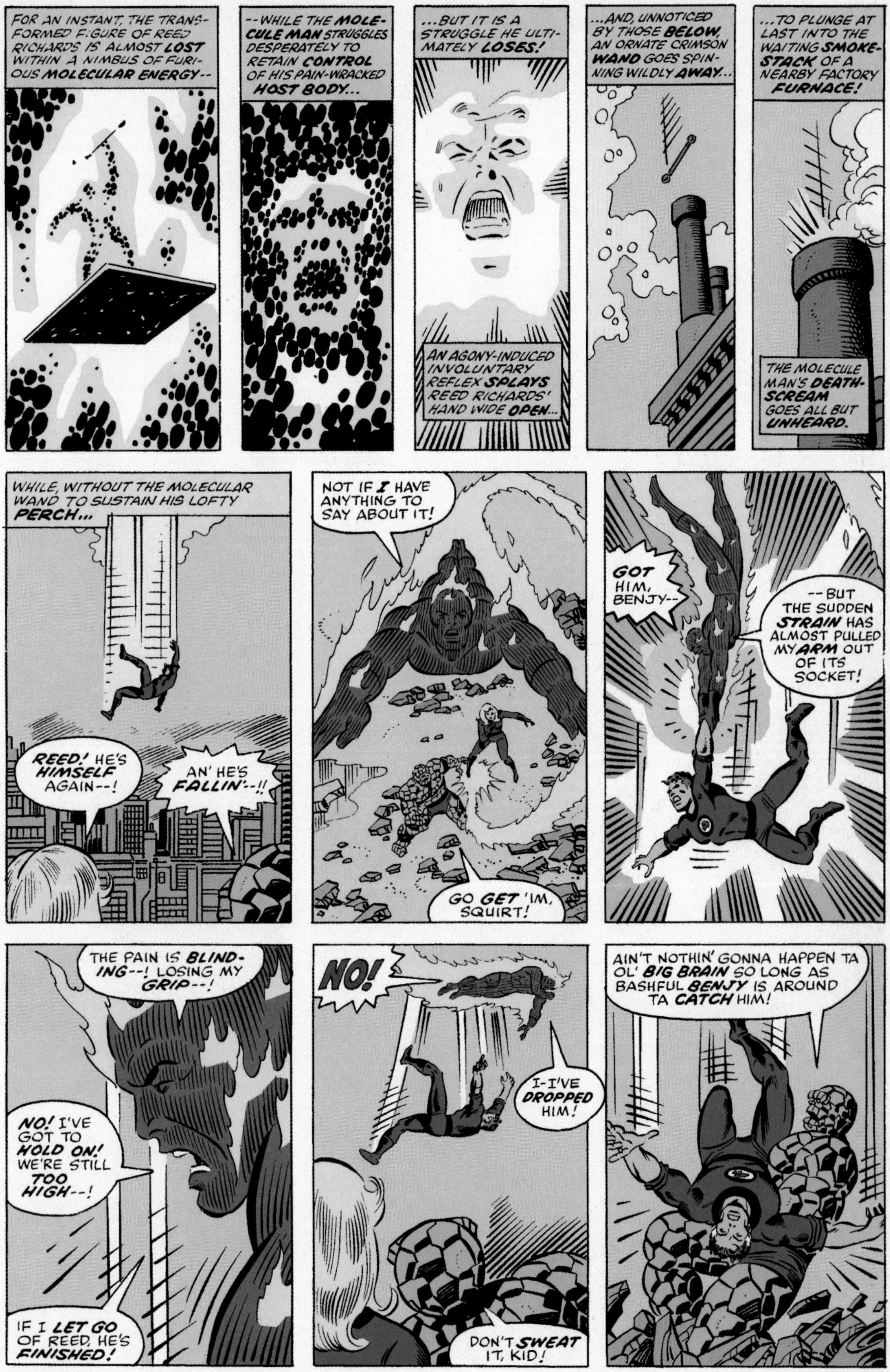

FOR AN INSTANT, THE TRANS-FORMED FIGURE OF REED RICHARDS IS ALMOST LOST WITHIN A NIMBUS OF FURI-OUS MOLECULAR ENERGY--
--WHILE THE MOLE-CULE MAN STRUGGLES DESPERATELY TO RETAIN CONTROL OF HIS PAIN-WRACKED HOST BODY...
...BUT IT IS A STRUGGLE HE ULTI-MATELY LOSES!
AN AGONY-INDUCED INVOLUNTARY REFLEX SPLAYS REED RICHARDS' HAND WIDE OPEN...
...AND, UNNOTICED BY THOSE BELOW, AN ORNATE CRIMSON WAND GOES SPIN-NING WILDLY AWAY...
...TO PLUNGE AT LAST INTO THE WAITING SMOKE-STACK OF A NEARBY FACTORY FURNACE!
THE MOLECULE MAN'S DEATH-SCREAM GOES ALL BUT UNHEARD.
WHILE, WITHOUT THE MOLECULAR WAND TO SUSTAIN HIS LOFTY PERCH...
REED! HE'S HIMSELF AGAIN--!
AN' HE'S FALLIN'--!!
NOT IF I HAVE ANYTHING TO SAY ABOUT IT!
GO GET 'IM, SQUIRT!
GOT HIM, BENJY--
--BUT THE SUDDEN STRAIN HAS ALMOST PULLED MY ARM OUT OF ITS SOCKET!
THE PAIN IS BLIND-ING--! LOSING MY GRIP--!
NO! I'VE GOT TO HOLD ON! WE'RE STILL TOO HIGH--!
IF I LET GO OF REED, HE'S FINISHED!
NO!
I-I'VE DROPPED HIM!
DON'T SWEAT IT, KID!
AIN'T NOTHIN' GONNA HAPPEN TA OL' BIG BRAIN SO LONG AS BASHFUL BENJY IS AROUND TA CATCH HIM!

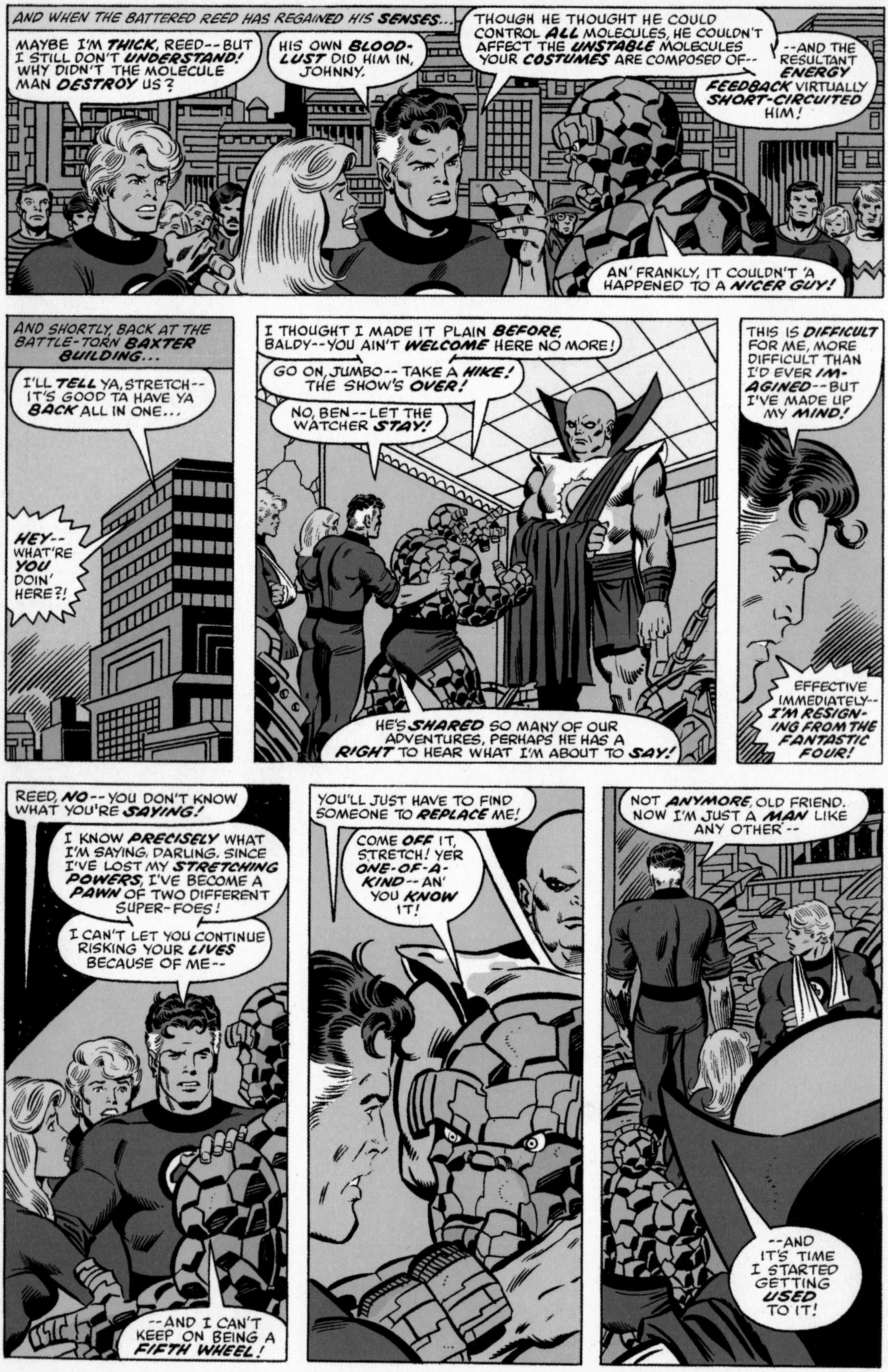
AND WHEN THE BATTERED REED HAS REGAINED HIS SENSES...
MAYBE I'M THICK, REED--BUT I STILL DON'T UNDERSTAND! WHY DIDN'T THE MOLECULE MAN DESTROY US?
HIS OWN BLOOD-LUST DID HIM IN, JOHNNY.
THOUGH HE THOUGHT HE COULD CONTROL ALL MOLECULES, HE COULDN'T AFFECT THE UNSTABLE MOLECULES YOUR COSTUMES ARE COMPOSED OF--
--AND THE RESULTANT ENERGY FEEDBACK VIRTUALLY SHORT-CIRCUITED HIM!
AN' FRANKLY, IT COULDN'T 'A HAPPENED TO A NICER GUY!
AND SHORTLY, BACK AT THE BATTLE-TORN BAXTER BUILDING...
I'LL TELL YA, STRETCH--IT'S GOOD TA HAVE YA BACK ALL IN ONE...
HEY--WHAT'RE YOU DOIN' HERE?!
I THOUGHT I MADE IT PLAIN BEFORE, BALDY--YOU AIN'T WELCOME HERE NO MORE!
GO ON, JUMBO--TAKE A HIKE! THE SHOW'S OVER!
NO, BEN--LET THE WATCHER STAY!
HE'S SHARED SO MANY OF OUR ADVENTURES, PERHAPS HE HAS A RIGHT TO HEAR WHAT I'M ABOUT TO SAY!
THIS IS DIFFICULT FOR ME, MORE DIFFICULT THAN I'D EVER IMAGINED--BUT I'VE MADE UP MY MIND!
EFFECTIVE IMMEDIATELY--I'M RESIGNING FROM THE FANTASTIC FOUR!
REED, NO--YOU DON'T KNOW WHAT YOU'RE SAYING!
I KNOW PRECISELY WHAT I'M SAYING, DARLING. SINCE I'VE LOST MY STRETCHING POWERS, I'VE BECOME A PAWN OF TWO DIFFERENT SUPER-FOES!
I CAN'T LET YOU CONTINUE RISKING YOUR LIVES BECAUSE OF ME--
--AND I CAN'T KEEP ON BEING A FIFTH WHEEL!
YOU'LL JUST HAVE TO FIND SOMEONE TO REPLACE ME!
COME OFF IT, STRETCH! YER ONE-OF-A-KIND--AN' YOU KNOW IT!
NOT ANYMORE, OLD FRIEND. NOW I'M JUST A MAN LIKE ANY OTHER--
--AND IT'S TIME I STARTED GETTING USED TO IT!

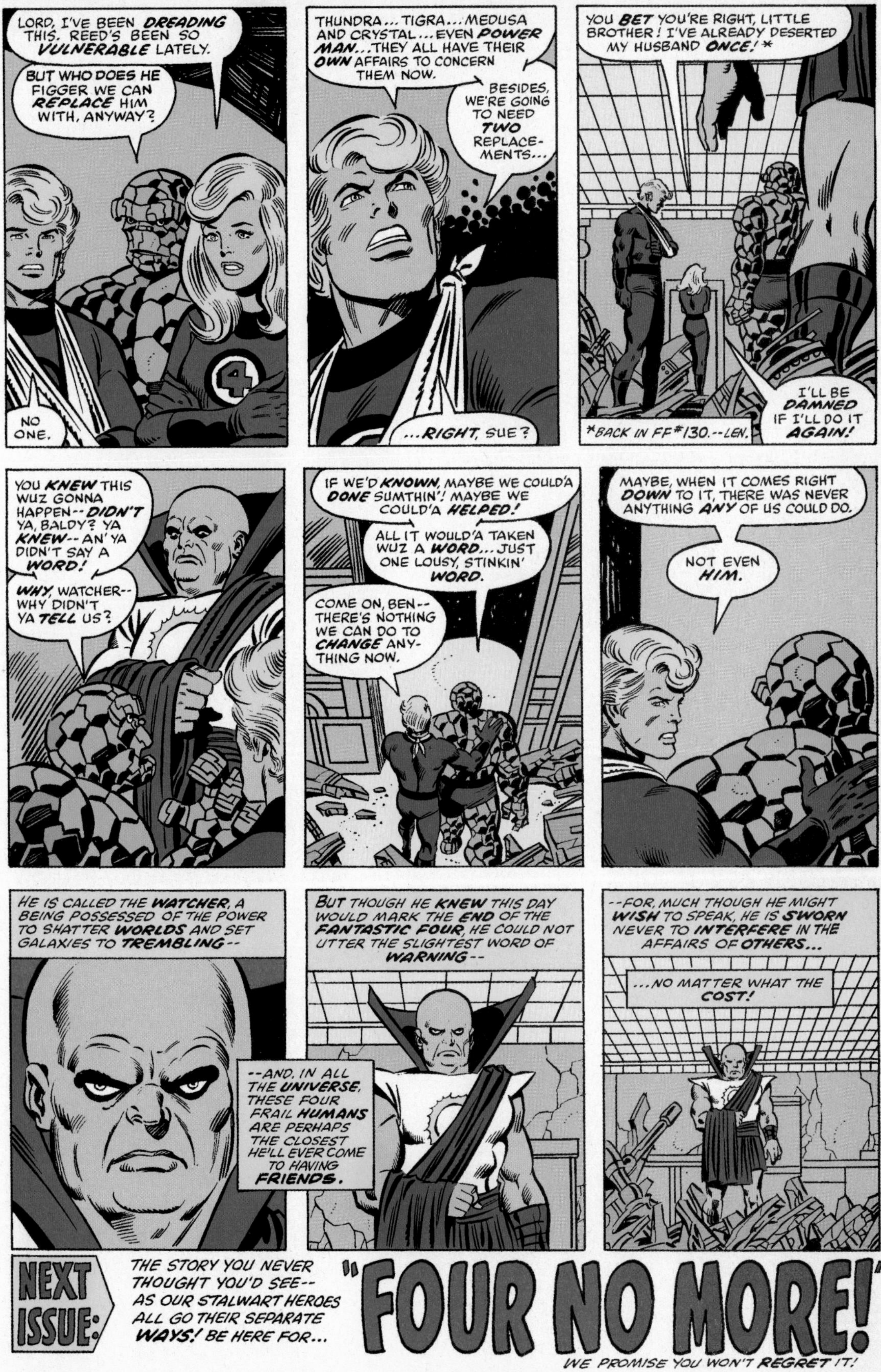
LORD, I'VE BEEN DREADING THIS. REED'S BEEN SO VULNERABLE LATELY.
BUT WHO DOES HE FIGGER WE CAN REPLACE HIM WITH, ANYWAY?
NO ONE.
THUNDRA... TIGRA... MEDUSA AND CRYSTAL... EVEN POWER MAN... THEY ALL HAVE THEIR OWN AFFAIRS TO CONCERN THEM NOW.
BESIDES, WE'RE GOING TO NEED TWO REPLACE-MENTS...
...RIGHT, SUE?
YOU BET YOU'RE RIGHT, LITTLE BROTHER! I'VE ALREADY DESERTED MY HUSBAND ONCE! *
I'LL BE DAMNED IF I'LL DO IT AGAIN!
*BACK IN FF #130.--LEN.
YOU KNEW THIS WUZ GONNA HAPPEN--DIDN'T YA, BALDY? YA KNEW--AN' YA DIDN'T SAY A WORD!
WHY, WATCHER--WHY DIDN'T YA TELL US?
IF WE'D KNOWN, MAYBE WE COULD'A DONE SUMTHIN'! MAYBE WE COULD'A HELPED!
ALL IT WOULD'A TAKEN WUZ A WORD... JUST ONE LOUSY, STINKIN' WORD.
COME ON, BEN--THERE'S NOTHING WE CAN DO TO CHANGE ANY-THING NOW.
MAYBE, WHEN IT COMES RIGHT DOWN TO IT, THERE WAS NEVER ANYTHING ANY OF US COULD DO.
NOT EVEN HIM.
HE IS CALLED THE WATCHER, A BEING POSSESSED OF THE POWER TO SHATTER WORLDS AND SET GALAXIES TO TREMBLING--
--AND, IN ALL THE UNIVERSE, THESE FOUR FRAIL HUMANS ARE PERHAPS THE CLOSEST HE'LL EVER COME TO HAVING FRIENDS.
BUT THOUGH HE KNEW THIS DAY WOULD MARK THE END OF THE FANTASTIC FOUR, HE COULD NOT UTTER THE SLIGHTEST WORD OF WARNING--
--FOR, MUCH THOUGH HE MIGHT WISH TO SPEAK, HE IS SWORN NEVER TO INTERFERE IN THE AFFAIRS OF OTHERS...
...NO MATTER WHAT THE COST!
NEXT ISSUE:
THE STORY YOU NEVER THOUGHT YOU'D SEE--AS OUR STALWART HEROES ALL GO THEIR SEPARATE WAYS! BE HERE FOR...
"FOUR NO MORE!"
WE PROMISE YOU WON'T REGRET IT!

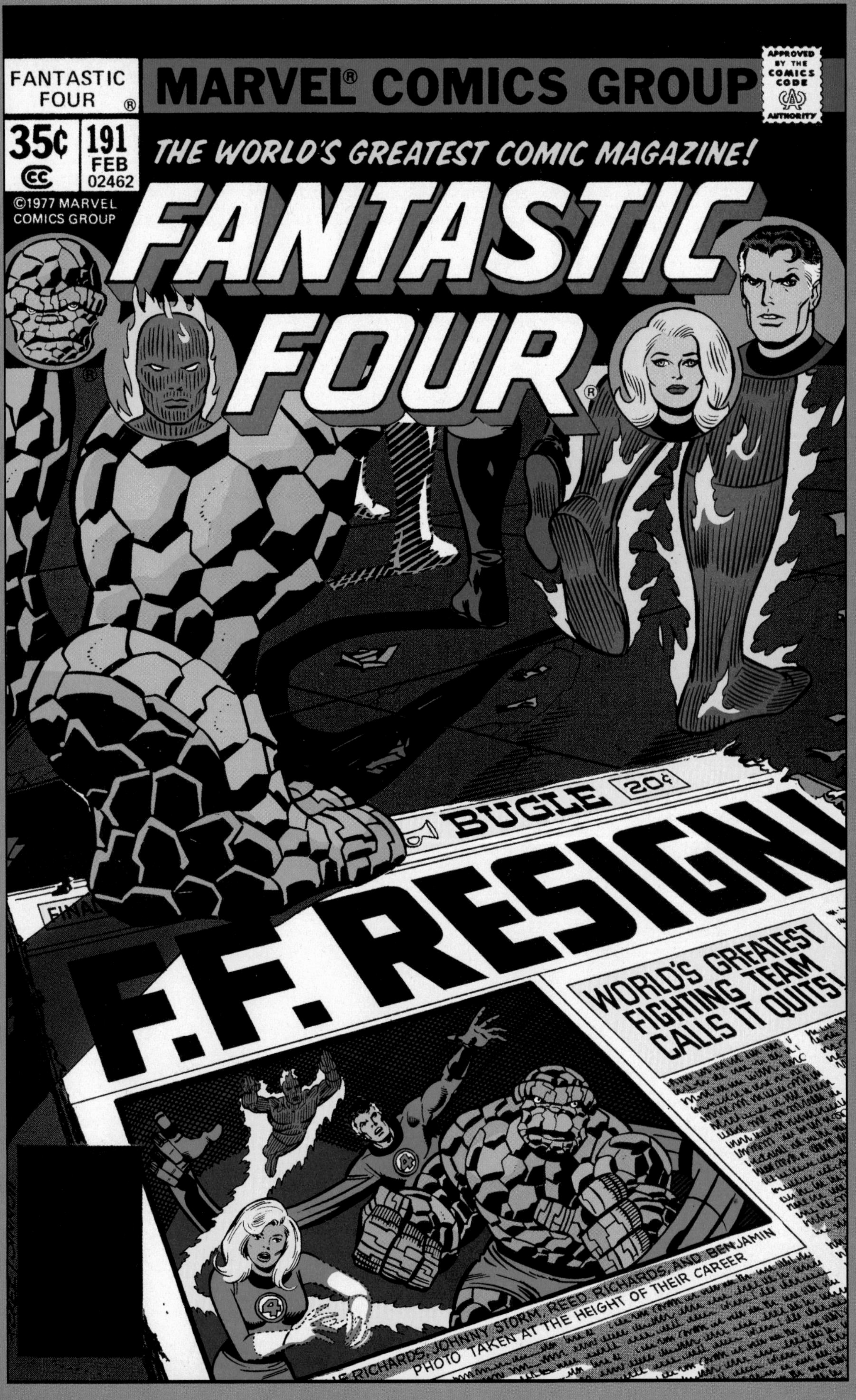

FANTASTIC FOUR
MARVEL® COMICS GROUP
APPROVED BY THE COMICS CODE AUTHORITY
35¢
191 FEB 02462
©1977 MARVEL COMICS GROUP
THE WORLD'S GREATEST COMIC MAGAZINE!
FANTASTIC FOUR
BUGLE 20¢
F.F. RESIGN
WORLD'S GREATEST FIGHTING TEAM CALLS IT QUITS!
RICHARDS, JOHNNY STORM, REED RICHARDS AND BENJAMIN
PHOTO TAKEN AT THE HEIGHT OF THEIR CAREER

A brilliant scientist— his best friend— the woman he loves— and her fiery-tempered kid brother! Together, they braved the unknown terrors of outer space, and were changed by cosmic rays into something more than merely human!
MR. FANTASTIC! THE THING! THE INVISIBLE GIRL! THE HUMAN TORCH! Now they are the FANTASTIC FOUR— and the world will never be the same again!

Stan Lee PRESENTS: THE FANTASTIC FOUR!™

LEN WEIN, WRITER/EDITOR * GEORGE PEREZ & JOE SINNOTT, ARTISTS/STORYTELLERS * GLYNIS WEIN, colorist * JOHN COSTANZA, letterer

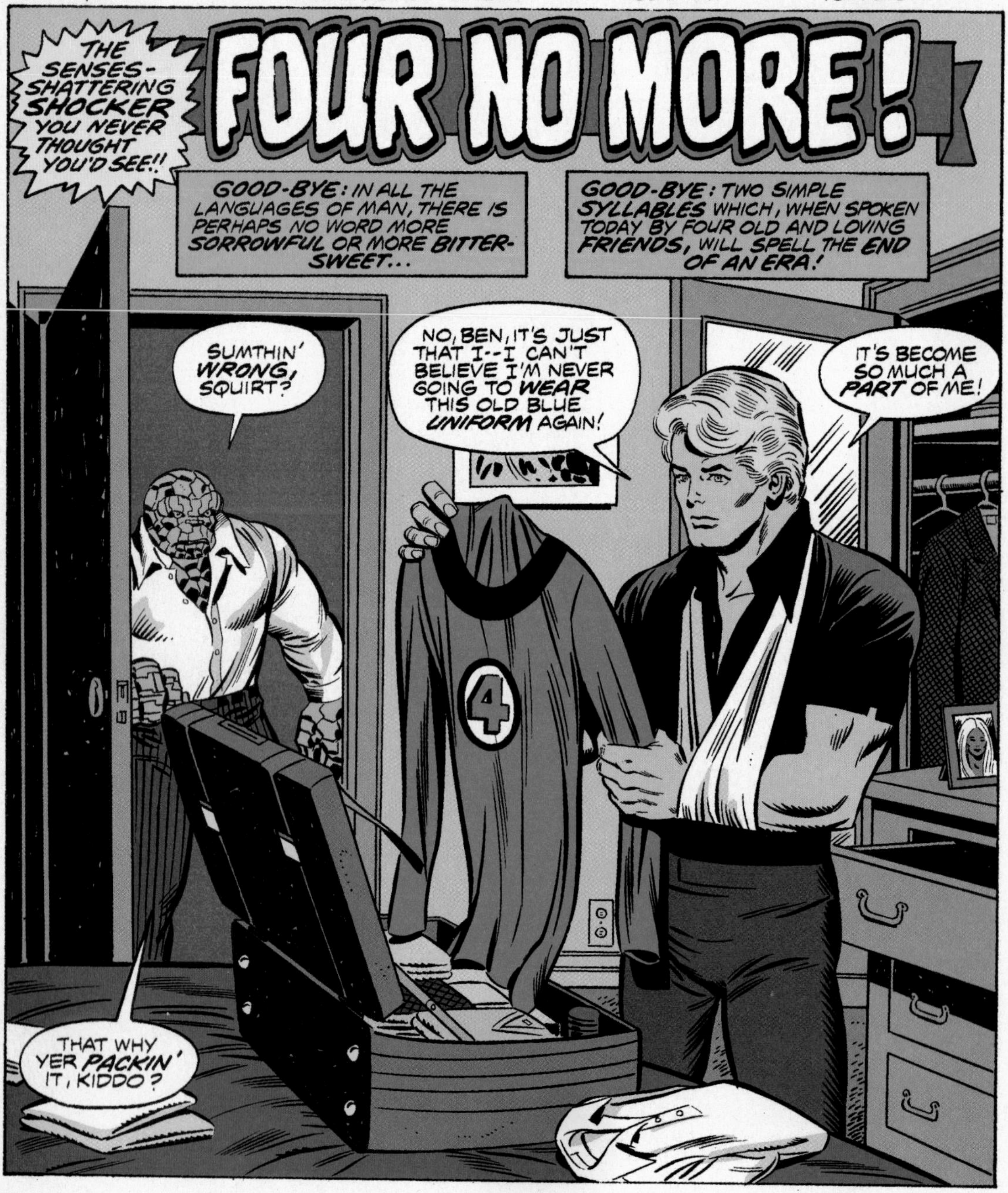

THE SENSES-SHATTERING SHOCKER YOU NEVER THOUGHT YOU'D SEE!!
FOUR NO MORE!
GOOD-BYE: IN ALL THE LANGUAGES OF MAN, THERE IS PERHAPS NO WORD MORE SORROWFUL OR MORE BITTER-SWEET...
GOOD-BYE: TWO SIMPLE SYLLABLES WHICH, WHEN SPOKEN TODAY BY FOUR OLD AND LOVING FRIENDS, WILL SPELL THE END OF AN ERA!
SUMTHIN' WRONG, SQUIRT?
NO, BEN, IT'S JUST THAT I--I CAN'T BELIEVE I'M NEVER GOING TO WEAR THIS OLD BLUE UNIFORM AGAIN!
IT'S BECOME SO MUCH A PART OF ME!
THAT WHY YER PACKIN' IT, KIDDO?

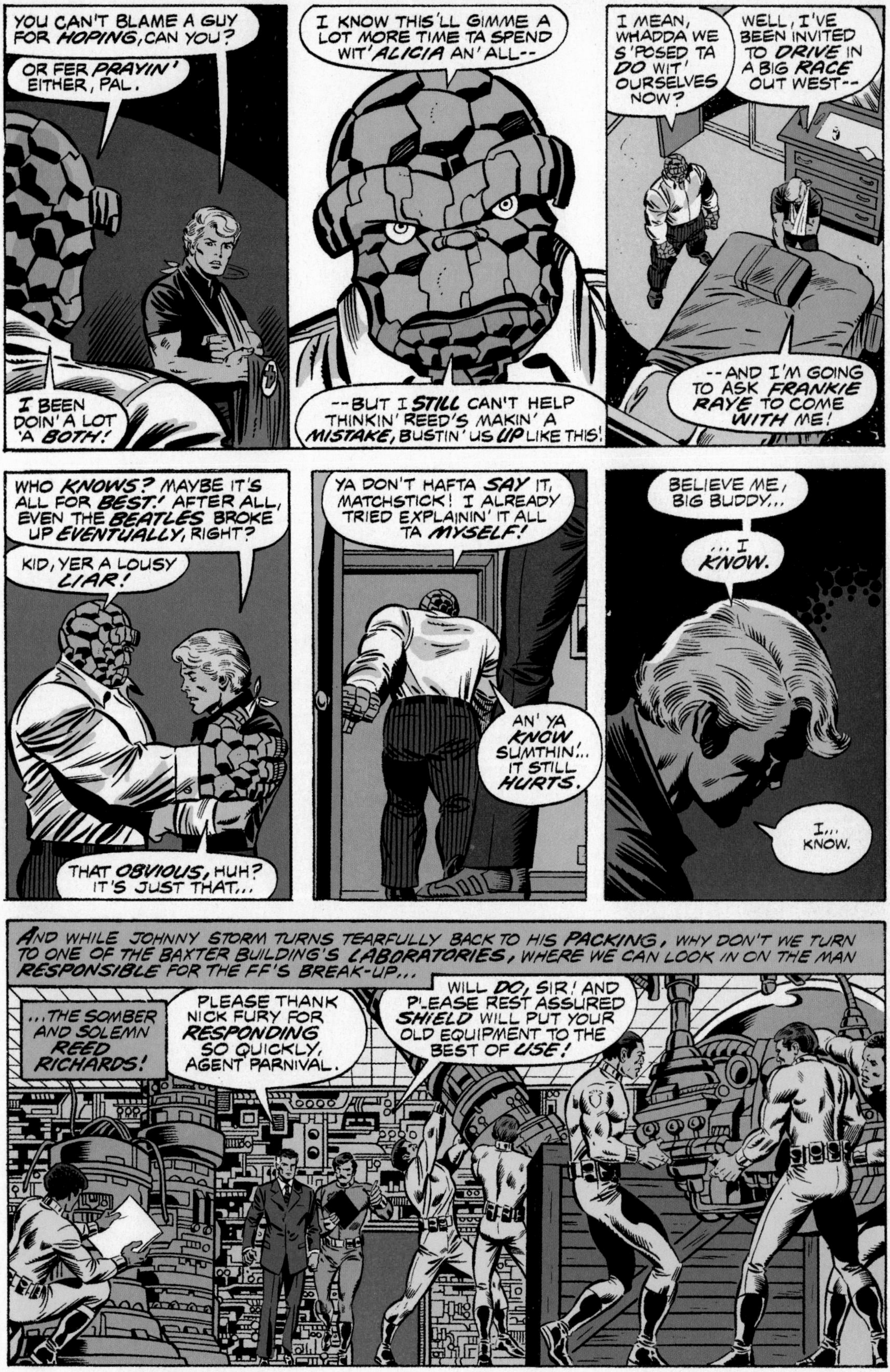
YOU CAN'T BLAME A GUY FOR HOPING, CAN YOU?
OR FER PRAYIN' EITHER, PAL.
I BEEN DOIN' A LOT 'A BOTH!
I KNOW THIS'LL GIMME A LOT MORE TIME TA SPEND WIT' ALICIA AN' ALL--
--BUT I STILL CAN'T HELP THINKIN' REED'S MAKIN' A MISTAKE, BUSTIN' US UP LIKE THIS!
I MEAN, WHADDA WE S'POSED TA DO WIT' OURSELVES NOW?
WELL, I'VE BEEN INVITED TO DRIVE IN A BIG RACE OUT WEST--
--AND I'M GOING TO ASK FRANKIE RAYE TO COME WITH ME!
WHO KNOWS? MAYBE IT'S ALL FOR BEST! AFTER ALL, EVEN THE BEATLES BROKE UP EVENTUALLY, RIGHT?
KID, YER A LOUSY LIAR!
THAT OBVIOUS, HUH? IT'S JUST THAT...
YA DON'T HAFTA SAY IT, MATCHSTICK! I ALREADY TRIED EXPLAININ' IT ALL TA MYSELF!
AN' YA KNOW SUMTHIN'... IT STILL HURTS.
BELIEVE ME, BIG BUDDY...
... I KNOW.
I... KNOW.
AND WHILE JOHNNY STORM TURNS TEARFULLY BACK TO HIS PACKING, WHY DON'T WE TURN TO ONE OF THE BAXTER BUILDING'S LABORATORIES, WHERE WE CAN LOOK IN ON THE MAN RESPONSIBLE FOR THE FF'S BREAK-UP...
...THE SOMBER AND SOLEMN REED RICHARDS!
PLEASE THANK NICK FURY FOR RESPONDING SO QUICKLY, AGENT PARNIVAL.
WILL DO, SIR! AND PLEASE REST ASSURED SHIELD WILL PUT YOUR OLD EQUIPMENT TO THE BEST OF USE!

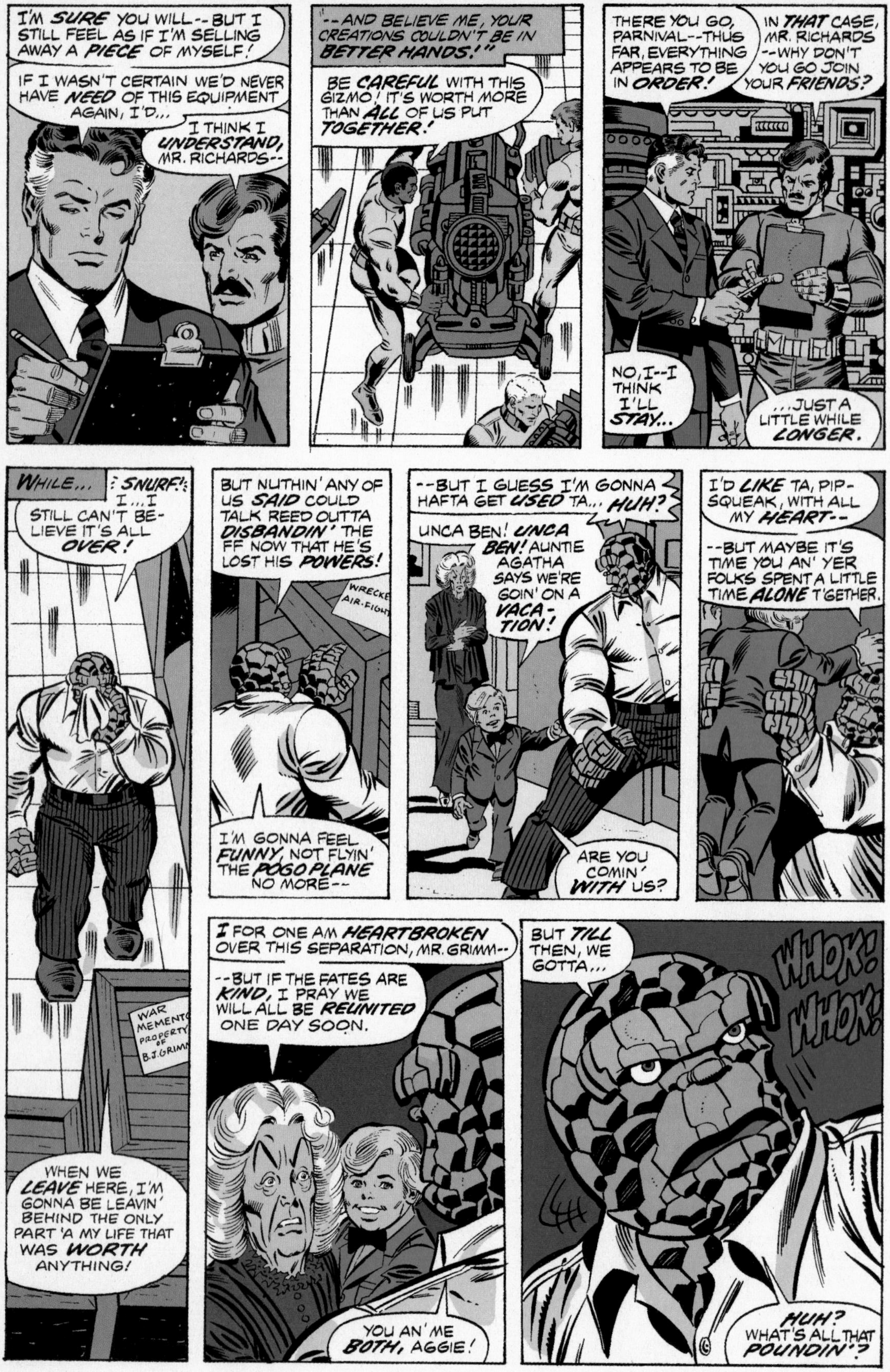

I'M SURE YOU WILL--BUT I STILL FEEL AS IF I'M SELLING AWAY A PIECE OF MYSELF!
IF I WASN'T CERTAIN WE'D NEVER HAVE NEED OF THIS EQUIPMENT AGAIN, I'D...
I THINK I UNDERSTAND, MR. RICHARDS--
--AND BELIEVE ME, YOUR CREATIONS COULDN'T BE IN BETTER HANDS!"
BE CAREFUL WITH THIS GIZMO! IT'S WORTH MORE THAN ALL OF US PUT TOGETHER!
THERE YOU GO, PARNIVAL--THUS FAR, EVERYTHING APPEARS TO BE IN ORDER!
IN THAT CASE, MR. RICHARDS --WHY DON'T YOU GO JOIN YOUR FRIENDS?
NO, I--I THINK I'LL STAY...
...JUST A LITTLE WHILE LONGER.
WHILE...
SNURF! I...I STILL CAN'T BELIEVE IT'S ALL OVER!
WAR MEMENTO PROPERTY OF B.J. GRIMM
WHEN WE LEAVE HERE, I'M GONNA BE LEAVIN' BEHIND THE ONLY PART 'A MY LIFE THAT WAS WORTH ANYTHING!
BUT NUTHIN' ANY OF US SAID COULD TALK REED OUTTA DISBANDIN' THE FF NOW THAT HE'S LOST HIS POWERS!
WRECKE AIR-FIGHT
I'M GONNA FEEL FUNNY, NOT FLYIN' THE POGO PLANE NO MORE--
--BUT I GUESS I'M GONNA HAFTA GET USED TA... HUH?
UNCA BEN! UNCA BEN! AUNTIE AGATHA SAYS WE'RE GOIN' ON A VACATION!
ARE YOU COMIN' WITH US?
I'D LIKE TA, PIP-SQUEAK, WITH ALL MY HEART--
--BUT MAYBE IT'S TIME YOU AN' YER FOLKS SPENT A LITTLE TIME ALONE T'GETHER.
I FOR ONE AM HEARTBROKEN OVER THIS SEPARATION, MR. GRIMM--
--BUT IF THE FATES ARE KIND, I PRAY WE WILL ALL BE REUNITED ONE DAY SOON.
YOU AN' ME BOTH, AGGIE!
BUT TILL THEN, WE GOTTA...
WHOK! WHOK!
HUH? WHAT'S ALL THAT POUNDIN'?

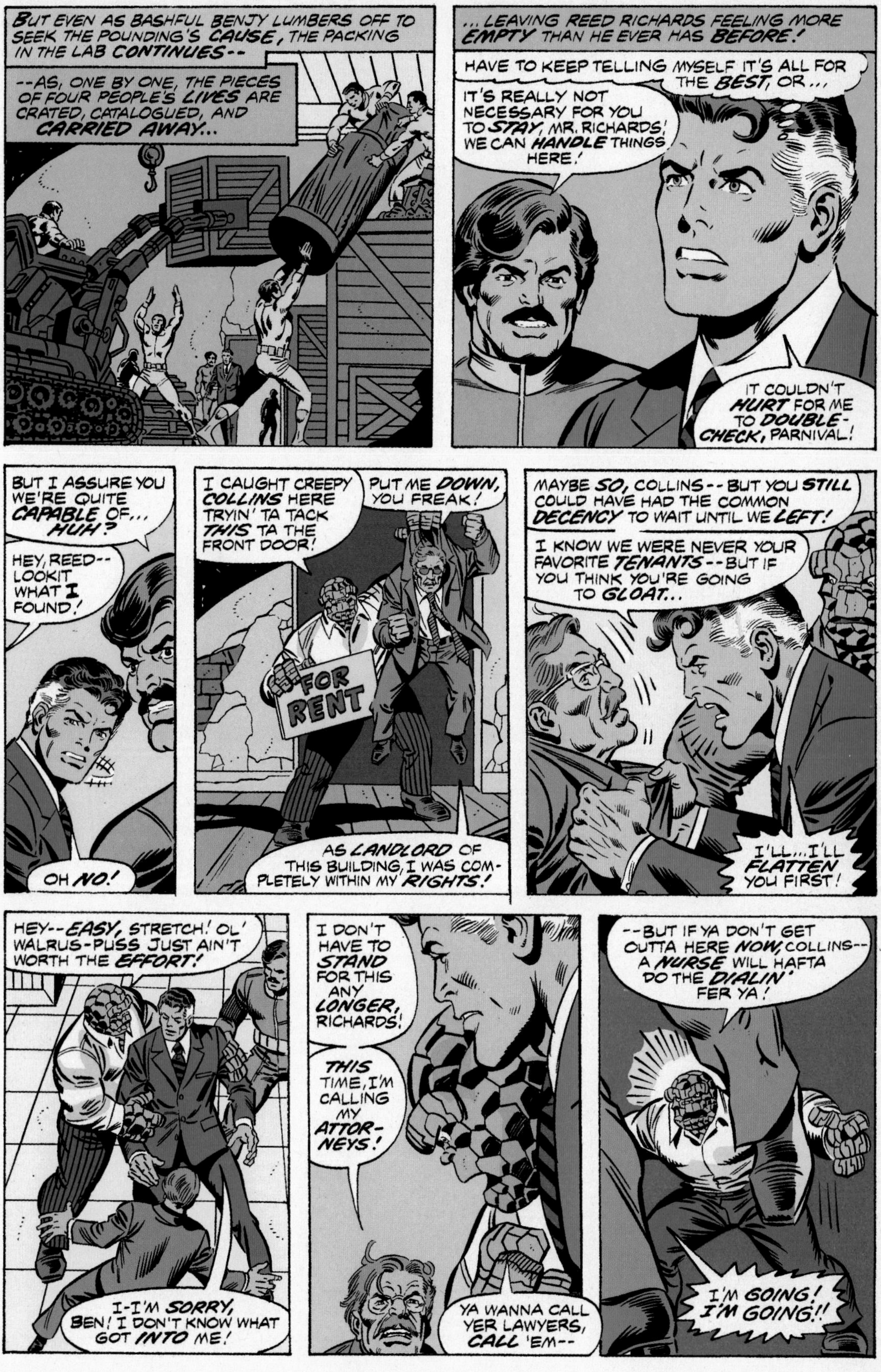
BUT EVEN AS BASHFUL BENJY LUMBERS OFF TO SEEK THE POUNDING'S CAUSE, THE PACKING IN THE LAB CONTINUES--
--AS, ONE BY ONE, THE PIECES OF FOUR PEOPLE'S LIVES ARE CRATED, CATALOGUED, AND CARRIED AWAY...
...LEAVING REED RICHARDS FEELING MORE EMPTY THAN HE EVER HAS BEFORE!
HAVE TO KEEP TELLING MYSELF IT'S ALL FOR THE BEST, OR...
IT'S REALLY NOT NECESSARY FOR YOU TO STAY, MR. RICHARDS! WE CAN HANDLE THINGS HERE!
IT COULDN'T HURT FOR ME TO DOUBLE-CHECK, PARNIVAL!
BUT I ASSURE YOU WE'RE QUITE CAPABLE OF... HUH?
HEY, REED-- LOOKIT WHAT I FOUND!
OH NO!
I CAUGHT CREEPY COLLINS HERE TRYIN' TA TACK THIS TA THE FRONT DOOR!
PUT ME DOWN, YOU FREAK!
FOR RENT
AS LANDLORD OF THIS BUILDING, I WAS COMPLETELY WITHIN MY RIGHTS!
MAYBE SO, COLLINS-- BUT YOU STILL COULD HAVE HAD THE COMMON DECENCY TO WAIT UNTIL WE LEFT!
I KNOW WE WERE NEVER YOUR FAVORITE TENANTS-- BUT IF YOU THINK YOU'RE GOING TO GLOAT...
I'LL... I'LL FLATTEN YOU FIRST!
HEY-- EASY, STRETCH! OL' WALRUS-PUSS JUST AIN'T WORTH THE EFFORT!
I-I'M SORRY, BEN! I DON'T KNOW WHAT GOT INTO ME!
I DON'T HAVE TO STAND FOR THIS ANY LONGER, RICHARDS!
THIS TIME, I'M CALLING MY ATTORNEYS!
YA WANNA CALL YER LAWYERS, CALL 'EM--
--BUT IF YA DON'T GET OUTTA HERE NOW, COLLINS-- A NURSE WILL HAFTA DO THE DIALIN' FER YA!
I'M GOING! I'M GOING!!

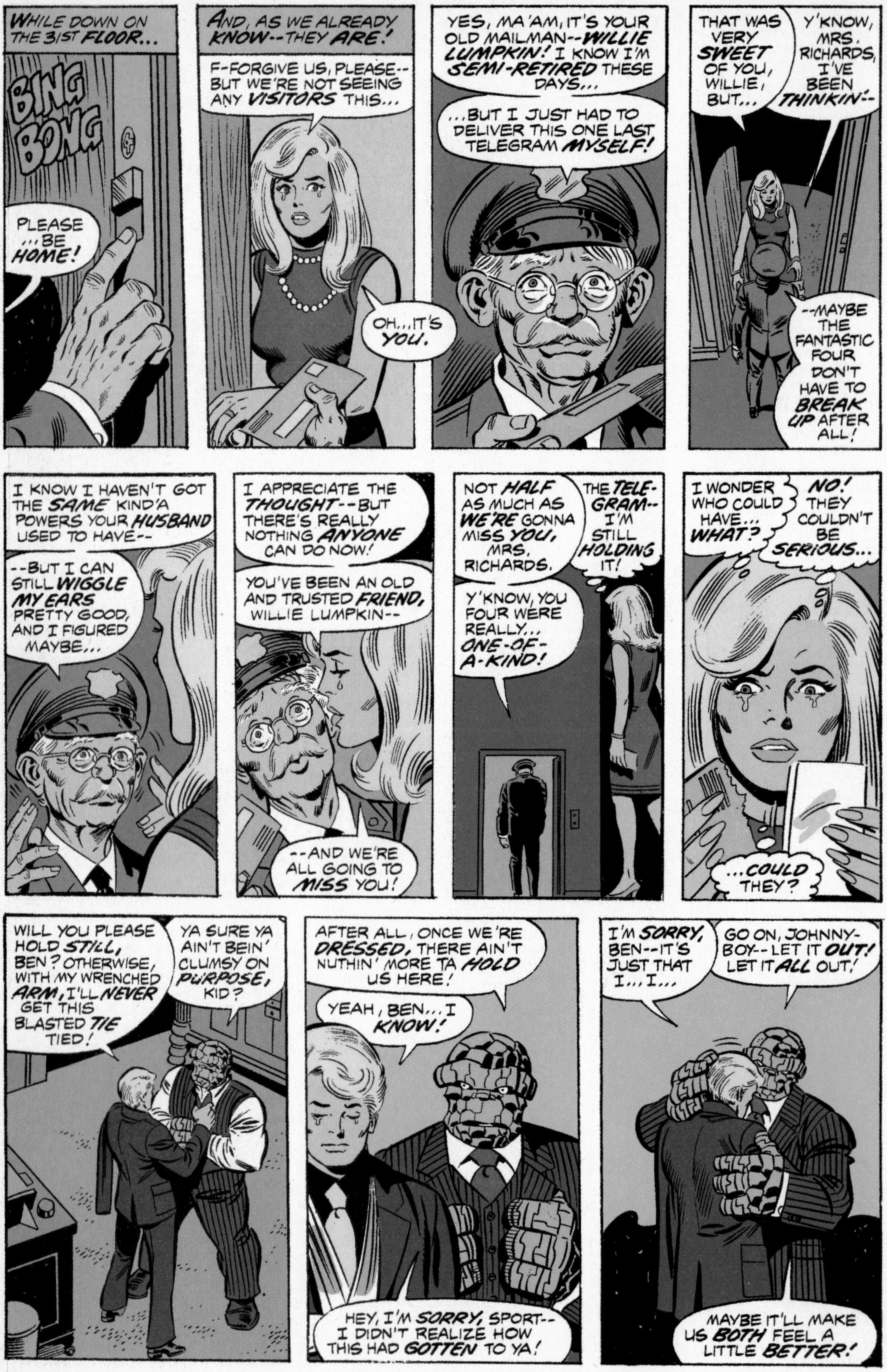
WHILE DOWN ON THE 31ST FLOOR...
BING BONG
PLEASE ...BE HOME!
AND, AS WE ALREADY KNOW--THEY ARE!
F-FORGIVE US, PLEASE--BUT WE'RE NOT SEEING ANY VISITORS THIS...
OH...IT'S YOU.
YES, MA'AM, IT'S YOUR OLD MAILMAN--WILLIE LUMPKIN! I KNOW I'M SEMI-RETIRED THESE DAYS...
...BUT I JUST HAD TO DELIVER THIS ONE LAST TELEGRAM MYSELF!
THAT WAS VERY SWEET OF YOU, WILLIE, BUT...
Y'KNOW, MRS. RICHARDS, I'VE BEEN THINKIN'--
--MAYBE THE FANTASTIC FOUR DON'T HAVE TO BREAK UP AFTER ALL!
I KNOW I HAVEN'T GOT THE SAME KIND'A POWERS YOUR HUSBAND USED TO HAVE--
--BUT I CAN STILL WIGGLE MY EARS PRETTY GOOD, AND I FIGURED MAYBE...
I APPRECIATE THE THOUGHT--BUT THERE'S REALLY NOTHING ANYONE CAN DO NOW!
YOU'VE BEEN AN OLD AND TRUSTED FRIEND, WILLIE LUMPKIN--
--AND WE'RE ALL GOING TO MISS YOU!
NOT HALF AS MUCH AS WE'RE GONNA MISS YOU, MRS. RICHARDS.
THE TELE-GRAM--I'M STILL HOLDING IT!
Y'KNOW, YOU FOUR WERE REALLY... ONE-OF-A-KIND!
I WONDER WHO COULD HAVE... WHAT?
NO! THEY COULDN'T BE SERIOUS...
...COULD THEY?
WILL YOU PLEASE HOLD STILL, BEN? OTHERWISE, WITH MY WRENCHED ARM, I'LL NEVER GET THIS BLASTED TIE TIED!
YA SURE YA AIN'T BEIN' CLUMSY ON PURPOSE, KID?
AFTER ALL, ONCE WE'RE DRESSED, THERE AIN'T NUTHIN' MORE TA HOLD US HERE!
YEAH, BEN... I KNOW!
HEY, I'M SORRY, SPORT--I DIDN'T REALIZE HOW THIS HAD GOTTEN TO YA!
I'M SORRY, BEN--IT'S JUST THAT I...I...
GO ON, JOHNNY-BOY--LET IT OUT! LET IT ALL OUT!
MAYBE IT'LL MAKE US BOTH FEEL A LITTLE BETTER!

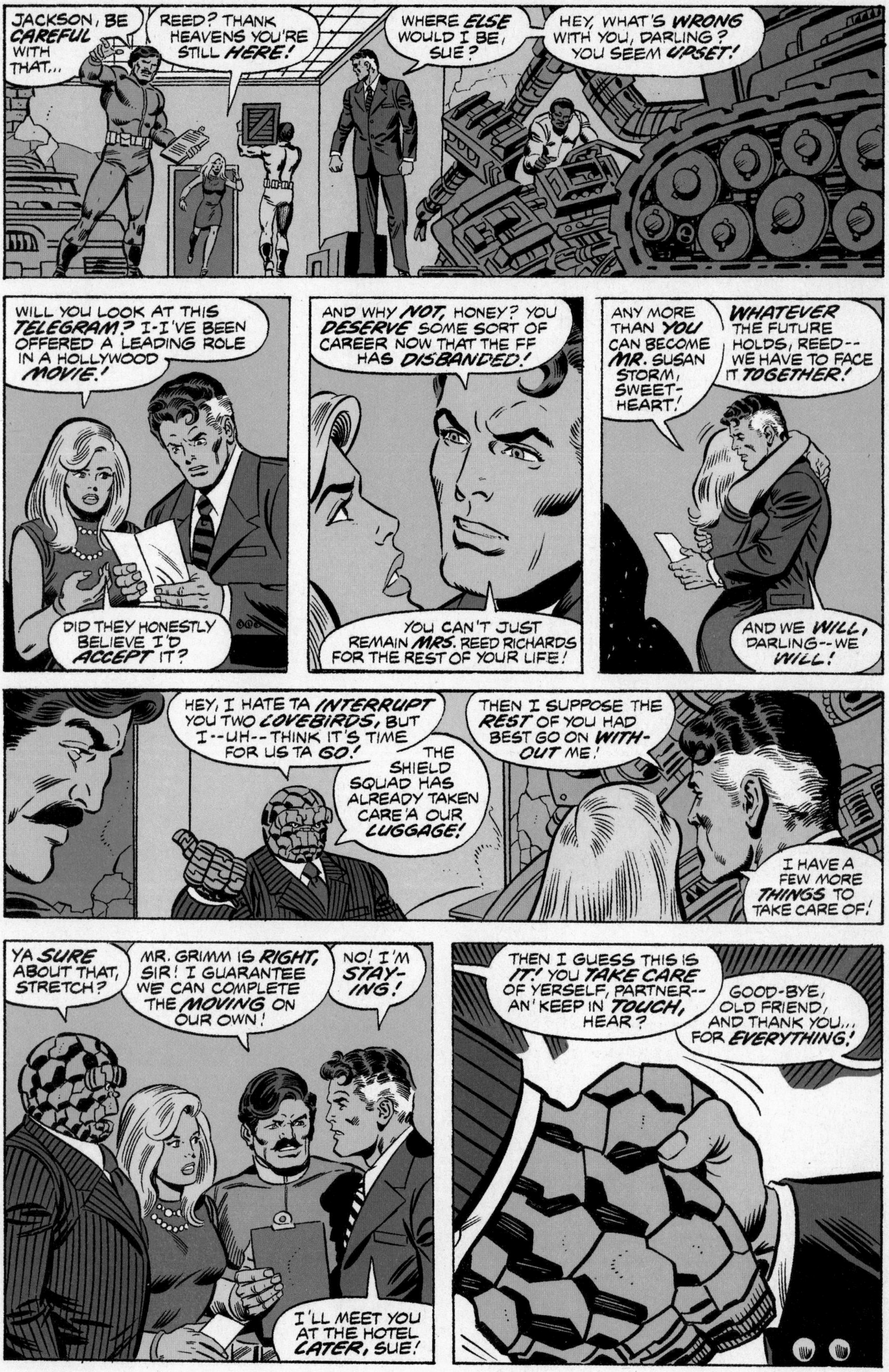
JACKSON, BE CAREFUL WITH THAT...
REED? THANK HEAVENS YOU'RE STILL HERE!
WHERE ELSE WOULD I BE, SUE?
HEY, WHAT'S WRONG WITH YOU, DARLING? YOU SEEM UPSET!
WILL YOU LOOK AT THIS TELEGRAM? I-I'VE BEEN OFFERED A LEADING ROLE IN A HOLLYWOOD MOVIE!
DID THEY HONESTLY BELIEVE I'D ACCEPT IT?
AND WHY NOT, HONEY? YOU DESERVE SOME SORT OF CAREER NOW THAT THE FF HAS DISBANDED!
YOU CAN'T JUST REMAIN MRS. REED RICHARDS FOR THE REST OF YOUR LIFE!
ANY MORE THAN YOU CAN BECOME MR. SUSAN STORM, SWEET-HEART!
WHATEVER THE FUTURE HOLDS, REED-- WE HAVE TO FACE IT TOGETHER!
AND WE WILL, DARLING--WE WILL!
HEY, I HATE TA INTERRUPT YOU TWO LOVEBIRDS, BUT I--UH--THINK IT'S TIME FOR US TA GO!
THE SHIELD SQUAD HAS ALREADY TAKEN CARE'A OUR LUGGAGE!
THEN I SUPPOSE THE REST OF YOU HAD BEST GO ON WITH-OUT ME!
I HAVE A FEW MORE THINGS TO TAKE CARE OF!
YA SURE ABOUT THAT, STRETCH?
MR. GRIMM IS RIGHT, SIR! I GUARANTEE WE CAN COMPLETE THE MOVING ON OUR OWN!
NO! I'M STAY-ING!
I'LL MEET YOU AT THE HOTEL LATER, SUE!
THEN I GUESS THIS IS IT! YOU TAKE CARE OF YERSELF, PARTNER-- AN' KEEP IN TOUCH, HEAR?
GOOD-BYE, OLD FRIEND, AND THANK YOU... FOR EVERYTHING!

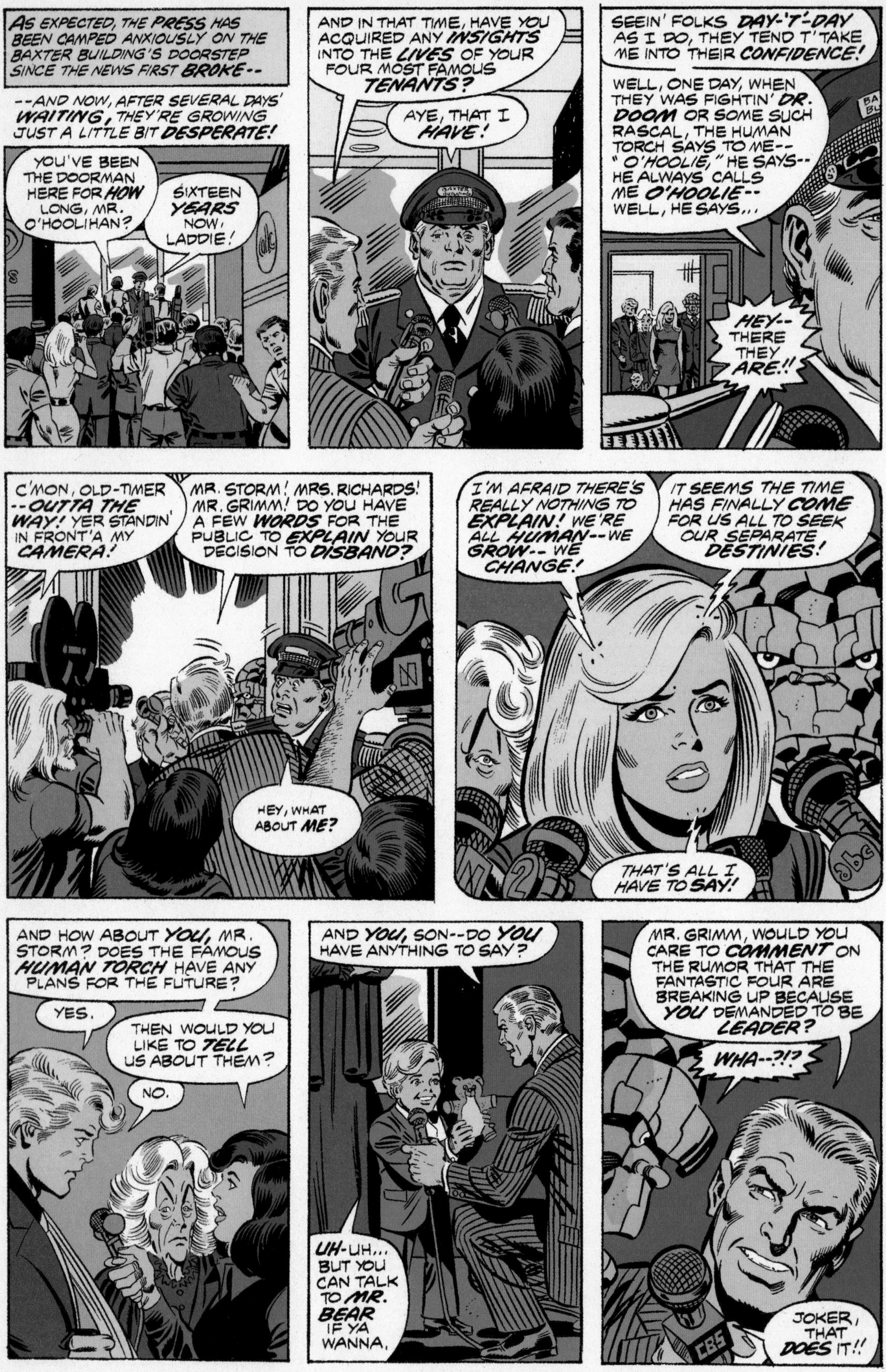

AS EXPECTED, THE PRESS HAS BEEN CAMPED ANXIOUSLY ON THE BAXTER BUILDING'S DOORSTEP SINCE THE NEWS FIRST BROKE--
--AND NOW, AFTER SEVERAL DAYS' WAITING, THEY'RE GROWING JUST A LITTLE BIT DESPERATE!
YOU'VE BEEN THE DOORMAN HERE FOR HOW LONG, MR. O'HOOLIHAN?
SIXTEEN YEARS NOW, LADDIE!
AND IN THAT TIME, HAVE YOU ACQUIRED ANY INSIGHTS INTO THE LIVES OF YOUR FOUR MOST FAMOUS TENANTS?
AYE, THAT I HAVE!
SEEIN' FOLKS DAY-'T'-DAY AS I DO, THEY TEND T' TAKE ME INTO THEIR CONFIDENCE!
WELL, ONE DAY, WHEN THEY WAS FIGHTIN' DR. DOOM OR SOME SUCH RASCAL, THE HUMAN TORCH SAYS TO ME-- "O'HOOLIE," HE SAYS-- HE ALWAYS CALLS ME O'HOOLIE-- WELL, HE SAYS...
HEY-- THERE THEY ARE!!
C'MON, OLD-TIMER --OUTTA THE WAY! YER STANDIN' IN FRONT'A MY CAMERA!
MR. STORM! MRS. RICHARDS! MR. GRIMM! DO YOU HAVE A FEW WORDS FOR THE PUBLIC TO EXPLAIN YOUR DECISION TO DISBAND?
HEY, WHAT ABOUT ME?
I'M AFRAID THERE'S REALLY NOTHING TO EXPLAIN! WE'RE ALL HUMAN--WE GROW-- WE CHANGE!
IT SEEMS THE TIME HAS FINALLY COME FOR US ALL TO SEEK OUR SEPARATE DESTINIES!
THAT'S ALL I HAVE TO SAY!
AND HOW ABOUT YOU, MR. STORM? DOES THE FAMOUS HUMAN TORCH HAVE ANY PLANS FOR THE FUTURE?
YES.
THEN WOULD YOU LIKE TO TELL US ABOUT THEM?
NO.
AND YOU, SON--DO YOU HAVE ANYTHING TO SAY?
UH-UH... BUT YOU CAN TALK TO MR. BEAR IF YA WANNA.
MR. GRIMM, WOULD YOU CARE TO COMMENT ON THE RUMOR THAT THE FANTASTIC FOUR ARE BREAKING UP BECAUSE YOU DEMANDED TO BE LEADER?
WHA--?!?
JOKER, THAT DOES IT!!

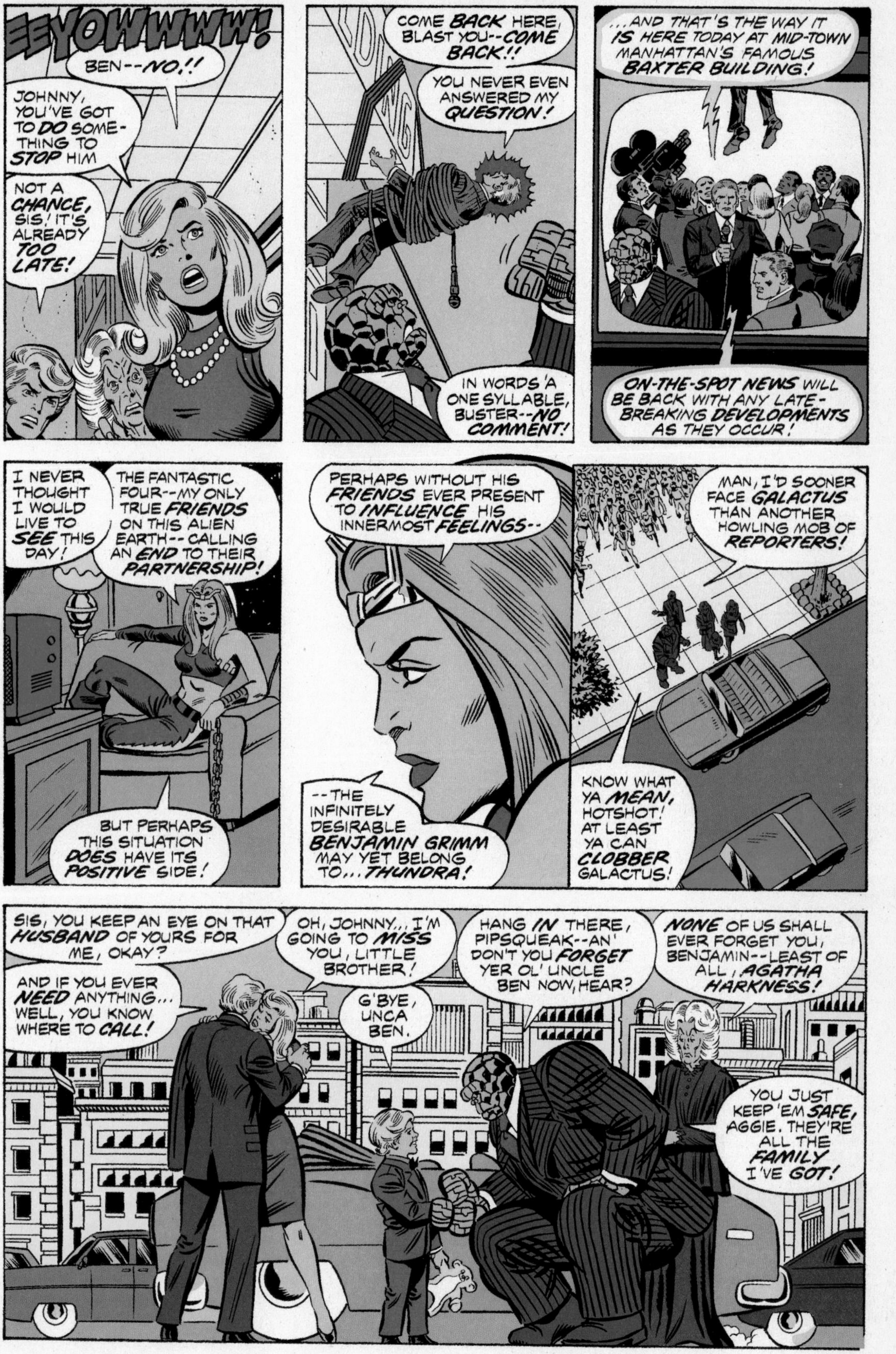

EEYOWWWW!
BEN--NO!!
JOHNNY, YOU'VE GOT TO DO SOME-THING TO STOP HIM
NOT A CHANCE, SIS! IT'S ALREADY TOO LATE!
COME BACK HERE, BLAST YOU--COME BACK!!
YOU NEVER EVEN ANSWERED MY QUESTION!
IN WORDS 'A ONE SYLLABLE, BUSTER--NO COMMENT!
...AND THAT'S THE WAY IT IS HERE TODAY AT MID-TOWN MANHATTAN'S FAMOUS BAXTER BUILDING!
ON-THE-SPOT NEWS WILL BE BACK WITH ANY LATE-BREAKING DEVELOPMENTS AS THEY OCCUR!
I NEVER THOUGHT I WOULD LIVE TO SEE THIS DAY!
THE FANTASTIC FOUR--MY ONLY TRUE FRIENDS ON THIS ALIEN EARTH--CALLING AN END TO THEIR PARTNERSHIP!
BUT PERHAPS THIS SITUATION DOES HAVE ITS POSITIVE SIDE!
PERHAPS WITHOUT HIS FRIENDS EVER PRESENT TO INFLUENCE HIS INNERMOST FEELINGS--
--THE INFINITELY DESIRABLE BENJAMIN GRIMM MAY YET BELONG TO... THUNDRA!
MAN, I'D SOONER FACE GALACTUS THAN ANOTHER HOWLING MOB OF REPORTERS!
KNOW WHAT YA MEAN, HOTSHOT! AT LEAST YA CAN CLOBBER GALACTUS!
SIS, YOU KEEP AN EYE ON THAT HUSBAND OF YOURS FOR ME, OKAY?
AND IF YOU EVER NEED ANYTHING... WELL, YOU KNOW WHERE TO CALL!
OH, JOHNNY... I'M GOING TO MISS YOU, LITTLE BROTHER!
G'BYE, UNCA BEN.
HANG IN THERE, PIPSQUEAK--AN' DON'T YOU FORGET YER OL' UNCLE BEN NOW, HEAR?
NONE OF US SHALL EVER FORGET YOU, BENJAMIN--LEAST OF ALL, AGATHA HARKNESS!
YOU JUST KEEP 'EM SAFE, AGGIE. THEY'RE ALL THE FAMILY I'VE GOT!

WELL, THERE THEY *GO!* THE FF IS OFFICIALLY *DEFUNCT!*

HEY, BITE YER *TONGUE,* HOTSHOT!

GIVE YER SISTER A LITTLE *CREDIT,* HUH? IF *ANYBODY* CAN CONVINCE STRETCH SPLITTIN' UP WUZ A *MISTAKE,* IT'S *SUZIE!*

JUST WAIT AN' *SEE,* KID, WE'LL ALL BE BACK T'GETHER BEFORE YA *KNOW* IT!

SURE, BEN,... ...SURE.

WELL, WHILE WE'RE *WAITIN',* I'M GONNA GO SEE *ALICIA!*

TAXI? HEY-- *TAXI!!*

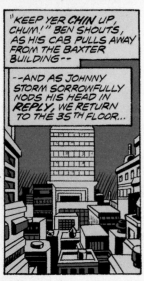

"KEEP YER *CHIN* UP, CHUM!" BEN SHOUTS, AS HIS CAB PULLS AWAY FROM THE BAXTER BUILDING--

--AND AS JOHNNY STORM SORROWFULLY NODS HIS HEAD IN *REPLY,* WE RETURN TO THE 35TH FLOOR...

FOR THE LAST TIME, PARNIVAL-- I'M NOT *LEAVING* TILL YOUR WORK HERE IS *FINISHED!*

PLEASE, RICHARDS-- YOU'RE REALLY MAKING THIS *DIFFICULT* FOR US!

MY MEN ARE COM-PLAINING YOU KEEP GETTING IN THEIR *WAY!*

I'M *SORRY* ABOUT THAT, BUT *STILL...*

HEY, *WATCH OUT* FOR THAT...

CRIPES!!

SKRASH!

SORRY BOSS, WE DIDN'T *MEAN* TA...

BE *QUIET,* YOU FOOL! IF THAT VIBRANIUM CASING WAS *DAM-AGED,* I'LL...

WHAT--?!?

THERE'S SOME-THING VERY *WRONG* HERE!

52

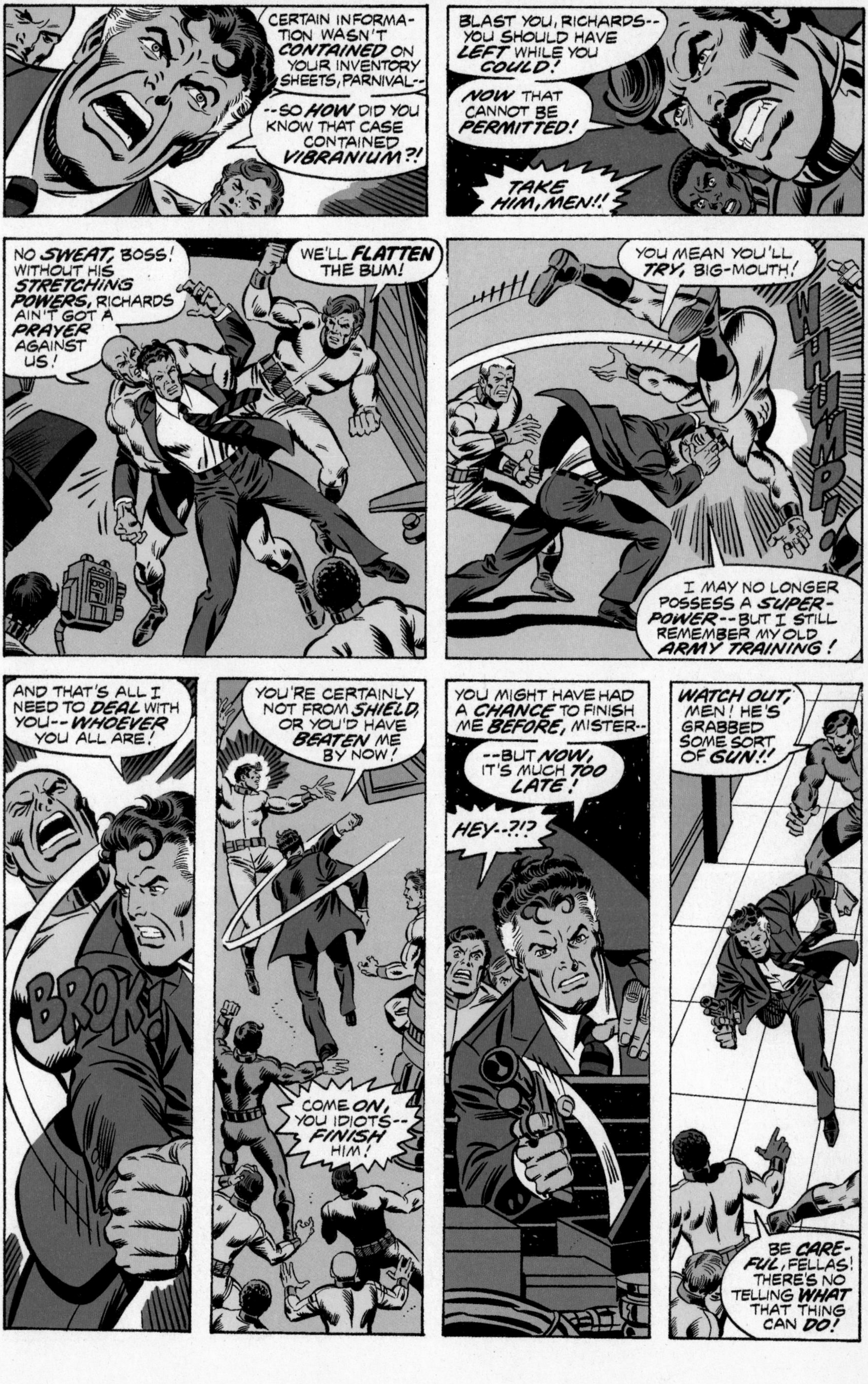

CERTAIN INFORMATION WASN'T CONTAINED ON YOUR INVENTORY SHEETS, PARNIVAL--
--SO HOW DID YOU KNOW THAT CASE CONTAINED VIBRANIUM?!
BLAST YOU, RICHARDS--YOU SHOULD HAVE LEFT WHILE YOU COULD!
NOW THAT CANNOT BE PERMITTED!
TAKE HIM, MEN!!
NO SWEAT, BOSS! WITHOUT HIS STRETCHING POWERS, RICHARDS AIN'T GOT A PRAYER AGAINST US!
WE'LL FLATTEN THE BUM!
YOU MEAN YOU'LL TRY, BIG-MOUTH!
WHUMP!
I MAY NO LONGER POSSESS A SUPER-POWER--BUT I STILL REMEMBER MY OLD ARMY TRAINING!
AND THAT'S ALL I NEED TO DEAL WITH YOU--WHOEVER YOU ALL ARE!
BROK!
YOU'RE CERTAINLY NOT FROM SHIELD, OR YOU'D HAVE BEATEN ME BY NOW!
COME ON, YOU IDIOTS--FINISH HIM!
YOU MIGHT HAVE HAD A CHANCE TO FINISH ME BEFORE, MISTER--
--BUT NOW, IT'S MUCH TOO LATE!
HEY--?!?
WATCH OUT, MEN! HE'S GRABBED SOME SORT OF GUN!!
BE CAREFUL, FELLAS! THERE'S NO TELLING WHAT THAT THING CAN DO!

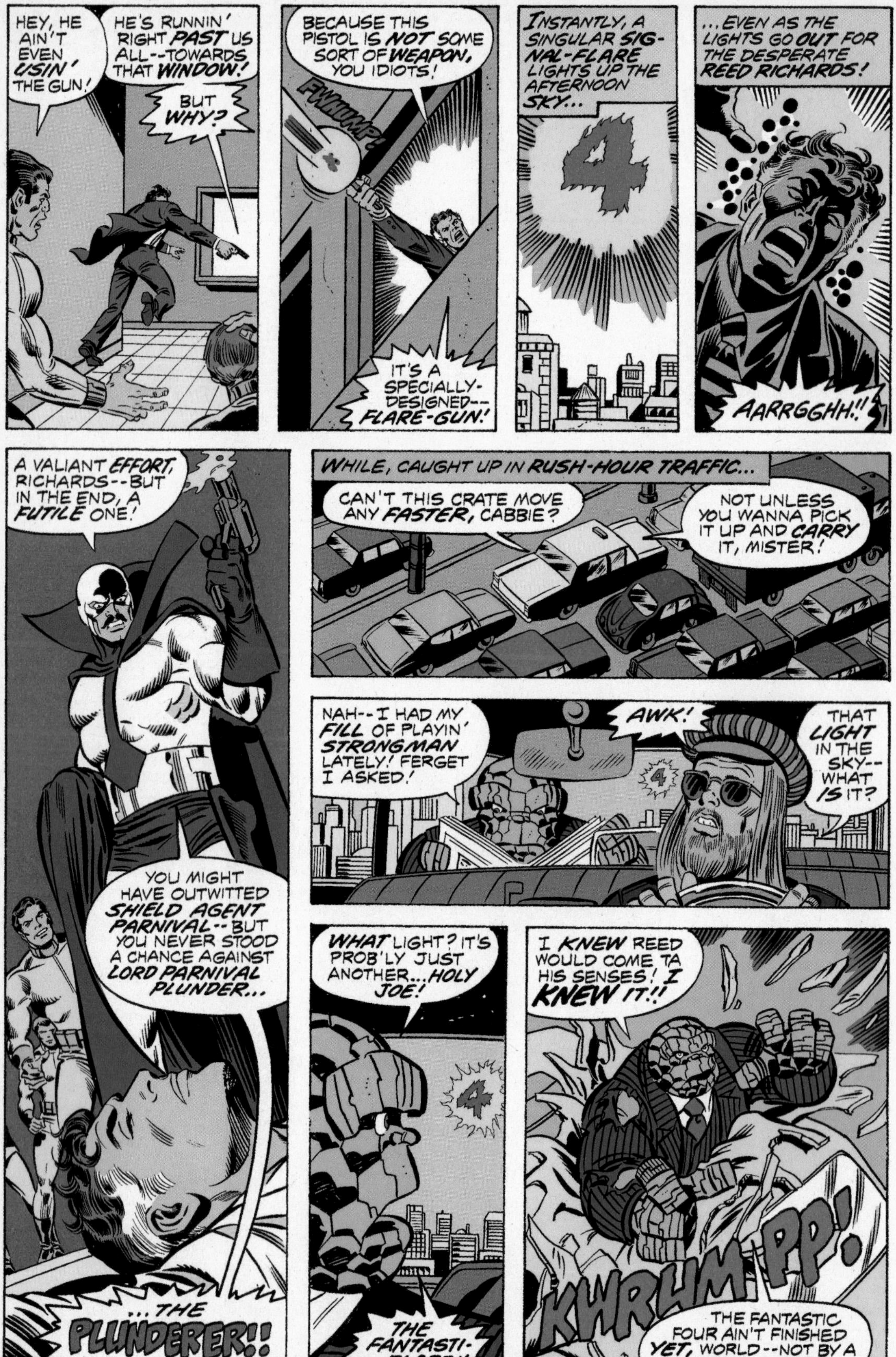

HEY, HE AIN'T EVEN USIN' THE GUN!
HE'S RUNNIN' RIGHT PAST US ALL--TOWARDS THAT WINDOW!
BUT WHY?
BECAUSE THIS PISTOL IS NOT SOME SORT OF WEAPON, YOU IDIOTS!
FWHUMP!
IT'S A SPECIALLY-DESIGNED--FLARE-GUN!
INSTANTLY, A SINGULAR SIGNAL-FLARE LIGHTS UP THE AFTERNOON SKY...
4
...EVEN AS THE LIGHTS GO OUT FOR THE DESPERATE REED RICHARDS!
AARRGGHH!!
A VALIANT EFFORT, RICHARDS--BUT IN THE END, A FUTILE ONE!
YOU MIGHT HAVE OUTWITTED SHIELD AGENT PARNIVAL--BUT YOU NEVER STOOD A CHANCE AGAINST LORD PARNIVAL PLUNDER...
...THE PLUNDERER!!
WHILE, CAUGHT UP IN RUSH-HOUR TRAFFIC...
CAN'T THIS CRATE MOVE ANY FASTER, CABBIE?
NOT UNLESS YOU WANNA PICK IT UP AND CARRY IT, MISTER!
NAH--I HAD MY FILL OF PLAYIN' STRONGMAN LATELY! FERGET I ASKED!
AWK!
THAT LIGHT IN THE SKY--WHAT IS IT?
WHAT LIGHT? IT'S PROB'LY JUST ANOTHER...HOLY JOE!
THE FANTASTI-FLARE!!
I KNEW REED WOULD COME TA HIS SENSES! I KNEW IT!!
KWRUMPP!
THE FANTASTIC FOUR AIN'T FINISHED YET, WORLD--NOT BY A LONG SHOT!

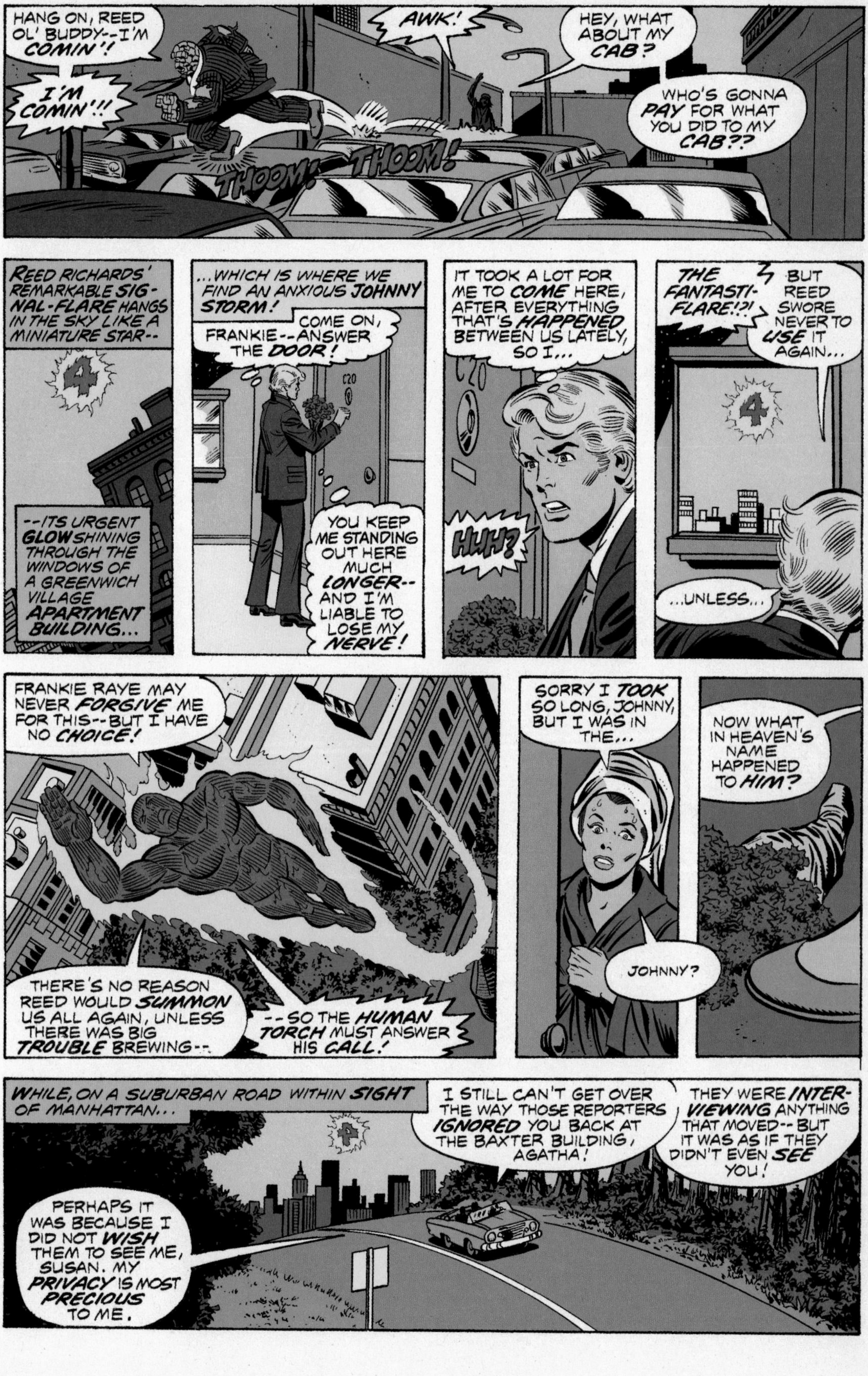
HANG ON, REED OL' BUDDY--I'M COMIN'!
I'M COMIN'!!
AWK!
HEY, WHAT ABOUT MY CAB?
WHO'S GONNA PAY FOR WHAT YOU DID TO MY CAB??
THOOM! THOOM!
REED RICHARDS' REMARKABLE SIG-NAL-FLARE HANGS IN THE SKY LIKE A MINIATURE STAR--
--ITS URGENT GLOW SHINING THROUGH THE WINDOWS OF A GREENWICH VILLAGE APARTMENT BUILDING...
...WHICH IS WHERE WE FIND AN ANXIOUS JOHNNY STORM!
COME ON, FRANKIE--ANSWER THE DOOR!
C20
YOU KEEP ME STANDING OUT HERE MUCH LONGER--AND I'M LIABLE TO LOSE MY NERVE!
IT TOOK A LOT FOR ME TO COME HERE, AFTER EVERYTHING THAT'S HAPPENED BETWEEN US LATELY, SO I...
HUH?
THE FANTASTI-FLARE!?!
BUT REED SWORE NEVER TO USE IT AGAIN...
...UNLESS...
FRANKIE RAYE MAY NEVER FORGIVE ME FOR THIS--BUT I HAVE NO CHOICE!
THERE'S NO REASON REED WOULD SUMMON US ALL AGAIN, UNLESS THERE WAS BIG TROUBLE BREWING--
--SO THE HUMAN TORCH MUST ANSWER HIS CALL!
SORRY I TOOK SO LONG, JOHNNY, BUT I WAS IN THE...
JOHNNY?
NOW WHAT IN HEAVEN'S NAME HAPPENED TO HIM?
WHILE, ON A SUBURBAN ROAD WITHIN SIGHT OF MANHATTAN...
I STILL CAN'T GET OVER THE WAY THOSE REPORTERS IGNORED YOU BACK AT THE BAXTER BUILDING, AGATHA!
THEY WERE INTER-VIEWING ANYTHING THAT MOVED--BUT IT WAS AS IF THEY DIDN'T EVEN SEE YOU!
PERHAPS IT WAS BECAUSE I DID NOT WISH THEM TO SEE ME, SUSAN. MY PRIVACY IS MOST PRECIOUS TO ME.

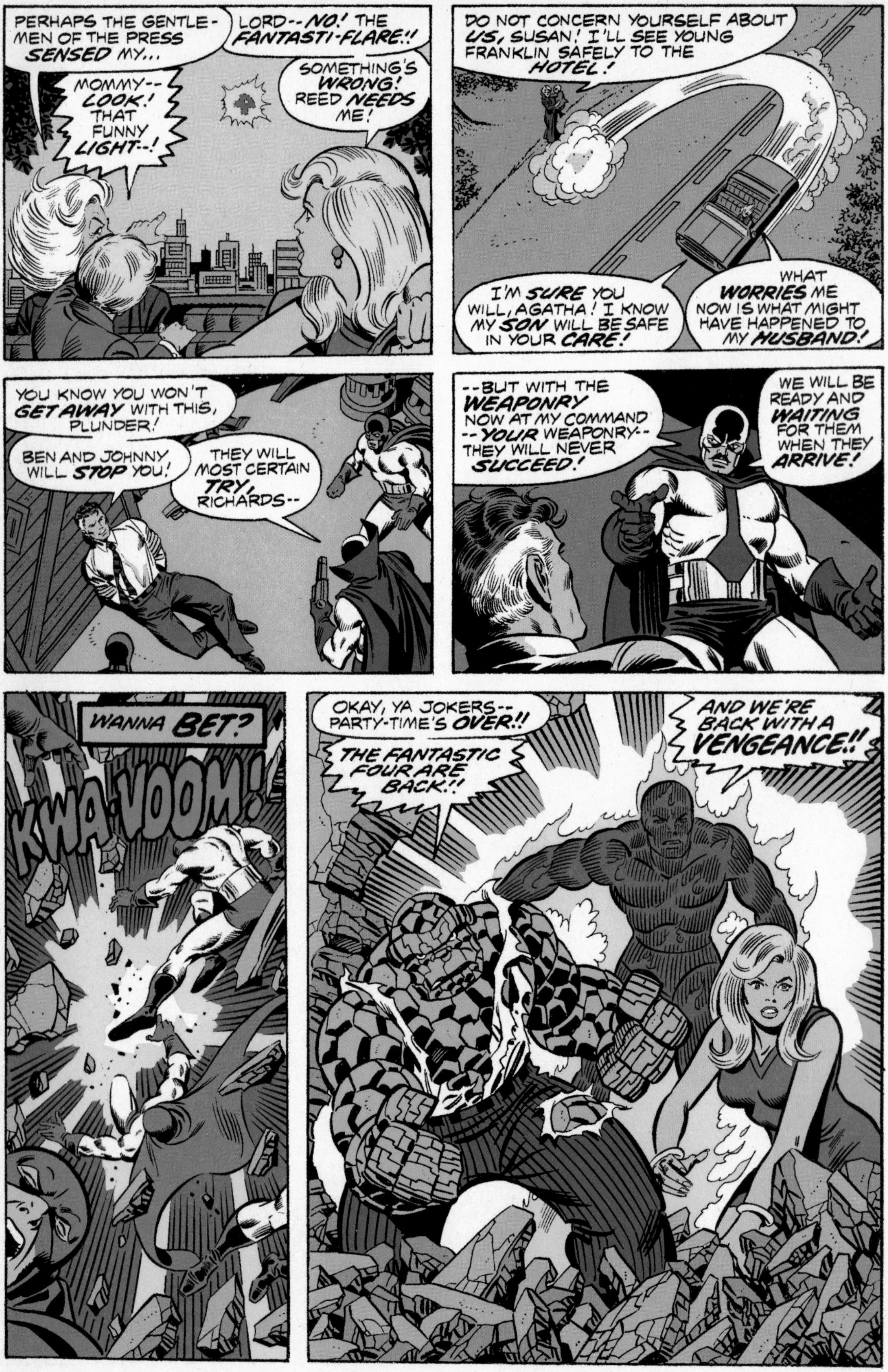
PERHAPS THE GENTLE-MEN OF THE PRESS SENSED MY...
LORD--NO! THE FANTASTI-FLARE!!
MOMMY--LOOK! THAT FUNNY LIGHT--!
SOMETHING'S WRONG! REED NEEDS ME!
DO NOT CONCERN YOURSELF ABOUT US, SUSAN! I'LL SEE YOUNG FRANKLIN SAFELY TO THE HOTEL!
I'M SURE YOU WILL, AGATHA! I KNOW MY SON WILL BE SAFE IN YOUR CARE!
WHAT WORRIES ME NOW IS WHAT MIGHT HAVE HAPPENED TO MY HUSBAND!
YOU KNOW YOU WON'T GET AWAY WITH THIS, PLUNDER!
BEN AND JOHNNY WILL STOP YOU!
THEY WILL MOST CERTAIN TRY, RICHARDS--
--BUT WITH THE WEAPONRY NOW AT MY COMMAND --YOUR WEAPONRY-- THEY WILL NEVER SUCCEED!
WE WILL BE READY AND WAITING FOR THEM WHEN THEY ARRIVE!
WANNA BET?
KWA-VOOM!
OKAY, YA JOKERS--PARTY-TIME'S OVER!!
THE FANTASTIC FOUR ARE BACK!!
AND WE'RE BACK WITH A VENGEANCE!!

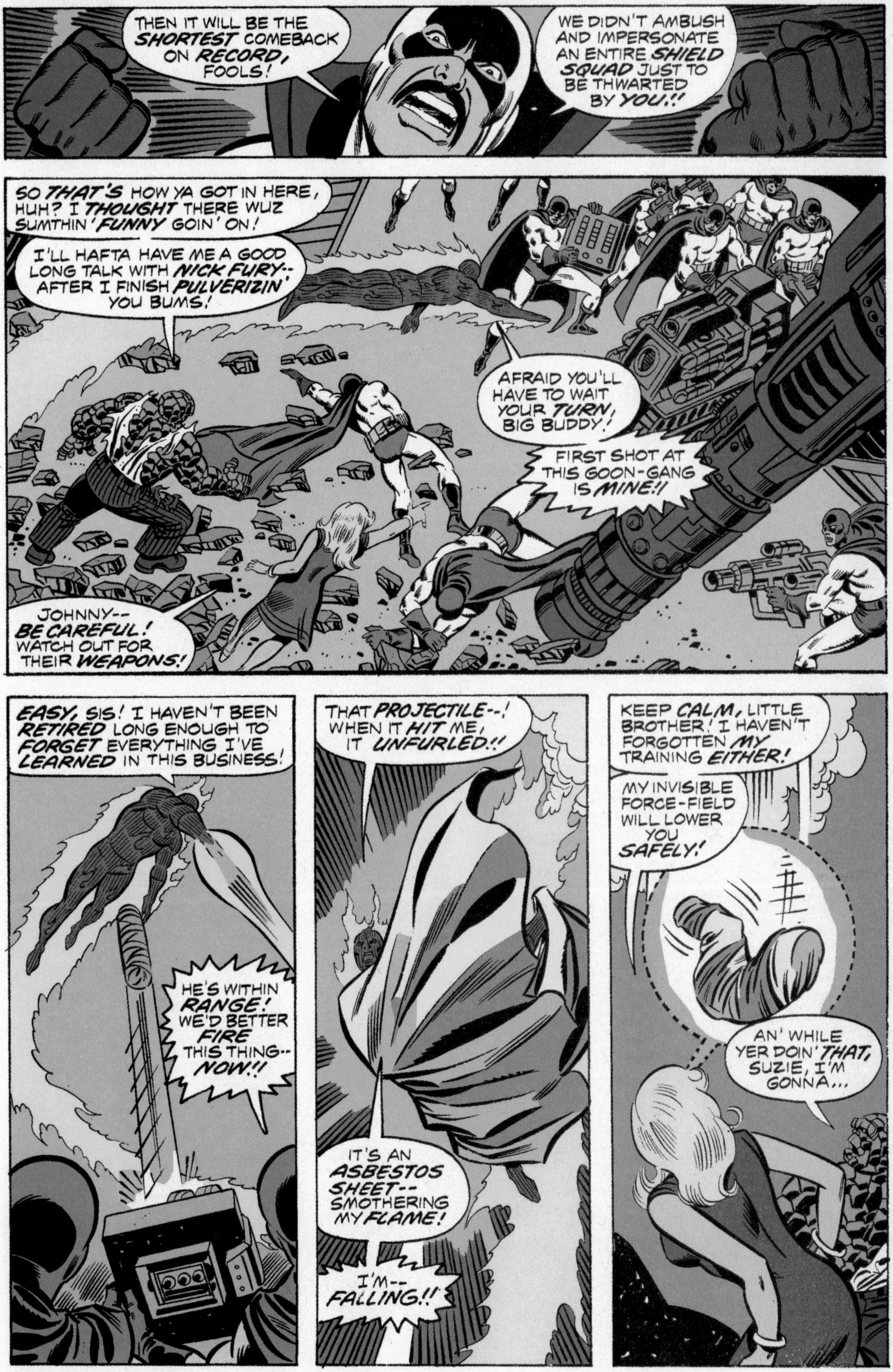
THEN IT WILL BE THE SHORTEST COMEBACK ON RECORD, FOOLS!
WE DIDN'T AMBUSH AND IMPERSONATE AN ENTIRE SHIELD SQUAD JUST TO BE THWARTED BY YOU!!
SO THAT'S HOW YA GOT IN HERE, HUH? I THOUGHT THERE WUZ SUMTHIN' FUNNY GOIN' ON!
I'LL HAFTA HAVE ME A GOOD LONG TALK WITH NICK FURY-- AFTER I FINISH PULVERIZIN' YOU BUMS!
AFRAID YOU'LL HAVE TO WAIT YOUR TURN, BIG BUDDY!
FIRST SHOT AT THIS GOON-GANG IS MINE!!
JOHNNY-- BE CAREFUL! WATCH OUT FOR THEIR WEAPONS!
EASY, SIS! I HAVEN'T BEEN RETIRED LONG ENOUGH TO FORGET EVERYTHING I'VE LEARNED IN THIS BUSINESS!
HE'S WITHIN RANGE! WE'D BETTER FIRE THIS THING-- NOW!!
THAT PROJECTILE--! WHEN IT HIT ME, IT UNFURLED!!
IT'S AN ASBESTOS SHEET-- SMOTHERING MY FLAME!
I'M-- FALLING!!
KEEP CALM, LITTLE BROTHER! I HAVEN'T FORGOTTEN MY TRAINING EITHER!
MY INVISIBLE FORCE-FIELD WILL LOWER YOU SAFELY!
AN' WHILE YER DOIN' THAT, SUZIE, I'M GONNA...

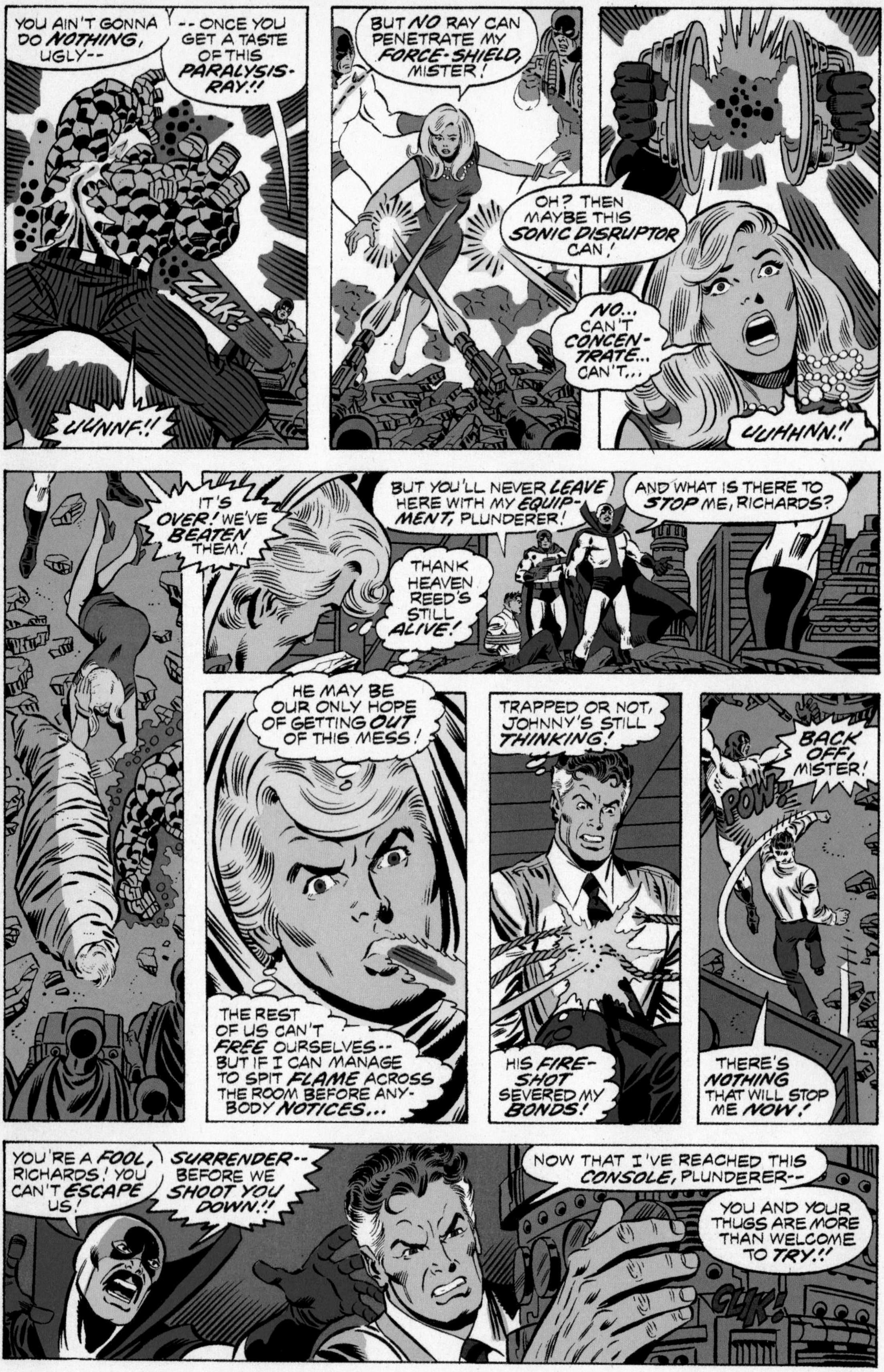
YOU AIN'T GONNA DO NOTHING, UGLY--
-- ONCE YOU GET A TASTE OF THIS PARALYSIS-RAY!!
ZAK!
UUNNF!!
BUT NO RAY CAN PENETRATE MY FORCE-SHIELD, MISTER!
OH? THEN MAYBE THIS SONIC DISRUPTOR CAN!
NO... CAN'T CONCEN-TRATE... CAN'T...
UUHHNN!!
IT'S OVER! WE'VE BEATEN THEM!
BUT YOU'LL NEVER LEAVE HERE WITH MY EQUIP-MENT, PLUNDERER!
AND WHAT IS THERE TO STOP ME, RICHARDS?
THANK HEAVEN REED'S STILL ALIVE!
HE MAY BE OUR ONLY HOPE OF GETTING OUT OF THIS MESS!
THE REST OF US CAN'T FREE OURSELVES-- BUT IF I CAN MANAGE TO SPIT FLAME ACROSS THE ROOM BEFORE ANY-BODY NOTICES...
TRAPPED OR NOT, JOHNNY'S STILL THINKING!
HIS FIRE-SHOT SEVERED MY BONDS!
BACK OFF, MISTER!
POW!
THERE'S NOTHING THAT WILL STOP ME NOW!
YOU'RE A FOOL, RICHARDS! YOU CAN'T ESCAPE US!
SURRENDER-- BEFORE WE SHOOT YOU DOWN!!
NOW THAT I'VE REACHED THIS CONSOLE, PLUNDERER--
YOU AND YOUR THUGS ARE MORE THAN WELCOME TO TRY!!
CLIK!

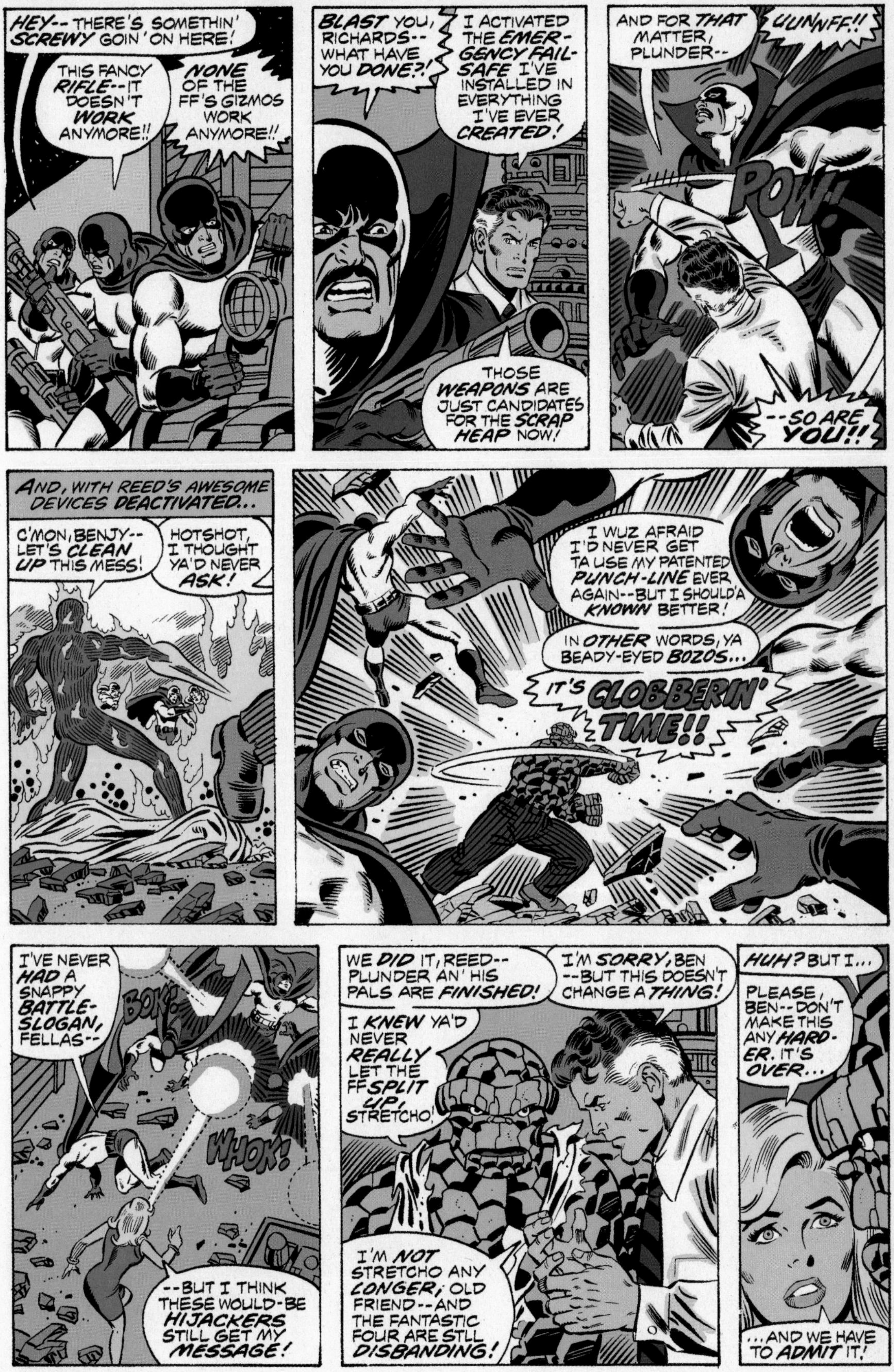
HEY-- THERE'S SOMETHIN' SCREWY GOIN' ON HERE!
THIS FANCY RIFLE--IT DOESN'T WORK ANYMORE!!
NONE OF THE FF'S GIZMOS WORK ANYMORE!!
BLAST YOU, RICHARDS-- WHAT HAVE YOU DONE?!
I ACTIVATED THE EMERGENCY FAIL-SAFE I'VE INSTALLED IN EVERYTHING I'VE EVER CREATED!
THOSE WEAPONS ARE JUST CANDIDATES FOR THE SCRAP HEAP NOW!
AND FOR THAT MATTER, PLUNDER--
UUNNFF!!
POW!
--SO ARE YOU!!
AND, WITH REED'S AWESOME DEVICES DEACTIVATED...
C'MON, BENJY-- LET'S CLEAN UP THIS MESS!
HOTSHOT, I THOUGHT YA'D NEVER ASK!
I WUZ AFRAID I'D NEVER GET TA USE MY PATENTED PUNCH-LINE EVER AGAIN--BUT I SHOULD'A KNOWN BETTER!
IN OTHER WORDS, YA BEADY-EYED BOZOS...
IT'S CLOBBERIN' TIME!!
I'VE NEVER HAD A SNAPPY BATTLE-SLOGAN, FELLAS--
BOK!
WHOK!
--BUT I THINK THESE WOULD-BE HIJACKERS STILL GET MY MESSAGE!
WE DID IT, REED-- PLUNDER AN' HIS PALS ARE FINISHED!
I KNEW YA'D NEVER REALLY LET THE FF SPLIT UP, STRETCHO!
I'M SORRY, BEN --BUT THIS DOESN'T CHANGE A THING!
I'M NOT STRETCHO ANY LONGER, OLD FRIEND--AND THE FANTASTIC FOUR ARE STILL DISBANDING!
HUH? BUT I...
PLEASE, BEN-- DON'T MAKE THIS ANY HARDER. IT'S OVER...
...AND WE HAVE TO ADMIT IT!

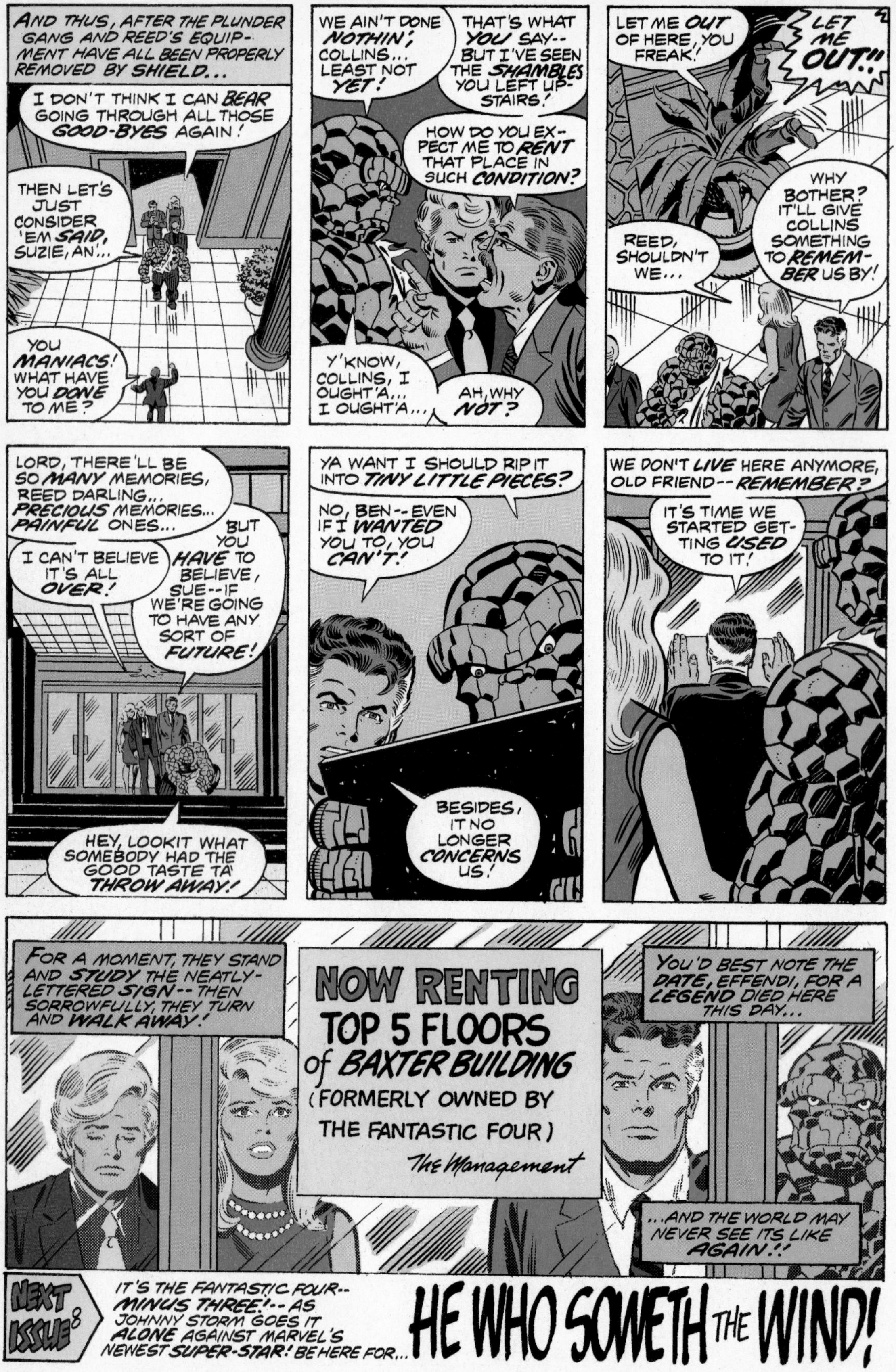
AND THUS, AFTER THE PLUNDER GANG AND REED'S EQUIPMENT HAVE ALL BEEN PROPERLY REMOVED BY SHIELD...
I DON'T THINK I CAN BEAR GOING THROUGH ALL THOSE GOOD-BYES AGAIN!
THEN LET'S JUST CONSIDER 'EM SAID, SUZIE, AN'...
YOU MANIACS! WHAT HAVE YOU DONE TO ME?
WE AIN'T DONE NOTHIN', COLLINS... LEAST NOT YET!
THAT'S WHAT YOU SAY-- BUT I'VE SEEN THE SHAMBLES YOU LEFT UPSTAIRS!
HOW DO YOU EXPECT ME TO RENT THAT PLACE IN SUCH CONDITION?
Y'KNOW, COLLINS, I OUGHT'A... I OUGHT'A...
AH, WHY NOT?
LET ME OUT OF HERE, YOU FREAK!
LET ME OUT!!
REED, SHOULDN'T WE...
WHY BOTHER? IT'LL GIVE COLLINS SOMETHING TO REMEMBER US BY!
LORD, THERE'LL BE SO MANY MEMORIES, REED DARLING... PRECIOUS MEMORIES... PAINFUL ONES...
I CAN'T BELIEVE IT'S ALL OVER!
BUT YOU HAVE TO BELIEVE, SUE--IF WE'RE GOING TO HAVE ANY SORT OF FUTURE!
HEY, LOOKIT WHAT SOMEBODY HAD THE GOOD TASTE TA' THROW AWAY!
YA WANT I SHOULD RIP IT INTO TINY LITTLE PIECES?
NO, BEN--EVEN IF I WANTED YOU TO, YOU CAN'T!
BESIDES, IT NO LONGER CONCERNS US!
WE DON'T LIVE HERE ANYMORE, OLD FRIEND--REMEMBER?
IT'S TIME WE STARTED GETTING USED TO IT!
FOR A MOMENT, THEY STAND AND STUDY THE NEATLY-LETTERED SIGN--THEN SORROWFULLY, THEY TURN AND WALK AWAY!
NOW RENTING
TOP 5 FLOORS
of BAXTER BUILDING
(FORMERLY OWNED BY THE FANTASTIC FOUR)
The Management
YOU'D BEST NOTE THE DATE, EFFENDI, FOR A LEGEND DIED HERE THIS DAY...
...AND THE WORLD MAY NEVER SEE ITS LIKE AGAIN!!
NEXT ISSUE
IT'S THE FANTASTIC FOUR--MINUS THREE!--AS JOHNNY STORM GOES IT ALONE AGAINST MARVEL'S NEWEST SUPER-STAR! BE HERE FOR...
HE WHO SOWETH THE WIND!

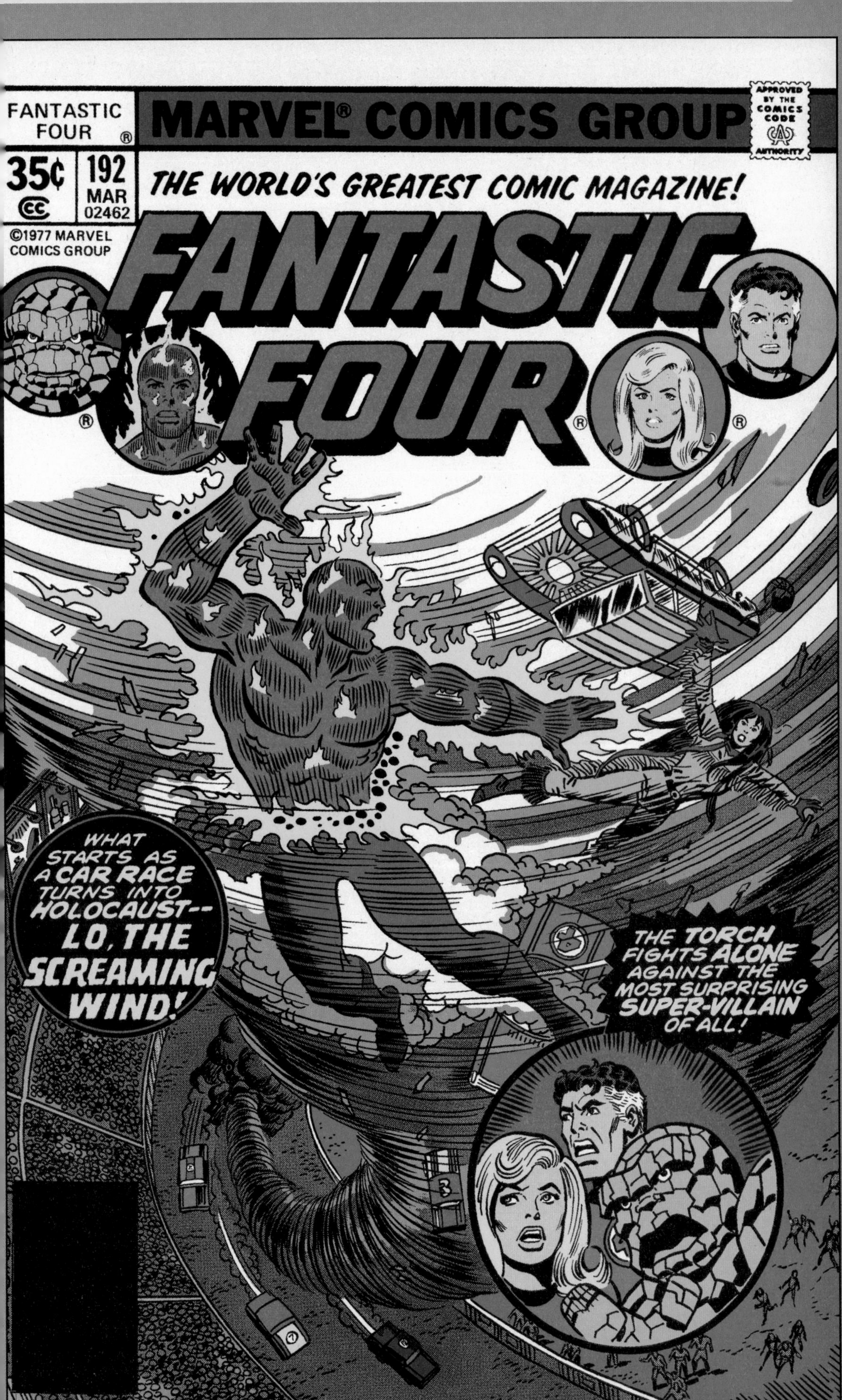
FANTASTIC FOUR ®
MARVEL® COMICS GROUP
APPROVED BY THE COMICS CODE AUTHORITY
35¢
192 MAR 02462
©1977 MARVEL COMICS GROUP
THE WORLD'S GREATEST COMIC MAGAZINE!
FANTASTIC FOUR®
WHAT STARTS AS A CAR RACE TURNS INTO HOLOCAUST-- LO, THE SCREAMING WIND!
THE TORCH FIGHTS ALONE AGAINST THE MOST SURPRISING SUPER-VILLAIN OF ALL!

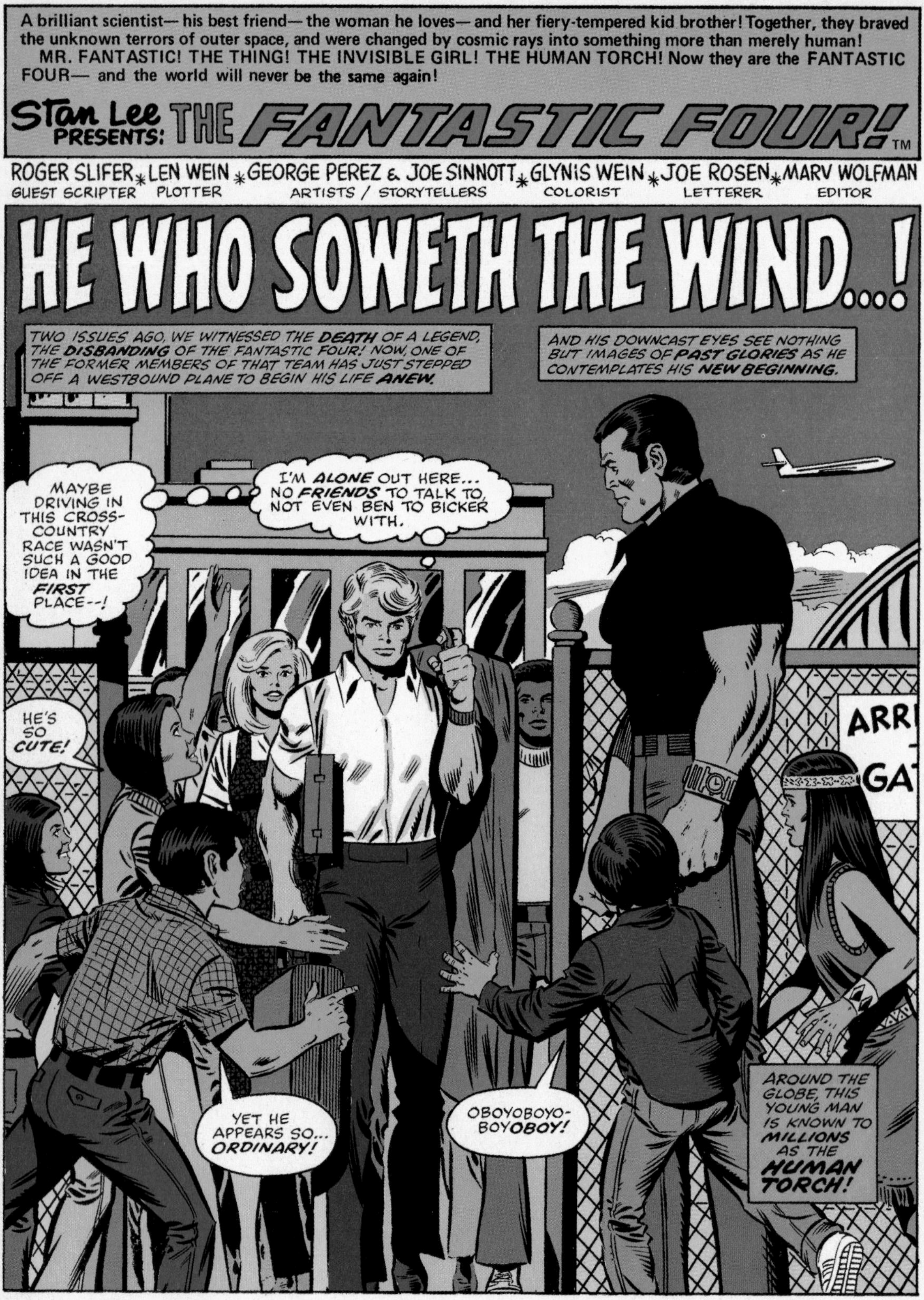
A brilliant scientist— his best friend— the woman he loves— and her fiery-tempered kid brother! Together, they braved the unknown terrors of outer space, and were changed by cosmic rays into something more than merely human!
MR. FANTASTIC! THE THING! THE INVISIBLE GIRL! THE HUMAN TORCH! Now they are the FANTASTIC FOUR— and the world will never be the same again!
Stan Lee PRESENTS: THE FANTASTIC FOUR! TM
ROGER SLIFER GUEST SCRIPTER * LEN WEIN PLOTTER * GEORGE PEREZ & JOE SINNOTT ARTISTS / STORYTELLERS * GLYNIS WEIN COLORIST * JOE ROSEN LETTERER * MARV WOLFMAN EDITOR
HE WHO SOWETH THE WIND...!
TWO ISSUES AGO, WE WITNESSED THE DEATH OF A LEGEND, THE DISBANDING OF THE FANTASTIC FOUR! NOW, ONE OF THE FORMER MEMBERS OF THAT TEAM HAS JUST STEPPED OFF A WESTBOUND PLANE TO BEGIN HIS LIFE ANEW.
AND HIS DOWNCAST EYES SEE NOTHING BUT IMAGES OF PAST GLORIES AS HE CONTEMPLATES HIS NEW BEGINNING.
I'M ALONE OUT HERE... NO FRIENDS TO TALK TO, NOT EVEN BEN TO BICKER WITH.
MAYBE DRIVING IN THIS CROSS-COUNTRY RACE WASN'T SUCH A GOOD IDEA IN THE FIRST PLACE--!
HE'S SO CUTE!
YET HE APPEARS SO... ORDINARY!
OBOYOBOYO-BOYOBOY!
AROUND THE GLOBE, THIS YOUNG MAN IS KNOWN TO MILLIONS AS THE HUMAN TORCH!

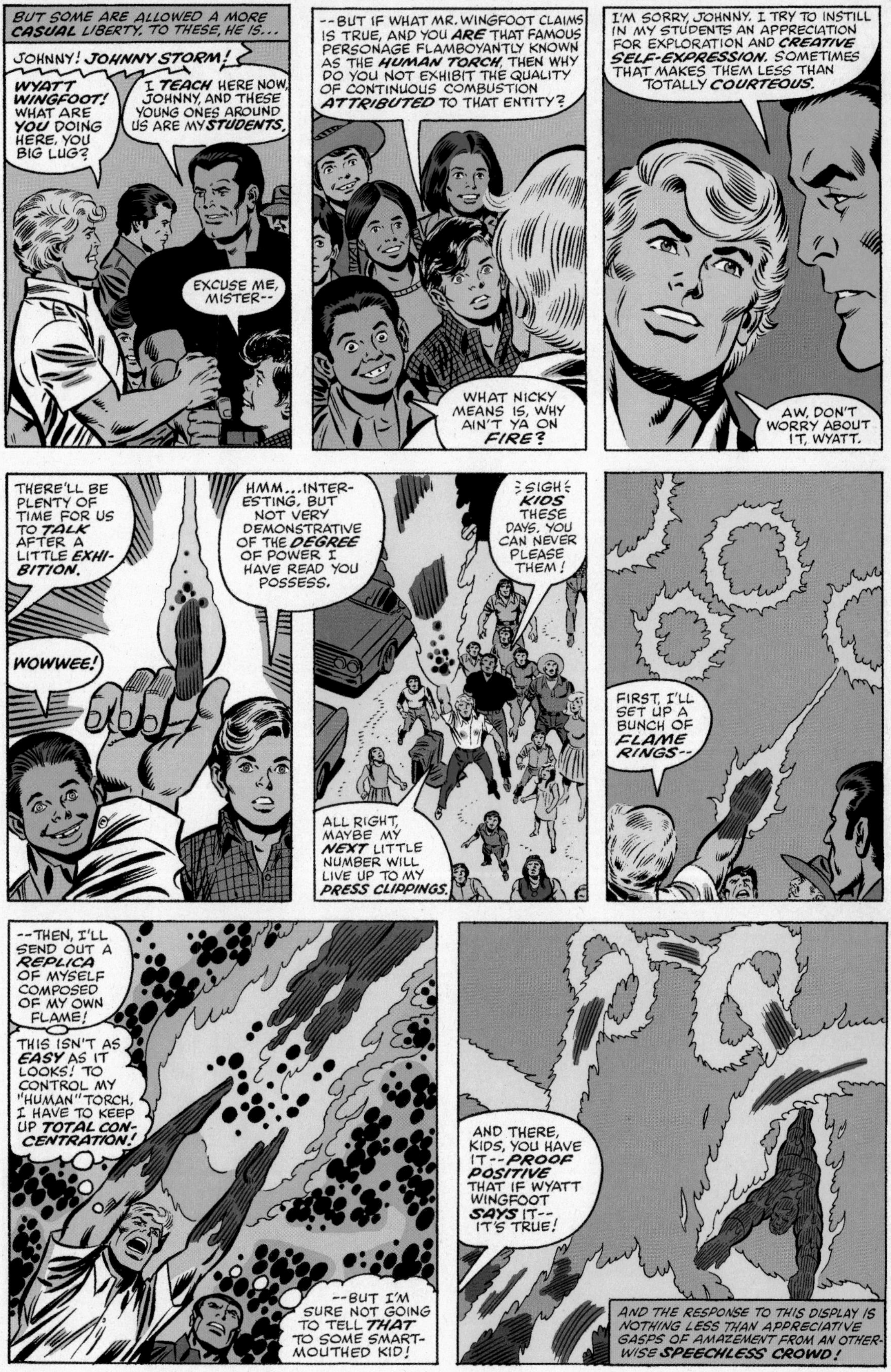

BUT SOME ARE ALLOWED A MORE CASUAL LIBERTY. TO THESE, HE IS...
JOHNNY! JOHNNY STORM!
WYATT WINGFOOT! WHAT ARE YOU DOING HERE, YOU BIG LUG?
I TEACH HERE NOW, JOHNNY, AND THESE YOUNG ONES AROUND US ARE MY STUDENTS.
EXCUSE ME, MISTER--
--BUT IF WHAT MR. WINGFOOT CLAIMS IS TRUE, AND YOU ARE THAT FAMOUS PERSONAGE FLAMBOYANTLY KNOWN AS THE HUMAN TORCH, THEN WHY DO YOU NOT EXHIBIT THE QUALITY OF CONTINUOUS COMBUSTION ATTRIBUTED TO THAT ENTITY?
WHAT NICKY MEANS IS, WHY AIN'T YA ON FIRE?
I'M SORRY, JOHNNY. I TRY TO INSTILL IN MY STUDENTS AN APPRECIATION FOR EXPLORATION AND CREATIVE SELF-EXPRESSION. SOMETIMES THAT MAKES THEM LESS THAN TOTALLY COURTEOUS.
AW, DON'T WORRY ABOUT IT, WYATT.
THERE'LL BE PLENTY OF TIME FOR US TO TALK AFTER A LITTLE EXHIBITION.
WOWWEE!
HMM... INTERESTING, BUT NOT VERY DEMONSTRATIVE OF THE DEGREE OF POWER I HAVE READ YOU POSSESS.
SIGH KIDS THESE DAYS. YOU CAN NEVER PLEASE THEM!
ALL RIGHT, MAYBE MY NEXT LITTLE NUMBER WILL LIVE UP TO MY PRESS CLIPPINGS.
FIRST, I'LL SET UP A BUNCH OF FLAME RINGS--
--THEN, I'LL SEND OUT A REPLICA OF MYSELF COMPOSED OF MY OWN FLAME!
THIS ISN'T AS EASY AS IT LOOKS! TO CONTROL MY "HUMAN" TORCH, I HAVE TO KEEP UP TOTAL CONCENTRATION!
--BUT I'M SURE NOT GOING TO TELL THAT TO SOME SMART-MOUTHED KID!
AND THERE, KIDS, YOU HAVE IT--PROOF POSITIVE THAT IF WYATT WINGFOOT SAYS IT--IT'S TRUE!
AND THE RESPONSE TO THIS DISPLAY IS NOTHING LESS THAN APPRECIATIVE GASPS OF AMAZEMENT FROM AN OTHERWISE SPEECHLESS CROWD!

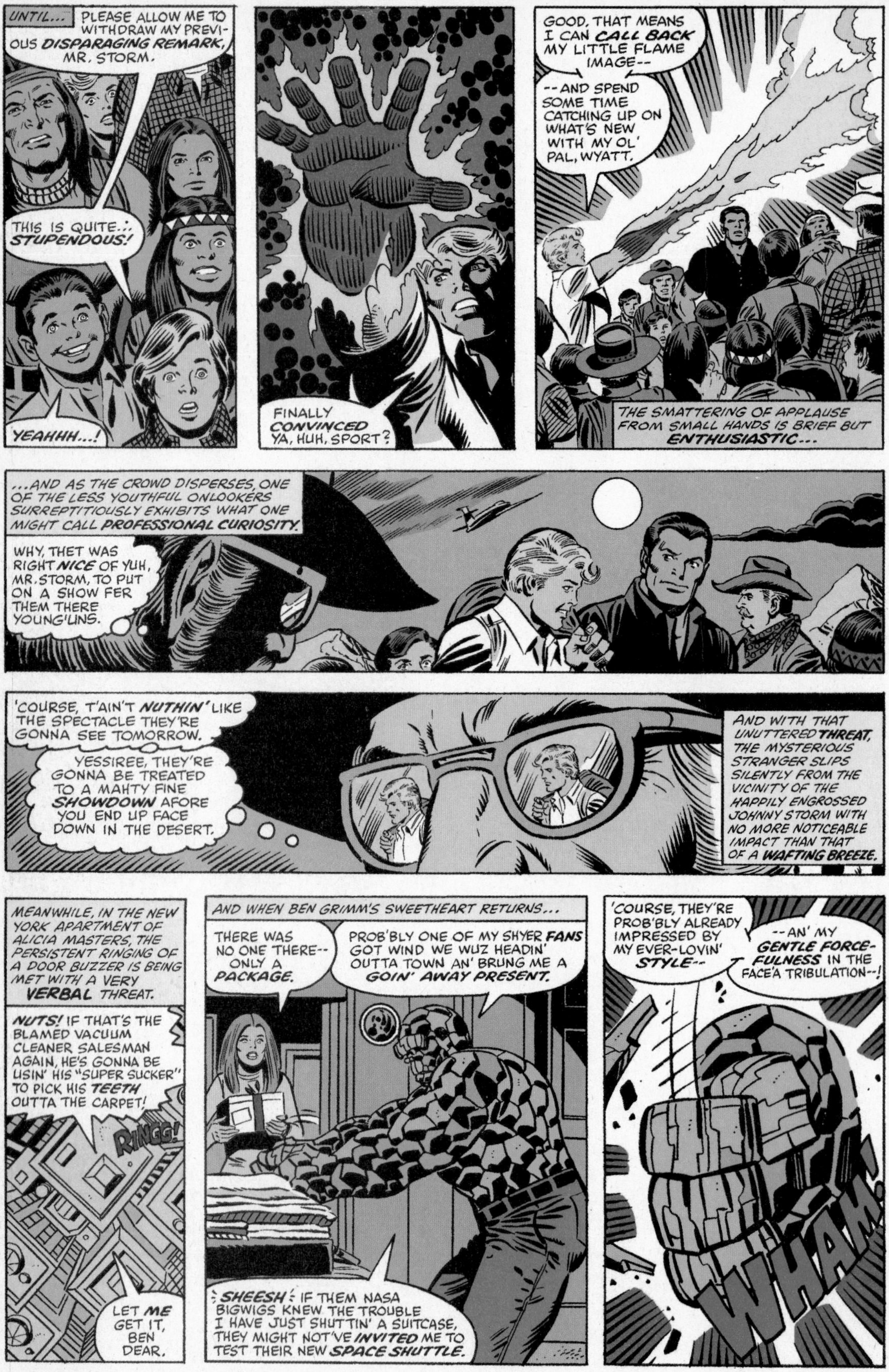

UNTIL...
PLEASE ALLOW ME TO WITHDRAW MY PREVIOUS DISPARAGING REMARK, MR. STORM.
THIS IS QUITE... STUPENDOUS!
YEAHHH...!
FINALLY CONVINCED YA, HUH, SPORT?
GOOD, THAT MEANS I CAN CALL BACK MY LITTLE FLAME IMAGE--
--AND SPEND SOME TIME CATCHING UP ON WHAT'S NEW WITH MY OL' PAL, WYATT.
THE SMATTERING OF APPLAUSE FROM SMALL HANDS IS BRIEF BUT ENTHUSIASTIC...
...AND AS THE CROWD DISPERSES, ONE OF THE LESS YOUTHFUL ONLOOKERS SURREPTITIOUSLY EXHIBITS WHAT ONE MIGHT CALL PROFESSIONAL CURIOSITY.
WHY, THET WAS RIGHT NICE OF YUH, MR. STORM, TO PUT ON A SHOW FER THEM THERE YOUNG'UNS.
'COURSE, T'AIN'T NUTHIN' LIKE THE SPECTACLE THEY'RE GONNA SEE TOMORROW.
YESSIREE, THEY'RE GONNA BE TREATED TO A MAHTY FINE SHOWDOWN AFORE YOU END UP FACE DOWN IN THE DESERT.
AND WITH THAT UNUTTERED THREAT, THE MYSTERIOUS STRANGER SLIPS SILENTLY FROM THE VICINITY OF THE HAPPILY ENGROSSED JOHNNY STORM WITH NO MORE NOTICEABLE IMPACT THAN THAT OF A WAFTING BREEZE.
MEANWHILE, IN THE NEW YORK APARTMENT OF ALICIA MASTERS, THE PERSISTENT RINGING OF A DOOR BUZZER IS BEING MET WITH A VERY VERBAL THREAT.
NUTS! IF THAT'S THE BLAMED VACUUM CLEANER SALESMAN AGAIN, HE'S GONNA BE USIN' HIS "SUPER SUCKER" TO PICK HIS TEETH OUTTA THE CARPET!
RINGG!
LET ME GET IT, BEN DEAR.
AND WHEN BEN GRIMM'S SWEETHEART RETURNS...
THERE WAS NO ONE THERE-- ONLY A PACKAGE.
PROB'BLY ONE OF MY SHYER FANS GOT WIND WE WUZ HEADIN' OUTTA TOWN AN' BRUNG ME A GOIN' AWAY PRESENT.
SHEESH! IF THEM NASA BIGWIGS KNEW THE TROUBLE I HAVE JUST SHUTTIN' A SUITCASE, THEY MIGHT NOT'VE INVITED ME TO TEST THEIR NEW SPACE SHUTTLE.
'COURSE, THEY'RE PROB'BLY ALREADY IMPRESSED BY MY EVER-LOVIN' STYLE--
--AN' MY GENTLE FORCE-FULNESS IN THE FACE'A TRIBULATION--!
WHAM!

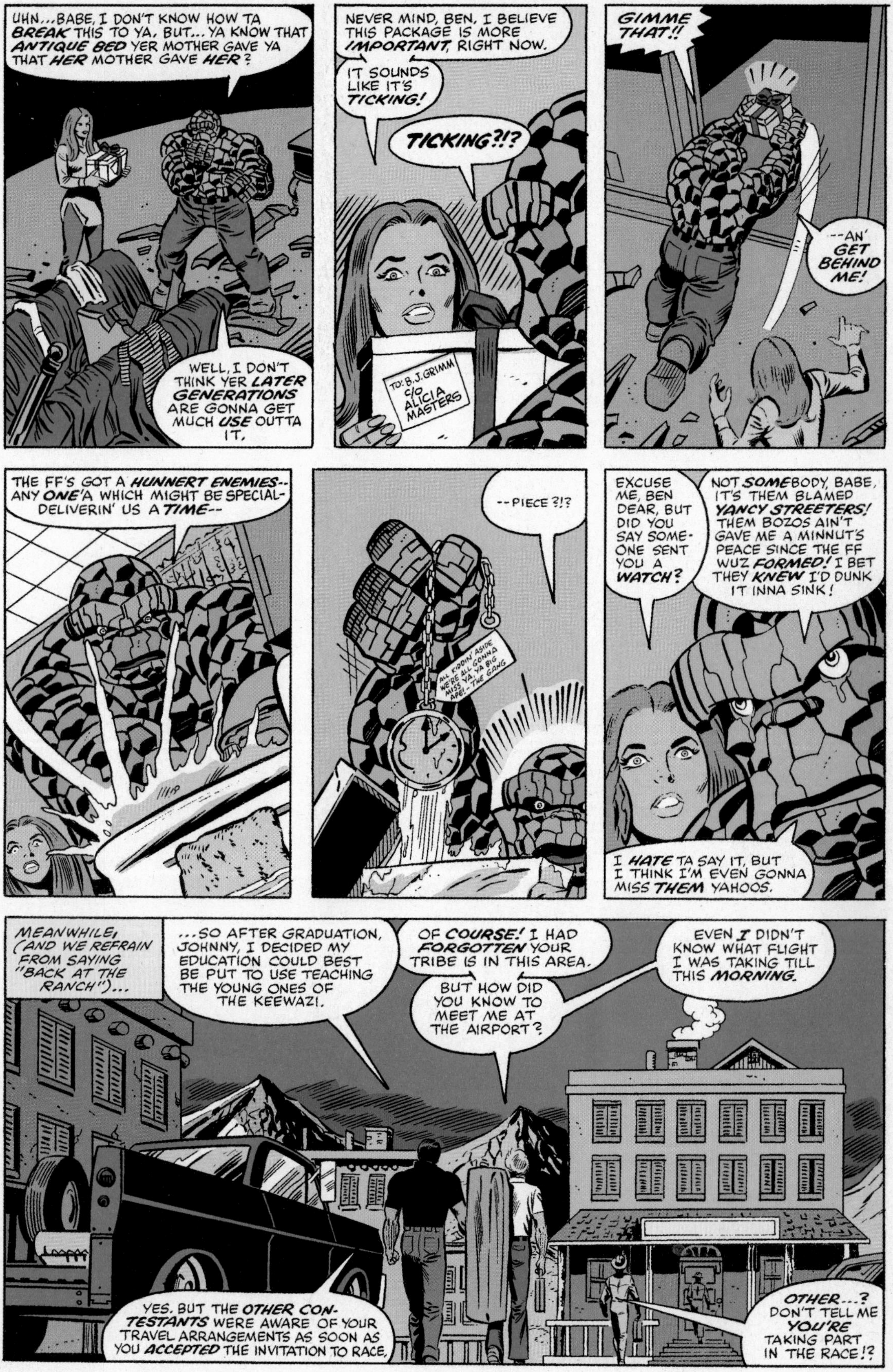

UHN...BABE, I DON'T KNOW HOW TA BREAK THIS TO YA, BUT... YA KNOW THAT ANTIQUE BED YER MOTHER GAVE YA THAT HER MOTHER GAVE HER?
WELL, I DON'T THINK YER LATER GENERATIONS ARE GONNA GET MUCH USE OUTTA IT.
NEVER MIND, BEN, I BELIEVE THIS PACKAGE IS MORE IMPORTANT, RIGHT NOW.
IT SOUNDS LIKE IT'S TICKING!
TICKING?!?
TO: B.J. GRIMM c/o ALICIA MASTERS
GIMME THAT!!
--AN' GET BEHIND ME!
THE FF'S GOT A HUNNERT ENEMIES--ANY ONE'A WHICH MIGHT BE SPECIAL-DELIVERIN' US A TIME--
--PIECE?!?
ALL KIDDIN' ASIDE WE'RE ALL GONNA MISS YA YA BIG APE! - THE GANG
EXCUSE ME, BEN DEAR, BUT DID YOU SAY SOME-ONE SENT YOU A WATCH?
NOT SOMEBODY, BABE, IT'S THEM BLAMED YANCY STREETERS! THEM BOZOS AIN'T GAVE ME A MINNUT'S PEACE SINCE THE FF WUZ FORMED! I BET THEY KNEW I'D DUNK IT INNA SINK!
I HATE TA SAY IT, BUT I THINK I'M EVEN GONNA MISS THEM YAHOOS.
MEANWHILE, (AND WE REFRAIN FROM SAYING "BACK AT THE RANCH")...
...SO AFTER GRADUATION, JOHNNY, I DECIDED MY EDUCATION COULD BEST BE PUT TO USE TEACHING THE YOUNG ONES OF THE KEEWAZI.
OF COURSE! I HAD FORGOTTEN YOUR TRIBE IS IN THIS AREA.
BUT HOW DID YOU KNOW TO MEET ME AT THE AIRPORT?
EVEN I DIDN'T KNOW WHAT FLIGHT I WAS TAKING TILL THIS MORNING.
YES. BUT THE OTHER CON-TESTANTS WERE AWARE OF YOUR TRAVEL ARRANGEMENTS AS SOON AS YOU ACCEPTED THE INVITATION TO RACE.
OTHER...? DON'T TELL ME YOU'RE TAKING PART IN THE RACE!?

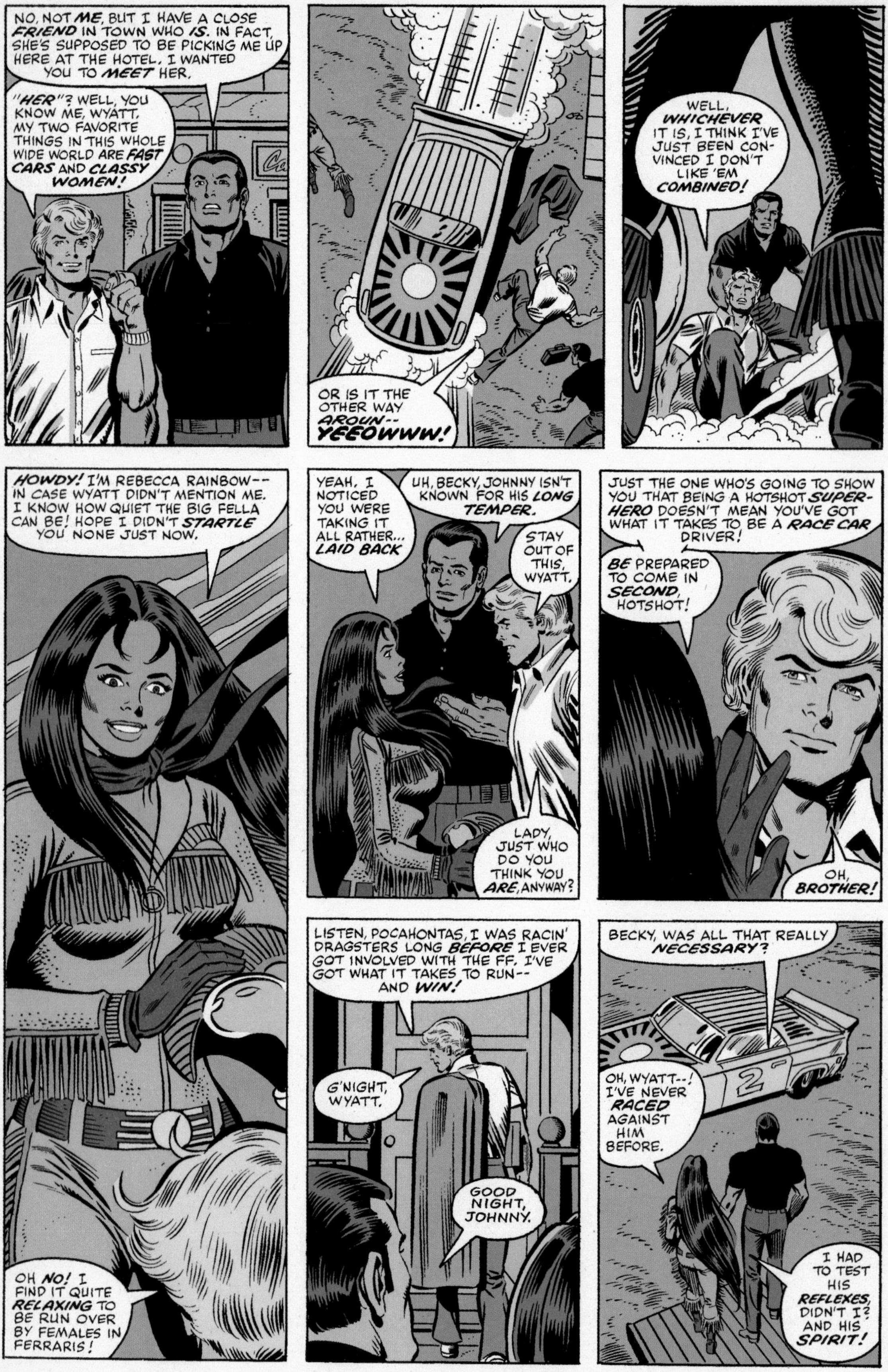
NO, NOT ME, BUT I HAVE A CLOSE FRIEND IN TOWN WHO IS. IN FACT, SHE'S SUPPOSED TO BE PICKING ME UP HERE AT THE HOTEL. I WANTED YOU TO MEET HER.
"HER"? WELL, YOU KNOW ME, WYATT. MY TWO FAVORITE THINGS IN THIS WHOLE WIDE WORLD ARE FAST CARS AND CLASSY WOMEN!
OR IS IT THE OTHER WAY AROUN-- YEEOWWW!
WELL, WHICHEVER IT IS, I THINK I'VE JUST BEEN CONVINCED I DON'T LIKE 'EM COMBINED!
HOWDY! I'M REBECCA RAINBOW-- IN CASE WYATT DIDN'T MENTION ME. I KNOW HOW QUIET THE BIG FELLA CAN BE! HOPE I DIDN'T STARTLE YOU NONE JUST NOW.
OH NO! I FIND IT QUITE RELAXING TO BE RUN OVER BY FEMALES IN FERRARIS!
YEAH, I NOTICED YOU WERE TAKING IT ALL RATHER... LAID BACK
UH, BECKY, JOHNNY ISN'T KNOWN FOR HIS LONG TEMPER.
STAY OUT OF THIS, WYATT.
LADY, JUST WHO DO YOU THINK YOU ARE, ANYWAY?
JUST THE ONE WHO'S GOING TO SHOW YOU THAT BEING A HOTSHOT SUPER-HERO DOESN'T MEAN YOU'VE GOT WHAT IT TAKES TO BE A RACE CAR DRIVER!
BE PREPARED TO COME IN SECOND, HOTSHOT!
OH, BROTHER!
LISTEN, POCAHONTAS, I WAS RACIN' DRAGSTERS LONG BEFORE I EVER GOT INVOLVED WITH THE FF. I'VE GOT WHAT IT TAKES TO RUN-- AND WIN!
G'NIGHT, WYATT.
GOOD NIGHT, JOHNNY.
BECKY, WAS ALL THAT REALLY NECESSARY?
OH, WYATT--! I'VE NEVER RACED AGAINST HIM BEFORE.
I HAD TO TEST HIS REFLEXES, DIDN'T I? AND HIS SPIRIT!

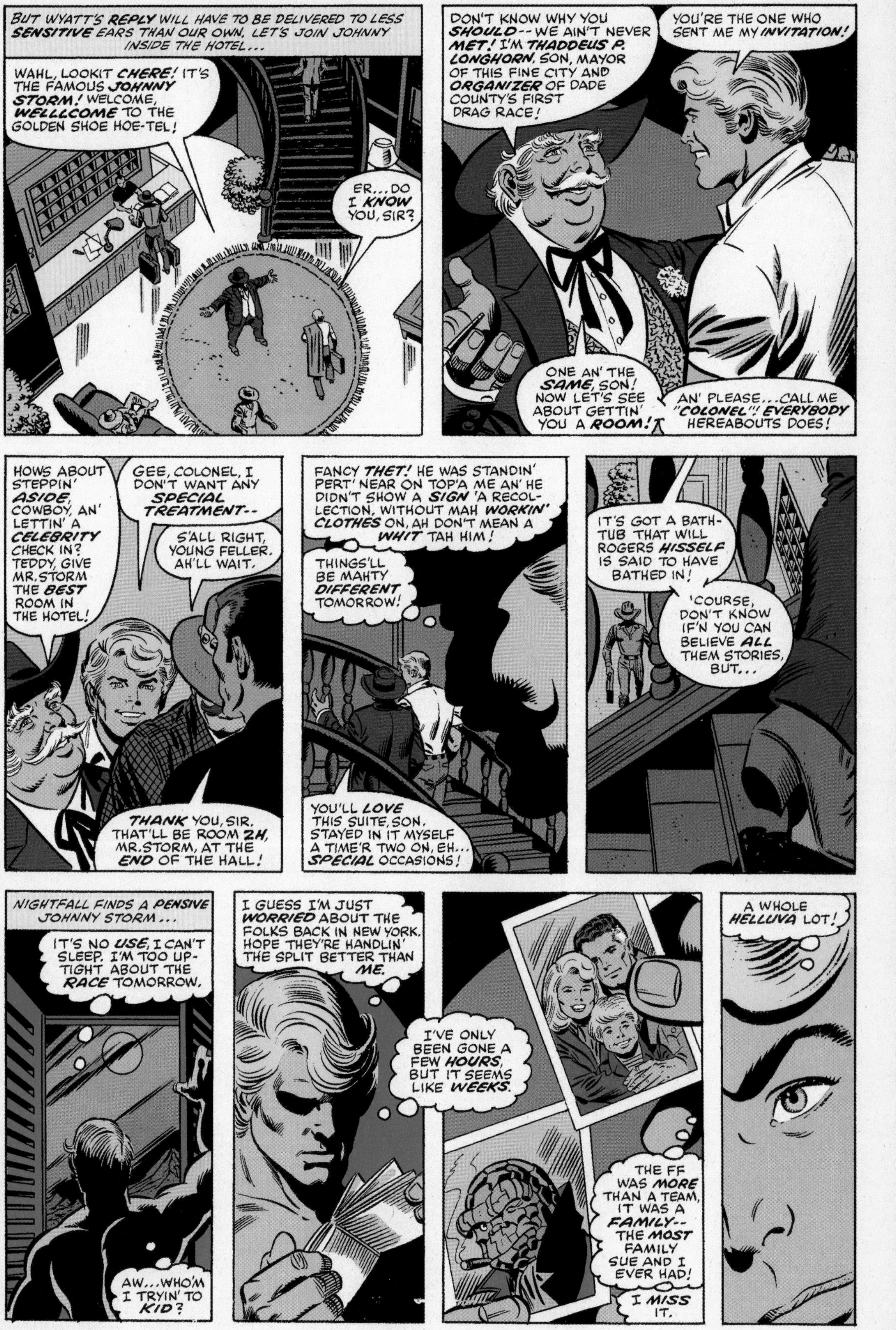
BUT WYATT'S REPLY WILL HAVE TO BE DELIVERED TO LESS SENSITIVE EARS THAN OUR OWN. LET'S JOIN JOHNNY INSIDE THE HOTEL...
WAHL, LOOKIT CHERE! IT'S THE FAMOUS JOHNNY STORM! WELCOME, WELLLCOME TO THE GOLDEN SHOE HOE-TEL!
ER... DO I KNOW YOU, SIR?
DON'T KNOW WHY YOU SHOULD-- WE AIN'T NEVER MET! I'M THADDEUS P. LONGHORN, SON, MAYOR OF THIS FINE CITY AND ORGANIZER OF DADE COUNTY'S FIRST DRAG RACE!
YOU'RE THE ONE WHO SENT ME MY INVITATION!
ONE AN' THE SAME, SON! NOW LET'S SEE ABOUT GETTIN' YOU A ROOM!
AN' PLEASE... CALL ME "COLONEL"! EVERYBODY HEREABOUTS DOES!
HOWS ABOUT STEPPIN' ASIDE, COWBOY, AN' LETTIN' A CELEBRITY CHECK IN? TEDDY, GIVE MR. STORM THE BEST ROOM IN THE HOTEL!
GEE, COLONEL, I DON'T WANT ANY SPECIAL TREATMENT--
S'ALL RIGHT, YOUNG FELLER. AH'LL WAIT.
THANK YOU, SIR. THAT'LL BE ROOM 2H, MR. STORM, AT THE END OF THE HALL!
FANCY THET! HE WAS STANDIN' PERT' NEAR ON TOP'A ME AN' HE DIDN'T SHOW A SIGN 'A RECOLLECTION. WITHOUT MAH WORKIN' CLOTHES ON, AH DON'T MEAN A WHIT TAH HIM!
THINGS'LL BE MAHTY DIFFERENT TOMORROW!
YOU'LL LOVE THIS SUITE, SON. STAYED IN IT MYSELF A TIME'R TWO ON, EH... SPECIAL OCCASIONS!
IT'S GOT A BATH-TUB THAT WILL ROGERS HISSELF IS SAID TO HAVE BATHED IN!
'COURSE, DON'T KNOW IF'N YOU CAN BELIEVE ALL THEM STORIES, BUT...
NIGHTFALL FINDS A PENSIVE JOHNNY STORM...
IT'S NO USE, I CAN'T SLEEP. I'M TOO UP-TIGHT ABOUT THE RACE TOMORROW.
AW... WHO'M I TRYIN' TO KID?
I GUESS I'M JUST WORRIED ABOUT THE FOLKS BACK IN NEW YORK. HOPE THEY'RE HANDLIN' THE SPLIT BETTER THAN ME.
I'VE ONLY BEEN GONE A FEW HOURS, BUT IT SEEMS LIKE WEEKS.
THE FF WAS MORE THAN A TEAM, IT WAS A FAMILY-- THE MOST FAMILY SUE AND I EVER HAD!
I MISS IT.
A WHOLE HELLUVA LOT!

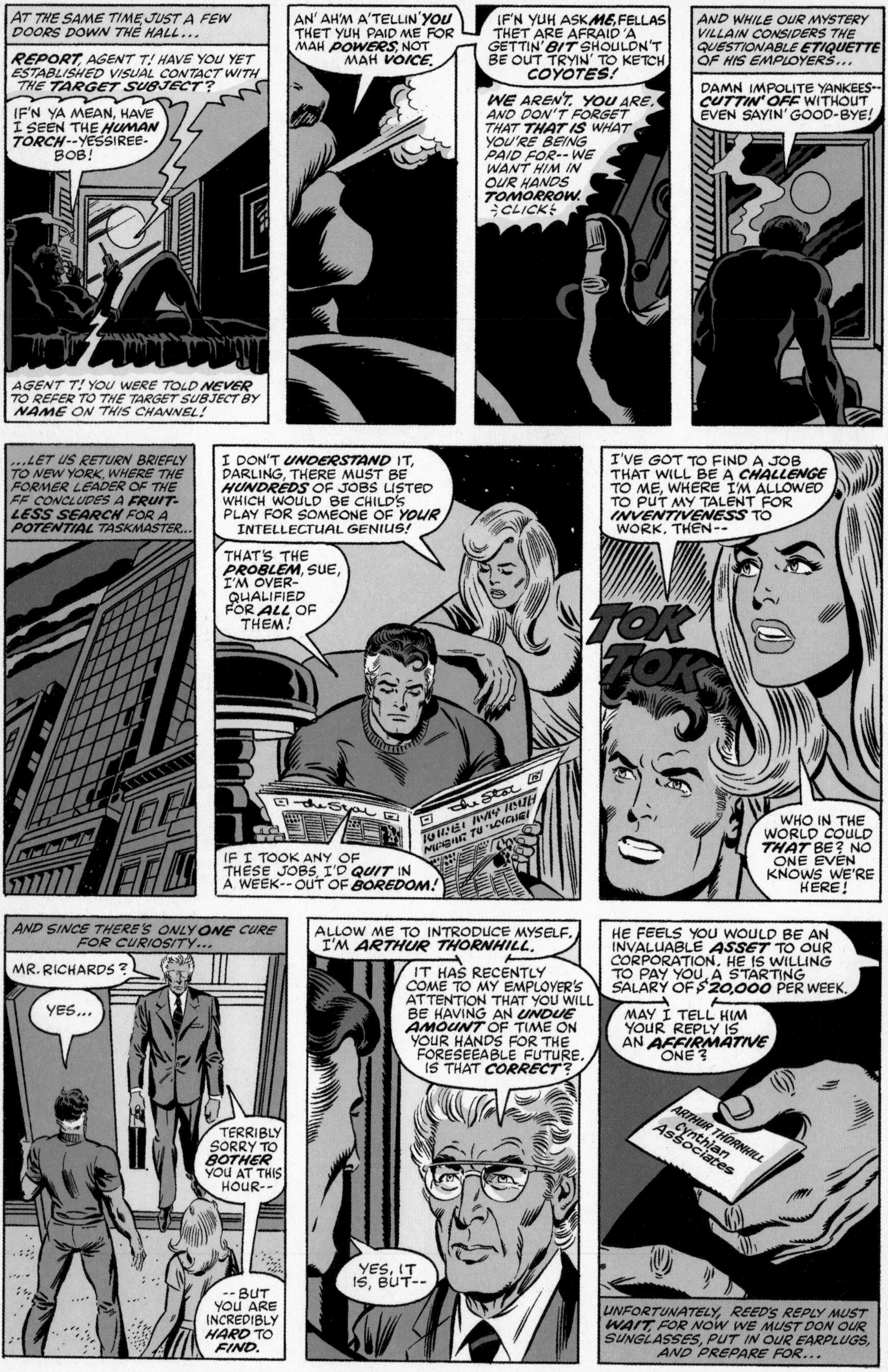

AT THE SAME TIME, JUST A FEW DOORS DOWN THE HALL...
REPORT, AGENT T! HAVE YOU YET ESTABLISHED VISUAL CONTACT WITH THE TARGET SUBJECT?
IF'N YA MEAN, HAVE I SEEN THE HUMAN TORCH--YESSIREE-BOB!
AGENT T! YOU WERE TOLD NEVER TO REFER TO THE TARGET SUBJECT BY NAME ON THIS CHANNEL!
AN' AH'M A'TELLIN' YOU THET YUH PAID ME FOR MAH POWERS, NOT MAH VOICE.
IF'N YUH ASK ME, FELLAS THET ARE AFRAID 'A GETTIN' BIT SHOULDN'T BE OUT TRYIN' TO KETCH COYOTES!
WE AREN'T. YOU ARE. AND DON'T FORGET THAT THAT IS WHAT YOU'RE BEING PAID FOR--WE WANT HIM IN OUR HANDS TOMORROW.
CLICK
AND WHILE OUR MYSTERY VILLAIN CONSIDERS THE QUESTIONABLE ETIQUETTE OF HIS EMPLOYERS...
DAMN IMPOLITE YANKEES--CUTTIN' OFF WITHOUT EVEN SAYIN' GOOD-BYE!
...LET US RETURN BRIEFLY TO NEW YORK, WHERE THE FORMER LEADER OF THE FF CONCLUDES A FRUITLESS SEARCH FOR A POTENTIAL TASKMASTER...
I DON'T UNDERSTAND IT, DARLING, THERE MUST BE HUNDREDS OF JOBS LISTED WHICH WOULD BE CHILD'S PLAY FOR SOMEONE OF YOUR INTELLECTUAL GENIUS!
THAT'S THE PROBLEM, SUE, I'M OVER-QUALIFIED FOR ALL OF THEM!
IF I TOOK ANY OF THESE JOBS, I'D QUIT IN A WEEK--OUT OF BOREDOM!
I'VE GOT TO FIND A JOB THAT WILL BE A CHALLENGE TO ME, WHERE I'M ALLOWED TO PUT MY TALENT FOR INVENTIVENESS TO WORK. THEN--
TOK TOK
WHO IN THE WORLD COULD THAT BE? NO ONE EVEN KNOWS WE'RE HERE!
AND SINCE THERE'S ONLY ONE CURE FOR CURIOSITY...
MR. RICHARDS?
YES...
TERRIBLY SORRY TO BOTHER YOU AT THIS HOUR--
--BUT YOU ARE INCREDIBLY HARD TO FIND.
ALLOW ME TO INTRODUCE MYSELF. I'M ARTHUR THORNHILL.
IT HAS RECENTLY COME TO MY EMPLOYER'S ATTENTION THAT YOU WILL BE HAVING AN UNDUE AMOUNT OF TIME ON YOUR HANDS FOR THE FORESEEABLE FUTURE. IS THAT CORRECT?
YES, IT IS, BUT--
HE FEELS YOU WOULD BE AN INVALUABLE ASSET TO OUR CORPORATION. HE IS WILLING TO PAY YOU A STARTING SALARY OF $20,000 PER WEEK.
MAY I TELL HIM YOUR REPLY IS AN AFFIRMATIVE ONE?
ARTHUR THORNHILL
Cynthian Associates
UNFORTUNATELY, REED'S REPLY MUST WAIT, FOR NOW WE MUST DON OUR SUNGLASSES, PUT IN OUR EARPLUGS, AND PREPARE FOR...

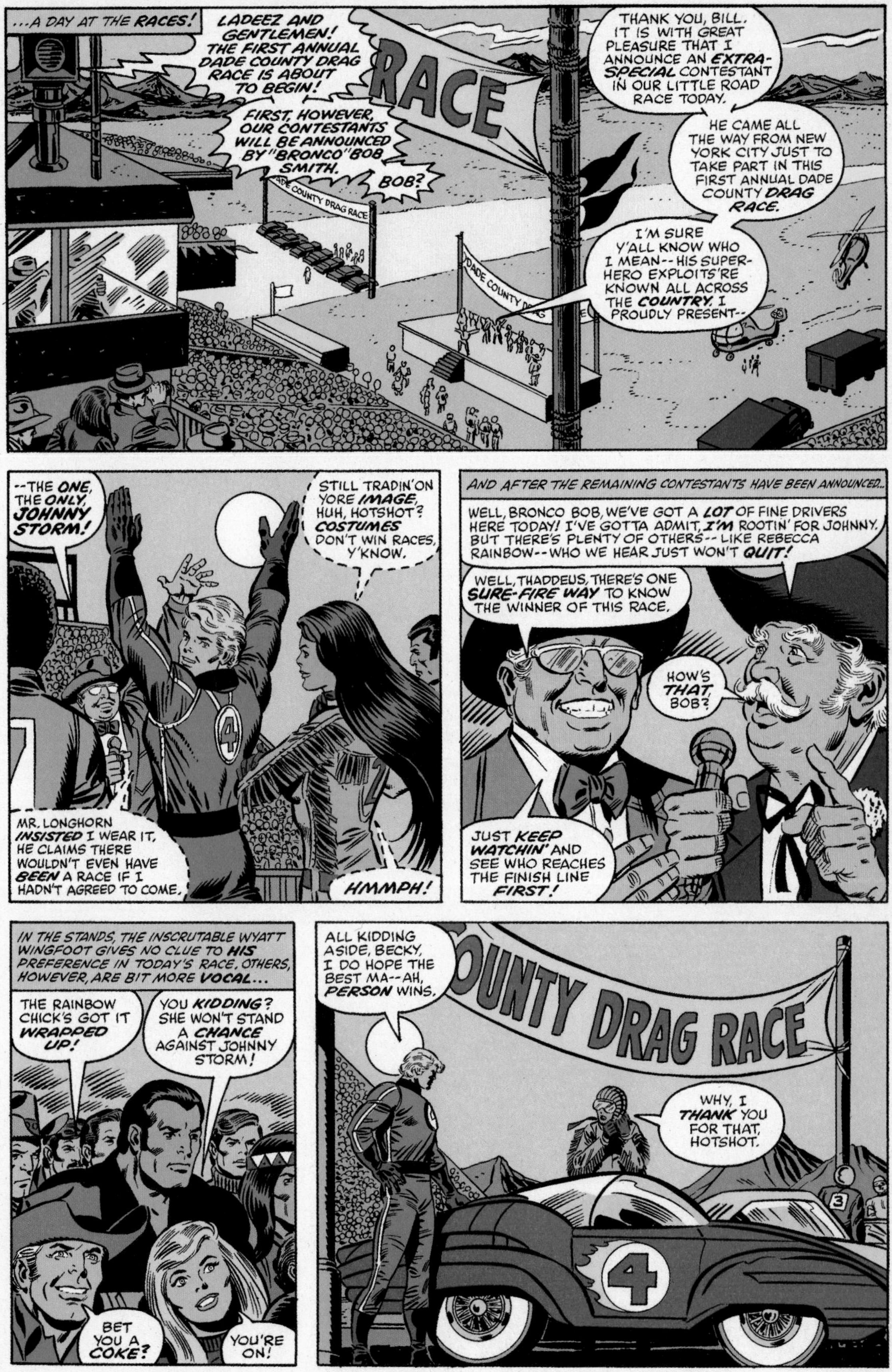

...A DAY AT THE RACES!
LADEEZ AND GENTLEMEN! THE FIRST ANNUAL DADE COUNTY DRAG RACE IS ABOUT TO BEGIN!
FIRST, HOWEVER, OUR CONTESTANTS WILL BE ANNOUNCED BY "BRONCO" BOB SMITH.
BOB?
RACE
DADE COUNTY DRAG RACE
THANK YOU, BILL. IT IS WITH GREAT PLEASURE THAT I ANNOUNCE AN EXTRA-SPECIAL CONTESTANT IN OUR LITTLE ROAD RACE TODAY.
HE CAME ALL THE WAY FROM NEW YORK CITY JUST TO TAKE PART IN THIS FIRST ANNUAL DADE COUNTY DRAG RACE.
I'M SURE Y'ALL KNOW WHO I MEAN--HIS SUPER-HERO EXPLOITS'RE KNOWN ALL ACROSS THE COUNTRY. I PROUDLY PRESENT--
--THE ONE, THE ONLY, JOHNNY STORM!
STILL TRADIN'ON YORE IMAGE, HUH, HOTSHOT? COSTUMES DON'T WIN RACES, Y'KNOW.
MR. LONGHORN INSISTED I WEAR IT. HE CLAIMS THERE WOULDN'T EVEN HAVE BEEN A RACE IF I HADN'T AGREED TO COME.
HMMPH!
AND AFTER THE REMAINING CONTESTANTS HAVE BEEN ANNOUNCED...
WELL, BRONCO BOB, WE'VE GOT A LOT OF FINE DRIVERS HERE TODAY! I'VE GOTTA ADMIT, I'M ROOTIN' FOR JOHNNY. BUT THERE'S PLENTY OF OTHERS--LIKE REBECCA RAINBOW--WHO WE HEAR JUST WON'T QUIT!
WELL, THADDEUS, THERE'S ONE SURE-FIRE WAY TO KNOW THE WINNER OF THIS RACE.
HOW'S THAT, BOB?
JUST KEEP WATCHIN' AND SEE WHO REACHES THE FINISH LINE FIRST!
IN THE STANDS, THE INSCRUTABLE WYATT WINGFOOT GIVES NO CLUE TO HIS PREFERENCE IN TODAY'S RACE. OTHERS, HOWEVER, ARE BIT MORE VOCAL...
THE RAINBOW CHICK'S GOT IT WRAPPED UP!
YOU KIDDING? SHE WON'T STAND A CHANCE AGAINST JOHNNY STORM!
BET YOU A COKE?
YOU'RE ON!
ALL KIDDING ASIDE, BECKY, I DO HOPE THE BEST MA--AH, PERSON WINS.
COUNTY DRAG RACE
WHY, I THANK YOU FOR THAT, HOTSHOT.

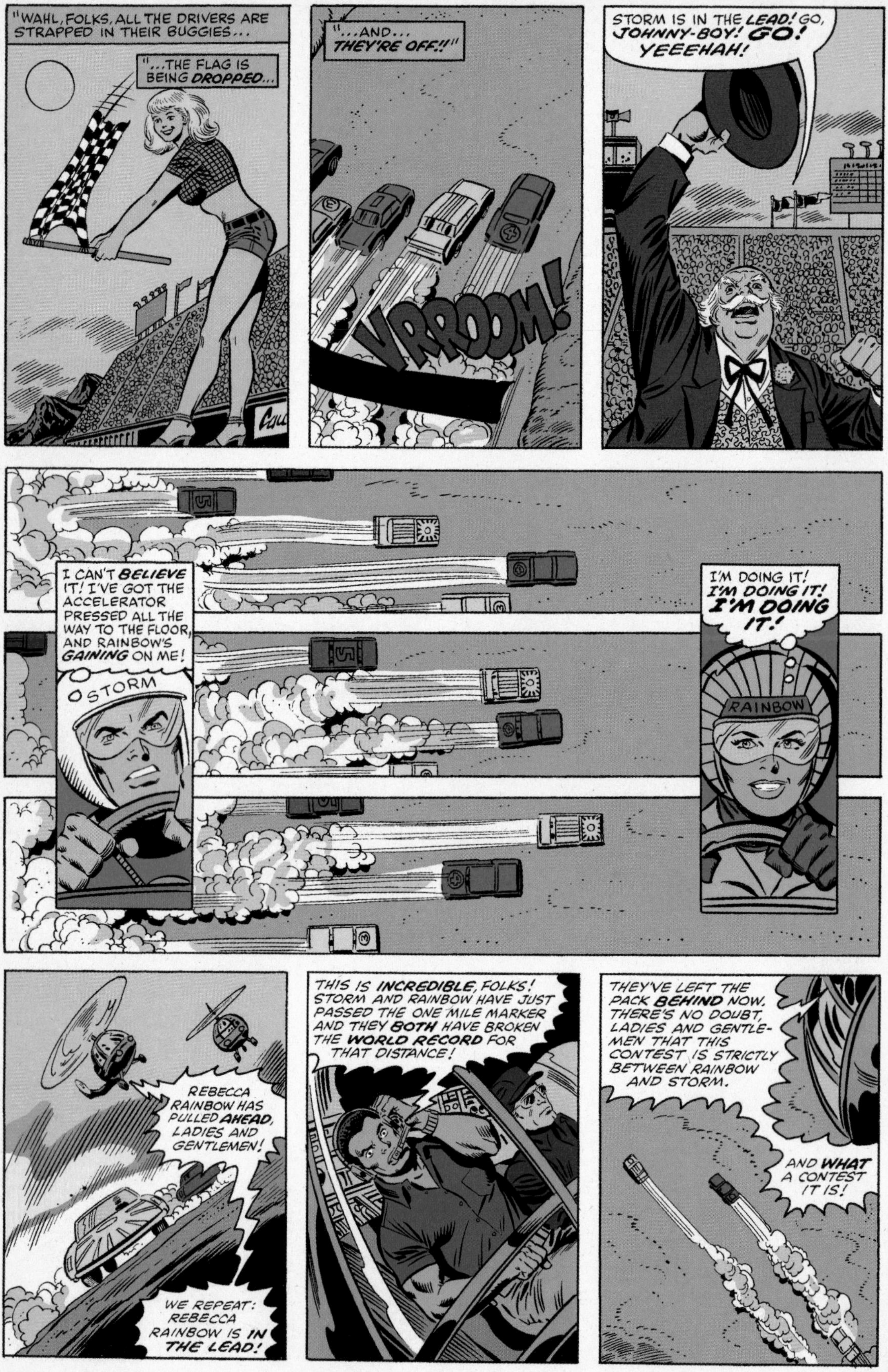
"WAHL, FOLKS, ALL THE DRIVERS ARE STRAPPED IN THEIR BUGGIES...
"...THE FLAG IS BEING DROPPED...
"...AND... THEY'RE OFF!!"
VRROOM!
STORM IS IN THE LEAD! GO, JOHNNY-BOY! GO! YEEEHAH!
I CAN'T BELIEVE IT! I'VE GOT THE ACCELERATOR PRESSED ALL THE WAY TO THE FLOOR, AND RAINBOW'S GAINING ON ME!
STORM
I'M DOING IT! I'M DOING IT! I'M DOING IT!
RAINBOW
REBECCA RAINBOW HAS PULLED AHEAD, LADIES AND GENTLEMEN!
WE REPEAT: REBECCA RAINBOW IS IN THE LEAD!
THIS IS INCREDIBLE, FOLKS! STORM AND RAINBOW HAVE JUST PASSED THE ONE MILE MARKER AND THEY BOTH HAVE BROKEN THE WORLD RECORD FOR THAT DISTANCE!
THEY'VE LEFT THE PACK BEHIND NOW. THERE'S NO DOUBT, LADIES AND GENTLE-MEN THAT THIS CONTEST IS STRICTLY BETWEEN RAINBOW AND STORM.
AND WHAT A CONTEST IT IS!

BUT *WAIT!* ON THE TRACK IN FRONT OF THEM, SPRINGING OUT OF *NOWHERE*--

--IT'S A *TWISTER!*

OH MY GOD! A *TORNADO* RIGHT IN *FRONT* OF US!

IT LOOKS LIKE STORM AND RAINBOW ARE *FINISHED!*

GOING TOO *FAST!* NO TIME TO *SWERVE!* WE'RE GOING TO SMACK INTO IT!

RAINBOW

SAVAGELY THE TWO CARS ARE *PLUCKED* FROM THE RACEWAY, *ENGULFED* BY THE TURBULENT GALES.

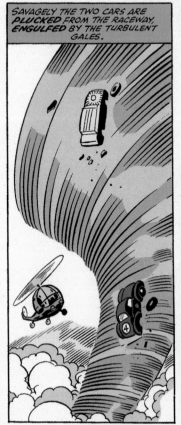

AND IT IS ONLY *CHANCE* THAT THE BATTERING WINDS THAT REND TIRE FROM AXLE, AXLE FROM FRAME ALSO SEND REBECCA *SAILING FREE!*

HELP ME! SOMEBODY *HELP ME!*

FREE, THAT IS, TO *PLUMMET* 200 HUNDRED FEET TO THE HARD EARTH BELOW!

SO *FANTASTIC* IS THE TABLEAU THAT EVEN THE ON-THE-SPOT ANNOUNCER-- TRAINED TO REPORT THROUGH EVEN THE MOST *BIZARRE* SPECTACLES--

--IS STRUCK *SPEECHLESS!*

ABRUPTLY, *ANOTHER* FIGURE ERUPTS FROM SWIRLING MADNESS...

FLAME ON!

BUT, IS HE IN *TIME?!*

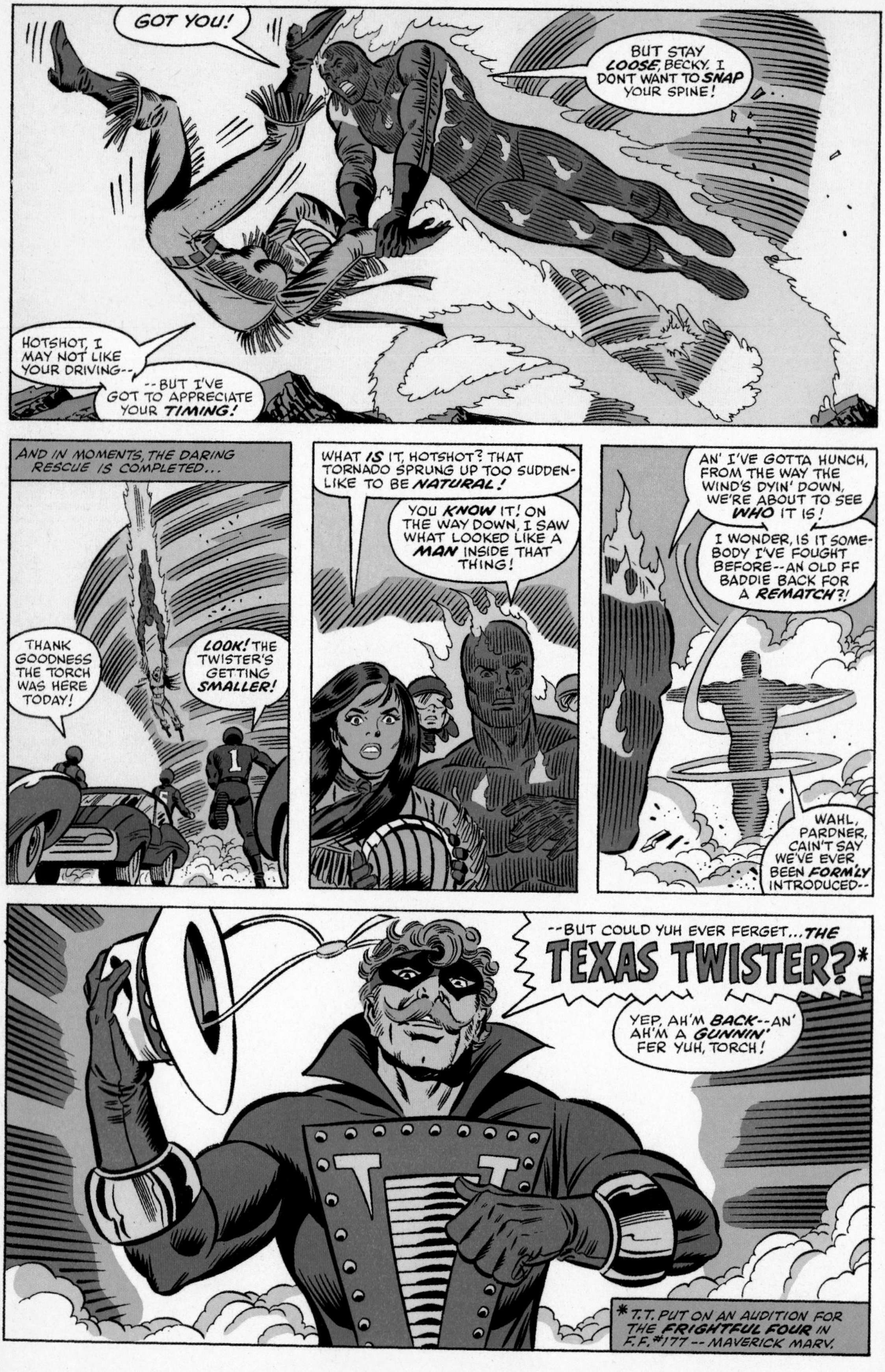
GOT YOU!
BUT STAY LOOSE, BECKY. I DONT WANT TO SNAP YOUR SPINE!
HOTSHOT, I MAY NOT LIKE YOUR DRIVING--
--BUT I'VE GOT TO APPRECIATE YOUR TIMING!
AND IN MOMENTS, THE DARING RESCUE IS COMPLETED...
THANK GOODNESS THE TORCH WAS HERE TODAY!
LOOK! THE TWISTER'S GETTING SMALLER!
WHAT IS IT, HOTSHOT? THAT TORNADO SPRUNG UP TOO SUDDEN-LIKE TO BE NATURAL!
YOU KNOW IT! ON THE WAY DOWN, I SAW WHAT LOOKED LIKE A MAN INSIDE THAT THING!
AN' I'VE GOTTA HUNCH, FROM THE WAY THE WIND'S DYIN' DOWN, WE'RE ABOUT TO SEE WHO IT IS!
I WONDER, IS IT SOMEBODY I'VE FOUGHT BEFORE--AN OLD FF BADDIE BACK FOR A REMATCH?!
WAHL, PARDNER, CAIN'T SAY WE'VE EVER BEEN FORM'LY INTRODUCED--
--BUT COULD YUH EVER FERGET... THE TEXAS TWISTER?*
YEP, AH'M BACK--AN' AH'M A GUNNIN' FER YUH, TORCH!
* T.T. PUT ON AN AUDITION FOR THE FRIGHTFUL FOUR IN F.F. #177 -- MAVERICK MARV.

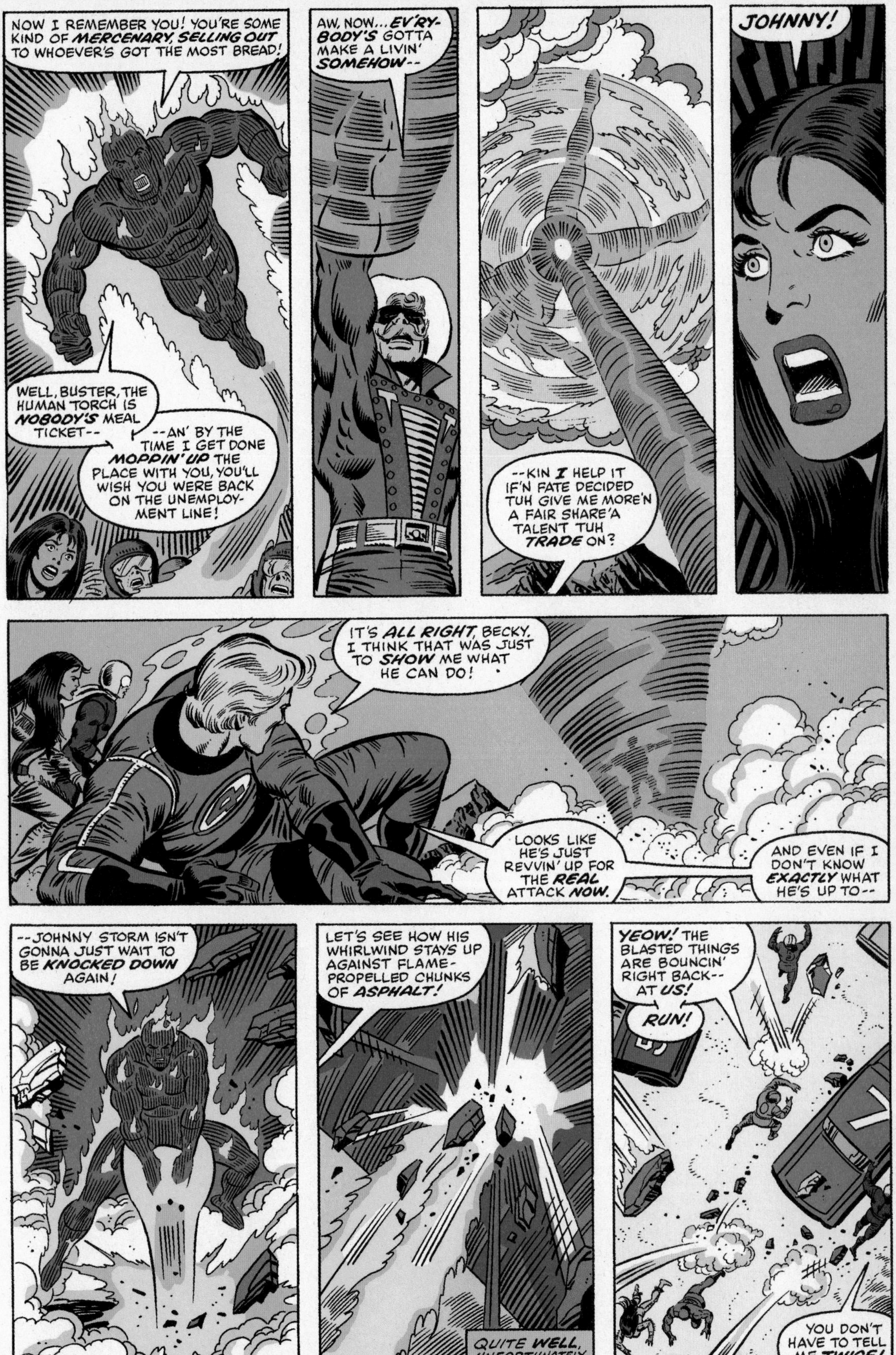
NOW I REMEMBER YOU! YOU'RE SOME KIND OF MERCENARY, SELLING OUT TO WHOEVER'S GOT THE MOST BREAD!
WELL, BUSTER, THE HUMAN TORCH IS NOBODY'S MEAL TICKET--
--AN' BY THE TIME I GET DONE MOPPIN' UP THE PLACE WITH YOU, YOU'LL WISH YOU WERE BACK ON THE UNEMPLOYMENT LINE!
AW, NOW... EV'RYBODY'S GOTTA MAKE A LIVIN' SOMEHOW--
--KIN I HELP IT IF'N FATE DECIDED TUH GIVE ME MORE'N A FAIR SHARE'A TALENT TUH TRADE ON?
JOHNNY!
IT'S ALL RIGHT, BECKY. I THINK THAT WAS JUST TO SHOW ME WHAT HE CAN DO!
LOOKS LIKE HE'S JUST REVVIN' UP FOR THE REAL ATTACK NOW.
AND EVEN IF I DON'T KNOW EXACTLY WHAT HE'S UP TO--
--JOHNNY STORM ISN'T GONNA JUST WAIT TO BE KNOCKED DOWN AGAIN!
LET'S SEE HOW HIS WHIRLWIND STAYS UP AGAINST FLAME-PROPELLED CHUNKS OF ASPHALT!
QUITE WELL, UNFORTUNATELY.
YEOW! THE BLASTED THINGS ARE BOUNCIN' RIGHT BACK-- AT US!
RUN!
YOU DON'T HAVE TO TELL ME TWICE!

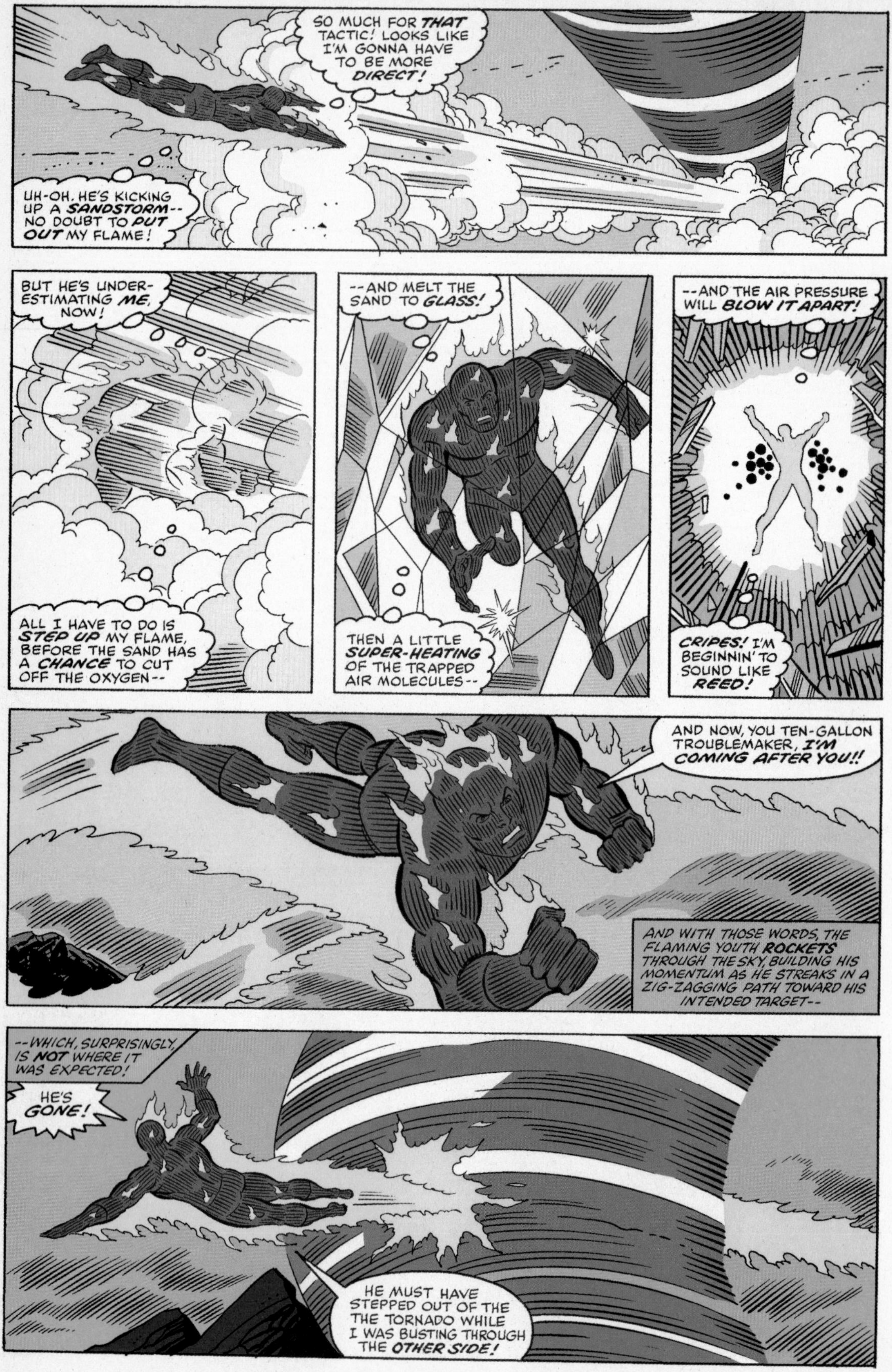
SO MUCH FOR THAT TACTIC! LOOKS LIKE I'M GONNA HAVE TO BE MORE DIRECT!
UH-OH. HE'S KICKING UP A SANDSTORM-- NO DOUBT TO PUT OUT MY FLAME!
BUT HE'S UNDER-ESTIMATING ME, NOW!
ALL I HAVE TO DO IS STEP UP MY FLAME, BEFORE THE SAND HAS A CHANCE TO CUT OFF THE OXYGEN--
--AND MELT THE SAND TO GLASS!
THEN A LITTLE SUPER-HEATING OF THE TRAPPED AIR MOLECULES--
--AND THE AIR PRESSURE WILL BLOW IT APART!
CRIPES! I'M BEGINNIN' TO SOUND LIKE REED!
AND NOW, YOU TEN-GALLON TROUBLEMAKER, I'M COMING AFTER YOU!!
AND WITH THOSE WORDS, THE FLAMING YOUTH ROCKETS THROUGH THE SKY, BUILDING HIS MOMENTUM AS HE STREAKS IN A ZIG-ZAGGING PATH TOWARD HIS INTENDED TARGET--
--WHICH, SURPRISINGLY, IS NOT WHERE IT WAS EXPECTED!
HE'S GONE!
HE MUST HAVE STEPPED OUT OF THE THE TORNADO WHILE I WAS BUSTING THROUGH THE OTHER SIDE!

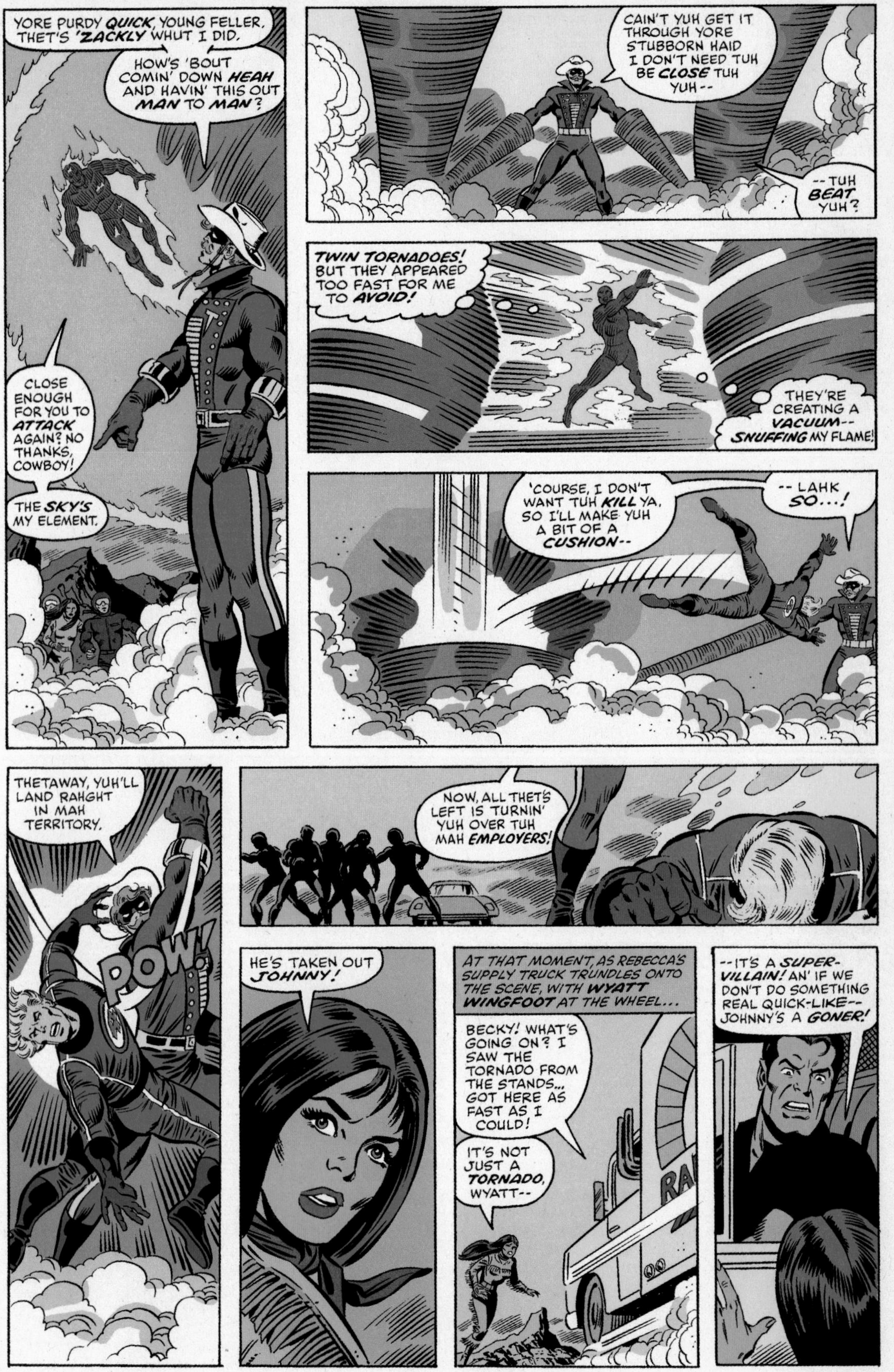
YORE PURDY QUICK, YOUNG FELLER, THET'S 'ZACKLY WHUT I DID.
HOW'S 'BOUT COMIN' DOWN HEAH AND HAVIN' THIS OUT MAN TO MAN?
CLOSE ENOUGH FOR YOU TO ATTACK AGAIN? NO THANKS, COWBOY!
THE SKY'S MY ELEMENT.
CAIN'T YUH GET IT THROUGH YORE STUBBORN HAID I DON'T NEED TUH BE CLOSE TUH YUH--
--TUH BEAT YUH?
TWIN TORNADOES! BUT THEY APPEARED TOO FAST FOR ME TO AVOID!
THEY'RE CREATING A VACUUM-- SNUFFING MY FLAME!
'COURSE, I DON'T WANT TUH KILL YA, SO I'LL MAKE YUH A BIT OF A CUSHION--
--LAHK SO...!
THETAWAY, YUH'LL LAND RAHGHT IN MAH TERRITORY.
POW!
NOW, ALL THET'S LEFT IS TURNIN' YUH OVER TUH MAH EMPLOYERS!
HE'S TAKEN OUT JOHNNY!
AT THAT MOMENT, AS REBECCA'S SUPPLY TRUCK TRUNDLES ONTO THE SCENE, WITH WYATT WINGFOOT AT THE WHEEL...
BECKY! WHAT'S GOING ON? I SAW THE TORNADO FROM THE STANDS... GOT HERE AS FAST AS I COULD!
IT'S NOT JUST A TORNADO, WYATT--
--IT'S A SUPER-VILLAIN! AN' IF WE DON'T DO SOMETHING REAL QUICK-LIKE-- JOHNNY'S A GONER!

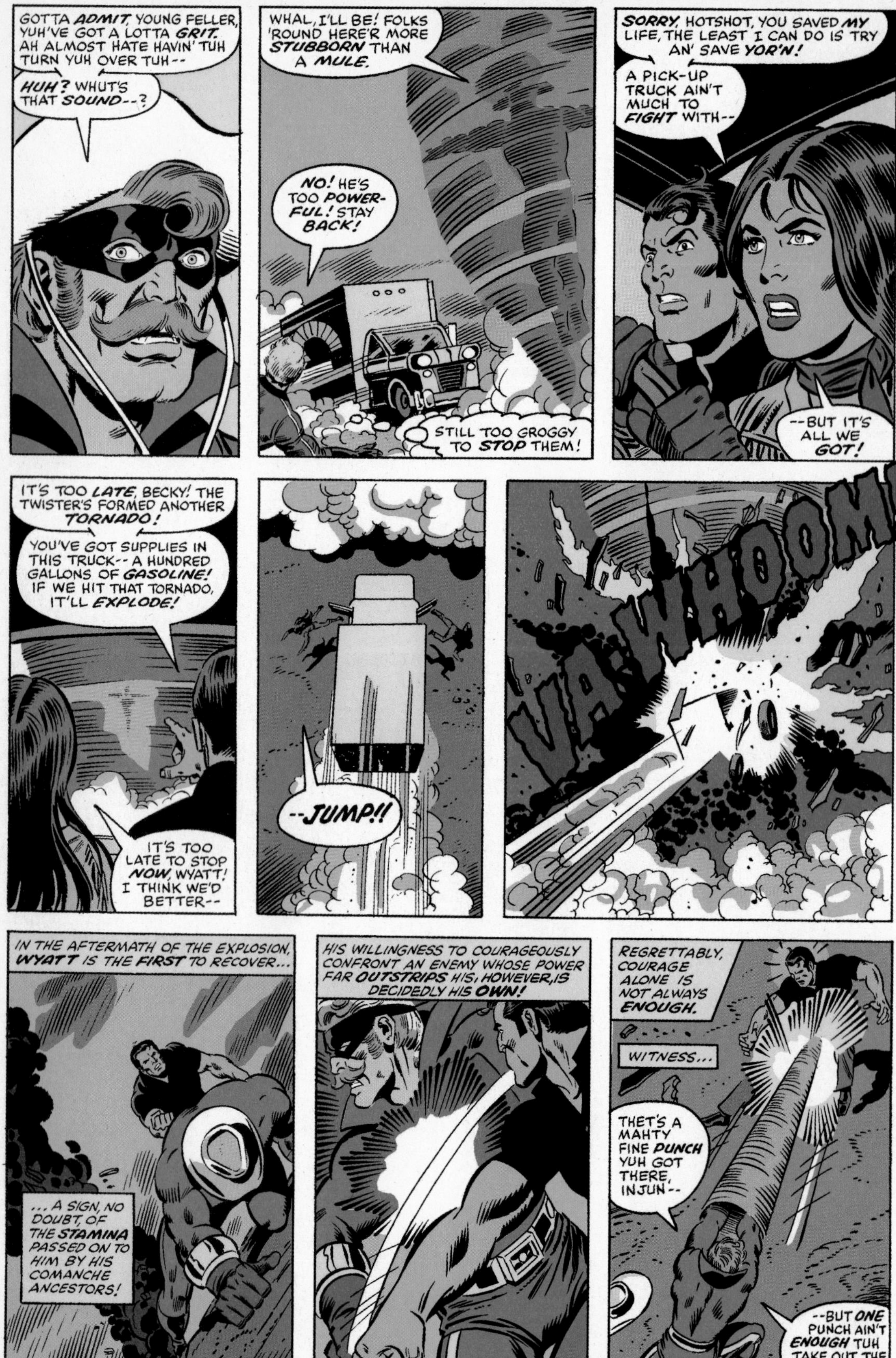
GOTTA ADMIT, YOUNG FELLER, YUH'VE GOT A LOTTA GRIT. AH ALMOST HATE HAVIN' TUH TURN YUH OVER TUH--
HUH? WHUT'S THAT SOUND--?
WHAL, I'LL BE! FOLKS 'ROUND HERE'R MORE STUBBORN THAN A MULE.
NO! HE'S TOO POWERFUL! STAY BACK!
STILL TOO GROGGY TO STOP THEM!
SORRY, HOTSHOT, YOU SAVED MY LIFE, THE LEAST I CAN DO IS TRY AN' SAVE YOR'N!
A PICK-UP TRUCK AIN'T MUCH TO FIGHT WITH--
--BUT IT'S ALL WE GOT!
IT'S TOO LATE, BECKY! THE TWISTER'S FORMED ANOTHER TORNADO!
YOU'VE GOT SUPPLIES IN THIS TRUCK-- A HUNDRED GALLONS OF GASOLINE! IF WE HIT THAT TORNADO, IT'LL EXPLODE!
IT'S TOO LATE TO STOP NOW, WYATT! I THINK WE'D BETTER--
--JUMP!!
VA-WHOOM!
IN THE AFTERMATH OF THE EXPLOSION, WYATT IS THE FIRST TO RECOVER...
...A SIGN, NO DOUBT, OF THE STAMINA PASSED ON TO HIM BY HIS COMANCHE ANCESTORS!
HIS WILLINGNESS TO COURAGEOUSLY CONFRONT AN ENEMY WHOSE POWER FAR OUTSTRIPS HIS, HOWEVER, IS DECIDEDLY HIS OWN!
REGRETTABLY, COURAGE ALONE IS NOT ALWAYS ENOUGH.
WITNESS...
THET'S A MAHTY FINE PUNCH YUH GOT THERE, INJUN--
--BUT ONE PUNCH AIN'T ENOUGH TUH TAKE OUT THE TEXAS TWISTER!

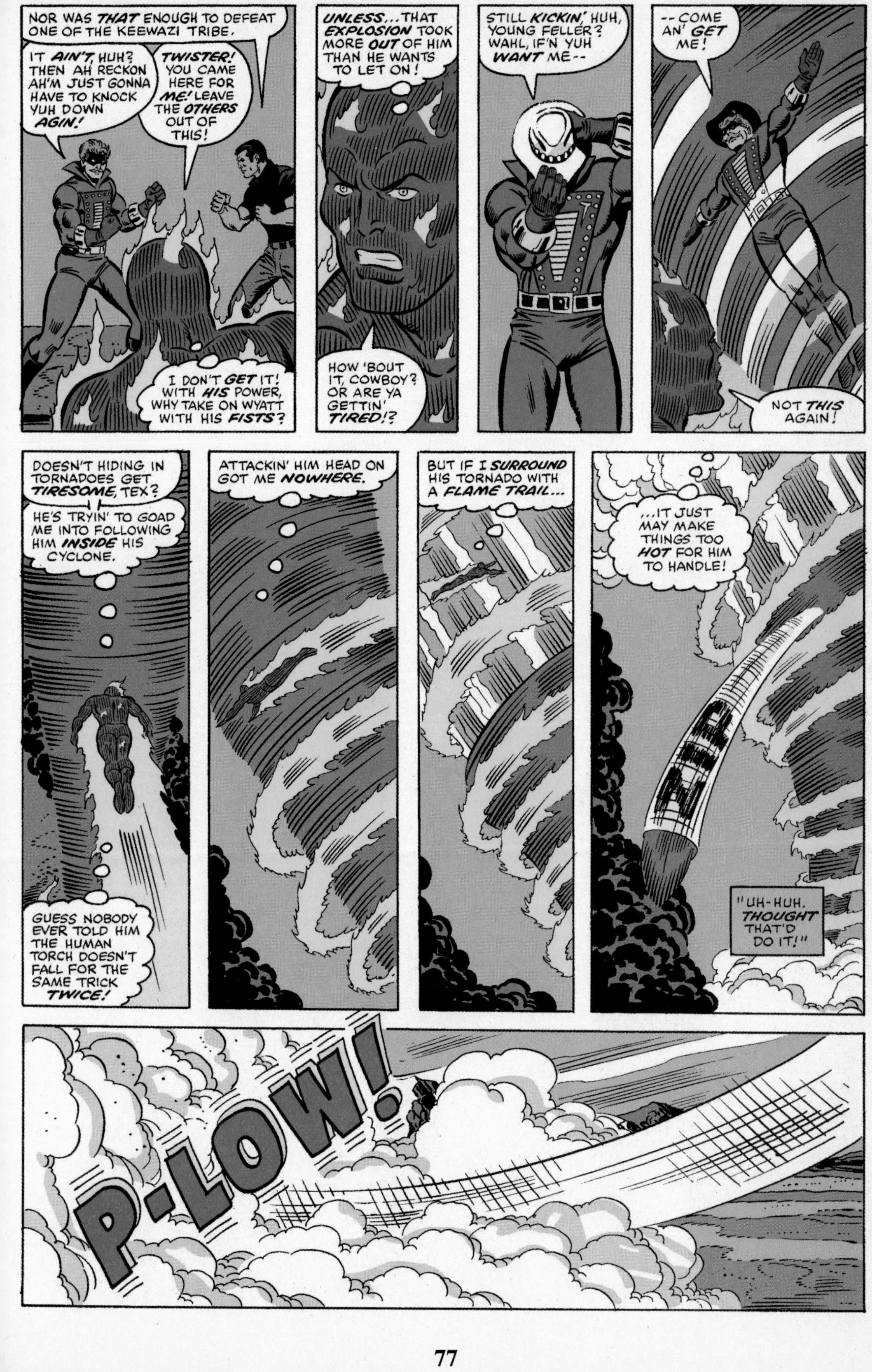
NOR WAS THAT ENOUGH TO DEFEAT ONE OF THE KEEWAZI TRIBE.
IT AIN'T, HUH? THEN AH RECKON AH'M JUST GONNA HAVE TO KNOCK YUH DOWN AGIN!
TWISTER! YOU CAME HERE FOR ME! LEAVE THE OTHERS OUT OF THIS!
I DON'T GET IT! WITH HIS POWER, WHY TAKE ON WYATT WITH HIS FISTS?
UNLESS... THAT EXPLOSION TOOK MORE OUT OF HIM THAN HE WANTS TO LET ON!
HOW 'BOUT IT, COWBOY? OR ARE YA GETTIN' TIRED!?
STILL KICKIN', HUH, YOUNG FELLER? WAHL, IF'N YUH WANT ME--
--COME AN' GET ME!
NOT THIS AGAIN!
DOESN'T HIDING IN TORNADOES GET TIRESOME, TEX?
HE'S TRYIN' TO GOAD ME INTO FOLLOWING HIM INSIDE HIS CYCLONE.
GUESS NOBODY EVER TOLD HIM THE HUMAN TORCH DOESN'T FALL FOR THE SAME TRICK TWICE!
ATTACKIN' HIM HEAD ON GOT ME NOWHERE.
BUT IF I SURROUND HIS TORNADO WITH A FLAME TRAIL...
...IT JUST MAY MAKE THINGS TOO HOT FOR HIM TO HANDLE!
"UH-HUH. THOUGHT THAT'D DO IT!"
P-LOW!

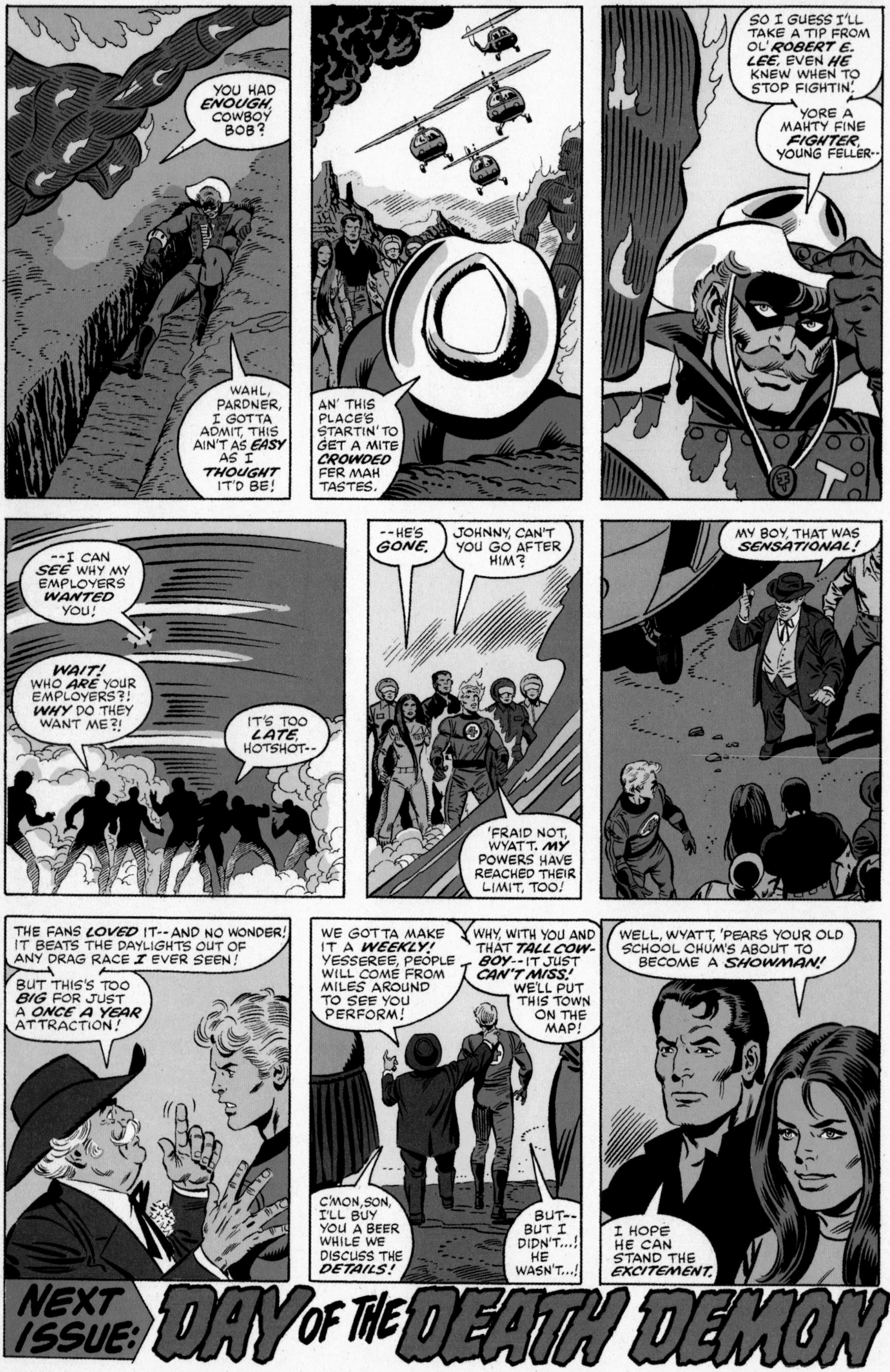
YOU HAD ENOUGH, COWBOY BOB?
WAHL, PARDNER, I GOTTA ADMIT, THIS AIN'T AS EASY AS I THOUGHT IT'D BE!
AN' THIS PLACE'S STARTIN' TO GET A MITE CROWDED FER MAH TASTES.
SO I GUESS I'LL TAKE A TIP FROM OL' ROBERT E. LEE. EVEN HE KNEW WHEN TO STOP FIGHTIN'.
YORE A MAHTY FINE FIGHTER, YOUNG FELLER--
--I CAN SEE WHY MY EMPLOYERS WANTED YOU!
WAIT! WHO ARE YOUR EMPLOYERS?! WHY DO THEY WANT ME?!
IT'S TOO LATE, HOTSHOT--
--HE'S GONE.
JOHNNY, CAN'T YOU GO AFTER HIM?
'FRAID NOT, WYATT. MY POWERS HAVE REACHED THEIR LIMIT, TOO!
MY BOY, THAT WAS SENSATIONAL!
THE FANS LOVED IT--AND NO WONDER! IT BEATS THE DAYLIGHTS OUT OF ANY DRAG RACE I EVER SEEN!
BUT THIS'S TOO BIG FOR JUST A ONCE A YEAR ATTRACTION!
WE GOTTA MAKE IT A WEEKLY! YESSEREE, PEOPLE WILL COME FROM MILES AROUND TO SEE YOU PERFORM!
WHY, WITH YOU AND THAT TALL COW-BOY--IT JUST CAN'T MISS! WE'LL PUT THIS TOWN ON THE MAP!
C'MON, SON, I'LL BUY YOU A BEER WHILE WE DISCUSS THE DETAILS!
BUT--BUT I DIDN'T...! HE WASN'T...!
WELL, WYATT, 'PEARS YOUR OLD SCHOOL CHUM'S ABOUT TO BECOME A SHOWMAN!
I HOPE HE CAN STAND THE EXCITEMENT.
NEXT ISSUE: DAY OF THE DEATH DEMON

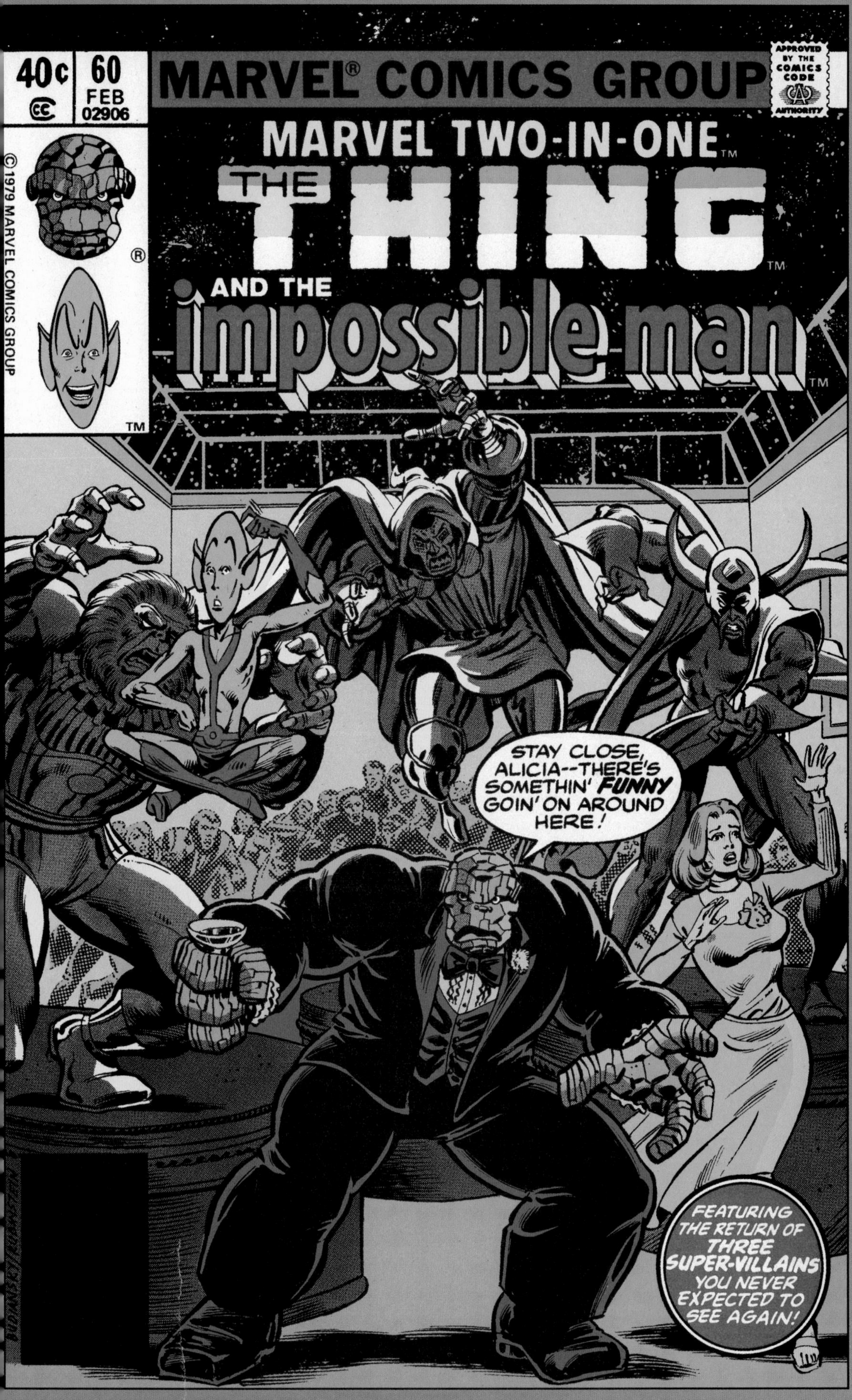
40¢
60
FEB
02906
MARVEL® COMICS GROUP
APPROVED BY THE COMICS CODE AUTHORITY
© 1979 MARVEL COMICS GROUP
MARVEL TWO-IN-ONE™
THE THING™
AND THE impossible man™
STAY CLOSE, ALICIA--THERE'S SOMETHIN' FUNNY GOIN' ON AROUND HERE!
FEATURING THE RETURN OF THREE SUPER-VILLAINS YOU NEVER EXPECTED TO SEE AGAIN!

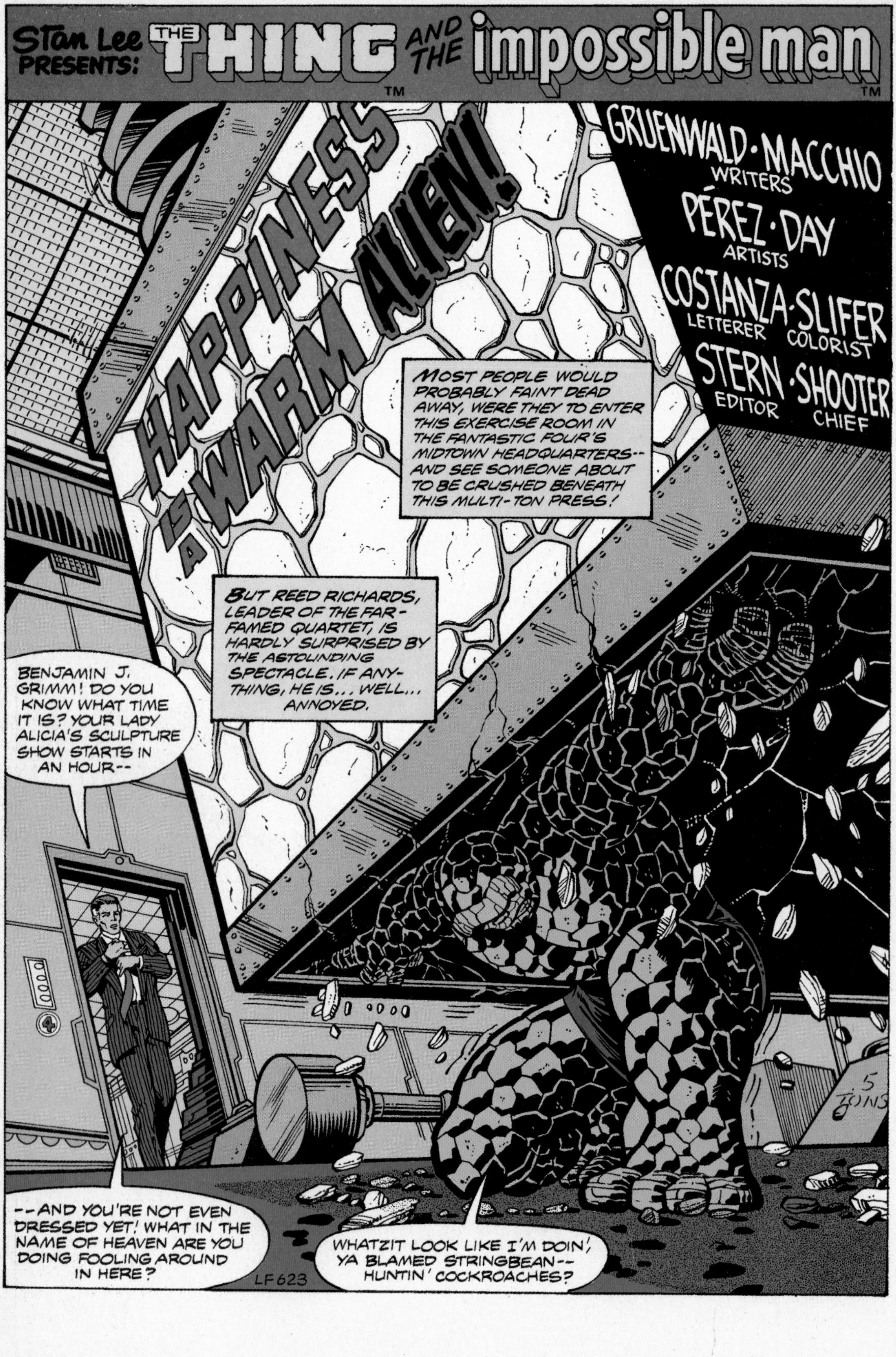
Stan Lee PRESENTS: THE THING™ AND THE impossible man™
HAPPINESS IS A WARM ALIEN!
GRUENWALD · MACCHIO WRITERS
PÉREZ · DAY ARTISTS
COSTANZA · SLIFER LETTERER COLORIST
STERN · SHOOTER EDITOR CHIEF
MOST PEOPLE WOULD PROBABLY FAINT DEAD AWAY, WERE THEY TO ENTER THIS EXERCISE ROOM IN THE FANTASTIC FOUR'S MIDTOWN HEADQUARTERS-- AND SEE SOMEONE ABOUT TO BE CRUSHED BENEATH THIS MULTI-TON PRESS!
BUT REED RICHARDS, LEADER OF THE FAR-FAMED QUARTET, IS HARDLY SURPRISED BY THE ASTOUNDING SPECTACLE. IF ANYTHING, HE IS... WELL... ANNOYED.
BENJAMIN J. GRIMM! DO YOU KNOW WHAT TIME IT IS? YOUR LADY ALICIA'S SCULPTURE SHOW STARTS IN AN HOUR--
--AND YOU'RE NOT EVEN DRESSED YET! WHAT IN THE NAME OF HEAVEN ARE YOU DOING FOOLING AROUND IN HERE?
WHATZIT LOOK LIKE I'M DOIN', YA BLAMED STRINGBEAN-- HUNTIN' COCKROACHES?
5 TONS
LF623

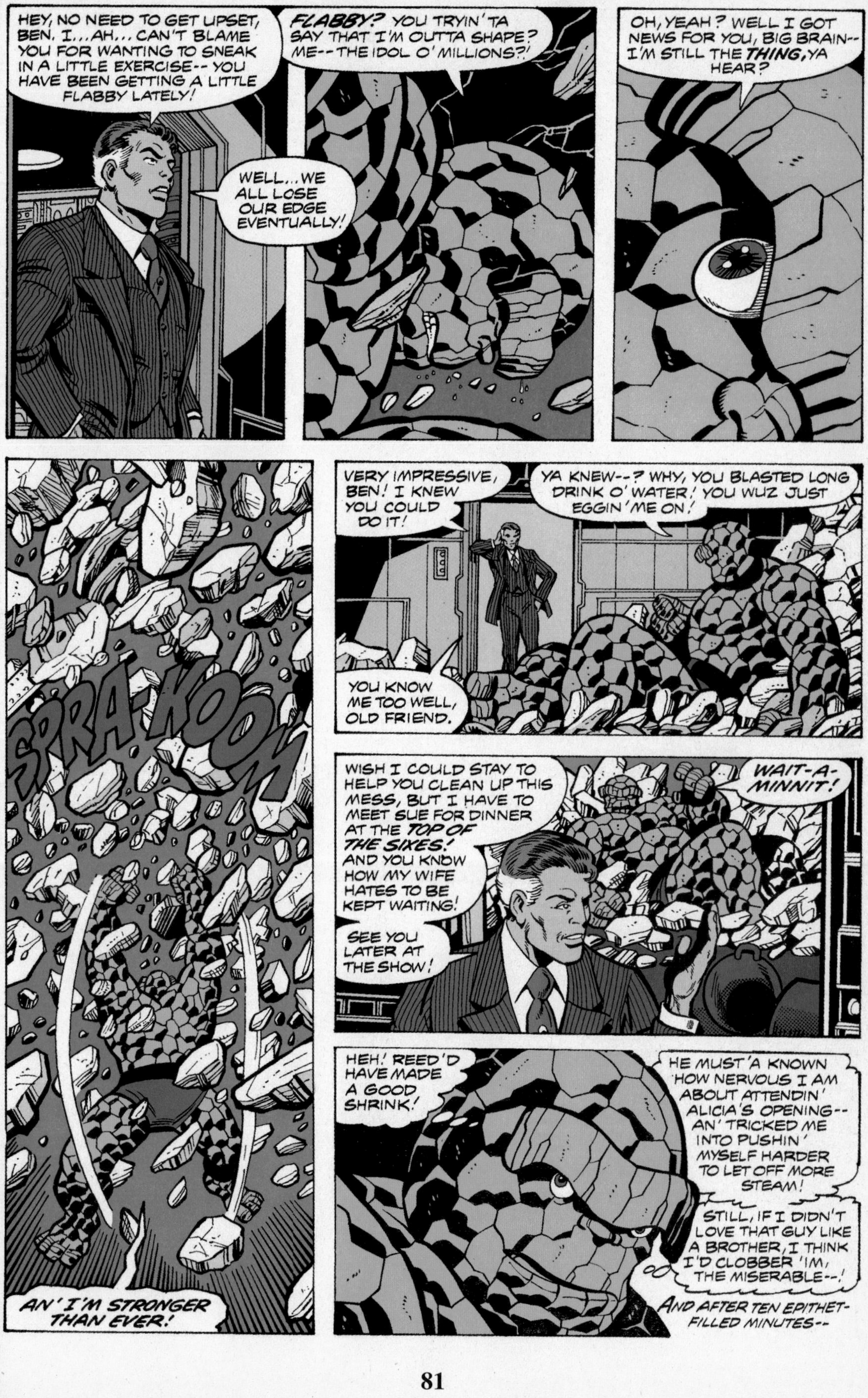
HEY, NO NEED TO GET UPSET, BEN. I... AH... CAN'T BLAME YOU FOR WANTING TO SNEAK IN A LITTLE EXERCISE-- YOU HAVE BEEN GETTING A LITTLE FLABBY LATELY!
WELL... WE ALL LOSE OUR EDGE EVENTUALLY!
FLABBY? YOU TRYIN' TA SAY THAT I'M OUTTA SHAPE? ME-- THE IDOL O' MILLIONS?!
OH, YEAH? WELL I GOT NEWS FOR YOU, BIG BRAIN-- I'M STILL THE THING, YA HEAR?
SPRA-KOOM
AN' I'M STRONGER THAN EVER!
VERY IMPRESSIVE, BEN! I KNEW YOU COULD DO IT!
YA KNEW--? WHY, YOU BLASTED LONG DRINK O' WATER! YOU WUZ JUST EGGIN' ME ON!
YOU KNOW ME TOO WELL, OLD FRIEND.
WISH I COULD STAY TO HELP YOU CLEAN UP THIS MESS, BUT I HAVE TO MEET SUE FOR DINNER AT THE TOP OF THE SIXES! AND YOU KNOW HOW MY WIFE HATES TO BE KEPT WAITING!
SEE YOU LATER AT THE SHOW!
WAIT-A-MINNIT!
HEH! REED'D HAVE MADE A GOOD SHRINK!
HE MUST'A KNOWN HOW NERVOUS I AM ABOUT ATTENDIN' ALICIA'S OPENING-- AN' TRICKED ME INTO PUSHIN' MYSELF HARDER TO LET OFF MORE STEAM!
STILL, IF I DIDN'T LOVE THAT GUY LIKE A BROTHER, I THINK I'D CLOBBER 'IM, THE MISERABLE--!
AND AFTER TEN EPITHET-FILLED MINUTES--

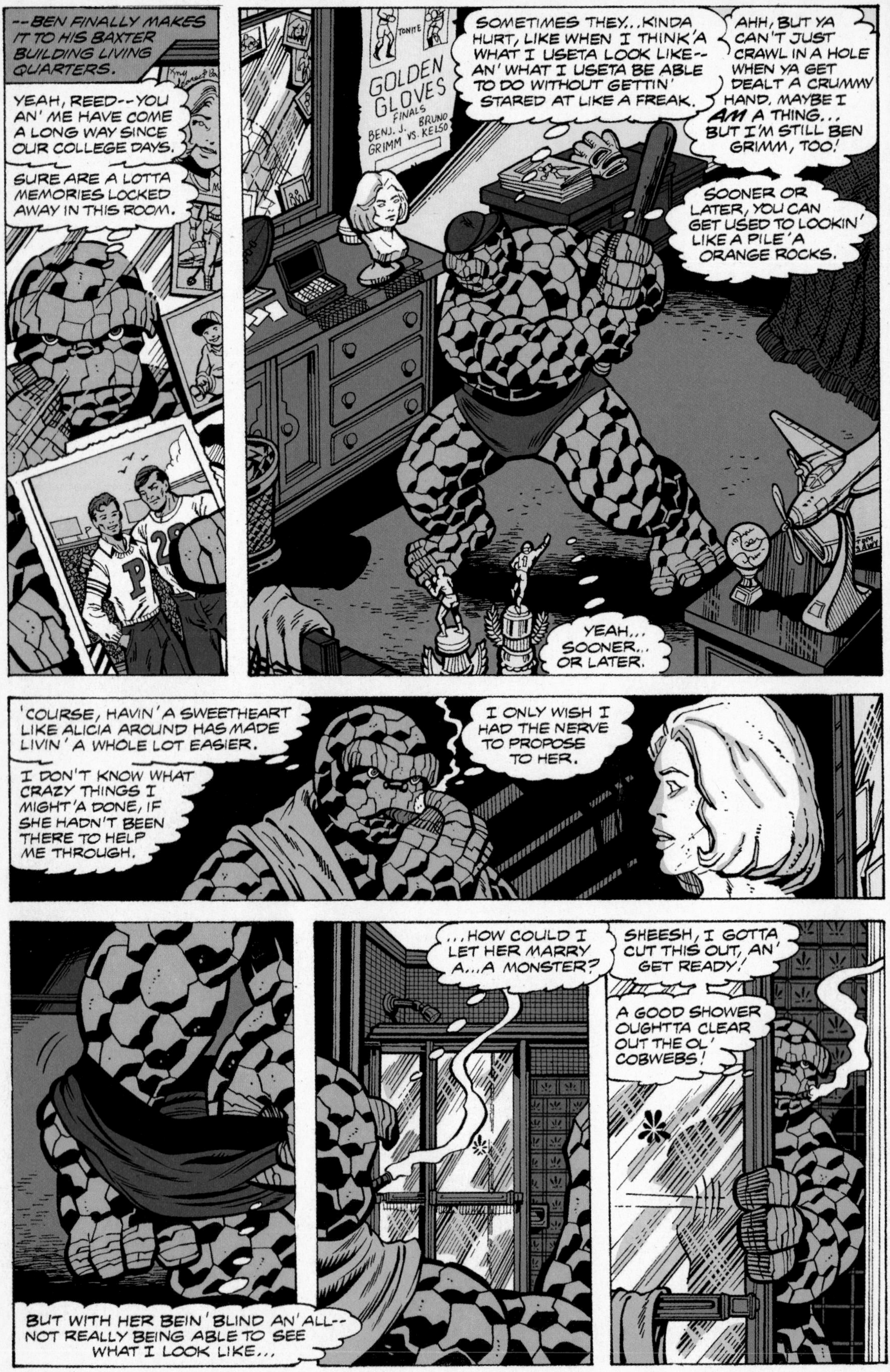
--BEN FINALLY MAKES IT TO HIS BAXTER BUILDING LIVING QUARTERS.
YEAH, REED--YOU AN' ME HAVE COME A LONG WAY SINCE OUR COLLEGE DAYS.
SURE ARE A LOTTA MEMORIES LOCKED AWAY IN THIS ROOM.
GOLDEN GLOVES FINALS BENJ. J. GRIMM VS. BRUNO KELSO
TONITE
SOMETIMES THEY...KINDA HURT, LIKE WHEN I THINK'A WHAT I USETA LOOK LIKE--AN' WHAT I USETA BE ABLE TO DO WITHOUT GETTIN' STARED AT LIKE A FREAK.
AHH, BUT YA CAN'T JUST CRAWL IN A HOLE WHEN YA GET DEALT A CRUMMY HAND. MAYBE I AM A THING... BUT I'M STILL BEN GRIMM, TOO!
SOONER OR LATER, YOU CAN GET USED TO LOOKIN' LIKE A PILE'A ORANGE ROCKS.
YEAH... SOONER... OR LATER.
'COURSE, HAVIN' A SWEETHEART LIKE ALICIA AROUND HAS MADE LIVIN' A WHOLE LOT EASIER.
I DON'T KNOW WHAT CRAZY THINGS I MIGHT'A DONE, IF SHE HADN'T BEEN THERE TO HELP ME THROUGH.
I ONLY WISH I HAD THE NERVE TO PROPOSE TO HER.
BUT WITH HER BEIN' BLIND AN' ALL--NOT REALLY BEING ABLE TO SEE WHAT I LOOK LIKE...
...HOW COULD I LET HER MARRY A...A MONSTER?
SHEESH, I GOTTA CUT THIS OUT, AN' GET READY!
A GOOD SHOWER OUGHTTA CLEAR OUT THE OL' COBWEBS!

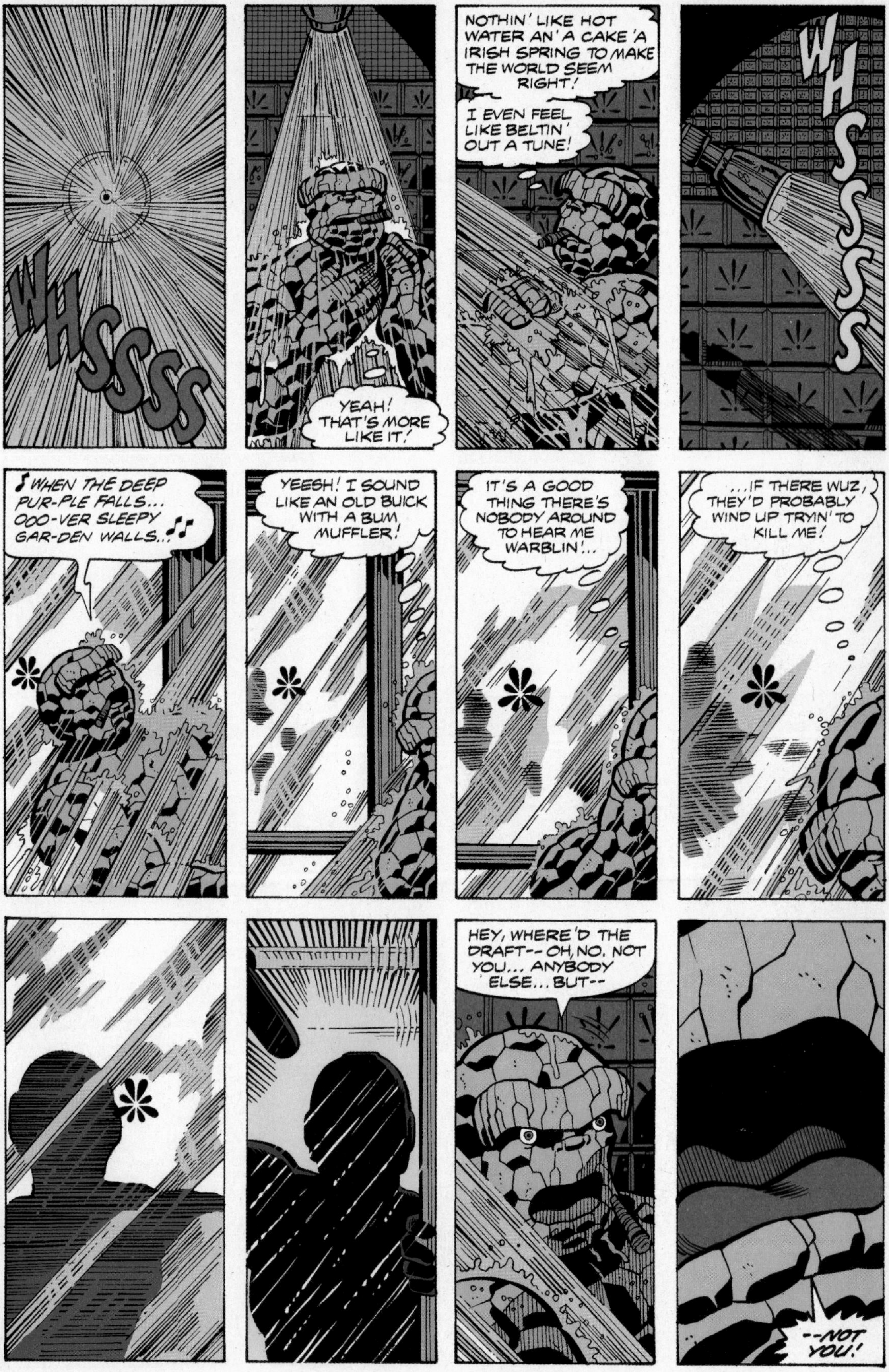
WHSSSSS
NOTHIN' LIKE HOT WATER AN' A CAKE 'A IRISH SPRING TO MAKE THE WORLD SEEM RIGHT!
I EVEN FEEL LIKE BELTIN' OUT A TUNE!
YEAH! THAT'S MORE LIKE IT!
WHSSSS
♪ WHEN THE DEEP PUR-PLE FALLS... OOO-VER SLEEPY GAR-DEN WALLS..♫
YEESH! I SOUND LIKE AN OLD BUICK WITH A BUM MUFFLER!
IT'S A GOOD THING THERE'S NOBODY AROUND TO HEAR ME WARBLIN'...
...IF THERE WUZ, THEY'D PROBABLY WIND UP TRYIN' TO KILL ME!
HEY, WHERE'D THE DRAFT-- OH, NO. NOT YOU... ANYBODY ELSE... BUT--
--NOT YOU!

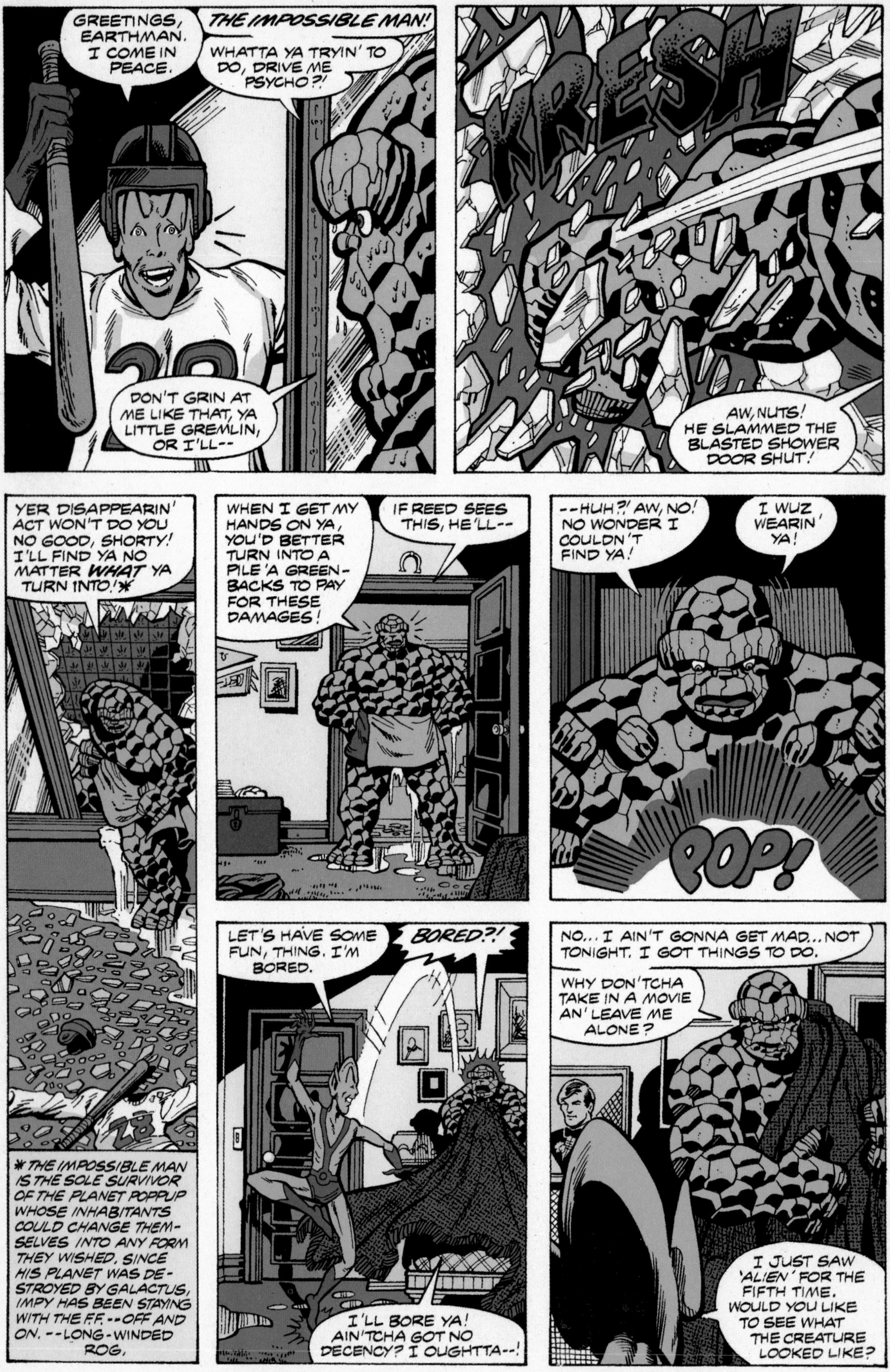
GREETINGS, EARTHMAN. I COME IN PEACE.
THE IMPOSSIBLE MAN!
WHATTA YA TRYIN' TO DO, DRIVE ME PSYCHO?!
DON'T GRIN AT ME LIKE THAT, YA LITTLE GREMLIN, OR I'LL--
KRESH
AW, NUTS! HE SLAMMED THE BLASTED SHOWER DOOR SHUT!
YER DISAPPEARIN' ACT WON'T DO YOU NO GOOD, SHORTY! I'LL FIND YA NO MATTER WHAT YA TURN INTO!*
WHEN I GET MY HANDS ON YA, YOU'D BETTER TURN INTO A PILE 'A GREEN-BACKS TO PAY FOR THESE DAMAGES!
IF REED SEES THIS, HE'LL--
--HUH?! AW, NO! NO WONDER I COULDN'T FIND YA!
I WUZ WEARIN' YA!
POP!
*THE IMPOSSIBLE MAN IS THE SOLE SURVIVOR OF THE PLANET POPPUP WHOSE INHABITANTS COULD CHANGE THEM-SELVES INTO ANY FORM THEY WISHED. SINCE HIS PLANET WAS DE-STROYED BY GALACTUS, IMPY HAS BEEN STAYING WITH THE F.F. --OFF AND ON. --LONG-WINDED ROG.
LET'S HAVE SOME FUN, THING. I'M BORED.
BORED?!
I'LL BORE YA! AIN'TCHA GOT NO DECENCY? I OUGHTTA--!
NO... I AIN'T GONNA GET MAD... NOT TONIGHT. I GOT THINGS TO DO.
WHY DON'TCHA TAKE IN A MOVIE AN' LEAVE ME ALONE?
I JUST SAW 'ALIEN' FOR THE FIFTH TIME. WOULD YOU LIKE TO SEE WHAT THE CREATURE LOOKED LIKE?

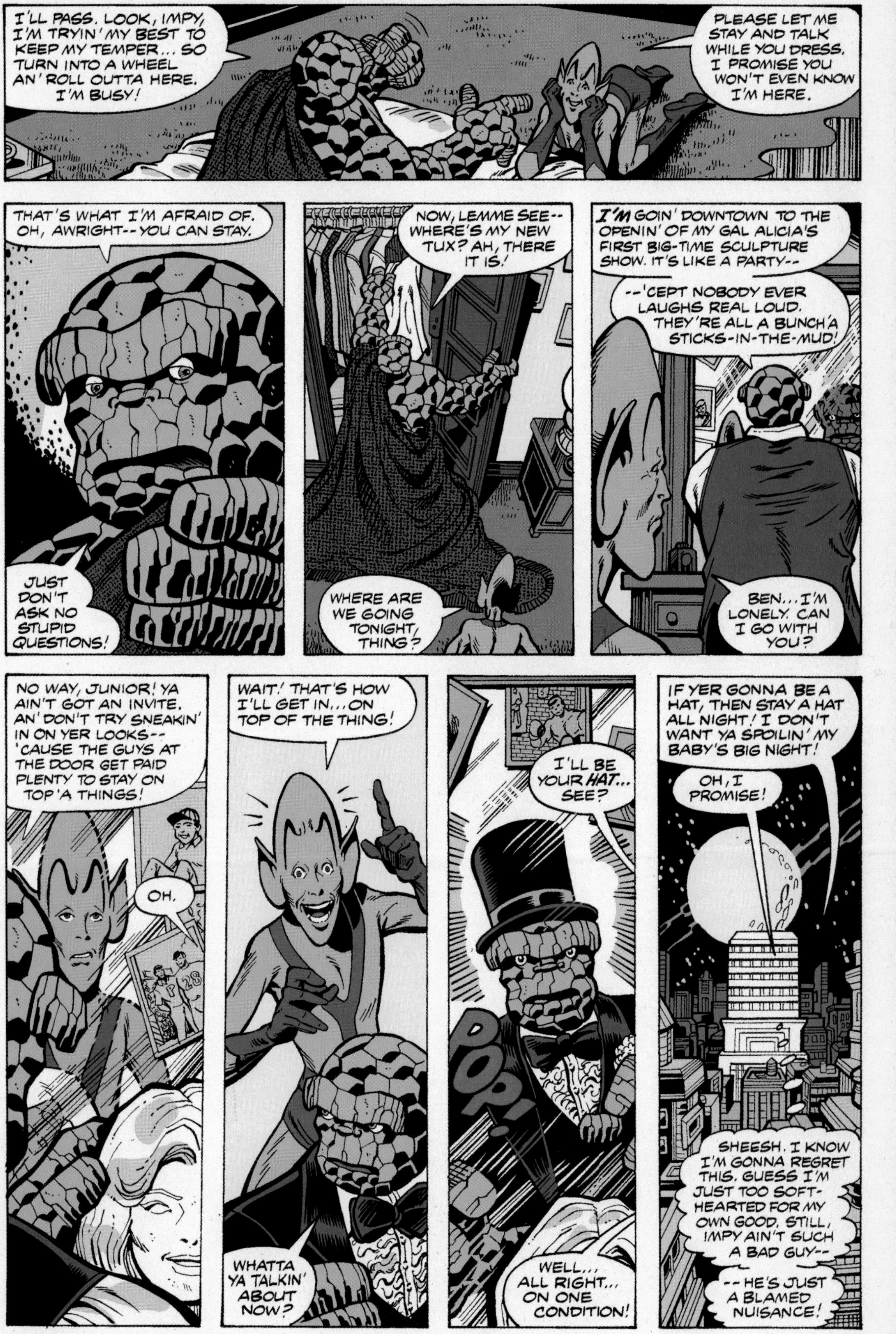
I'LL PASS. LOOK, IMPY, I'M TRYIN' MY BEST TO KEEP MY TEMPER... SO TURN INTO A WHEEL AN' ROLL OUTTA HERE. I'M BUSY!
PLEASE LET ME STAY AND TALK WHILE YOU DRESS. I PROMISE YOU WON'T EVEN KNOW I'M HERE.
THAT'S WHAT I'M AFRAID OF. OH, AWRIGHT--YOU CAN STAY.
JUST DON'T ASK NO STUPID QUESTIONS!
NOW, LEMME SEE--WHERE'S MY NEW TUX? AH, THERE IT IS!
WHERE ARE WE GOING TONIGHT, THING?
I'M GOIN' DOWNTOWN TO THE OPENIN' OF MY GAL ALICIA'S FIRST BIG-TIME SCULPTURE SHOW. IT'S LIKE A PARTY--
--'CEPT NOBODY EVER LAUGHS REAL LOUD. THEY'RE ALL A BUNCH'A STICKS-IN-THE-MUD!
BEN... I'M LONELY. CAN I GO WITH YOU?
NO WAY, JUNIOR! YA AIN'T GOT AN INVITE. AN' DON'T TRY SNEAKIN' IN ON YER LOOKS--'CAUSE THE GUYS AT THE DOOR GET PAID PLENTY TO STAY ON TOP'A THINGS!
OH.
WAIT! THAT'S HOW I'LL GET IN... ON TOP OF THE THING!
WHATTA YA TALKIN' ABOUT NOW?
I'LL BE YOUR HAT... SEE?
POP!
WELL... ALL RIGHT... ON ONE CONDITION!
IF YER GONNA BE A HAT, THEN STAY A HAT ALL NIGHT! I DON'T WANT YA SPOILIN' MY BABY'S BIG NIGHT!
OH, I PROMISE!
SHEESH. I KNOW I'M GONNA REGRET THIS. GUESS I'M JUST TOO SOFT-HEARTED FOR MY OWN GOOD. STILL, IMPY AIN'T SUCH A BAD GUY--
--HE'S JUST A BLAMED NUISANCE!

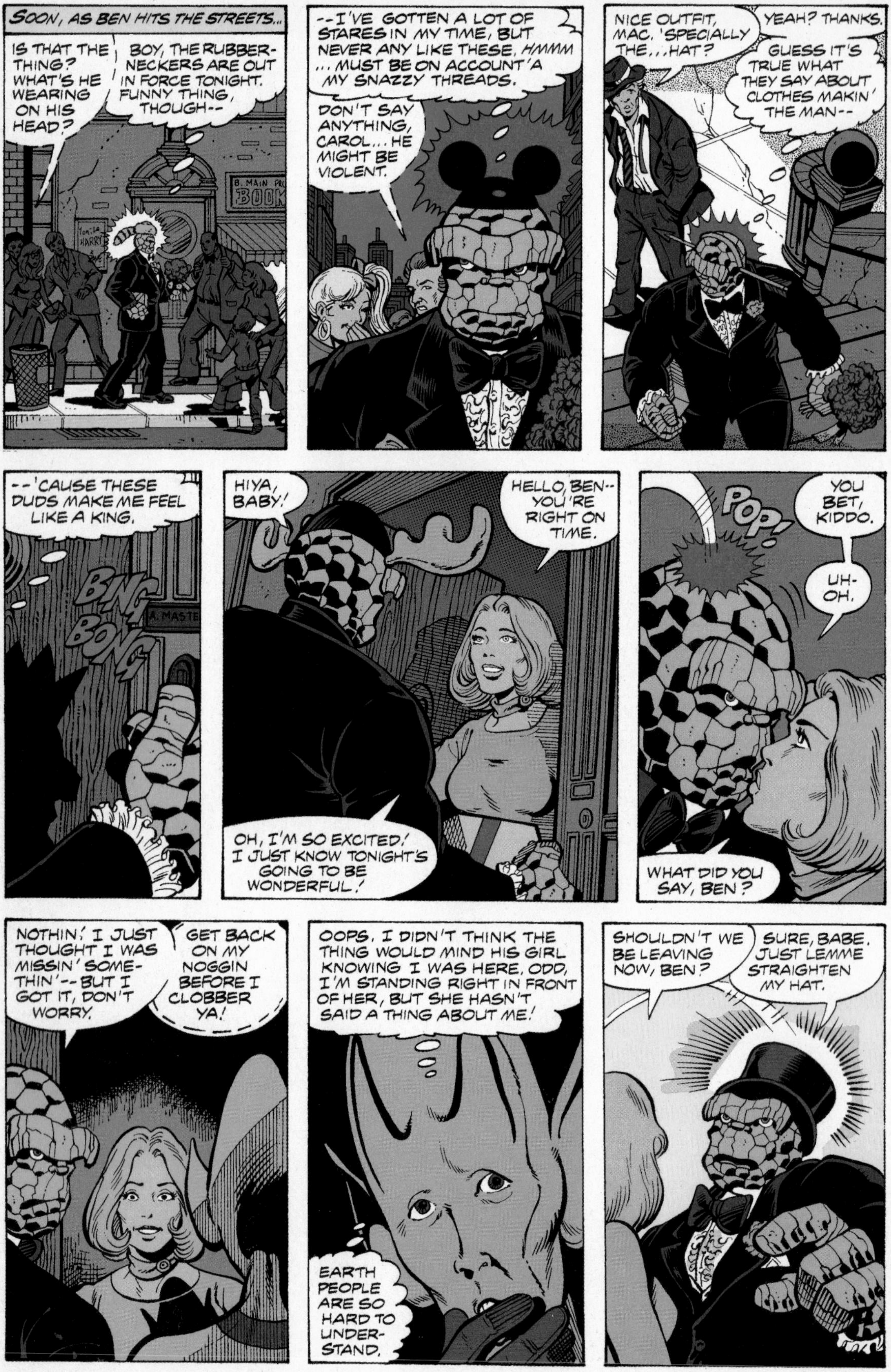

SOON, AS BEN HITS THE STREETS...
IS THAT THE THING? WHAT'S HE WEARING ON HIS HEAD?
BOY, THE RUBBER-NECKERS ARE OUT IN FORCE TONIGHT. FUNNY THING, THOUGH--
B. MAIN
BOOK
--I'VE GOTTEN A LOT OF STARES IN MY TIME, BUT NEVER ANY LIKE THESE. HMMM ... MUST BE ON ACCOUNT 'A MY SNAZZY THREADS.
DON'T SAY ANYTHING, CAROL... HE MIGHT BE VIOLENT.
NICE OUTFIT, MAC. 'SPECIALLY THE...HAT?
YEAH? THANKS.
GUESS IT'S TRUE WHAT THEY SAY ABOUT CLOTHES MAKIN' THE MAN--
--'CAUSE THESE DUDS MAKE ME FEEL LIKE A KING.
BING BONG
A. MASTE
HIYA, BABY!
HELLO, BEN-- YOU'RE RIGHT ON TIME.
OH, I'M SO EXCITED! I JUST KNOW TONIGHT'S GOING TO BE WONDERFUL!
POP!
YOU BET, KIDDO.
UH-OH.
WHAT DID YOU SAY, BEN?
NOTHIN'! I JUST THOUGHT I WAS MISSIN' SOME-THIN'--BUT I GOT IT, DON'T WORRY.
GET BACK ON MY NOGGIN BEFORE I CLOBBER YA!
OOPS. I DIDN'T THINK THE THING WOULD MIND HIS GIRL KNOWING I WAS HERE. ODD, I'M STANDING RIGHT IN FRONT OF HER, BUT SHE HASN'T SAID A THING ABOUT ME!
EARTH PEOPLE ARE SO HARD TO UNDER-STAND.
SHOULDN'T WE BE LEAVING NOW, BEN?
SURE, BABE. JUST LEMME STRAIGHTEN MY HAT.

MOMENTS LATER, SEVERAL BLOCKS DOWNTOWN...

HOPE YA DON'T MIND THE WALK, BABE-- IT'S JUST TOO NICE A NIGHT TO GET COOPED UP IN A CAB!

OF COURSE I DON'T MIND, BUT, BEN...YOU SEEM SO TENSE. WHAT'S WRONG?

YANCY STREET

PLEASE CURB YOUR DOG

AW, I JUST DIDN'T REALIZE WE'D BE WALKIN' THROUGH THIS NEIGHBORHOOD. THIS IS WHERE THE *YANCY STREET GANG* HANGS OUT.

THOSE CLOWNS HAVE BEEN A THORN IN MY SIDE SINCE THE WORD GO!

I'VE NEVER UNDER-STOOD, BEN-- JUST WHAT STARTED THIS ANIMOSITY THEY HAVE TOWARDS YOU?

A SAWBUCK SAYS YOU MISS THE HAT.

YOU'RE ON.

IT'S A LONG STORY, DOLL-- I DON'T WANNA BORE YA WITH IT TONIGHT.

YIKE!

THE BIGGEST PROBLEM I HAVE WITH THEM YANCY STREETERS IS THAT THEY'RE ALL SNEAKS --YA'D HAVE TO HAVE EYES IN THE BACK OF YER HEAD TO CATCH 'EM!

SPRONG

BOY, IF I EVER DO, THERE'S A COUPLE 'A FAVORS I WOULDN'T MIND RETURNIN' TO THEM CREEPS!

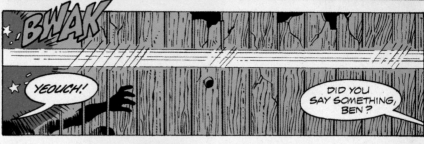

...BWAK

YEOUCH!

DID YOU SAY SOMETHING, BEN?

HEE-HEE-HEE!

SHUT UP, YOU!

NAW, IT WASN'T ME, KIDDO... BUT I GET THE FEELIN' THAT SOMETHIN' MIGHTY FISHY'S GOIN' ON AROUND HERE!

I AIN'T NEVER BEEN DOWN THIS STREET BEFORE WITHOUT AT LEAST HAVIN' A COUPLE 'A FRIENDLY BANANA PEELS TOSSED AT ME!

MAYBE YOU HAVE A GUARDIAN ANGEL WATCHING OVER YOU THIS EVENING.

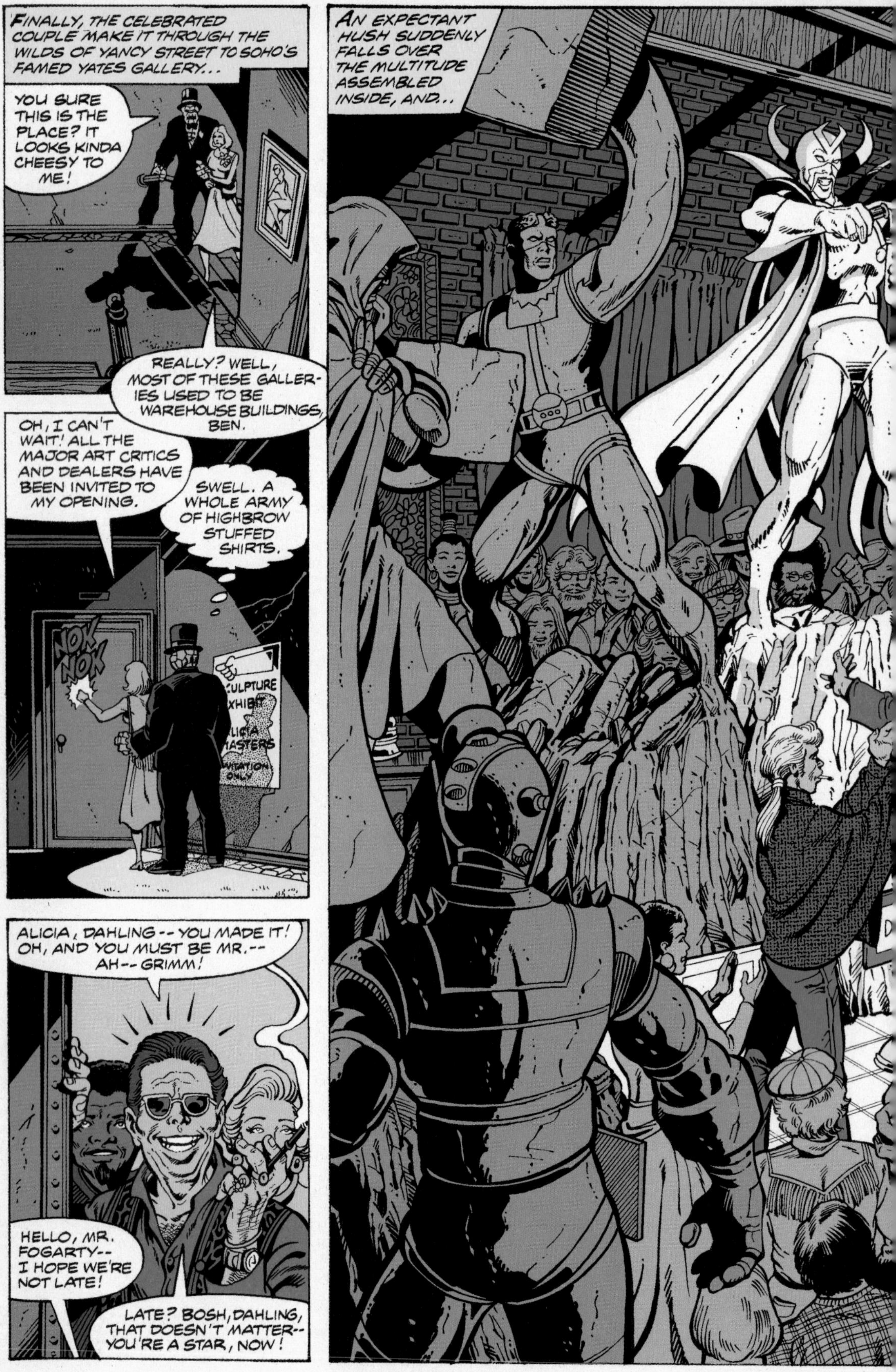
FINALLY, THE CELEBRATED COUPLE MAKE IT THROUGH THE WILDS OF YANCY STREET TO SOHO'S FAMED YATES GALLERY...
YOU SURE THIS IS THE PLACE? IT LOOKS KINDA CHEESY TO ME!
REALLY? WELL, MOST OF THESE GALLERIES USED TO BE WAREHOUSE BUILDINGS, BEN.
OH, I CAN'T WAIT! ALL THE MAJOR ART CRITICS AND DEALERS HAVE BEEN INVITED TO MY OPENING.
SWELL. A WHOLE ARMY OF HIGHBROW STUFFED SHIRTS.
NOK NOK
ALICIA, DAHLING -- YOU MADE IT! OH, AND YOU MUST BE MR.-- AH-- GRIMM!
HELLO, MR. FOGARTY-- I HOPE WE'RE NOT LATE!
LATE? BOSH, DAHLING, THAT DOESN'T MATTER-- YOU'RE A STAR, NOW!
AN EXPECTANT HUSH SUDDENLY FALLS OVER THE MULTITUDE ASSEMBLED INSIDE, AND...

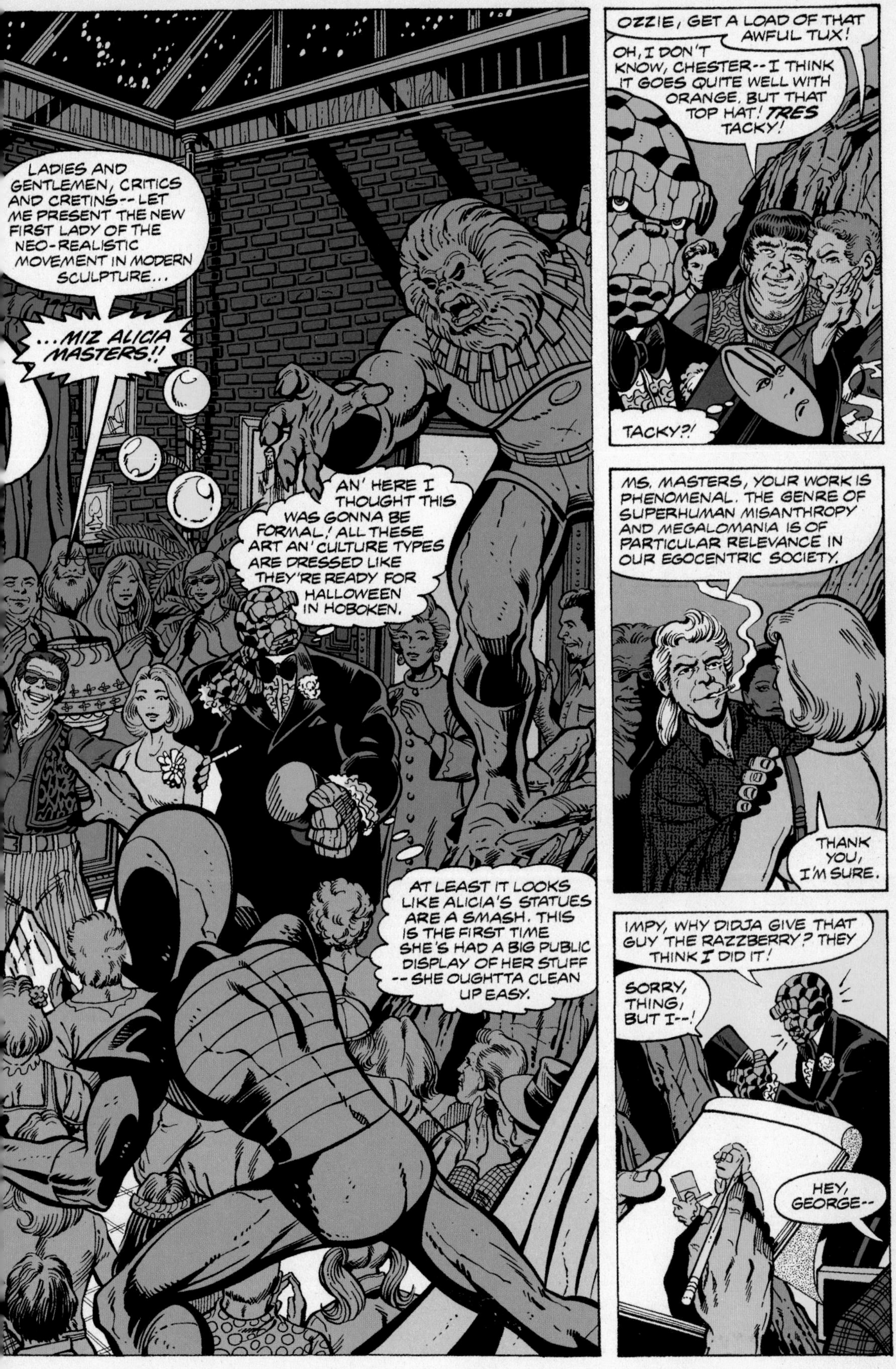
LADIES AND GENTLEMEN, CRITICS AND CRETINS-- LET ME PRESENT THE NEW FIRST LADY OF THE NEO-REALISTIC MOVEMENT IN MODERN SCULPTURE...
...MIZ ALICIA MASTERS!!
AN' HERE I THOUGHT THIS WAS GONNA BE FORMAL! ALL THESE ART AN' CULTURE TYPES ARE DRESSED LIKE THEY'RE READY FOR HALLOWEEN IN HOBOKEN.
AT LEAST IT LOOKS LIKE ALICIA'S STATUES ARE A SMASH. THIS IS THE FIRST TIME SHE'S HAD A BIG PUBLIC DISPLAY OF HER STUFF -- SHE OUGHTTA CLEAN UP EASY.
OZZIE, GET A LOAD OF THAT AWFUL TUX!
OH, I DON'T KNOW, CHESTER-- I THINK IT GOES QUITE WELL WITH ORANGE. BUT THAT TOP HAT! TRES TACKY!
TACKY?!
MS. MASTERS, YOUR WORK IS PHENOMENAL. THE GENRE OF SUPERHUMAN MISANTHROPY AND MEGALOMANIA IS OF PARTICULAR RELEVANCE IN OUR EGOCENTRIC SOCIETY.
THANK YOU, I'M SURE.
IMPY, WHY DIDJA GIVE THAT GUY THE RAZZBERRY? THEY THINK I DID IT!
SORRY, THING, BUT I--!
HEY, GEORGE--

Panel 1: --RALPH FINALLY SHOWED UP. LET'S TALK ABOUT THAT PLOT FOR ISSUE SIXTY, OKAY?

IN A MINUTE, MARK. IT ISN'T EVERY DAY I GET TO DRAW THE *REAL* THING... ARGUING WITH HIS HAT!

Panel 2: RALPH, WE GOTTA GET GEORGE AWAY FROM HIS SKETCHPAD AND BACK TO THE DRAWING BOARD. THIS BOOK IS LATE... *AGAIN!*

AHHH, IT'S JUST AS WELL.

Panel 3: I MEAN, HOW COULD WE EVER TOP THAT SIX-PART *PROJECT PEGASUS* STORY? IT HAD EVERYTHING-- DRAMA, HUMOR, IRONY, PATHOS, SATIRE--

BALONEY?

--BALONEY... *BALONEY?!*

Panel 4: *BUT SOON, AS THE BUFFET LINE BEGINS TO THIN...*

THE ACCURSED THING HAS ARRIVED. IT IS TIME TO BEGIN.

CHECK.

RIGHT, BOSS.

YOGI CATERING

Panel 5: *SWIFTLY, THE THREE 'CATERERS' TAKE THEIR PRE-ARRANGED POSITIONS BY THE STATUES OF THEIR CHOICE...*

"HANDSOME" HARRY PHILLIPS, MASTER CON MAN, SIDLES UP TO THE SCULPTURE OF THE DIABOLICAL DR. DOOM...

Panel 6: *...BRAWNY "BULL" BROGIN STANDS NEAR THE EFFIGY OF BLASTAAR, THE LIVING BOMB-BURST...*

Panel 7: *...AND SECRETING HIMSELF BEHIND THE ICON OF DIABLO, MASTER OF ALCHEMY, IS THE CRIMINAL FAKIR-- YOGI DAKOR!*

IT WAS THE THING WHO PUT US IN PRISON... THUS SHALL HE BE THE FIRST TO FALL!

Panel 8: *AT THE FAKIR'S SIGNAL, ALL THREE MEN CONCENTRATE--*

--AND THE SPECIAL POWERS OF MIND THAT YOGI DEVELOPED DURING HIS LONG INCARCERATION REACH OUT, TRANSFERRING THEIR VERY LIFE-FORCES INTO THE GRANITE FIGURES!

90

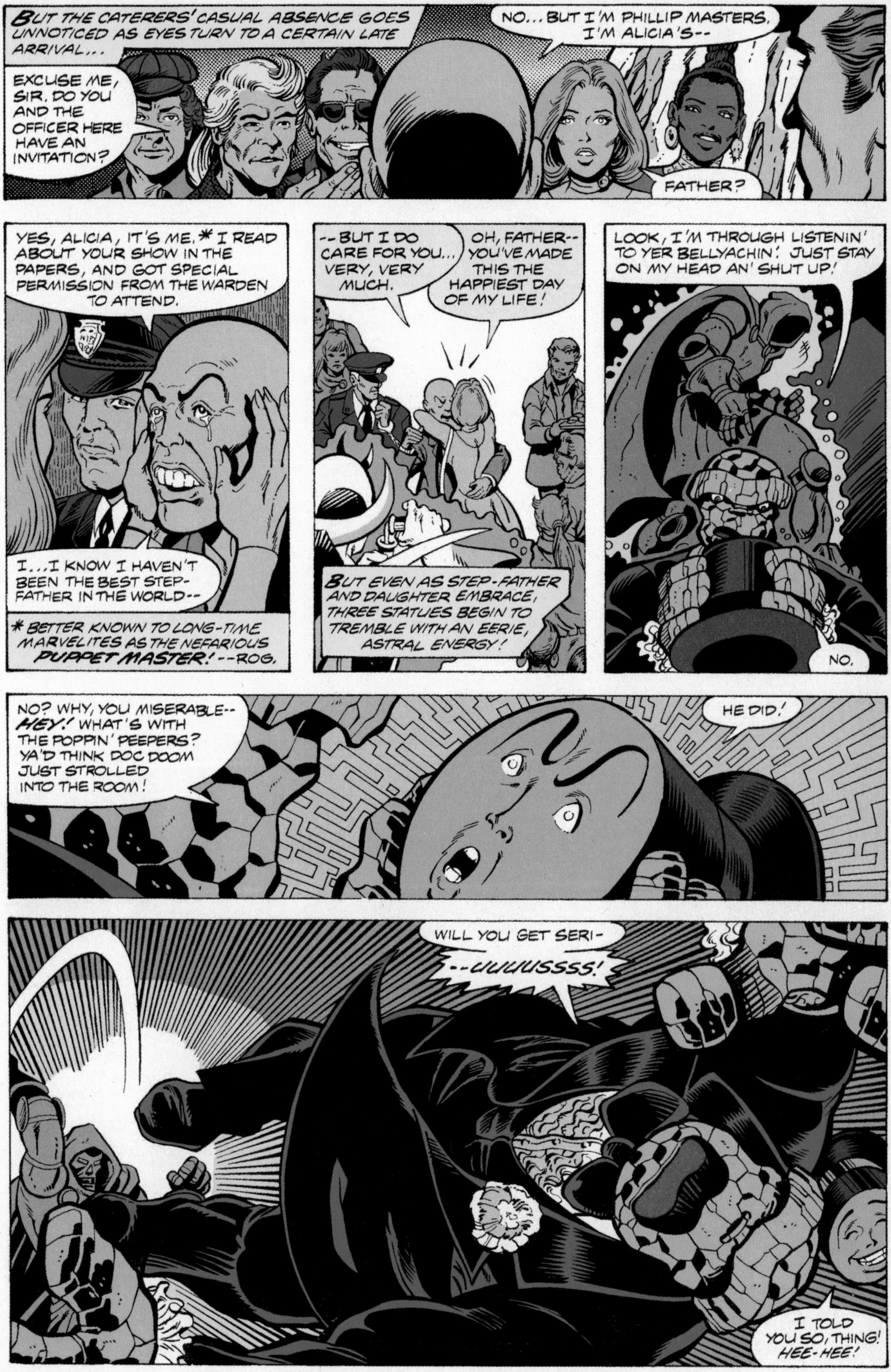
BUT THE CATERERS' CASUAL ABSENCE GOES UNNOTICED AS EYES TURN TO A CERTAIN LATE ARRIVAL...
EXCUSE ME, SIR. DO YOU AND THE OFFICER HERE HAVE AN INVITATION?
NO... BUT I'M PHILLIP MASTERS. I'M ALICIA'S--
FATHER?
YES, ALICIA, IT'S ME.* I READ ABOUT YOUR SHOW IN THE PAPERS, AND GOT SPECIAL PERMISSION FROM THE WARDEN TO ATTEND.
I...I KNOW I HAVEN'T BEEN THE BEST STEP-FATHER IN THE WORLD--
* BETTER KNOWN TO LONG-TIME MARVELITES AS THE NEFARIOUS PUPPET MASTER! --ROG.
--BUT I DO CARE FOR YOU... VERY, VERY MUCH.
OH, FATHER-- YOU'VE MADE THIS THE HAPPIEST DAY OF MY LIFE!
BUT EVEN AS STEP-FATHER AND DAUGHTER EMBRACE, THREE STATUES BEGIN TO TREMBLE WITH AN EERIE, ASTRAL ENERGY!
LOOK, I'M THROUGH LISTENIN' TO YER BELLYACHIN'! JUST STAY ON MY HEAD AN' SHUT UP!
NO.
NO? WHY, YOU MISERABLE-- HEY! WHAT'S WITH THE POPPIN' PEEPERS? YA'D THINK DOC DOOM JUST STROLLED INTO THE ROOM!
HE DID!
WILL YOU GET SERI-
--UUUUSSSS!
I TOLD YOU SO, THING! HEE-HEE!

AND I WASN'T JUST TALKING THROUGH MY HAT, SEE? HERE COMES ANOTHER ONE!

POP!

IZZAT SO? WELL, ONE SLUG, AND IT'LL BE ALL OVER... ALL OVER THE ROOM!

MR. GRIMM-- NO!!

THOSE STATUES ARE PRICELESS!

THEM BOZOS GOT A POINT. ALICIA PUT HER HEART AN' SOUL INTO THESE ROCKS! I CAN'T JUST GO BUSTIN' 'EM UP.

BUT IF I DON'T--

-- THEY MIGHT JUST ABOUT BUST ME!

UNGH! THAT CHUNK 'A GRANITE HITS ALMOST AS HARD AS THE REAL BLASTAAR!

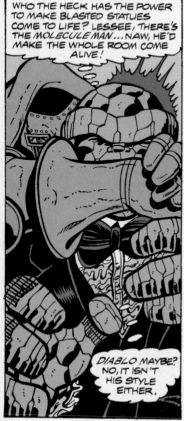

WHO THE HECK HAS THE POWER TO MAKE BLASTED STATUES COME TO LIFE? LESSEE, THERE'S THE MOLECULE MAN... NAW, HE'D MAKE THE WHOLE ROOM COME ALIVE!

DIABLO MAYBE? NO, IT ISN'T HIS STYLE EITHER.

:WHOUFF: PUNCHED INTO THE PUNCH BOWL... HOW HUMILIATIN'!

THE ONLY THING GOOD ABOUT WALTZIN' AROUND WITH THESE STATUES IS THAT THEY HAVEN'T STARTED MAKIN' A BUNCH 'A CORNBALL SPEECHES!

THE THING IS CERTAINLY TAKING A DRUBBING. I WONDER WHY HE DOESN'T FIGHT BACK. THIS ISN'T LIKE HIM.

BLDOOM!

"WHAT ARE THOSE AWFUL SOUNDS, BEN?!"

"IT'S YOUR STATUES, LADY-- SOMEHOW THEY'VE COME TO LIFE AND THEY'RE ATTACKING THE THING! B-BUT HE'S NOT FIGHTING BACK!"

"OF COURSE, HE'S NOT! WHY... THEY'RE WORKS OF ART!"

"OHHH! FATHER, PLEASE TELL ME YOU HAD NOTHING TO DO WITH THIS!"

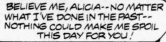

"BELIEVE ME, ALICIA--NO MATTER WHAT I'VE DONE IN THE PAST-- NOTHING COULD MAKE ME SPOIL THIS DAY FOR YOU!"

"BEN! BEN, MY DARLING, FIGHT THEM! DON'T LET THEM HURT YOU! THEY MEAN NOTHING TO ME... NOTHING COMPARED TO YOU!"

"OH, GAWD--I CAN'T LOOK!"

"I HEAR YA, BABY... I HEAR YA!"

"AN' THERE AIN'T EVER BEEN A WARNIN' THAT SOUNDED SO BEAUTIFUL!"

"AWRIGHT, YA WALKIN' ROCKPILES-- PLAYTIME'S OVER! YOU'RE THROUGH TAKIN' POTSHOTS AT GOOD-NATURED BENJY!"

"OH, BOY! WE'RE GOING TO HAVE SOME REAL FUN NOW!"

"I'D ADVISE ALL 'A YOU FOLKS TO GET UNDER COVER FOR A MINUTE--'CAUSE I'M GONNA STRAIGHTEN THINGS OUT WITH THESE TWO GRANITE GOOF-BALLS RIGHT NOW!"

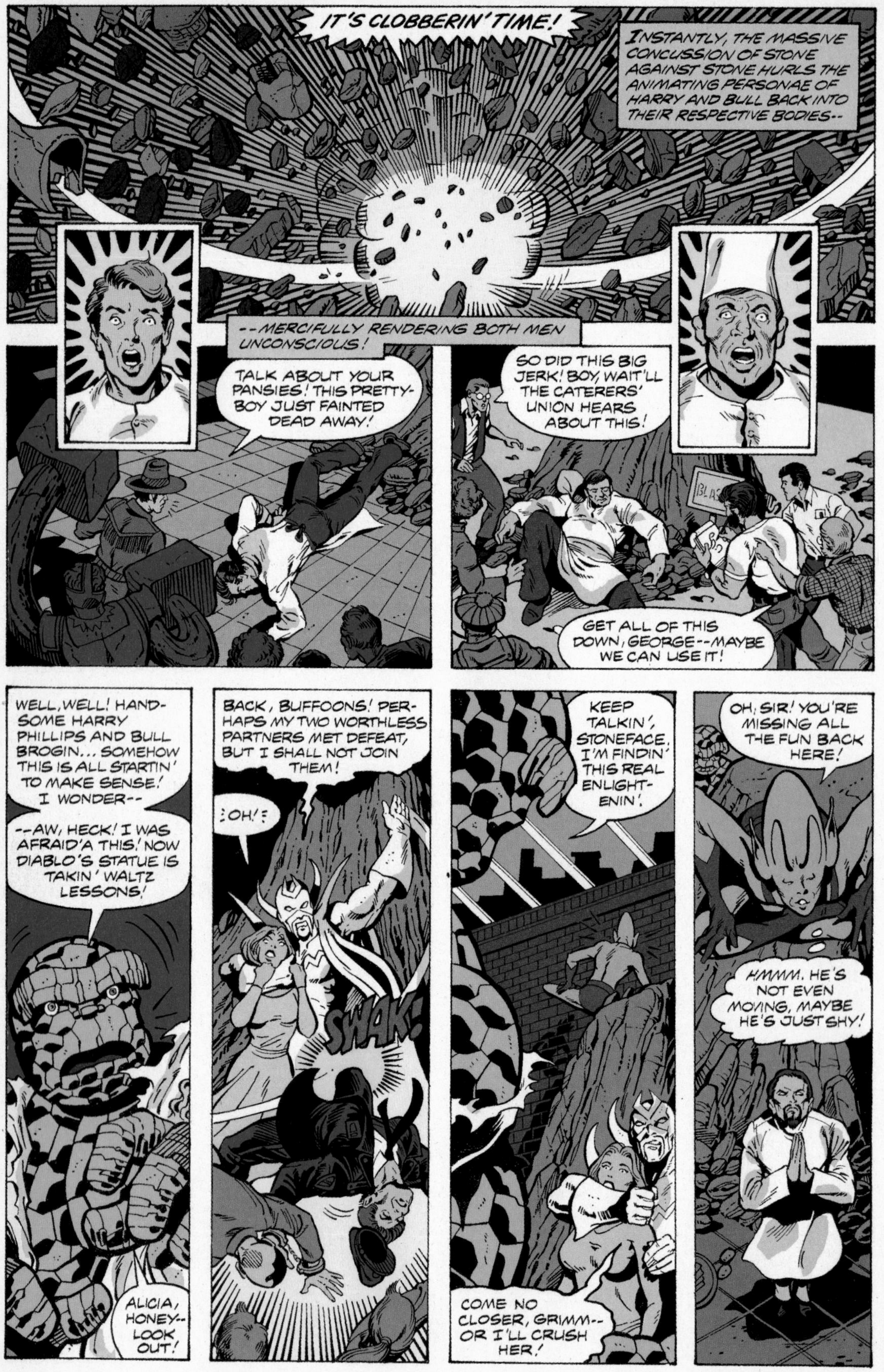
IT'S CLOBBERIN' TIME!
INSTANTLY, THE MASSIVE CONCUSSION OF STONE AGAINST STONE HURLS THE ANIMATING PERSONAE OF HARRY AND BULL BACK INTO THEIR RESPECTIVE BODIES--
--MERCIFULLY RENDERING BOTH MEN UNCONSCIOUS!
TALK ABOUT YOUR PANSIES! THIS PRETTY-BOY JUST FAINTED DEAD AWAY!
SO DID THIS BIG JERK! BOY, WAIT'LL THE CATERERS' UNION HEARS ABOUT THIS!
GET ALL OF THIS DOWN, GEORGE--MAYBE WE CAN USE IT!
WELL, WELL! HAND-SOME HARRY PHILLIPS AND BULL BROGIN... SOMEHOW THIS IS ALL STARTIN' TO MAKE SENSE! I WONDER--
--AW, HECK! I WAS AFRAID'A THIS! NOW DIABLO'S STATUE IS TAKIN' WALTZ LESSONS!
ALICIA, HONEY--LOOK OUT!
BACK, BUFFOONS! PER-HAPS MY TWO WORTHLESS PARTNERS MET DEFEAT, BUT I SHALL NOT JOIN THEM!
OH!
SWAK!
KEEP TALKIN', STONEFACE. I'M FINDIN' THIS REAL ENLIGHT-ENIN'.
COME NO CLOSER, GRIMM--OR I'LL CRUSH HER!
OH, SIR! YOU'RE MISSING ALL THE FUN BACK HERE!
HMMM. HE'S NOT EVEN MOVING, MAYBE HE'S JUST SHY!

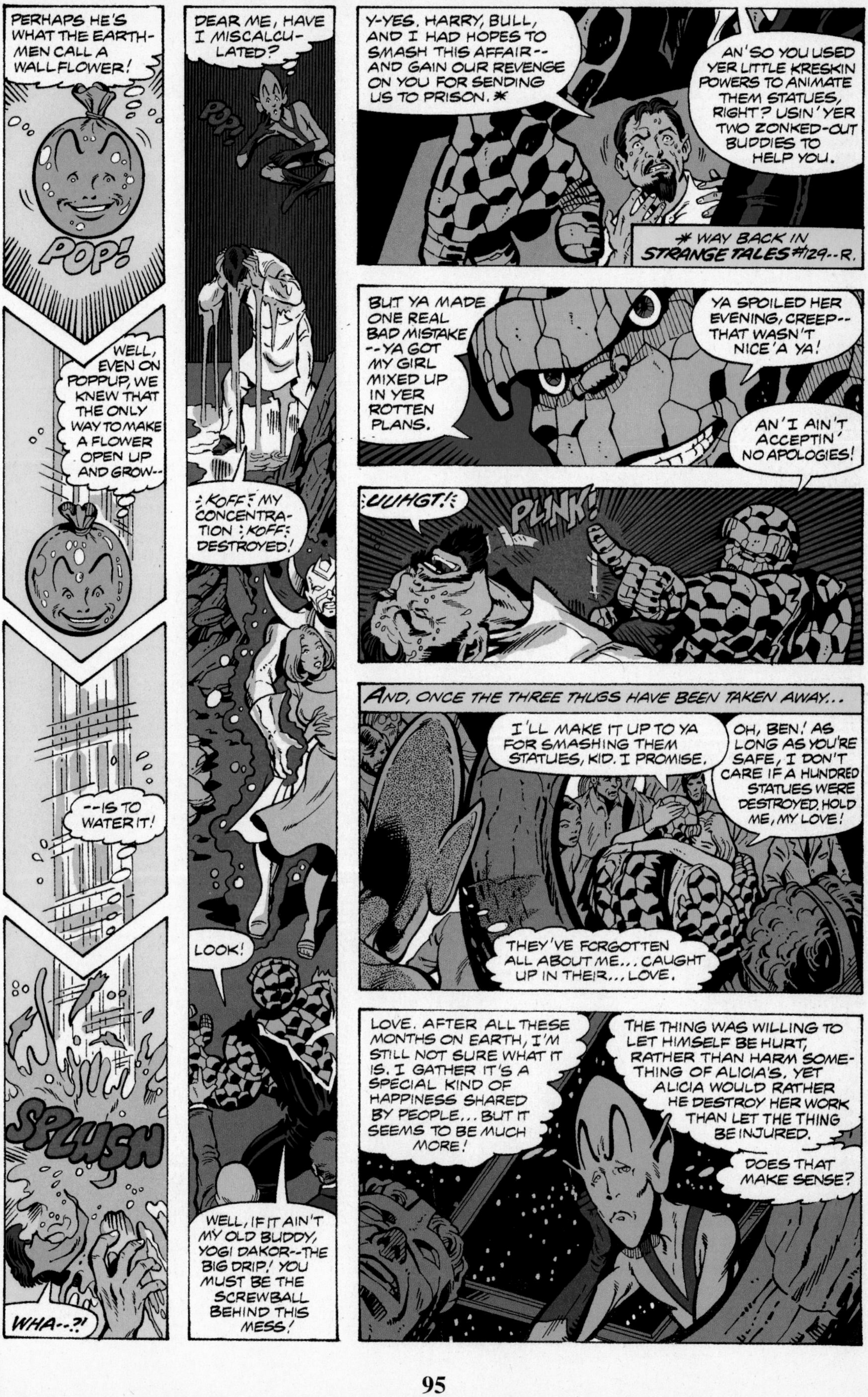
PERHAPS HE'S WHAT THE EARTH-MEN CALL A WALLFLOWER!
POP!
WELL, EVEN ON POPPUP, WE KNEW THAT THE ONLY WAY TO MAKE A FLOWER OPEN UP AND GROW--
--IS TO WATER IT!
SPLUSH
WHA--?!
DEAR ME, HAVE I MISCALCULATED?
POP!
:KOFF: MY CONCENTRATION :KOFF: DESTROYED!
LOOK!
WELL, IF IT AIN'T MY OLD BUDDY, YOGI DAKOR--THE BIG DRIP! YOU MUST BE THE SCREWBALL BEHIND THIS MESS!
Y-YES. HARRY, BULL, AND I HAD HOPES TO SMASH THIS AFFAIR--AND GAIN OUR REVENGE ON YOU FOR SENDING US TO PRISON. *
AN' SO YOU USED YER LITTLE KRESKIN POWERS TO ANIMATE THEM STATUES, RIGHT? USIN' YER TWO ZONKED-OUT BUDDIES TO HELP YOU.
* WAY BACK IN STRANGE TALES #129--R.
BUT YA MADE ONE REAL BAD MISTAKE--YA GOT MY GIRL MIXED UP IN YER ROTTEN PLANS.
YA SPOILED HER EVENING, CREEP--THAT WASN'T NICE'A YA!
AN' I AIN'T ACCEPTIN' NO APOLOGIES!
UUHGT!
PLINK!
AND, ONCE THE THREE THUGS HAVE BEEN TAKEN AWAY...
I'LL MAKE IT UP TO YA FOR SMASHING THEM STATUES, KID. I PROMISE.
OH, BEN! AS LONG AS YOU'RE SAFE, I DON'T CARE IF A HUNDRED STATUES WERE DESTROYED. HOLD ME, MY LOVE!
THEY'VE FORGOTTEN ALL ABOUT ME... CAUGHT UP IN THEIR... LOVE.
LOVE. AFTER ALL THESE MONTHS ON EARTH, I'M STILL NOT SURE WHAT IT IS. I GATHER IT'S A SPECIAL KIND OF HAPPINESS SHARED BY PEOPLE... BUT IT SEEMS TO BE MUCH MORE!
THE THING WAS WILLING TO LET HIMSELF BE HURT, RATHER THAN HARM SOMETHING OF ALICIA'S. YET ALICIA WOULD RATHER HE DESTROY HER WORK THAN LET THE THING BE INJURED.
DOES THAT MAKE SENSE?

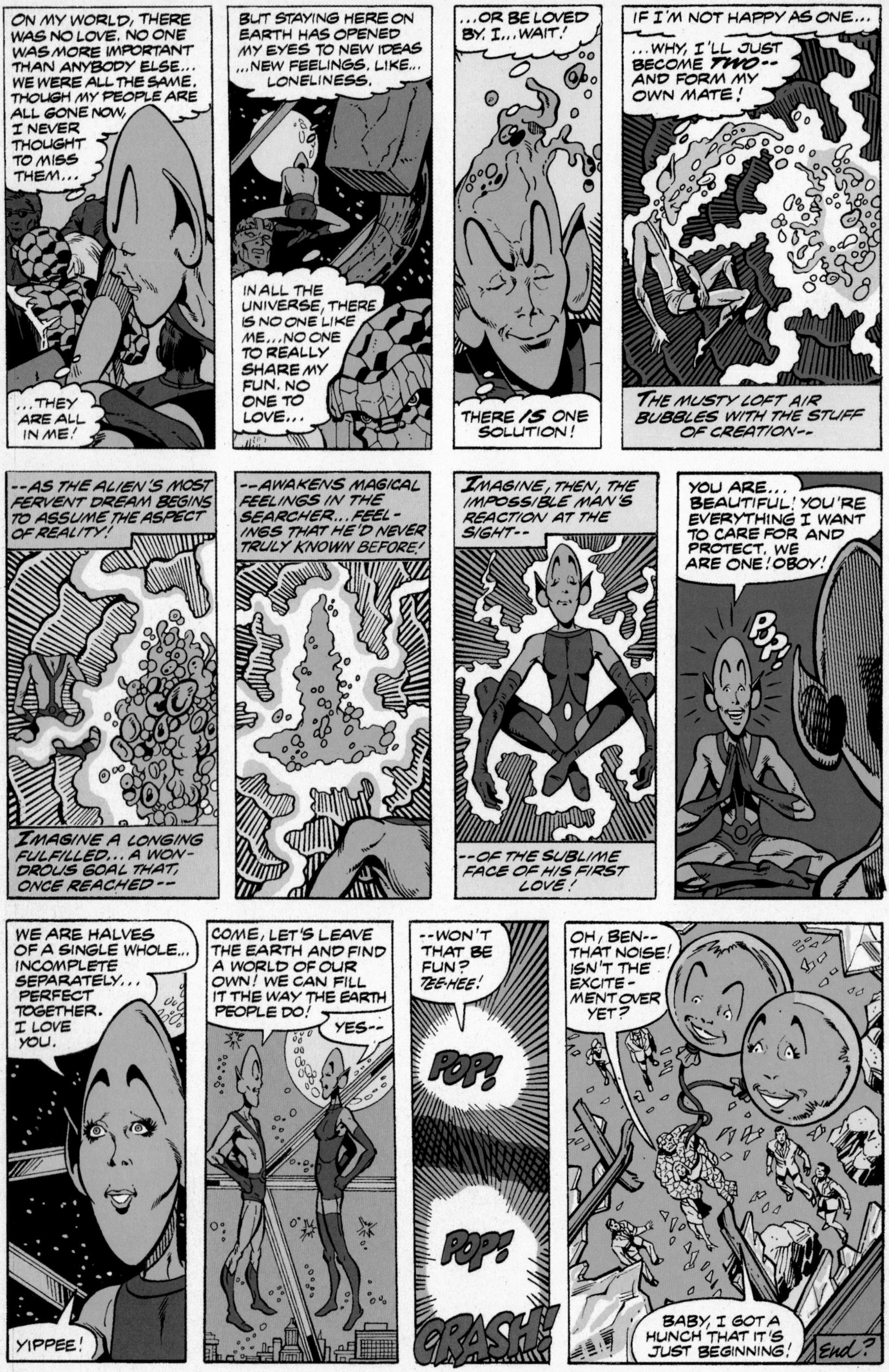
ON MY WORLD, THERE WAS NO LOVE. NO ONE WAS MORE IMPORTANT THAN ANYBODY ELSE... WE WERE ALL THE SAME. THOUGH MY PEOPLE ARE ALL GONE NOW, I NEVER THOUGHT TO MISS THEM...
...THEY ARE ALL IN ME!
BUT STAYING HERE ON EARTH HAS OPENED MY EYES TO NEW IDEAS ...NEW FEELINGS. LIKE... LONELINESS.
IN ALL THE UNIVERSE, THERE IS NO ONE LIKE ME...NO ONE TO REALLY SHARE MY FUN. NO ONE TO LOVE...
...OR BE LOVED BY. I...WAIT!
THERE IS ONE SOLUTION!
IF I'M NOT HAPPY AS ONE...
...WHY, I'LL JUST BECOME TWO-- AND FORM MY OWN MATE!
THE MUSTY LOFT AIR BUBBLES WITH THE STUFF OF CREATION--
--AS THE ALIEN'S MOST FERVENT DREAM BEGINS TO ASSUME THE ASPECT OF REALITY!
IMAGINE A LONGING FULFILLED... A WONDROUS GOAL THAT, ONCE REACHED--
--AWAKENS MAGICAL FEELINGS IN THE SEARCHER...FEELINGS THAT HE'D NEVER TRULY KNOWN BEFORE!
IMAGINE, THEN, THE IMPOSSIBLE MAN'S REACTION AT THE SIGHT--
--OF THE SUBLIME FACE OF HIS FIRST LOVE!
YOU ARE... BEAUTIFUL! YOU'RE EVERYTHING I WANT TO CARE FOR AND PROTECT. WE ARE ONE! OBOY!
POP!
WE ARE HALVES OF A SINGLE WHOLE... INCOMPLETE SEPARATELY... PERFECT TOGETHER. I LOVE YOU.
YIPPEE!
COME, LET'S LEAVE THE EARTH AND FIND A WORLD OF OUR OWN! WE CAN FILL IT THE WAY THE EARTH PEOPLE DO!
YES--
--WON'T THAT BE FUN? TEE-HEE!
POP!
POP!
CRASH!
OH, BEN-- THAT NOISE! ISN'T THE EXCITEMENT OVER YET?
BABY, I GOT A HUNCH THAT IT'S JUST BEGINNING!
End?

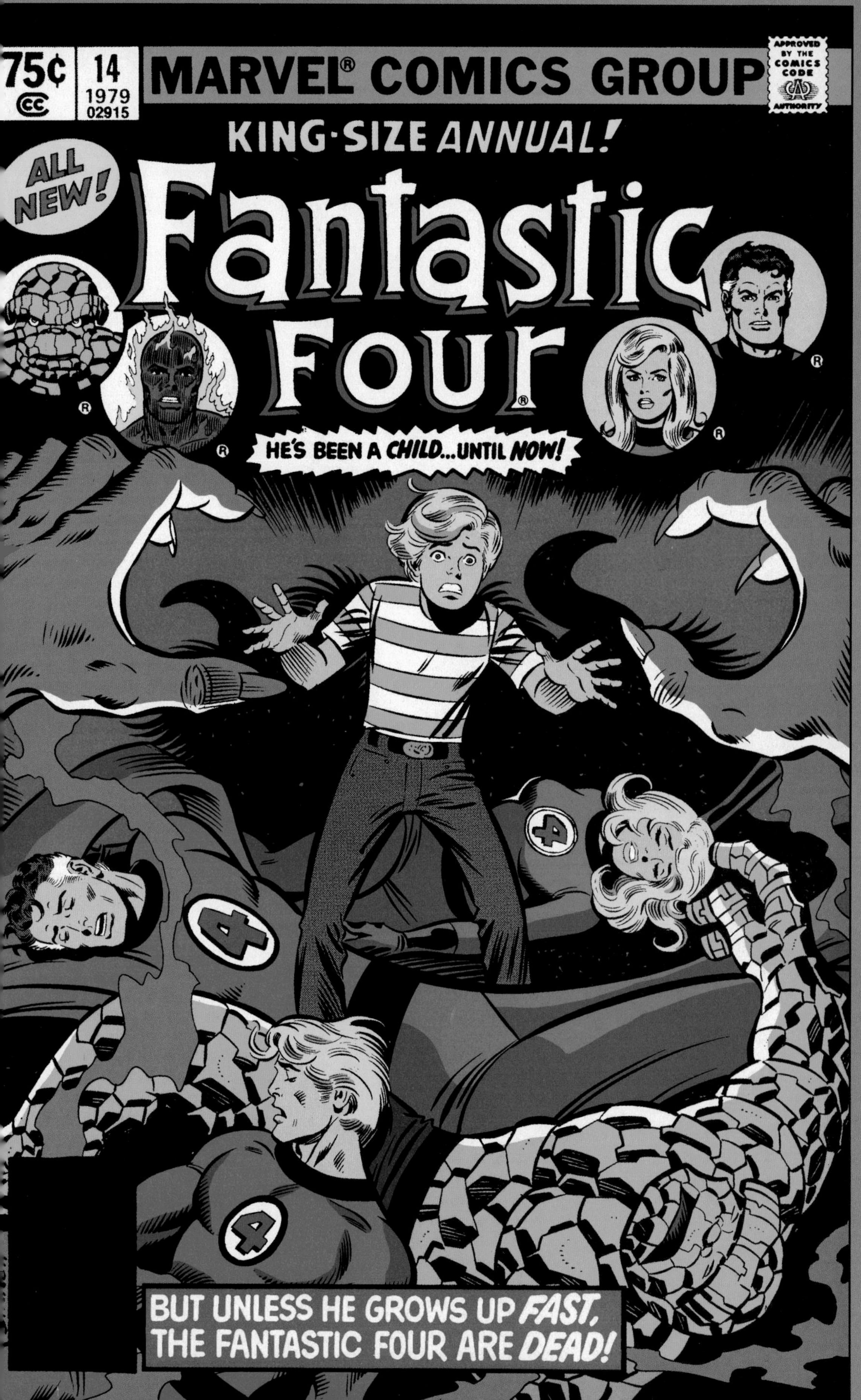

75¢
CC
14
1979
02915
MARVEL® COMICS GROUP
APPROVED BY THE COMICS CODE AUTHORITY
KING-SIZE ANNUAL!
ALL NEW!
Fantastic Four®
HE'S BEEN A CHILD...UNTIL NOW!
BUT UNLESS HE GROWS UP FAST,
THE FANTASTIC FOUR ARE DEAD!

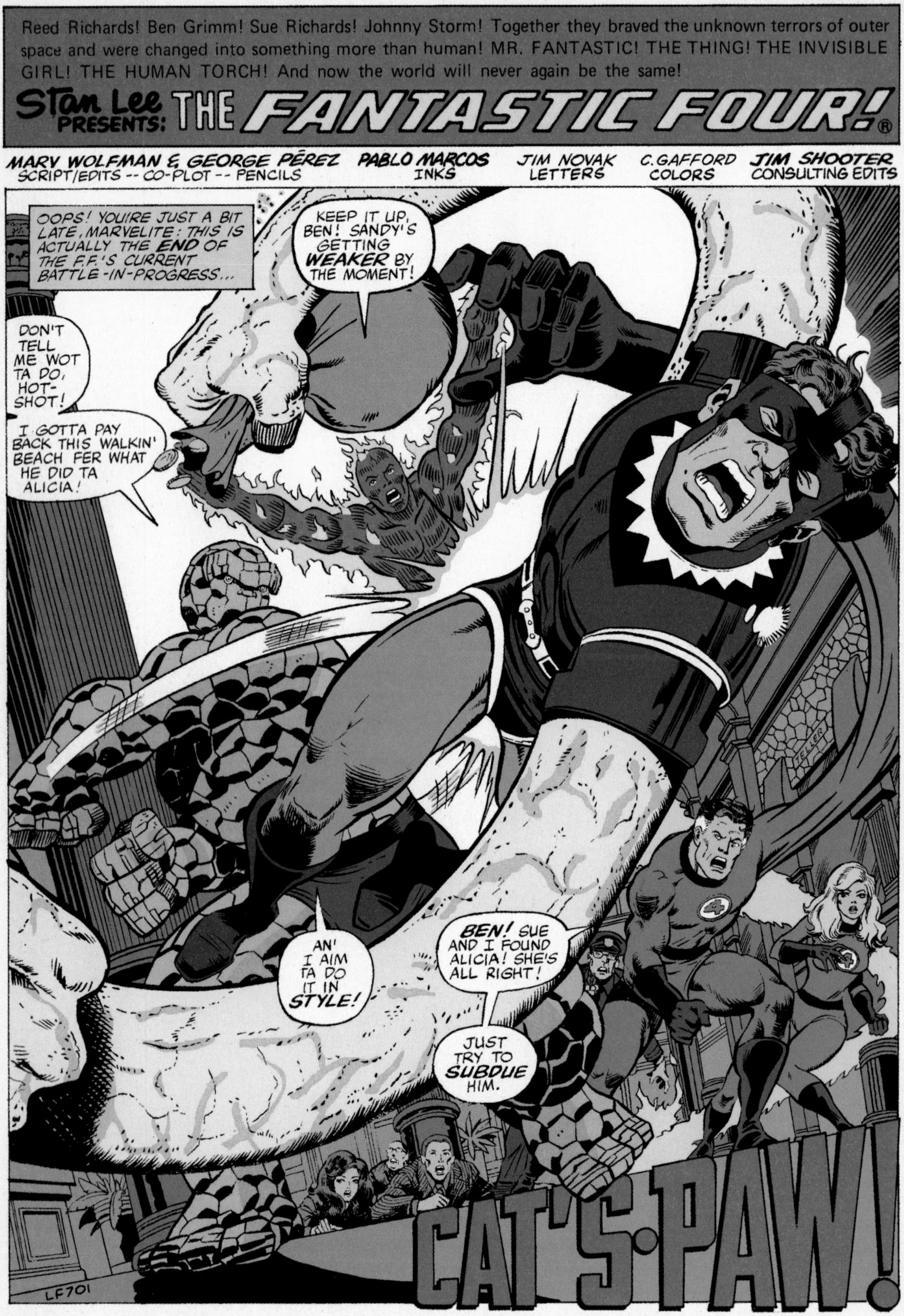
Reed Richards! Ben Grimm! Sue Richards! Johnny Storm! Together they braved the unknown terrors of outer space and were changed into something more than human! MR. FANTASTIC! THE THING! THE INVISIBLE GIRL! THE HUMAN TORCH! And now the world will never again be the same!
Stan Lee PRESENTS: THE FANTASTIC FOUR!®
MARV WOLFMAN & GEORGE PÉREZ SCRIPT/EDITS -- CO-PLOT -- PENCILS
PABLO MARCOS INKS
JIM NOVAK LETTERS
C.GAFFORD COLORS
JIM SHOOTER CONSULTING EDITS
OOPS! YOU'RE JUST A BIT LATE, MARVELITE: THIS IS ACTUALLY THE END OF THE F.F.'S CURRENT BATTLE-IN-PROGRESS...
KEEP IT UP, BEN! SANDY'S GETTING WEAKER BY THE MOMENT!
DON'T TELL ME WOT TA DO, HOT-SHOT!
I GOTTA PAY BACK THIS WALKIN' BEACH FER WHAT HE DID TA ALICIA!
AN' I AIM TA DO IT IN STYLE!
BEN! SUE AND I FOUND ALICIA! SHE'S ALL RIGHT!
JUST TRY TO SUBDUE HIM.
CAT'S-PAW!
LF701

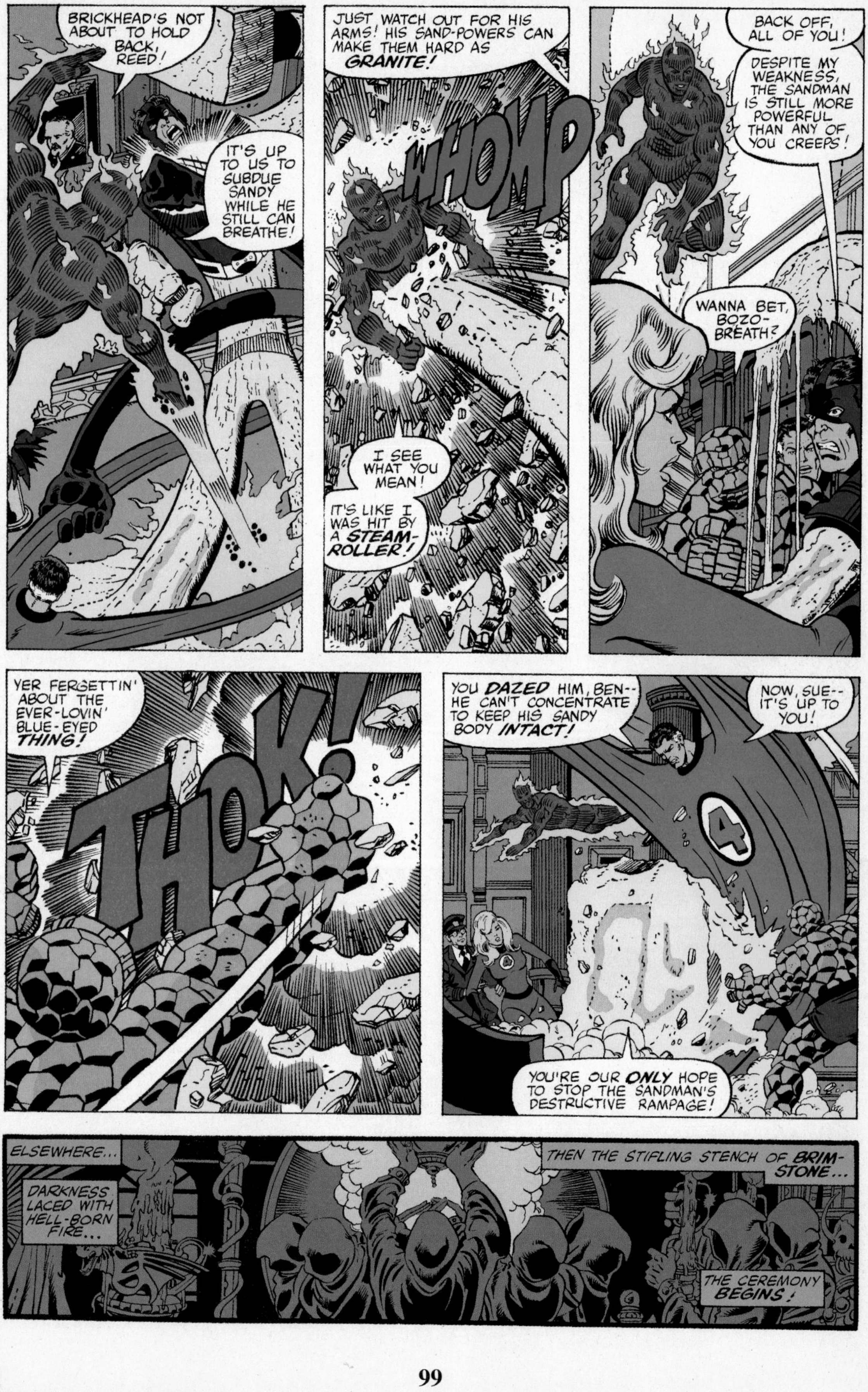

BRICKHEAD'S NOT ABOUT TO HOLD BACK, REED!
IT'S UP TO US TO SUBDUE SANDY WHILE HE STILL CAN BREATHE!
JUST WATCH OUT FOR HIS ARMS! HIS SAND-POWERS CAN MAKE THEM HARD AS GRANITE!
WHOMP
I SEE WHAT YOU MEAN!
IT'S LIKE I WAS HIT BY A STEAM-ROLLER!
BACK OFF, ALL OF YOU!
DESPITE MY WEAKNESS, THE SANDMAN IS STILL MORE POWERFUL THAN ANY OF YOU CREEPS!
WANNA BET, BOZO-BREATH?
YER FERGETTIN' ABOUT THE EVER-LOVIN' BLUE-EYED THING!
THOK!
YOU DAZED HIM, BEN-- HE CAN'T CONCENTRATE TO KEEP HIS SANDY BODY INTACT!
NOW, SUE-- IT'S UP TO YOU!
YOU'RE OUR ONLY HOPE TO STOP THE SANDMAN'S DESTRUCTIVE RAMPAGE!
ELSEWHERE...
DARKNESS LACED WITH HELL-BORN FIRE...
THEN THE STIFLING STENCH OF BRIM-STONE...
THE CEREMONY BEGINS!

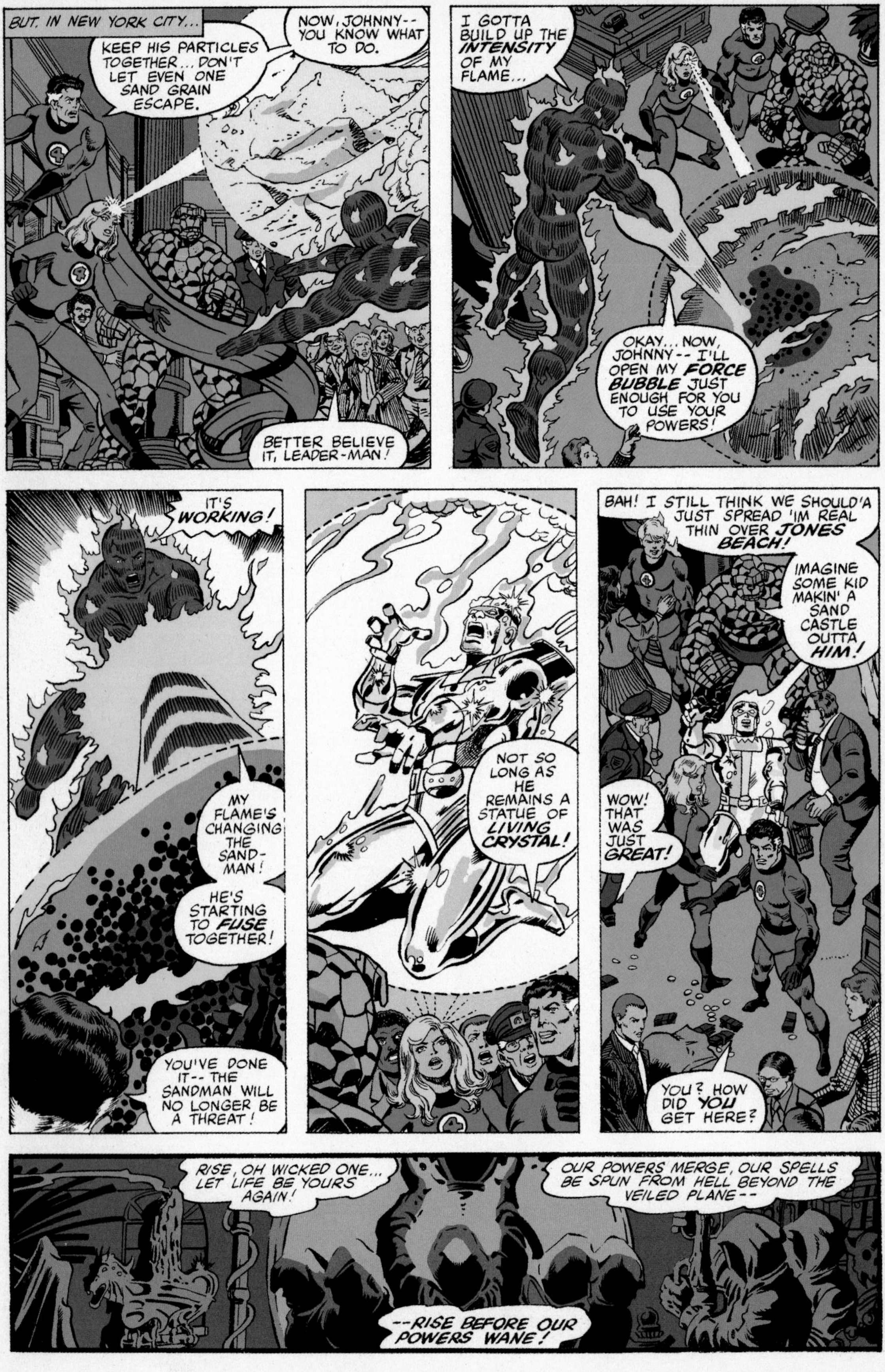
BUT, IN NEW YORK CITY...
KEEP HIS PARTICLES TOGETHER... DON'T LET EVEN ONE SAND GRAIN ESCAPE.
NOW, JOHNNY-- YOU KNOW WHAT TO DO.
BETTER BELIEVE IT, LEADER-MAN!
I GOTTA BUILD UP THE INTENSITY OF MY FLAME...
OKAY... NOW, JOHNNY-- I'LL OPEN MY FORCE BUBBLE JUST ENOUGH FOR YOU TO USE YOUR POWERS!
IT'S WORKING!
MY FLAME'S CHANGING THE SANDMAN!
HE'S STARTING TO FUSE TOGETHER!
YOU'VE DONE IT-- THE SANDMAN WILL NO LONGER BE A THREAT!
NOT SO LONG AS HE REMAINS A STATUE OF LIVING CRYSTAL!
BAH! I STILL THINK WE SHOULD'A JUST SPREAD 'IM REAL THIN OVER JONES BEACH!
IMAGINE SOME KID MAKIN' A SAND CASTLE OUTTA HIM!
WOW! THAT WAS JUST GREAT!
YOU? HOW DID YOU GET HERE?
RISE, OH WICKED ONE... LET LIFE BE YOURS AGAIN!
OUR POWERS MERGE, OUR SPELLS BE SPUN FROM HELL BEYOND THE VEILED PLANE--
--RISE BEFORE OUR POWERS WANE!

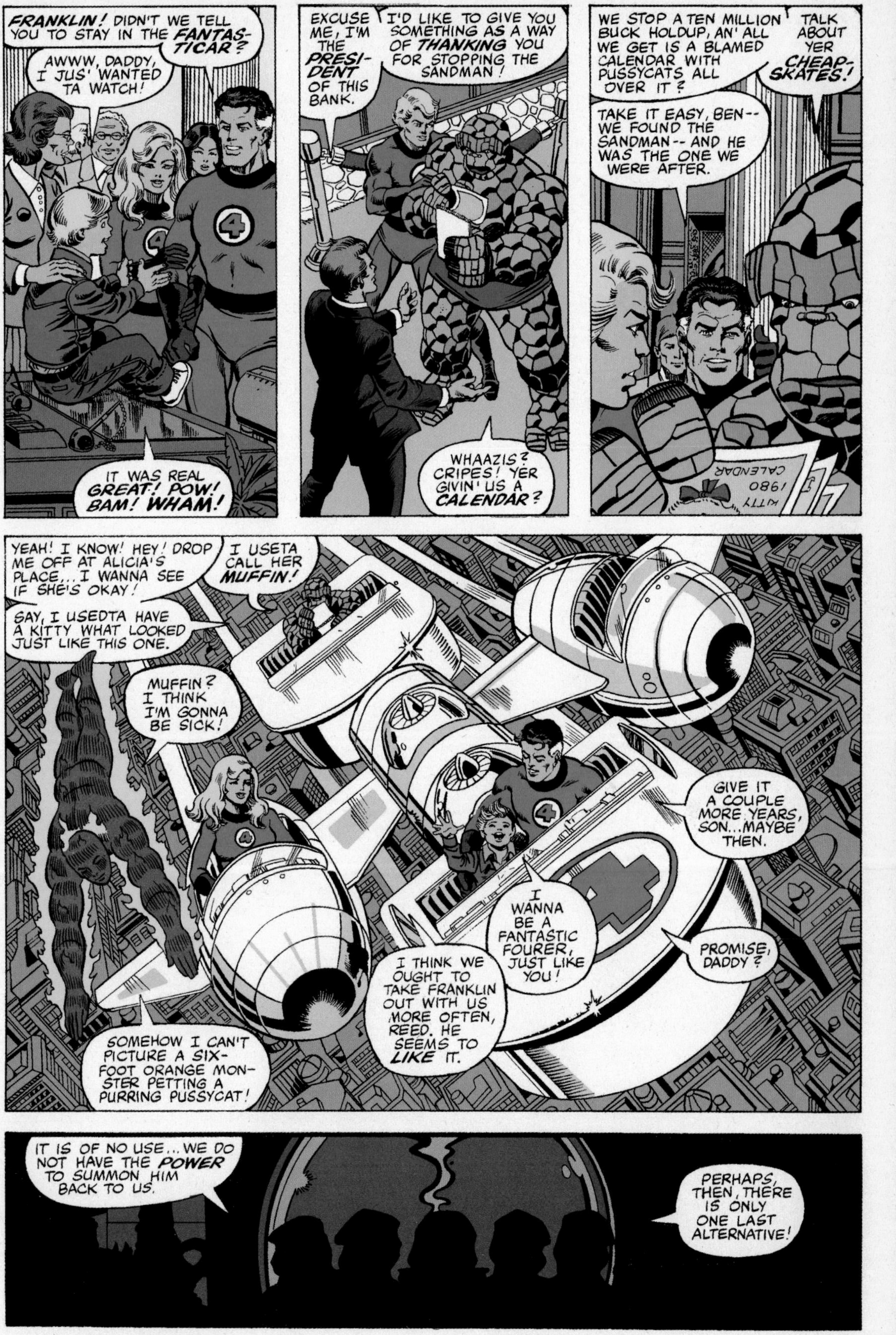
FRANKLIN! DIDN'T WE TELL YOU TO STAY IN THE FANTASTICAR?
AWWW, DADDY, I JUS' WANTED TA WATCH!
IT WAS REAL GREAT! POW! BAM! WHAM!
EXCUSE ME, I'M THE PRESIDENT OF THIS BANK.
I'D LIKE TO GIVE YOU SOMETHING AS A WAY OF THANKING YOU FOR STOPPING THE SANDMAN!
WHAAZIS? CRIPES! YER GIVIN' US A CALENDAR?
WE STOP A TEN MILLION BUCK HOLDUP, AN' ALL WE GET IS A BLAMED CALENDAR WITH PUSSYCATS ALL OVER IT?
TALK ABOUT YER CHEAPSKATES!
TAKE IT EASY, BEN-- WE FOUND THE SANDMAN-- AND HE WAS THE ONE WE WERE AFTER.
KITTY 1980 CALENDAR
YEAH! I KNOW! HEY! DROP ME OFF AT ALICIA'S PLACE,.. I WANNA SEE IF SHE'S OKAY!
SAY, I USEDTA HAVE A KITTY WHAT LOOKED JUST LIKE THIS ONE.
I USETA CALL HER MUFFIN!
MUFFIN? I THINK I'M GONNA BE SICK!
SOMEHOW I CAN'T PICTURE A SIX-FOOT ORANGE MONSTER PETTING A PURRING PUSSYCAT!
I THINK WE OUGHT TO TAKE FRANKLIN OUT WITH US MORE OFTEN, REED. HE SEEMS TO LIKE IT.
I WANNA BE A FANTASTIC FOURER, JUST LIKE YOU!
GIVE IT A COUPLE MORE YEARS, SON...MAYBE THEN.
PROMISE, DADDY?
IT IS OF NO USE... WE DO NOT HAVE THE POWER TO SUMMON HIM BACK TO US.
PERHAPS, THEN, THERE IS ONLY ONE LAST ALTERNATIVE!

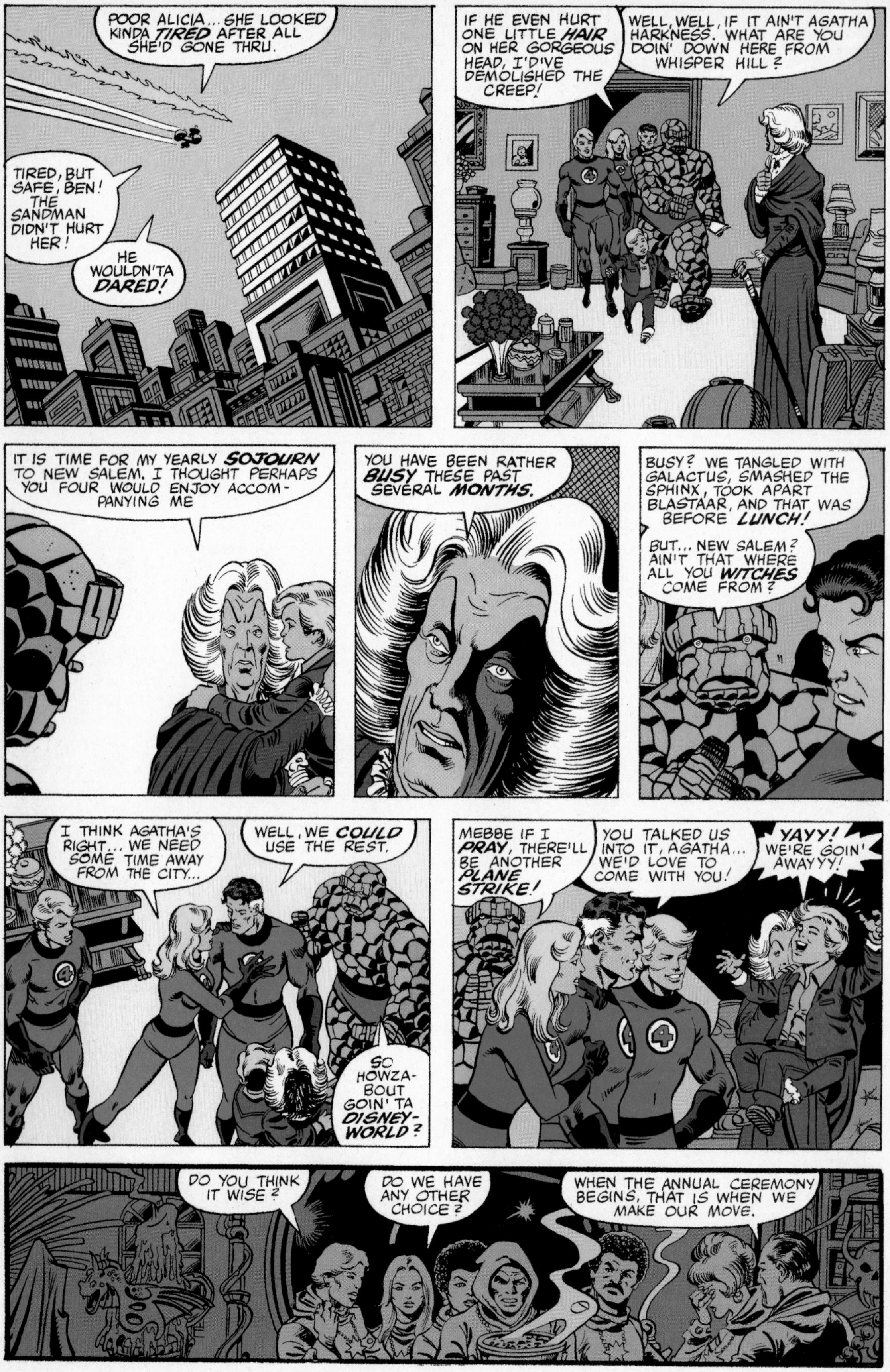
POOR ALICIA... SHE LOOKED KINDA TIRED AFTER ALL SHE'D GONE THRU.
TIRED, BUT SAFE, BEN! THE SANDMAN DIDN'T HURT HER!
HE WOULDN'TA DARED!
IF HE EVEN HURT ONE LITTLE HAIR ON HER GORGEOUS HEAD, I'D'VE DEMOLISHED THE CREEP!
WELL, WELL, IF IT AIN'T AGATHA HARKNESS. WHAT ARE YOU DOIN' DOWN HERE FROM WHISPER HILL?
IT IS TIME FOR MY YEARLY SOJOURN TO NEW SALEM. I THOUGHT PERHAPS YOU FOUR WOULD ENJOY ACCOMPANYING ME
YOU HAVE BEEN RATHER BUSY THESE PAST SEVERAL MONTHS.
BUSY? WE TANGLED WITH GALACTUS, SMASHED THE SPHINX, TOOK APART BLASTAAR, AND THAT WAS BEFORE LUNCH!
BUT... NEW SALEM? AIN'T THAT WHERE ALL YOU WITCHES COME FROM?
I THINK AGATHA'S RIGHT... WE NEED SOME TIME AWAY FROM THE CITY...
WELL, WE COULD USE THE REST.
SO HOWZABOUT GOIN' TA DISNEY-WORLD?
MEBBE IF I PRAY, THERE'LL BE ANOTHER PLANE STRIKE!
YOU TALKED US INTO IT, AGATHA... WE'D LOVE TO COME WITH YOU!
YAYY! WE'RE GOIN' AWAYYY!
DO YOU THINK IT WISE?
DO WE HAVE ANY OTHER CHOICE?
WHEN THE ANNUAL CEREMONY BEGINS, THAT IS WHEN WE MAKE OUR MOVE.

THERE'S STILL TIME TA GO TO DISNEYLAND! YA CAN STILL CHANGE YER MIND.

AFRAID? LISSEN, SQUIRT, I AIN'T AFRAID OF NOTHIN' THAT LIVES!

TROUBLE IS, I DON'T KNOW IF WITCHES AN' WARLOCKS IS ALL THAT WALKS AROUND THAT HAUNTED JOINT.

REED, SUE... SOMETHING TELLS ME BLUE-EYES HERE IS A TAD AFRAID OF VISITING NEW SALEM.

WOT IF THERE'S GHOSTS AN' GOBLINS AN'...

ARE WE THE ONLY ONES ON THIS FLIGHT, MISS? WHERE'S THE OTHER PASSENGERS?

OH, WHEN THEY HEARD THE FANTASTIC FOUR WAS ON BOARD, THEY ALL CHANGED THEIR RESERVATIONS.

THEY SAID THEY DIDN'T WANT TO GET INVOLVED IF ANY OF YOUR OLD ENEMIES ATTACKED.

EXCUSE ME, WOULD YOU CARE FOR SOME COFFEE, OR--

I ALREADY HAVE MY TEA, MISS. BUT, THANK YOU.

B-BUT... HOW DID--?

ARE THERE REALLY GHOSTS IN NEW SALEM, UNCLE BEN?

I WANNA SEE SOME GHOSTS, DADDY...

THERE AIN'T NO SUCH THINGS AS GHOSTS...THERE AIN'T NO SUCH THINGS AS GHOSTS...

MEBBE IF I SAY IT ENUFF, I START BELIEVIN' IT.

HOURS LATER, AFTER THE GIANT 747 LANDS AT THE SPRAWLING COLORADO AIRPORT...

I DON'T UNNERSTAN' THIS. I COULD'A SWORN NEW SALEM WAS JUST AROUND A BEND.

ONLY NOW THERE AIN'T EVEN A BEND HERE ANYMORE.

WE DISGUISED THE ROUTE TO OUR HOMELAND, MR. GRIMM.

MY PEOPLE HAVE ALWAYS BEEN SUSPICIOUS OF OUTSIDERS.

WE HAVE NEVER ENCOURAGED ANY MINGLING BETWEEN OUR PEOPLE AND HUMANS.

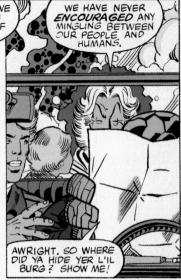

AWRIGHT. SO WHERE DID YA HIDE YER L'IL BURG? SHOW ME!

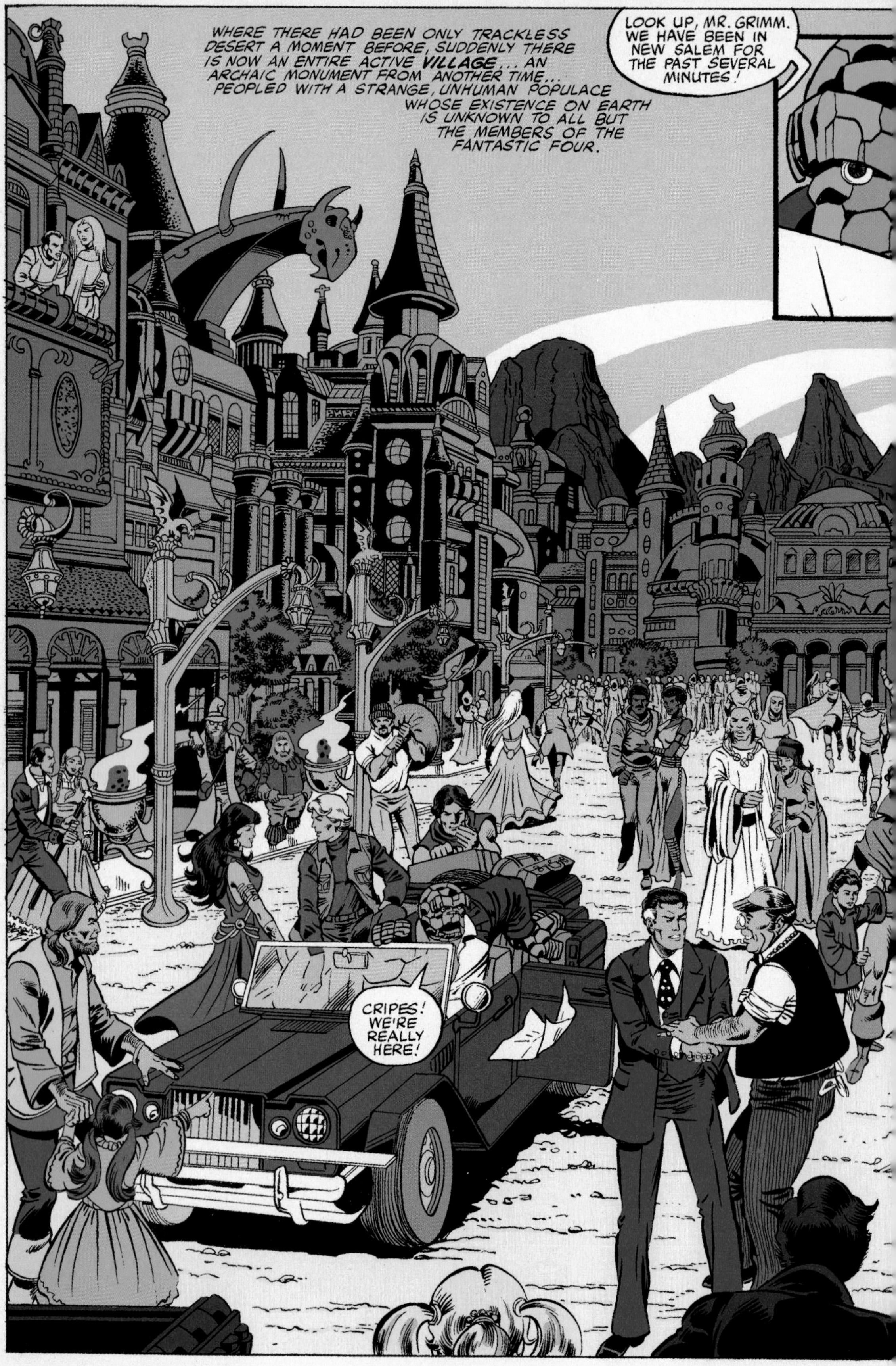
WHERE THERE HAD BEEN ONLY TRACKLESS DESERT A MOMENT BEFORE, SUDDENLY THERE IS NOW AN ENTIRE ACTIVE VILLAGE... AN ARCHAIC MONUMENT FROM ANOTHER TIME... PEOPLED WITH A STRANGE, UNHUMAN POPULACE WHOSE EXISTENCE ON EARTH IS UNKNOWN TO ALL BUT THE MEMBERS OF THE FANTASTIC FOUR.
LOOK UP, MR. GRIMM. WE HAVE BEEN IN NEW SALEM FOR THE PAST SEVERAL MINUTES!
CRIPES! WE'RE REALLY HERE!

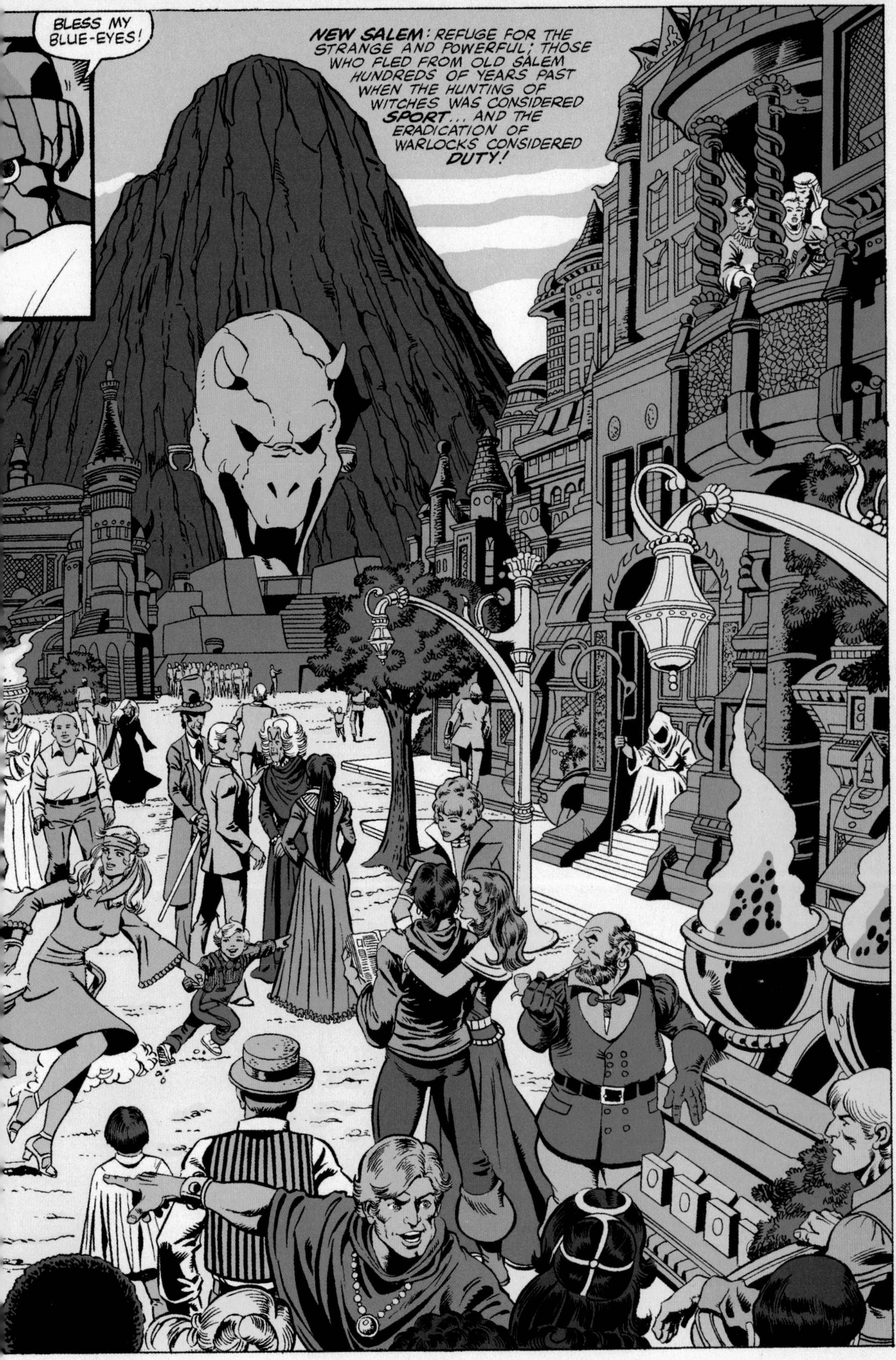
BLESS MY BLUE-EYES!
NEW SALEM: REFUGE FOR THE STRANGE AND POWERFUL; THOSE WHO FLED FROM OLD SALEM HUNDREDS OF YEARS PAST WHEN THE HUNTING OF WITCHES WAS CONSIDERED SPORT... AND THE ERADICATION OF WARLOCKS CONSIDERED DUTY!

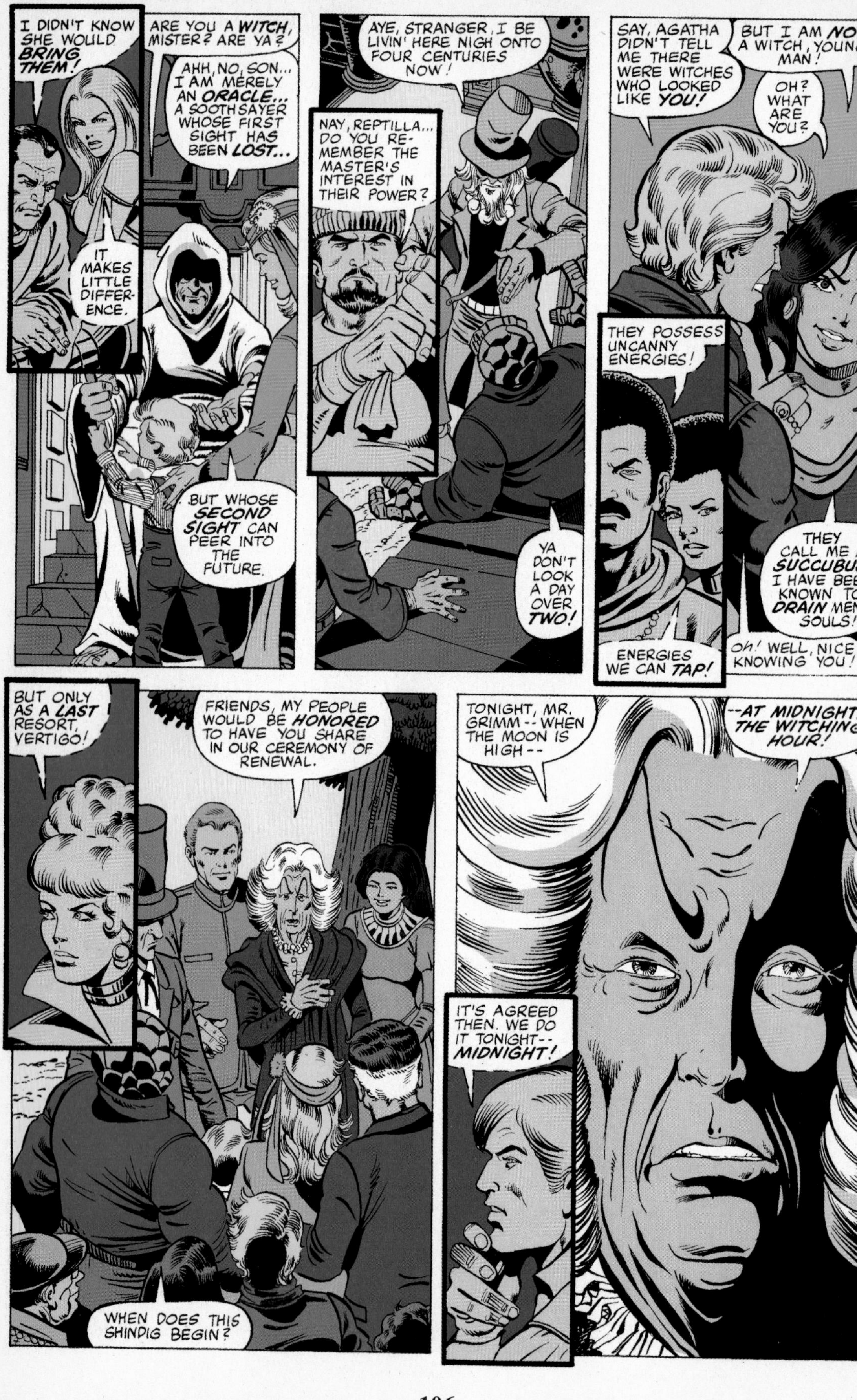
I DIDN'T KNOW SHE WOULD BRING THEM!
ARE YOU A WITCH, MISTER? ARE YA?
AHH, NO, SON... I AM MERELY AN ORACLE... A SOOTHSAYER WHOSE FIRST SIGHT HAS BEEN LOST...
IT MAKES LITTLE DIFFERENCE.
BUT WHOSE SECOND SIGHT CAN PEER INTO THE FUTURE.
AYE, STRANGER, I BE LIVIN' HERE NIGH ONTO FOUR CENTURIES NOW!
NAY, REPTILLA... DO YOU REMEMBER THE MASTER'S INTEREST IN THEIR POWER?
YA DON'T LOOK A DAY OVER TWO!
SAY, AGATHA DIDN'T TELL ME THERE WERE WITCHES WHO LOOKED LIKE YOU!
BUT I AM NOT A WITCH, YOUNG MAN!
OH? WHAT ARE YOU?
THEY POSSESS UNCANNY ENERGIES!
ENERGIES WE CAN TAP!
THEY CALL ME A SUCCUBUS! I HAVE BEEN KNOWN TO DRAIN MEN'S SOULS!
Oh! WELL, NICE KNOWING YOU!
BUT ONLY AS A LAST RESORT, VERTIGO!
FRIENDS, MY PEOPLE WOULD BE HONORED TO HAVE YOU SHARE IN OUR CEREMONY OF RENEWAL.
WHEN DOES THIS SHINDIG BEGIN?
TONIGHT, MR. GRIMM -- WHEN THE MOON IS HIGH --
--AT MIDNIGHT... THE WITCHING HOUR!
IT'S AGREED THEN. WE DO IT TONIGHT-- MIDNIGHT!

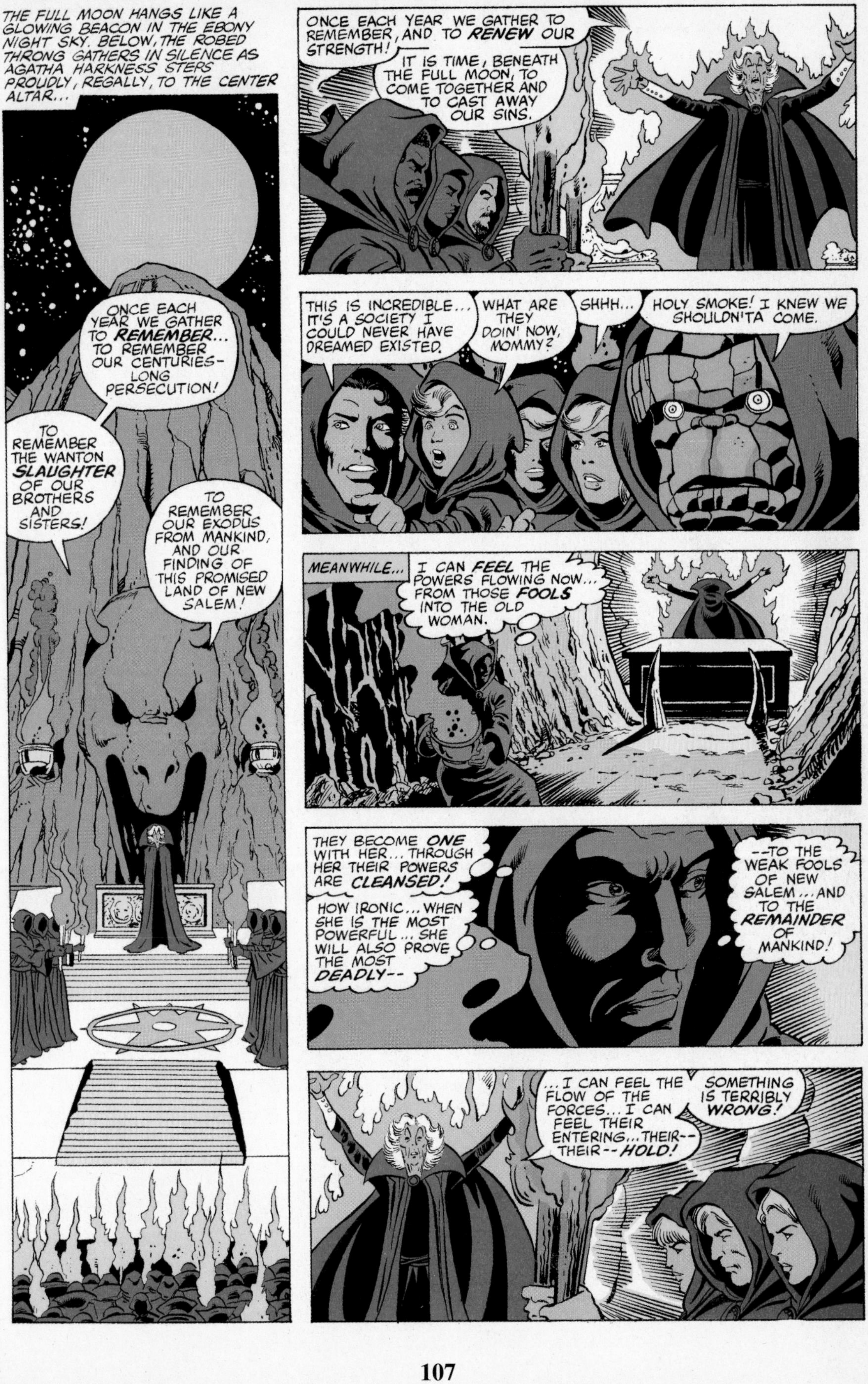
THE FULL MOON HANGS LIKE A GLOWING BEACON IN THE EBONY NIGHT SKY. BELOW, THE ROBED THRONG GATHERS IN SILENCE AS AGATHA HARKNESS STEPS PROUDLY, REGALLY, TO THE CENTER ALTAR...
ONCE EACH YEAR WE GATHER TO REMEMBER... TO REMEMBER OUR CENTURIES-LONG PERSECUTION!
TO REMEMBER THE WANTON SLAUGHTER OF OUR BROTHERS AND SISTERS!
TO REMEMBER OUR EXODUS FROM MANKIND, AND OUR FINDING OF THIS PROMISED LAND OF NEW SALEM!
ONCE EACH YEAR WE GATHER TO REMEMBER, AND TO RENEW OUR STRENGTH!
IT IS TIME, BENEATH THE FULL MOON, TO COME TOGETHER AND TO CAST AWAY OUR SINS.
THIS IS INCREDIBLE... IT'S A SOCIETY I COULD NEVER HAVE DREAMED EXISTED.
WHAT ARE THEY DOIN' NOW, MOMMY?
SHHH...
HOLY SMOKE! I KNEW WE SHOULDN'TA COME.
MEANWHILE...
I CAN FEEL THE POWERS FLOWING NOW... FROM THOSE FOOLS INTO THE OLD WOMAN.
THEY BECOME ONE WITH HER... THROUGH HER THEIR POWERS ARE CLEANSED!
HOW IRONIC... WHEN SHE IS THE MOST POWERFUL... SHE WILL ALSO PROVE THE MOST DEADLY--
--TO THE WEAK FOOLS OF NEW SALEM... AND TO THE REMAINDER OF MANKIND!
...I CAN FEEL THE FLOW OF THE FORCES... I CAN FEEL THEIR ENTERING... THEIR-- THEIR--HOLD!
SOMETHING IS TERRIBLY WRONG!

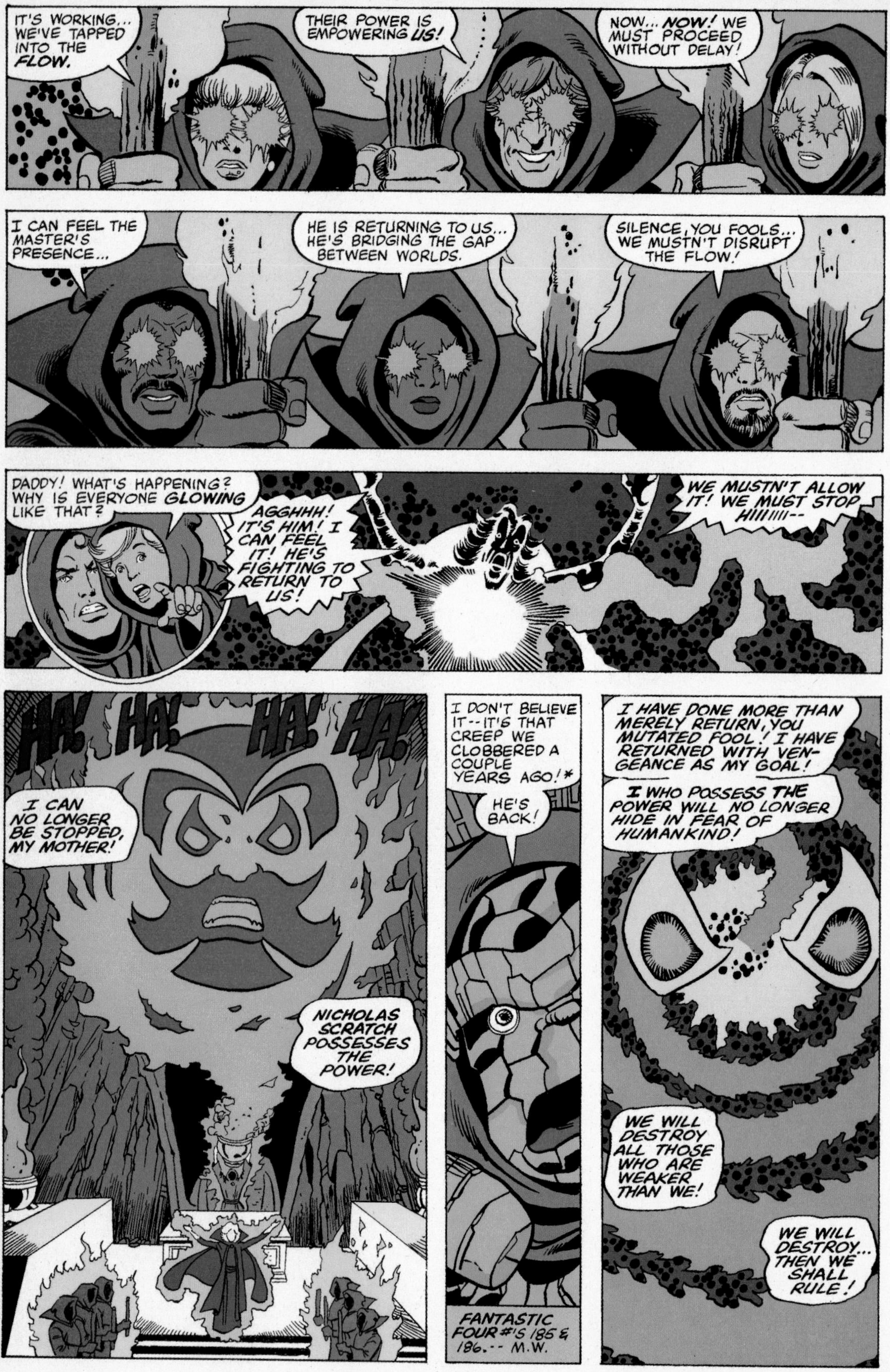
IT'S WORKING... WE'VE TAPPED INTO THE FLOW.
THEIR POWER IS EMPOWERING US!
NOW... NOW! WE MUST PROCEED WITHOUT DELAY!
I CAN FEEL THE MASTER'S PRESENCE...
HE IS RETURNING TO US... HE'S BRIDGING THE GAP BETWEEN WORLDS.
SILENCE, YOU FOOLS... WE MUSTN'T DISRUPT THE FLOW!
DADDY! WHAT'S HAPPENING? WHY IS EVERYONE GLOWING LIKE THAT?
AGGHHH! IT'S HIM! I CAN FEEL IT! HE'S FIGHTING TO RETURN TO US!
WE MUSTN'T ALLOW IT! WE MUST STOP HIIIIIII--
HA! HA! HA! HA!
I CAN NO LONGER BE STOPPED, MY MOTHER!
NICHOLAS SCRATCH POSSESSES THE POWER!
I DON'T BELIEVE IT--IT'S THAT CREEP WE CLOBBERED A COUPLE YEARS AGO!*
HE'S BACK!
FANTASTIC FOUR #'S 185 & 186.--M.W.
I HAVE DONE MORE THAN MERELY RETURN, YOU MUTATED FOOL! I HAVE RETURNED WITH VENGEANCE AS MY GOAL!
I WHO POSSESS THE POWER WILL NO LONGER HIDE IN FEAR OF HUMANKIND!
WE WILL DESTROY ALL THOSE WHO ARE WEAKER THAN WE!
WE WILL DESTROY... THEN WE SHALL RULE!

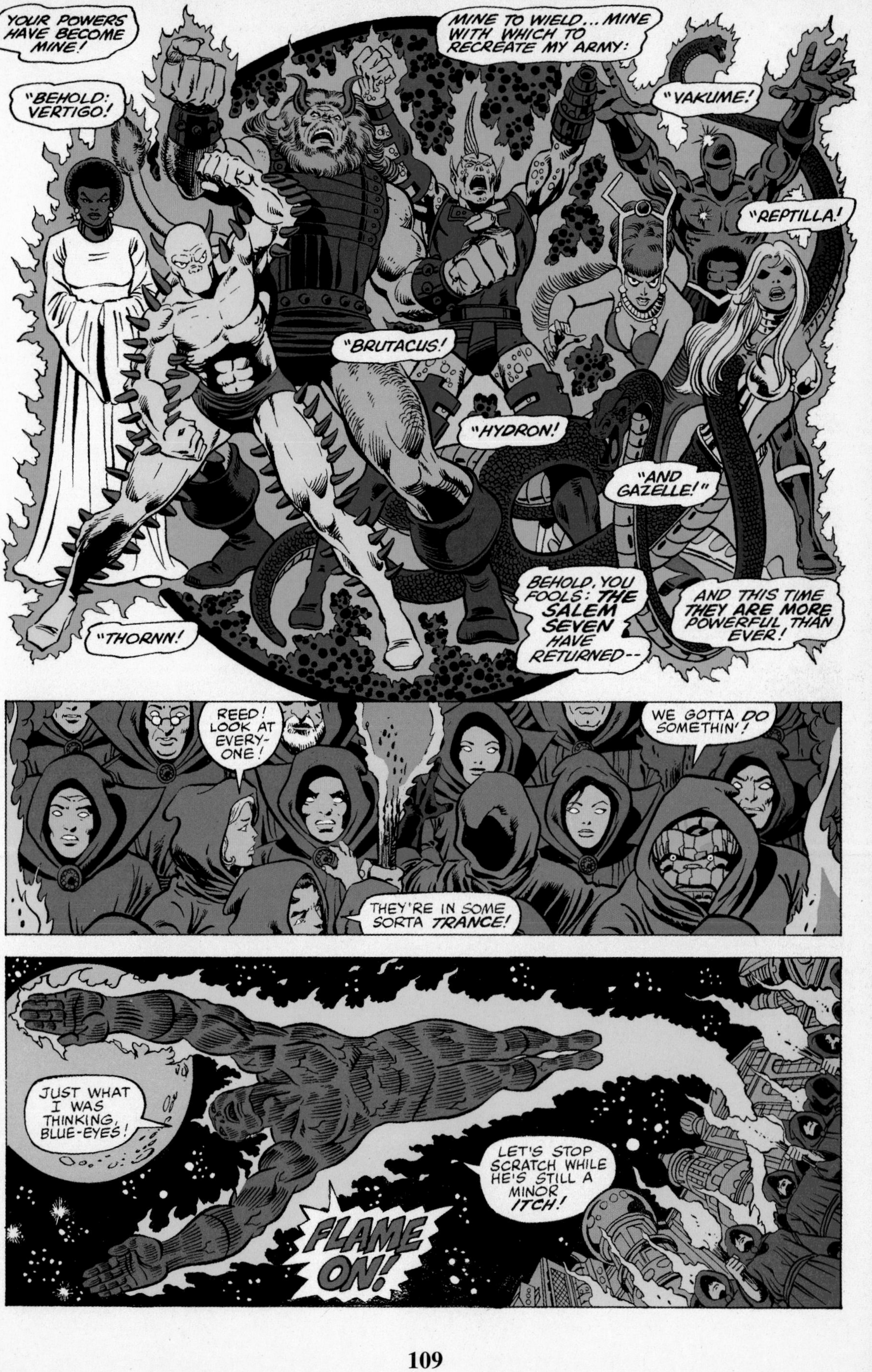
YOUR POWERS HAVE BECOME MINE!
MINE TO WIELD... MINE WITH WHICH TO RECREATE MY ARMY:
"BEHOLD: VERTIGO!
"YAKUME!
"REPTILLA!
"BRUTACUS!
"HYDRON!
"AND GAZELLE!"
"THORNN!
BEHOLD, YOU FOOLS: THE SALEM SEVEN HAVE RETURNED--
AND THIS TIME THEY ARE MORE POWERFUL THAN EVER!
REED! LOOK AT EVERY-ONE!
WE GOTTA DO SOMETHIN'!
THEY'RE IN SOME SORTA TRANCE!
JUST WHAT I WAS THINKING, BLUE-EYES!
LET'S STOP SCRATCH WHILE HE'S STILL A MINOR ITCH!
FLAME ON!

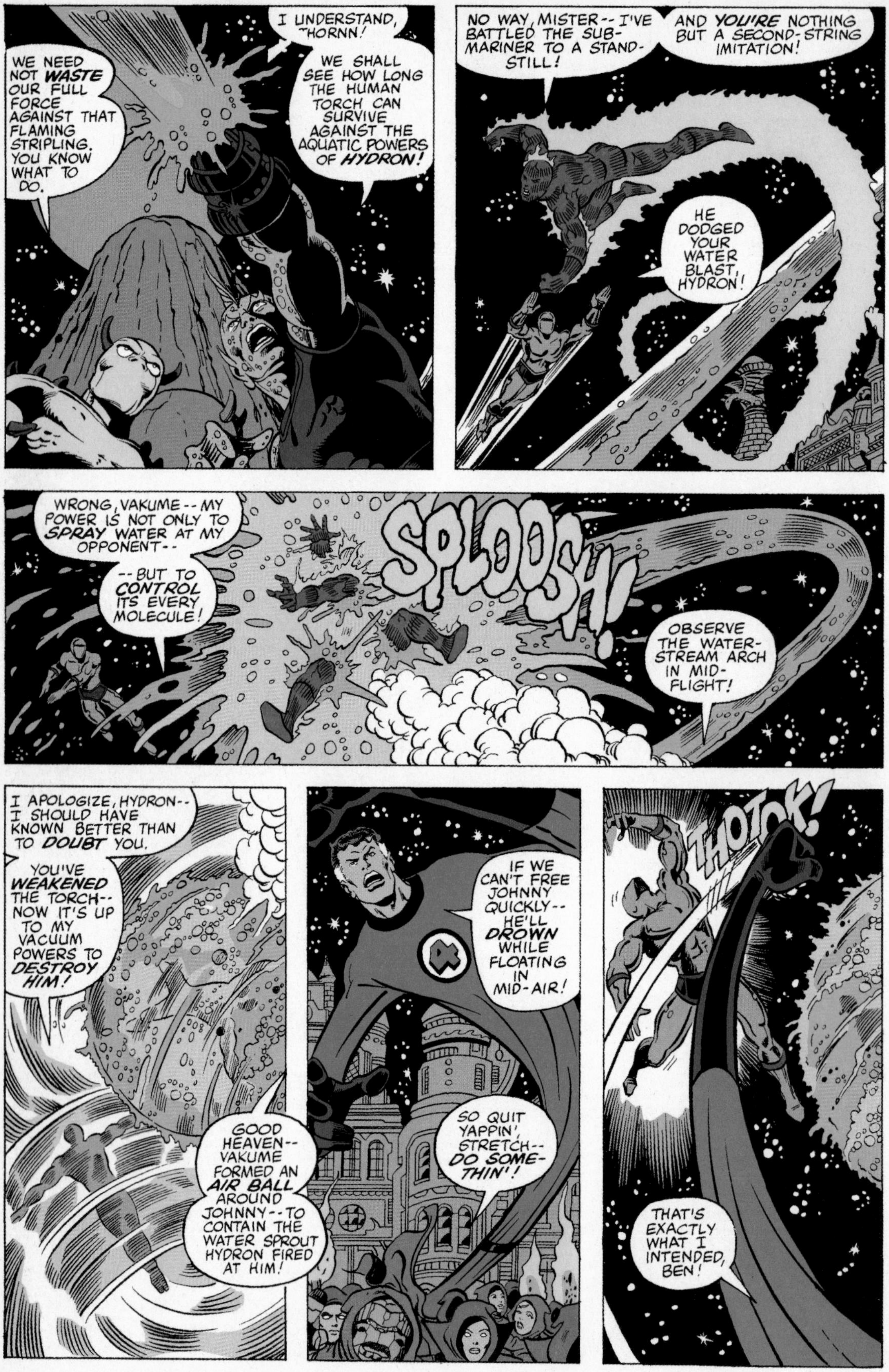
WE NEED NOT WASTE OUR FULL FORCE AGAINST THAT FLAMING STRIPLING. YOU KNOW WHAT TO DO.
I UNDERSTAND, THORNN!
WE SHALL SEE HOW LONG THE HUMAN TORCH CAN SURVIVE AGAINST THE AQUATIC POWERS OF HYDRON!
NO WAY, MISTER-- I'VE BATTLED THE SUB-MARINER TO A STAND-STILL!
AND YOU'RE NOTHING BUT A SECOND-STRING IMITATION!
HE DODGED YOUR WATER BLAST, HYDRON!
WRONG, VAKUME-- MY POWER IS NOT ONLY TO SPRAY WATER AT MY OPPONENT--
--BUT TO CONTROL ITS EVERY MOLECULE!
SPLOOSH!
OBSERVE THE WATER-STREAM ARCH IN MID-FLIGHT!
I APOLOGIZE, HYDRON-- I SHOULD HAVE KNOWN BETTER THAN TO DOUBT YOU.
YOU'VE WEAKENED THE TORCH-- NOW IT'S UP TO MY VACUUM POWERS TO DESTROY HIM!
GOOD HEAVEN-- VAKUME FORMED AN AIR BALL AROUND JOHNNY--TO CONTAIN THE WATER SPROUT HYDRON FIRED AT HIM!
IF WE CAN'T FREE JOHNNY QUICKLY-- HE'LL DROWN WHILE FLOATING IN MID-AIR!
SO QUIT YAPPIN', STRETCH-- DO SOME-THIN'!
THOTOK!
THAT'S EXACTLY WHAT I INTENDED, BEN!

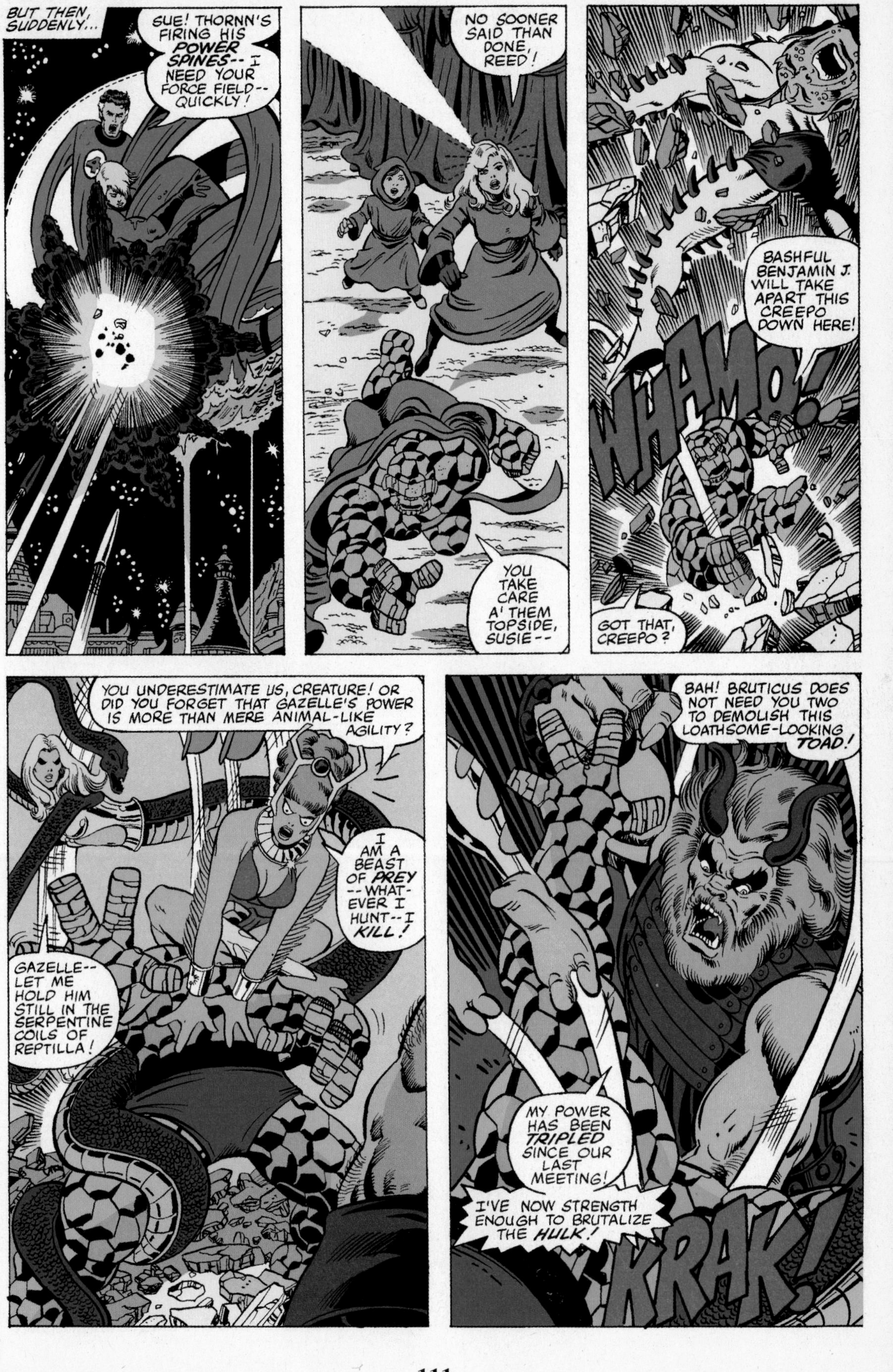

BUT THEN, SUDDENLY...
SUE! THORNN'S FIRING HIS POWER SPINES-- I NEED YOUR FORCE FIELD-- QUICKLY!
NO SOONER SAID THAN DONE, REED!
YOU TAKE CARE A' THEM TOPSIDE, SUSIE--
BASHFUL BENJAMIN J. WILL TAKE APART THIS CREEPO DOWN HERE!
WHAMO!
GOT THAT, CREEPO?
YOU UNDERESTIMATE US, CREATURE! OR DID YOU FORGET THAT GAZELLE'S POWER IS MORE THAN MERE ANIMAL-LIKE AGILITY?
I AM A BEAST OF PREY --WHAT-EVER I HUNT--I KILL!
GAZELLE-- LET ME HOLD HIM STILL IN THE SERPENTINE COILS OF REPTILLA!
BAH! BRUTICUS DOES NOT NEED YOU TWO TO DEMOLISH THIS LOATHSOME-LOOKING TOAD!
MY POWER HAS BEEN TRIPLED SINCE OUR LAST MEETING!
I'VE NOW STRENGTH ENOUGH TO BRUTALIZE THE HULK!
KRAK!

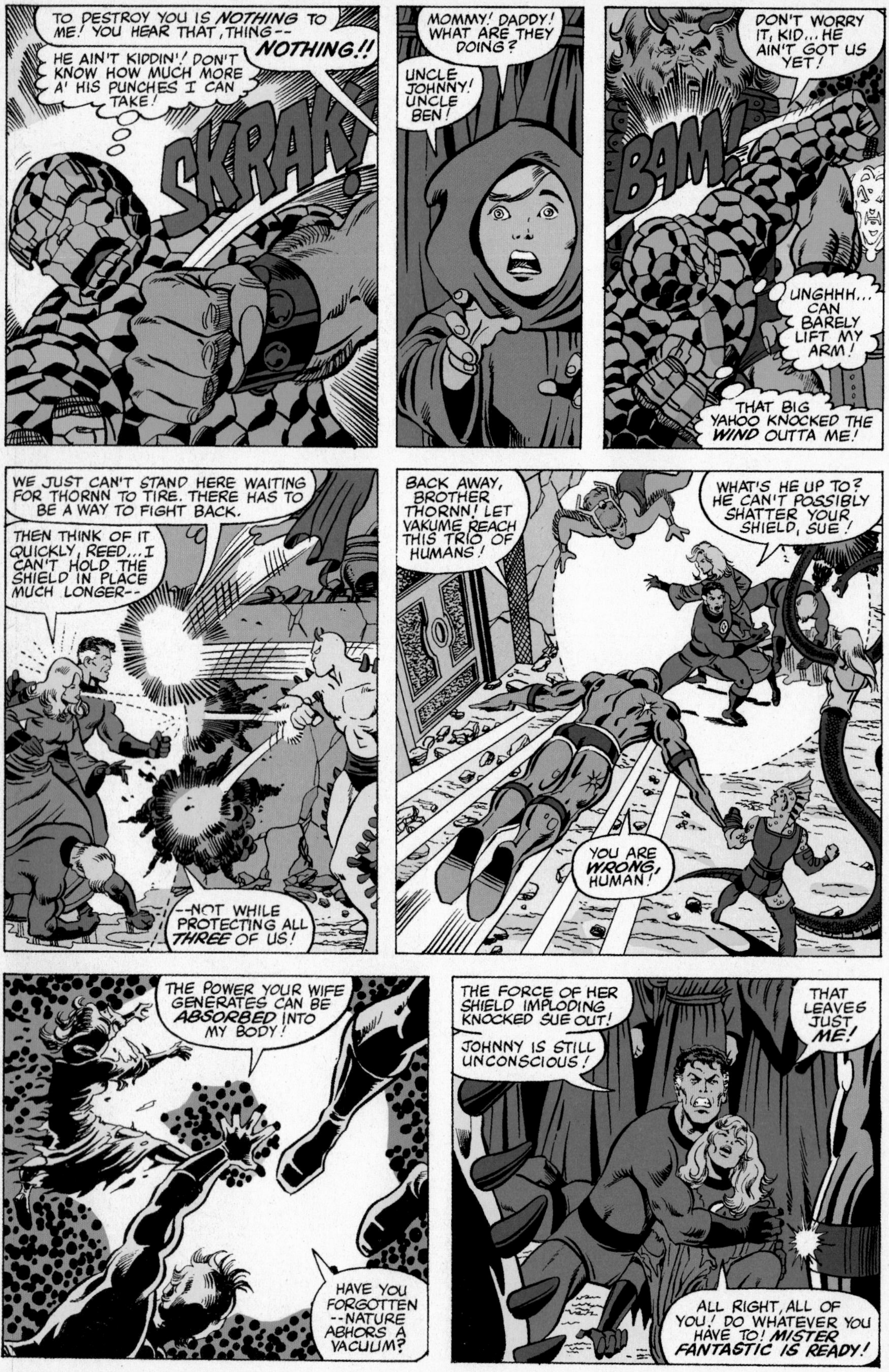
TO DESTROY YOU IS NOTHING TO ME! YOU HEAR THAT, THING-- NOTHING!!
HE AIN'T KIDDIN'! DON'T KNOW HOW MUCH MORE A' HIS PUNCHES I CAN TAKE!
SKRAK!
MOMMY! DADDY! WHAT ARE THEY DOING?
UNCLE JOHNNY! UNCLE BEN!
DON'T WORRY IT, KID... HE AIN'T GOT US YET!
BAM!
UNGHHH... CAN BARELY LIFT MY ARM!
THAT BIG YAHOO KNOCKED THE WIND OUTTA ME!
WE JUST CAN'T STAND HERE WAITING FOR THORNN TO TIRE. THERE HAS TO BE A WAY TO FIGHT BACK.
THEN THINK OF IT QUICKLY, REED... I CAN'T HOLD THE SHIELD IN PLACE MUCH LONGER--
--NOT WHILE PROTECTING ALL THREE OF US!
BACK AWAY, BROTHER THORNN! LET VAKUME REACH THIS TRIO OF HUMANS!
WHAT'S HE UP TO? HE CAN'T POSSIBLY SHATTER YOUR SHIELD, SUE!
YOU ARE WRONG, HUMAN!
THE POWER YOUR WIFE GENERATES CAN BE ABSORBED INTO MY BODY!
HAVE YOU FORGOTTEN --NATURE ABHORS A VACUUM?
THE FORCE OF HER SHIELD IMPLODING KNOCKED SUE OUT!
JOHNNY IS STILL UNCONSCIOUS!
THAT LEAVES JUST ME!
ALL RIGHT, ALL OF YOU! DO WHATEVER YOU HAVE TO! MISTER FANTASTIC IS READY!

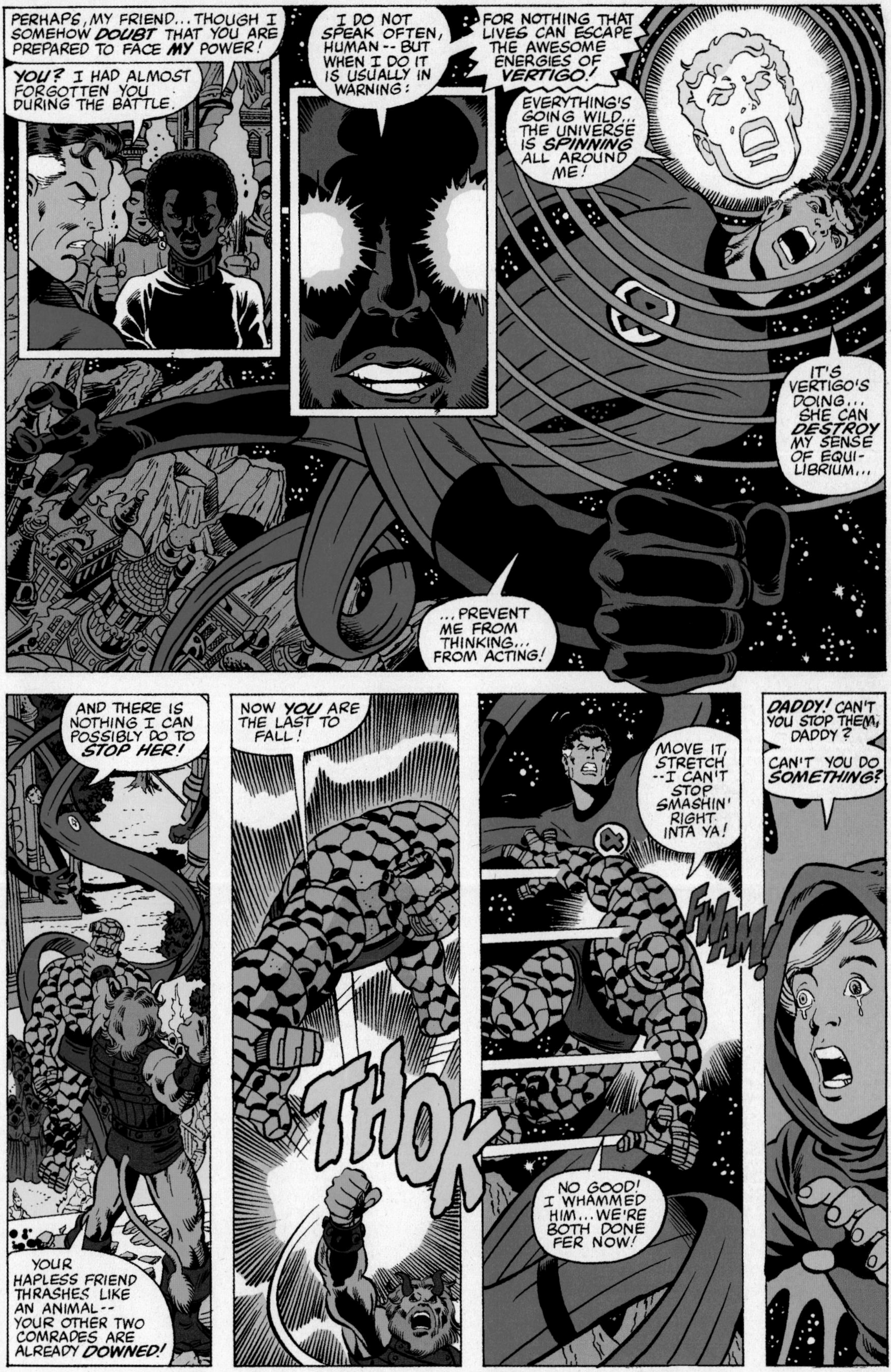
PERHAPS, MY FRIEND... THOUGH I SOMEHOW DOUBT THAT YOU ARE PREPARED TO FACE MY POWER!
YOU? I HAD ALMOST FORGOTTEN YOU DURING THE BATTLE.
I DO NOT SPEAK OFTEN, HUMAN -- BUT WHEN I DO IT IS USUALLY IN WARNING:
FOR NOTHING THAT LIVES CAN ESCAPE THE AWESOME ENERGIES OF VERTIGO!
EVERYTHING'S GOING WILD... THE UNIVERSE IS SPINNING ALL AROUND ME!
IT'S VERTIGO'S DOING... SHE CAN DESTROY MY SENSE OF EQUILIBRIUM...
...PREVENT ME FROM THINKING... FROM ACTING!
AND THERE IS NOTHING I CAN POSSIBLY DO TO STOP HER!
YOUR HAPLESS FRIEND THRASHES LIKE AN ANIMAL -- YOUR OTHER TWO COMRADES ARE ALREADY DOWNED!
NOW YOU ARE THE LAST TO FALL!
THOK
MOVE IT, STRETCH --I CAN'T STOP SMASHIN' RIGHT INTA YA!
FWAM!
NO GOOD! I WHAMMED HIM... WE'RE BOTH DONE FER NOW!
DADDY! CAN'T YOU STOP THEM, DADDY?
CAN'T YOU DO SOMETHING?

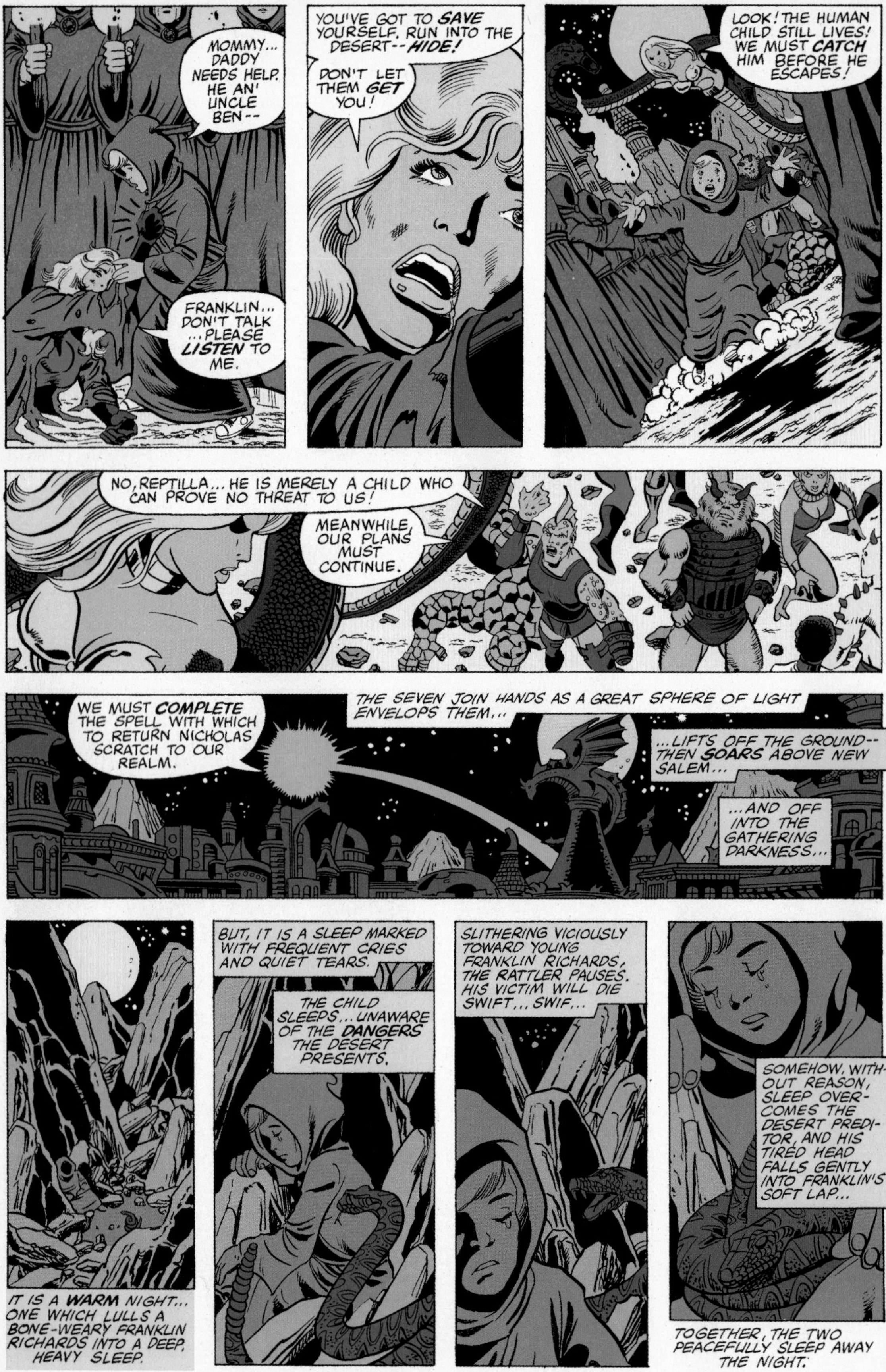
MOMMY... DADDY NEEDS HELP. HE AN' UNCLE BEN--
FRANKLIN... DON'T TALK ...PLEASE LISTEN TO ME.
YOU'VE GOT TO SAVE YOURSELF. RUN INTO THE DESERT--HIDE!
DON'T LET THEM GET YOU!
LOOK! THE HUMAN CHILD STILL LIVES! WE MUST CATCH HIM BEFORE HE ESCAPES!
NO, REPTILLA... HE IS MERELY A CHILD WHO CAN PROVE NO THREAT TO US!
MEANWHILE, OUR PLANS MUST CONTINUE.
WE MUST COMPLETE THE SPELL WITH WHICH TO RETURN NICHOLAS SCRATCH TO OUR REALM.
THE SEVEN JOIN HANDS AS A GREAT SPHERE OF LIGHT ENVELOPS THEM...
...LIFTS OFF THE GROUND--THEN SOARS ABOVE NEW SALEM...
...AND OFF INTO THE GATHERING DARKNESS...
IT IS A WARM NIGHT... ONE WHICH LULLS A BONE-WEARY FRANKLIN RICHARDS INTO A DEEP, HEAVY SLEEP.
BUT, IT IS A SLEEP MARKED WITH FREQUENT CRIES AND QUIET TEARS.
THE CHILD SLEEPS... UNAWARE OF THE DANGERS THE DESERT PRESENTS.
SLITHERING VICIOUSLY TOWARD YOUNG FRANKLIN RICHARDS, THE RATTLER PAUSES. HIS VICTIM WILL DIE SWIFT... SWIF...
SOMEHOW, WITHOUT REASON, SLEEP OVERCOMES THE DESERT PREDITOR, AND HIS TIRED HEAD FALLS GENTLY INTO FRANKLIN'S SOFT LAP...
TOGETHER, THE TWO PEACEFULLY SLEEP AWAY THE NIGHT.

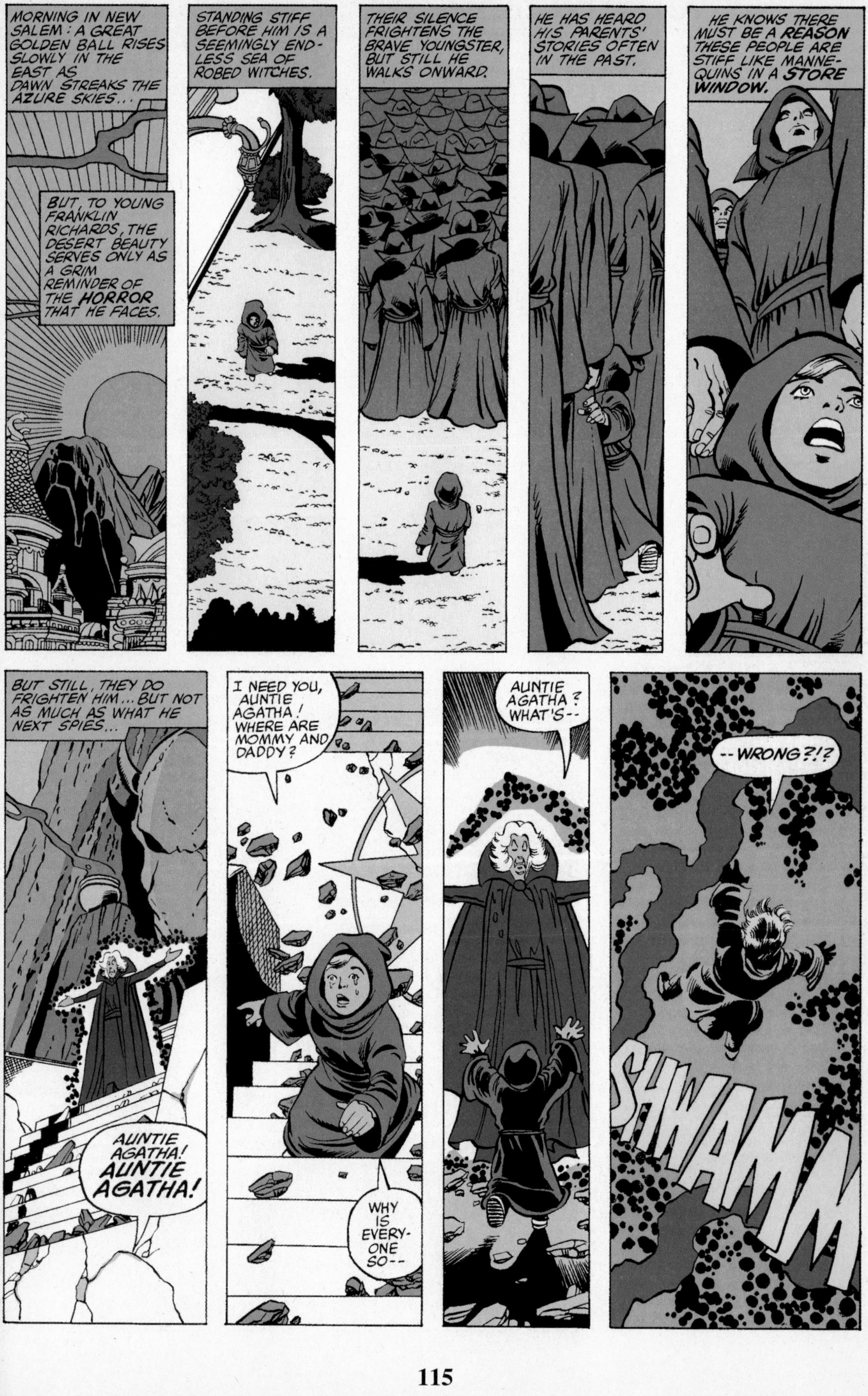
MORNING IN NEW SALEM: A GREAT GOLDEN BALL RISES SLOWLY IN THE EAST AS DAWN STREAKS THE AZURE SKIES...
BUT, TO YOUNG FRANKLIN RICHARDS, THE DESERT BEAUTY SERVES ONLY AS A GRIM REMINDER OF THE HORROR THAT HE FACES.
STANDING STIFF BEFORE HIM IS A SEEMINGLY ENDLESS SEA OF ROBED WITCHES.
THEIR SILENCE FRIGHTENS THE BRAVE YOUNGSTER, BUT STILL HE WALKS ONWARD.
HE HAS HEARD HIS PARENTS' STORIES OFTEN IN THE PAST.
HE KNOWS THERE MUST BE A REASON THESE PEOPLE ARE STIFF LIKE MANNEQUINS IN A STORE WINDOW.
BUT STILL, THEY DO FRIGHTEN HIM... BUT NOT AS MUCH AS WHAT HE NEXT SPIES...
AUNTIE AGATHA! AUNTIE AGATHA!
I NEED YOU, AUNTIE AGATHA! WHERE ARE MOMMY AND DADDY?
WHY IS EVERYONE SO--
AUNTIE AGATHA? WHAT'S--
--WRONG?!?
SHWAMM

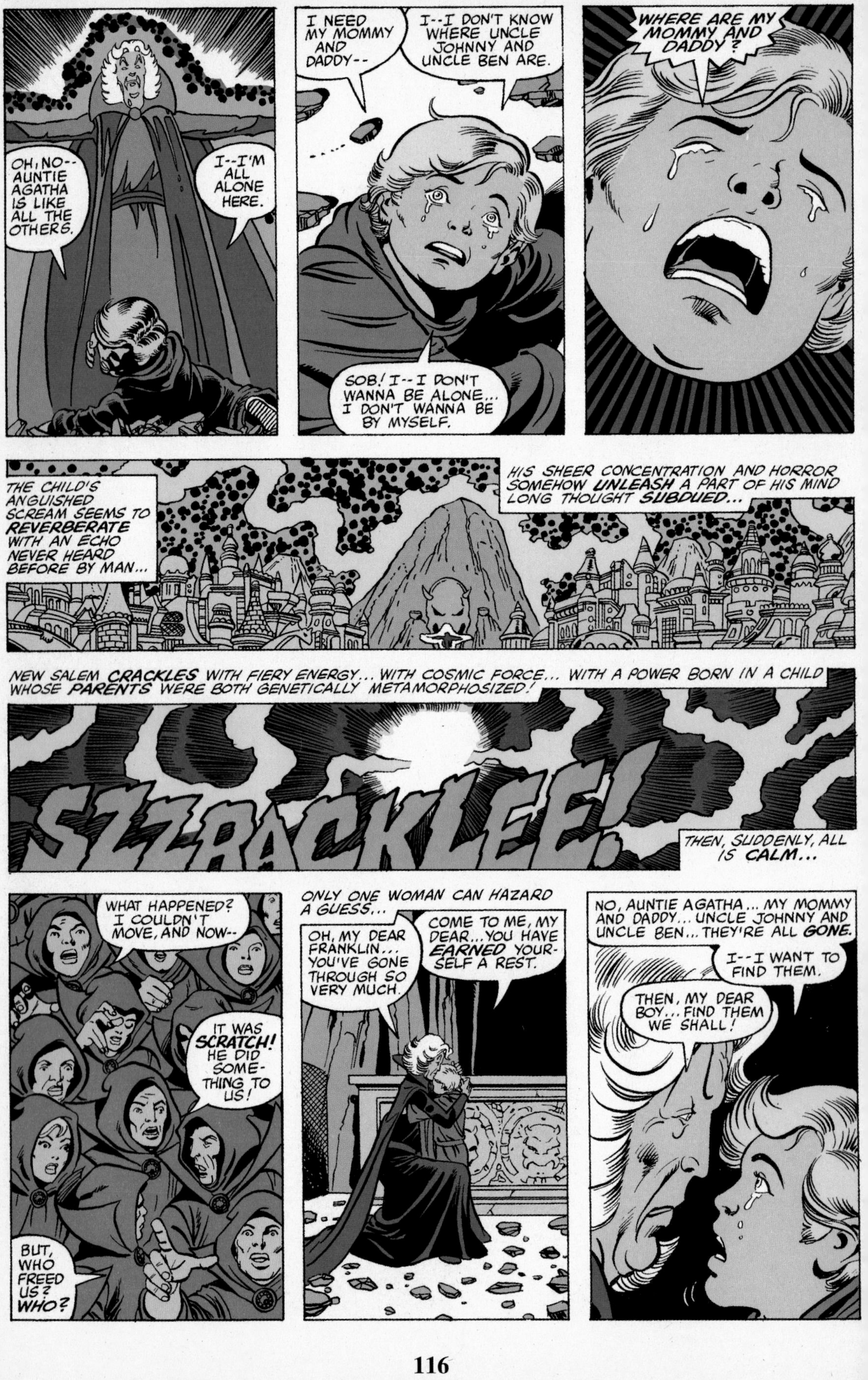
OH, NO--
AUNTIE AGATHA IS LIKE ALL THE OTHERS.
I--I'M ALL ALONE HERE.
I NEED MY MOMMY AND DADDY--
I--I DON'T KNOW WHERE UNCLE JOHNNY AND UNCLE BEN ARE.
SOB! I--I DON'T WANNA BE ALONE... I DON'T WANNA BE BY MYSELF.
WHERE ARE MY MOMMY AND DADDY?
THE CHILD'S ANGUISHED SCREAM SEEMS TO REVERBERATE WITH AN ECHO NEVER HEARD BEFORE BY MAN...
HIS SHEER CONCENTRATION AND HORROR SOMEHOW UNLEASH A PART OF HIS MIND LONG THOUGHT SUBDUED...
NEW SALEM CRACKLES WITH FIERY ENERGY... WITH COSMIC FORCE... WITH A POWER BORN IN A CHILD WHOSE PARENTS WERE BOTH GENETICALLY METAMORPHOSIZED!
SZZRACKLEE!
THEN, SUDDENLY, ALL IS CALM...
WHAT HAPPENED? I COULDN'T MOVE, AND NOW--
IT WAS SCRATCH! HE DID SOMETHING TO US!
BUT, WHO FREED US? WHO?
ONLY ONE WOMAN CAN HAZARD A GUESS...
OH, MY DEAR FRANKLIN... YOU'VE GONE THROUGH SO VERY MUCH.
COME TO ME, MY DEAR... YOU HAVE EARNED YOURSELF A REST.
NO, AUNTIE AGATHA... MY MOMMY AND DADDY... UNCLE JOHNNY AND UNCLE BEN... THEY'RE ALL GONE.
I--I WANT TO FIND THEM.
THEN, MY DEAR BOY... FIND THEM WE SHALL!

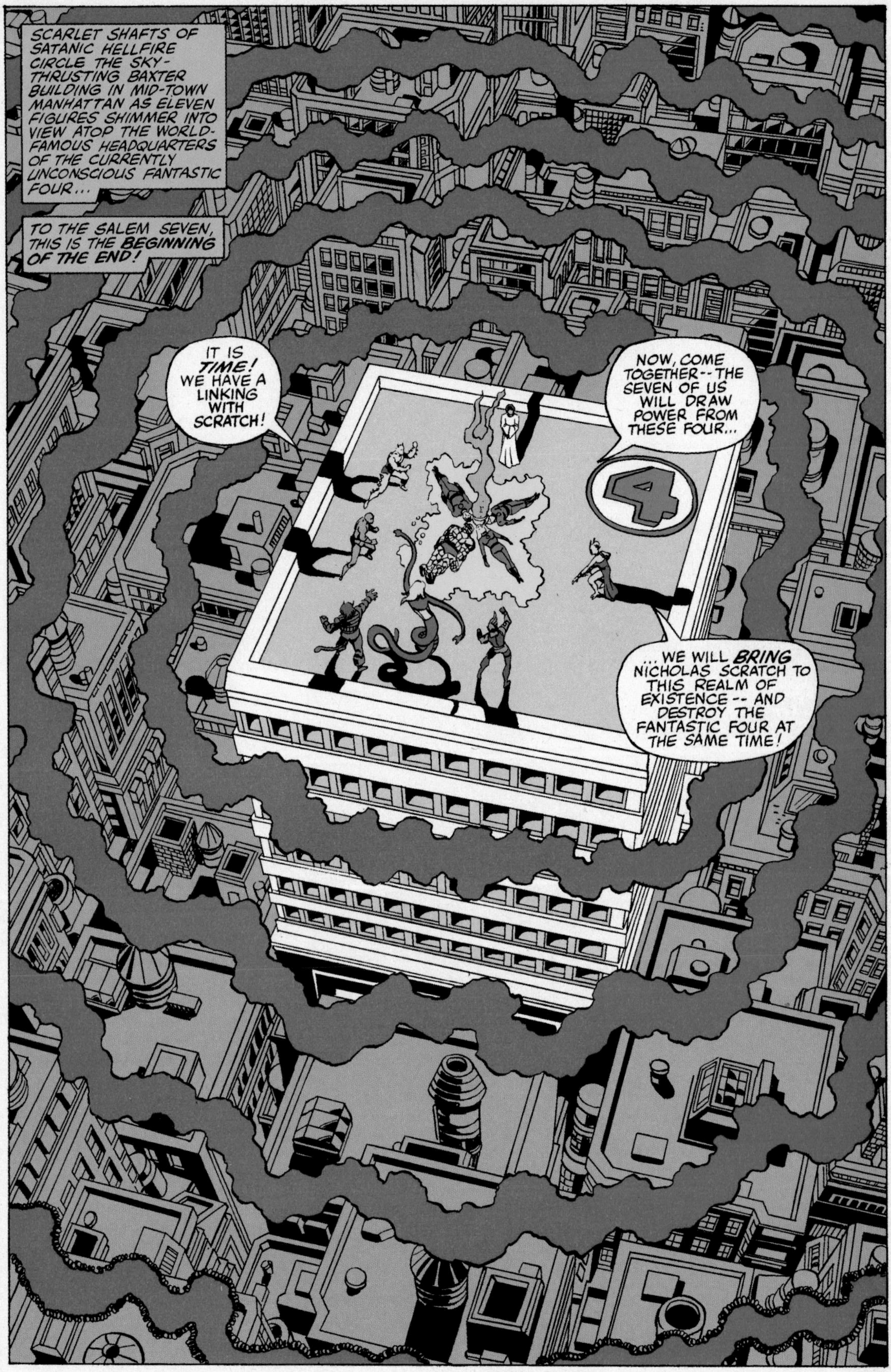
SCARLET SHAFTS OF SATANIC HELLFIRE CIRCLE THE SKY-THRUSTING BAXTER BUILDING IN MID-TOWN MANHATTAN AS ELEVEN FIGURES SHIMMER INTO VIEW ATOP THE WORLD-FAMOUS HEADQUARTERS OF THE CURRENTLY UNCONSCIOUS FANTASTIC FOUR...
TO THE SALEM SEVEN, THIS IS THE BEGINNING OF THE END!
IT IS TIME! WE HAVE A LINKING WITH SCRATCH!
NOW, COME TOGETHER--THE SEVEN OF US WILL DRAW POWER FROM THESE FOUR...
4
...WE WILL BRING NICHOLAS SCRATCH TO THIS REALM OF EXISTENCE -- AND DESTROY THE FANTASTIC FOUR AT THE SAME TIME!

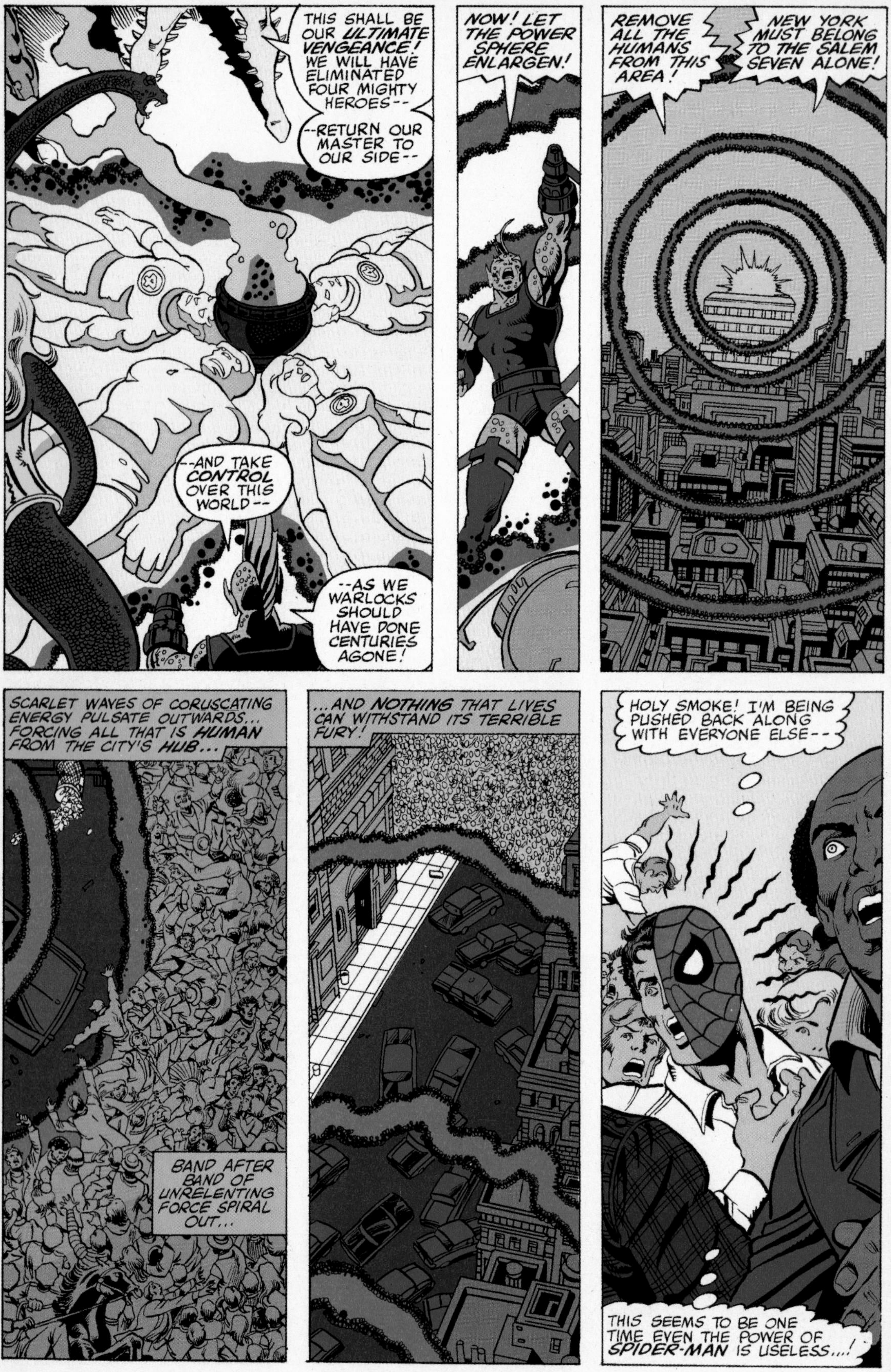
THIS SHALL BE OUR ULTIMATE VENGEANCE! WE WILL HAVE ELIMINATED FOUR MIGHTY HEROES--
--RETURN OUR MASTER TO OUR SIDE--
--AND TAKE CONTROL OVER THIS WORLD--
--AS WE WARLOCKS SHOULD HAVE DONE CENTURIES AGONE!
NOW! LET THE POWER SPHERE ENLARGEN!
REMOVE ALL THE HUMANS FROM THIS AREA!
NEW YORK MUST BELONG TO THE SALEM SEVEN ALONE!
SCARLET WAVES OF CORUSCATING ENERGY PULSATE OUTWARDS... FORCING ALL THAT IS HUMAN FROM THE CITY'S HUB...
BAND AFTER BAND OF UNRELENTING FORCE SPIRAL OUT...
...AND NOTHING THAT LIVES CAN WITHSTAND ITS TERRIBLE FURY!
HOLY SMOKE! I'M BEING PUSHED BACK ALONG WITH EVERYONE ELSE--
THIS SEEMS TO BE ONE TIME EVEN THE POWER OF SPIDER-MAN IS USELESS...!

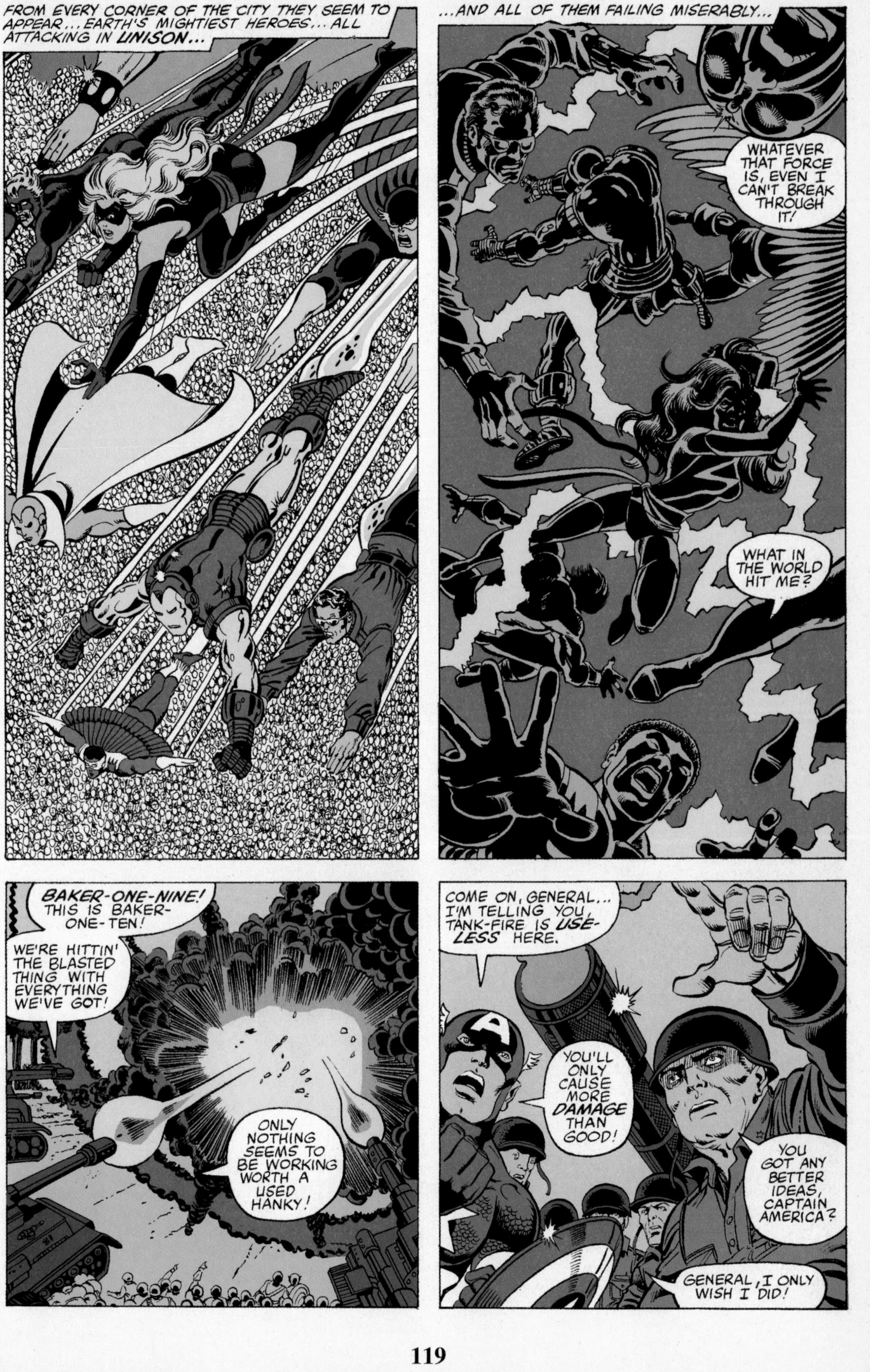
FROM EVERY CORNER OF THE CITY THEY SEEM TO APPEAR... EARTH'S MIGHTIEST HEROES... ALL ATTACKING IN UNISON...
...AND ALL OF THEM FAILING MISERABLY...
WHATEVER THAT FORCE IS, EVEN I CAN'T BREAK THROUGH IT!
WHAT IN THE WORLD HIT ME?
BAKER-ONE-NINE! THIS IS BAKER-ONE-TEN!
WE'RE HITTIN' THE BLASTED THING WITH EVERYTHING WE'VE GOT!
ONLY NOTHING SEEMS TO BE WORKING WORTH A USED HANKY!
COME ON, GENERAL... I'M TELLING YOU, TANK-FIRE IS USELESS HERE.
YOU'LL ONLY CAUSE MORE DAMAGE THAN GOOD!
YOU GOT ANY BETTER IDEAS, CAPTAIN AMERICA?
GENERAL, I ONLY WISH I DID!

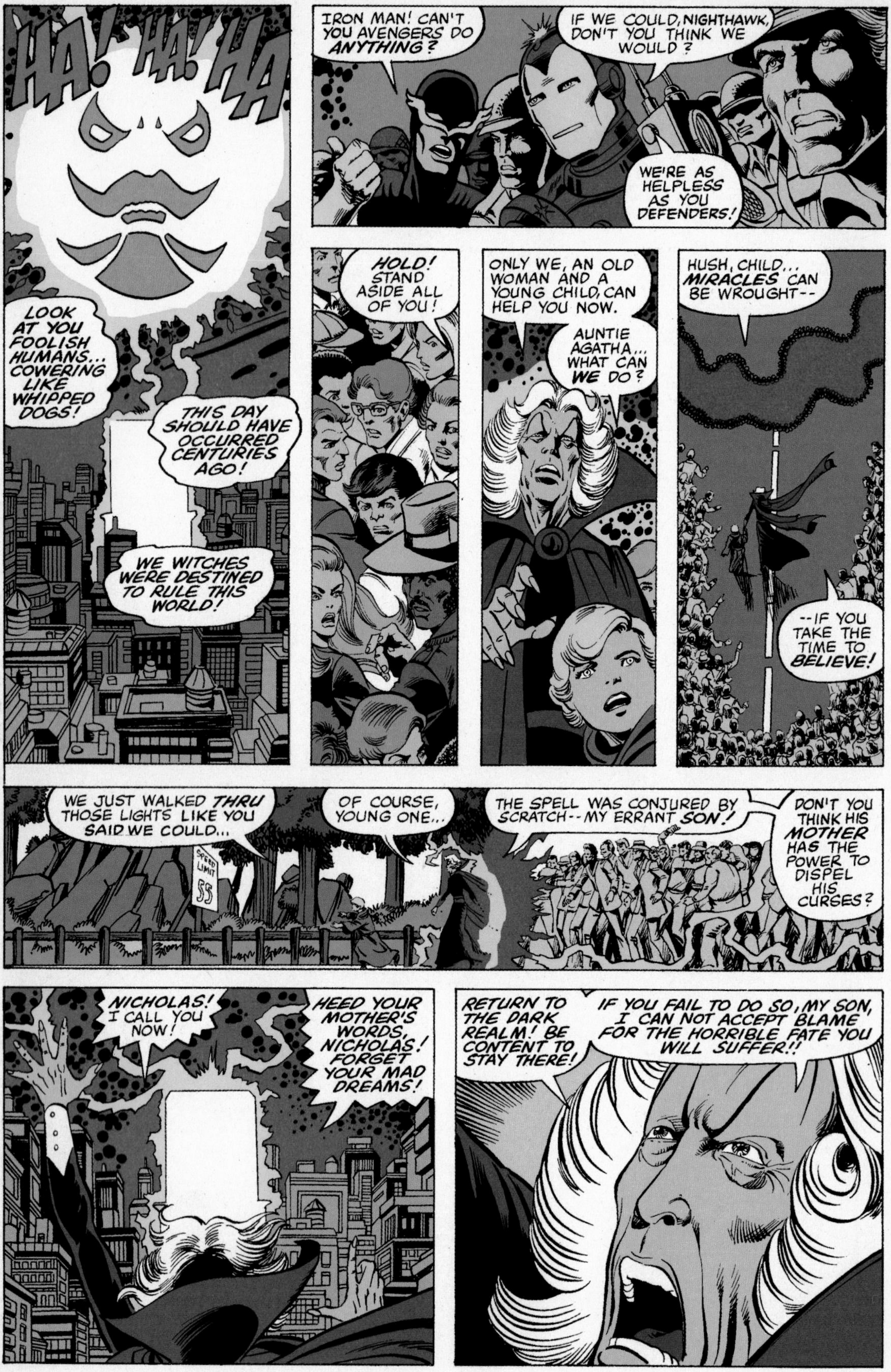
HA! HA! HA!
LOOK AT YOU FOOLISH HUMANS... COWERING LIKE WHIPPED DOGS!
THIS DAY SHOULD HAVE OCCURRED CENTURIES AGO!
WE WITCHES WERE DESTINED TO RULE THIS WORLD!
IRON MAN! CAN'T YOU AVENGERS DO ANYTHING?
IF WE COULD, NIGHTHAWK, DON'T YOU THINK WE WOULD?
WE'RE AS HELPLESS AS YOU DEFENDERS!
HOLD! STAND ASIDE ALL OF YOU!
ONLY WE, AN OLD WOMAN AND A YOUNG CHILD, CAN HELP YOU NOW.
AUNTIE AGATHA... WHAT CAN WE DO?
HUSH, CHILD... MIRACLES CAN BE WROUGHT--
--IF YOU TAKE THE TIME TO BELIEVE!
WE JUST WALKED THRU THOSE LIGHTS LIKE YOU SAID WE COULD...
SPEED LIMIT 55
OF COURSE, YOUNG ONE...
THE SPELL WAS CONJURED BY SCRATCH--MY ERRANT SON!
DON'T YOU THINK HIS MOTHER HAS THE POWER TO DISPEL HIS CURSES?
NICHOLAS! I CALL YOU NOW!
HEED YOUR MOTHER'S WORDS, NICHOLAS! FORGET YOUR MAD DREAMS!
RETURN TO THE DARK REALM! BE CONTENT TO STAY THERE!
IF YOU FAIL TO DO SO, MY SON, I CAN NOT ACCEPT BLAME FOR THE HORRIBLE FATE YOU WILL SUFFER!!

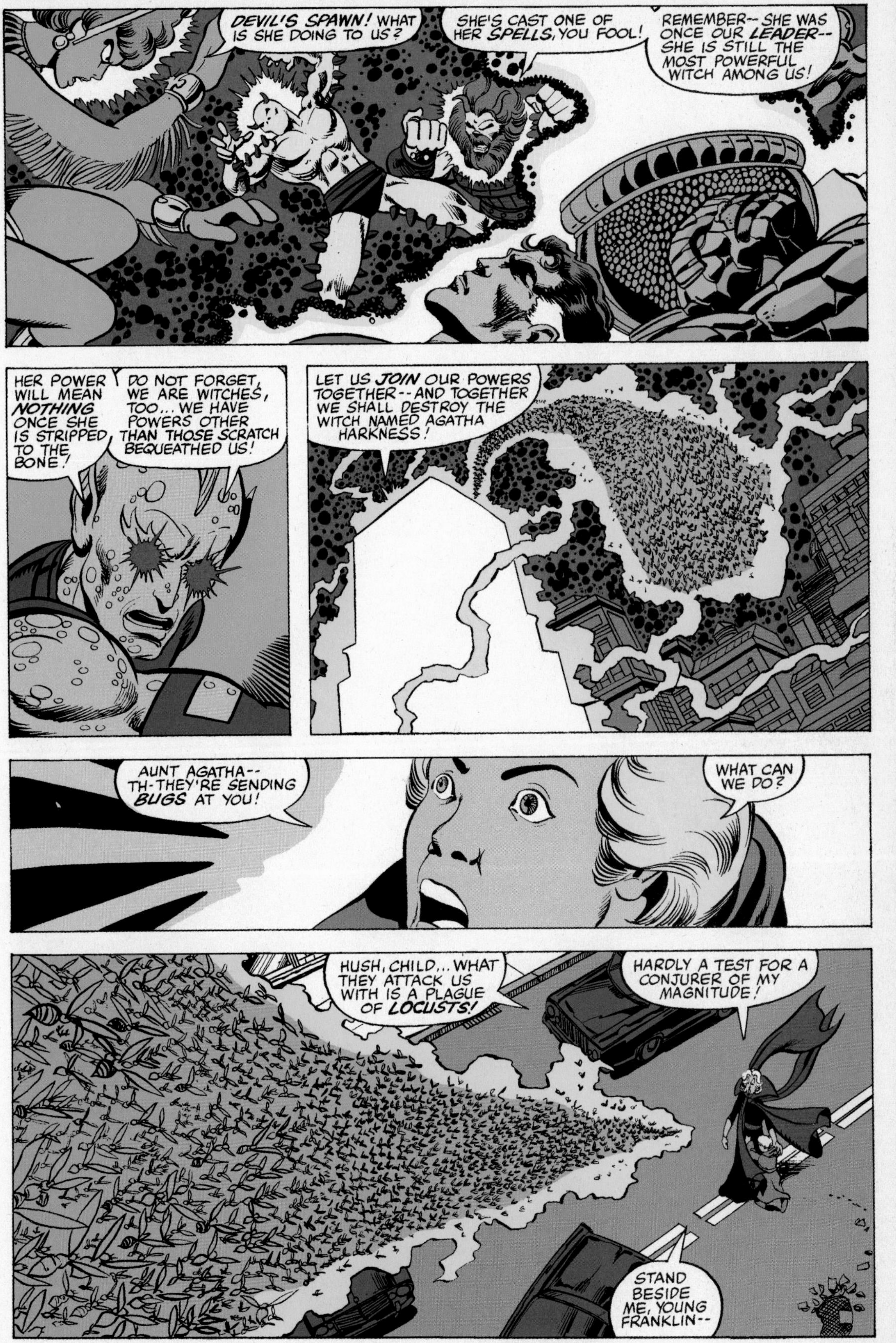
DEVIL'S SPAWN! WHAT IS SHE DOING TO US?
SHE'S CAST ONE OF HER SPELLS, YOU FOOL!
REMEMBER-- SHE WAS ONCE OUR LEADER-- SHE IS STILL THE MOST POWERFUL WITCH AMONG US!
HER POWER WILL MEAN NOTHING ONCE SHE IS STRIPPED TO THE BONE!
DO NOT FORGET, WE ARE WITCHES, TOO... WE HAVE POWERS OTHER THAN THOSE SCRATCH BEQUEATHED US!
LET US JOIN OUR POWERS TOGETHER-- AND TOGETHER WE SHALL DESTROY THE WITCH NAMED AGATHA HARKNESS!
AUNT AGATHA-- TH-THEY'RE SENDING BUGS AT YOU!
WHAT CAN WE DO?
HUSH, CHILD... WHAT THEY ATTACK US WITH IS A PLAGUE OF LOCUSTS!
HARDLY A TEST FOR A CONJURER OF MY MAGNITUDE!
STAND BESIDE ME, YOUNG FRANKLIN--

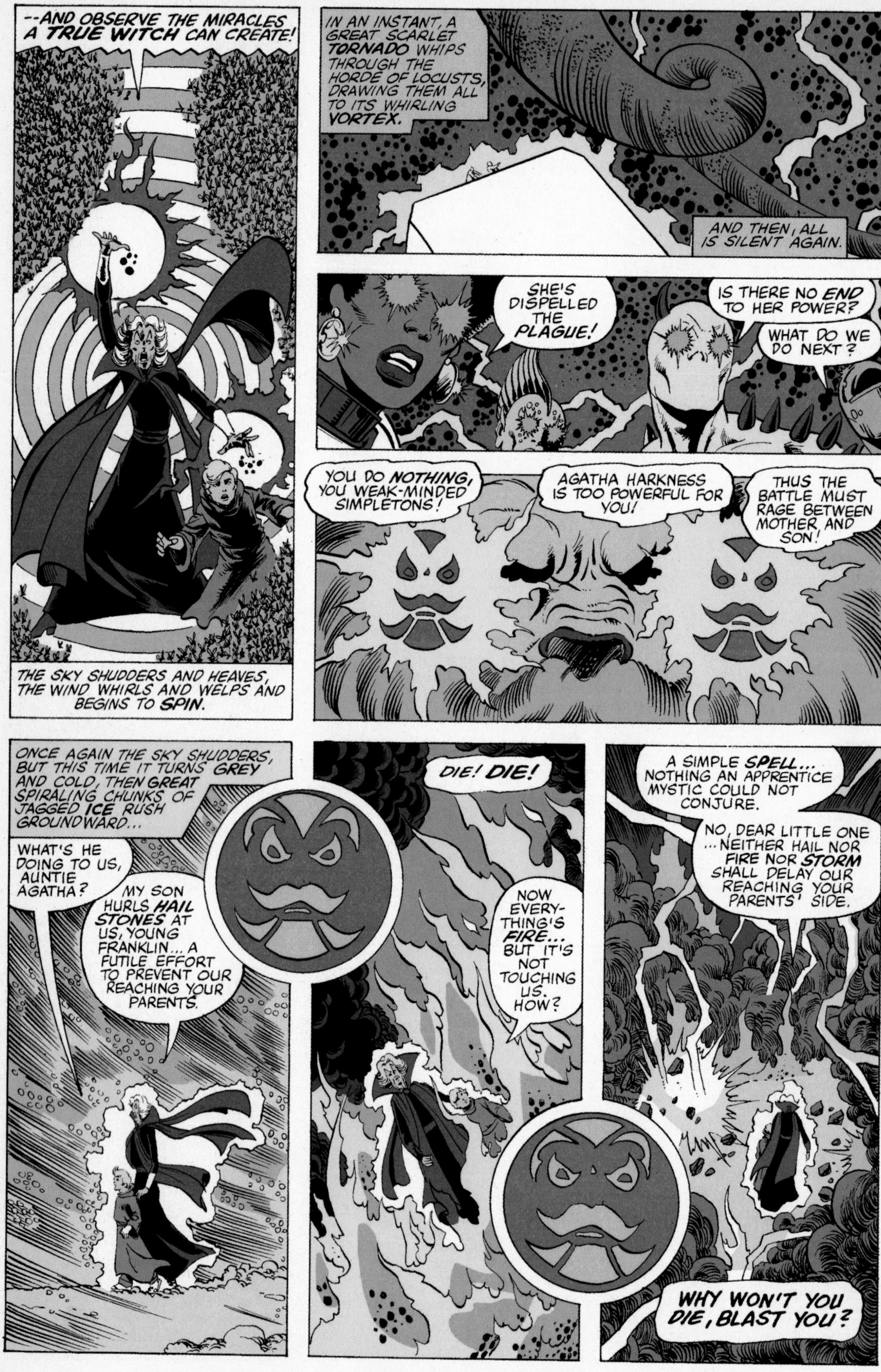
--AND OBSERVE THE MIRACLES A TRUE WITCH CAN CREATE!
THE SKY SHUDDERS AND HEAVES, THE WIND WHIRLS AND WELPS AND BEGINS TO SPIN.
IN AN INSTANT, A GREAT SCARLET TORNADO WHIPS THROUGH THE HORDE OF LOCUSTS, DRAWING THEM ALL TO ITS WHIRLING VORTEX.
AND THEN, ALL IS SILENT AGAIN.
SHE'S DISPELLED THE PLAGUE!
IS THERE NO END TO HER POWER?
WHAT DO WE DO NEXT?
YOU DO NOTHING, YOU WEAK-MINDED SIMPLETONS!
AGATHA HARKNESS IS TOO POWERFUL FOR YOU!
THUS THE BATTLE MUST RAGE BETWEEN MOTHER AND SON!
ONCE AGAIN THE SKY SHUDDERS, BUT THIS TIME IT TURNS GREY AND COLD, THEN GREAT SPIRALING CHUNKS OF JAGGED ICE RUSH GROUNDWARD...
WHAT'S HE DOING TO US, AUNTIE AGATHA?
MY SON HURLS HAIL STONES AT US, YOUNG FRANKLIN... A FUTILE EFFORT TO PREVENT OUR REACHING YOUR PARENTS.
DIE! DIE!
NOW EVERYTHING'S FIRE... BUT IT'S NOT TOUCHING US. HOW?
A SIMPLE SPELL... NOTHING AN APPRENTICE MYSTIC COULD NOT CONJURE.
NO, DEAR LITTLE ONE ...NEITHER HAIL NOR FIRE NOR STORM SHALL DELAY OUR REACHING YOUR PARENTS' SIDE.
WHY WON'T YOU DIE, BLAST YOU?

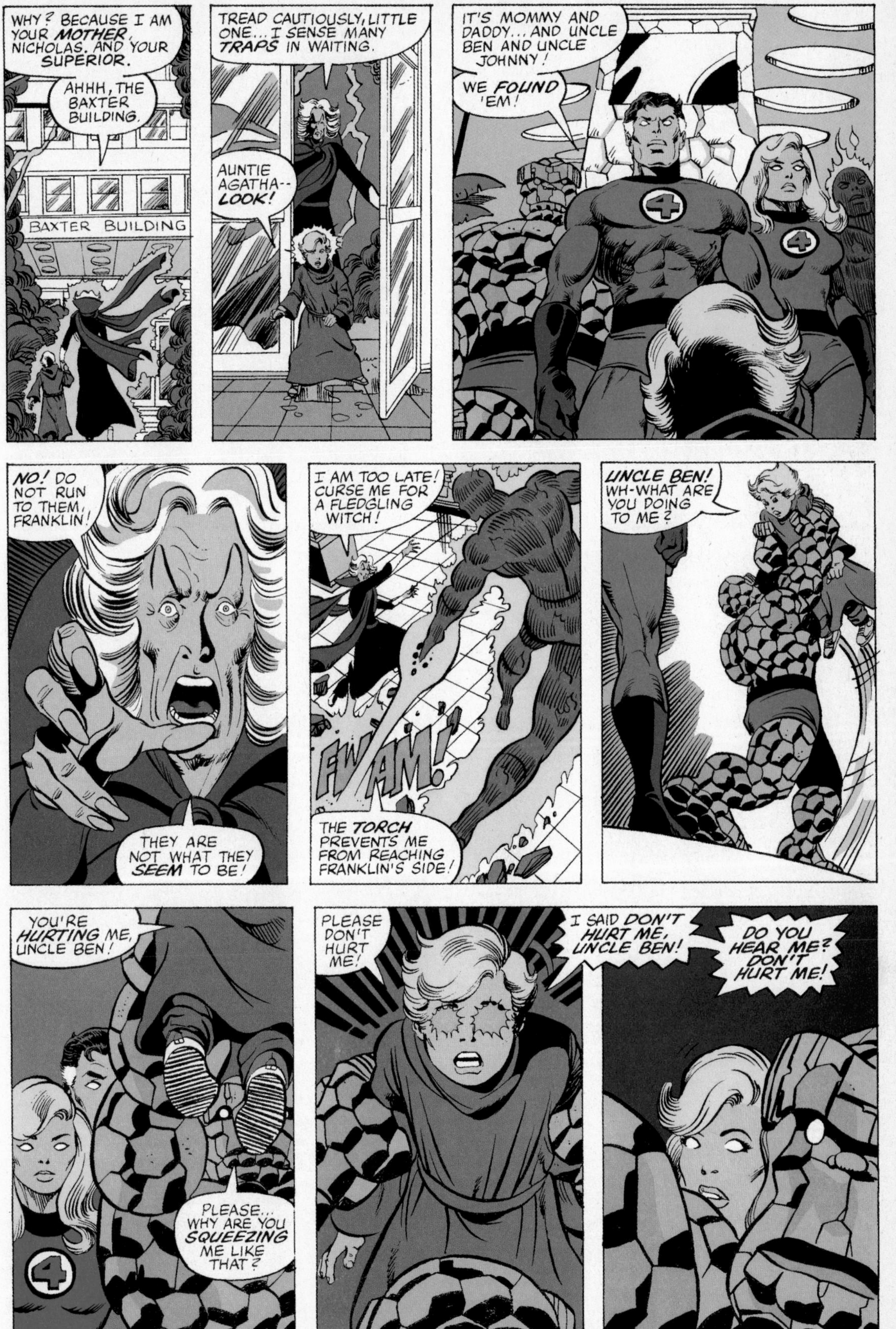
WHY? BECAUSE I AM YOUR MOTHER, NICHOLAS. AND YOUR SUPERIOR.
AHHH, THE BAXTER BUILDING.
BAXTER BUILDING
TREAD CAUTIOUSLY, LITTLE ONE... I SENSE MANY TRAPS IN WAITING.
AUNTIE AGATHA-- LOOK!
IT'S MOMMY AND DADDY... AND UNCLE BEN AND UNCLE JOHNNY!
WE FOUND 'EM!
NO! DO NOT RUN TO THEM, FRANKLIN!
THEY ARE NOT WHAT THEY SEEM TO BE!
I AM TOO LATE! CURSE ME FOR A FLEDGLING WITCH!
FWAM!
THE TORCH PREVENTS ME FROM REACHING FRANKLIN'S SIDE!
UNCLE BEN! WH-WHAT ARE YOU DOING TO ME?
YOU'RE HURTING ME, UNCLE BEN!
PLEASE... WHY ARE YOU SQUEEZING ME LIKE THAT?
PLEASE DON'T HURT ME!
I SAID DON'T HURT ME, UNCLE BEN!
DO YOU HEAR ME? DON'T HURT ME!

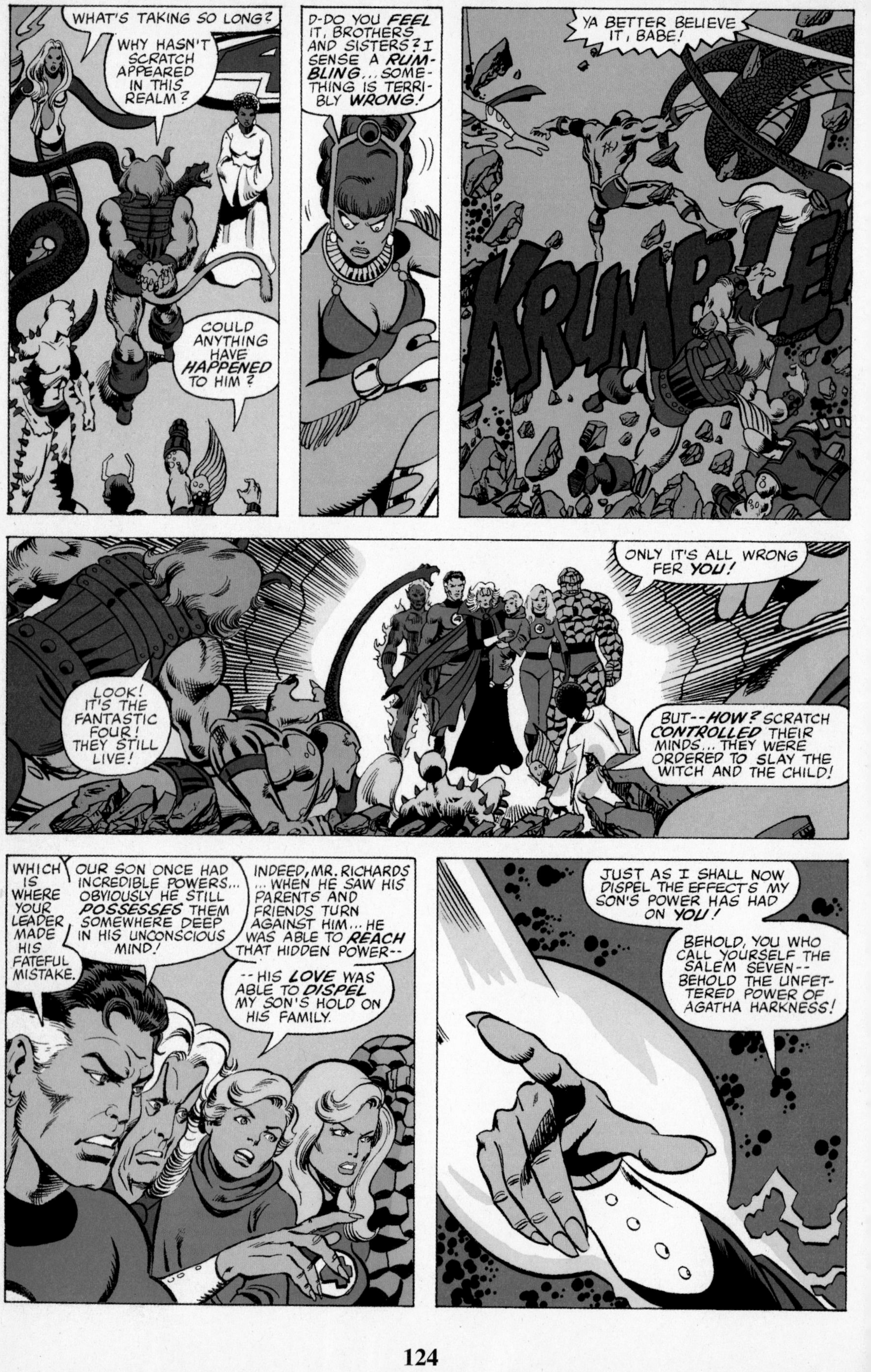
WHAT'S TAKING SO LONG?
WHY HASN'T SCRATCH APPEARED IN THIS REALM?
COULD ANYTHING HAVE HAPPENED TO HIM?
D-DO YOU FEEL IT, BROTHERS AND SISTERS? I SENSE A RUMBLING... SOMETHING IS TERRIBLY WRONG!
YA BETTER BELIEVE IT, BABE!
KRUMBLE!
ONLY IT'S ALL WRONG FER YOU!
LOOK! IT'S THE FANTASTIC FOUR! THEY STILL LIVE!
BUT--HOW? SCRATCH CONTROLLED THEIR MINDS... THEY WERE ORDERED TO SLAY THE WITCH AND THE CHILD!
WHICH IS WHERE YOUR LEADER MADE HIS FATEFUL MISTAKE.
OUR SON ONCE HAD INCREDIBLE POWERS... OBVIOUSLY HE STILL POSSESSES THEM SOMEWHERE DEEP IN HIS UNCONSCIOUS MIND!
INDEED, MR. RICHARDS ... WHEN HE SAW HIS PARENTS AND FRIENDS TURN AGAINST HIM... HE WAS ABLE TO REACH THAT HIDDEN POWER--
--HIS LOVE WAS ABLE TO DISPEL MY SON'S HOLD ON HIS FAMILY.
JUST AS I SHALL NOW DISPEL THE EFFECTS MY SON'S POWER HAS HAD ON YOU!
BEHOLD, YOU WHO CALL YOURSELF THE SALEM SEVEN--BEHOLD THE UNFETTERED POWER OF AGATHA HARKNESS!

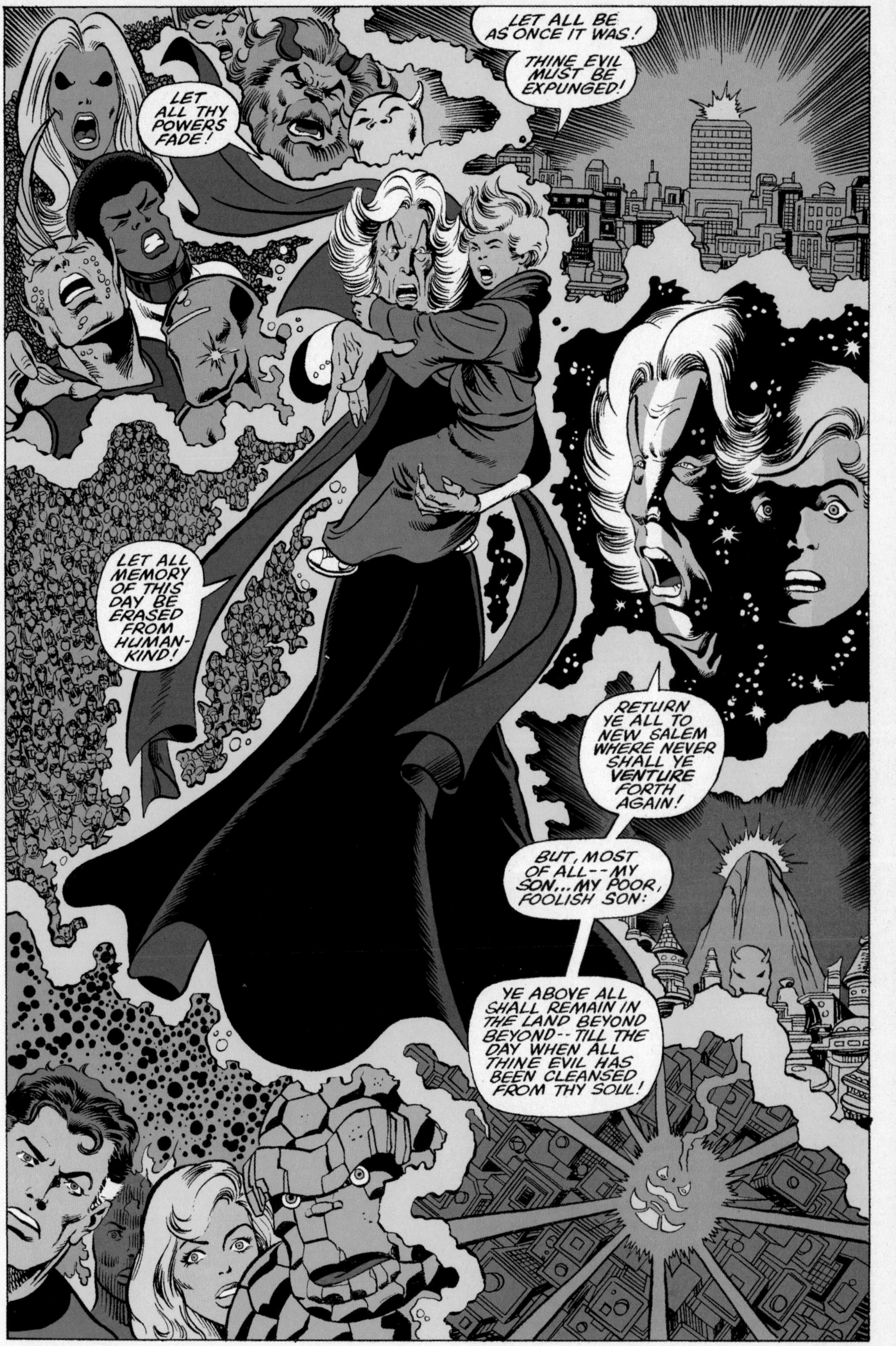
LET ALL BE AS ONCE IT WAS!
THINE EVIL MUST BE EXPUNGED!
LET ALL THY POWERS FADE!
LET ALL MEMORY OF THIS DAY BE ERASED FROM HUMAN-KIND!
RETURN YE ALL TO NEW SALEM WHERE NEVER SHALL YE VENTURE FORTH AGAIN!
BUT, MOST OF ALL--MY SON...MY POOR, FOOLISH SON:
YE ABOVE ALL SHALL REMAIN IN THE LAND BEYOND BEYOND--TILL THE DAY WHEN ALL THINE EVIL HAS BEEN CLEANSED FROM THY SOUL!

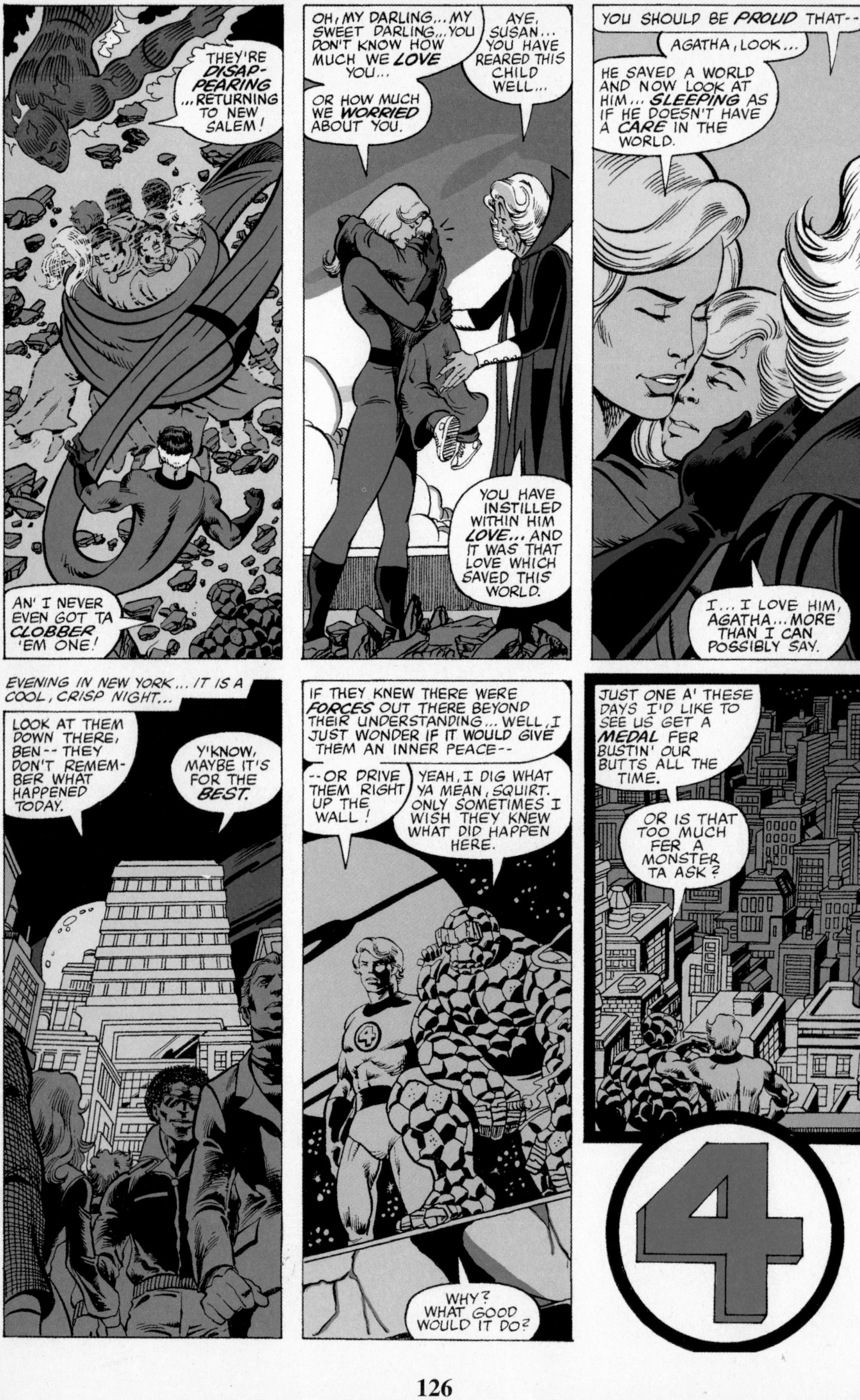
THEY'RE DISAPPEARING ...RETURNING TO NEW SALEM!
AN' I NEVER EVEN GOT TA CLOBBER 'EM ONE!
OH, MY DARLING... MY SWEET DARLING... YOU DON'T KNOW HOW MUCH WE LOVE YOU...
OR HOW MUCH WE WORRIED ABOUT YOU.
AYE, SUSAN... YOU HAVE REARED THIS CHILD WELL...
YOU HAVE INSTILLED WITHIN HIM LOVE... AND IT WAS THAT LOVE WHICH SAVED THIS WORLD.
YOU SHOULD BE PROUD THAT--
AGATHA, LOOK...
HE SAVED A WORLD AND NOW LOOK AT HIM... SLEEPING AS IF HE DOESN'T HAVE A CARE IN THE WORLD.
I... I LOVE HIM, AGATHA... MORE THAN I CAN POSSIBLY SAY.
EVENING IN NEW YORK... IT IS A COOL, CRISP NIGHT...
LOOK AT THEM DOWN THERE, BEN -- THEY DON'T REMEMBER WHAT HAPPENED TODAY.
Y'KNOW, MAYBE IT'S FOR THE BEST.
IF THEY KNEW THERE WERE FORCES OUT THERE BEYOND THEIR UNDERSTANDING... WELL, I JUST WONDER IF IT WOULD GIVE THEM AN INNER PEACE--
--OR DRIVE THEM RIGHT UP THE WALL!
YEAH, I DIG WHAT YA MEAN, SQUIRT. ONLY SOMETIMES I WISH THEY KNEW WHAT DID HAPPEN HERE.
WHY? WHAT GOOD WOULD IT DO?
JUST ONE A' THESE DAYS I'D LIKE TO SEE US GET A MEDAL FER BUSTIN' OUR BUTTS ALL THE TIME.
OR IS THAT TOO MUCH FER A MONSTER TA ASK?
4

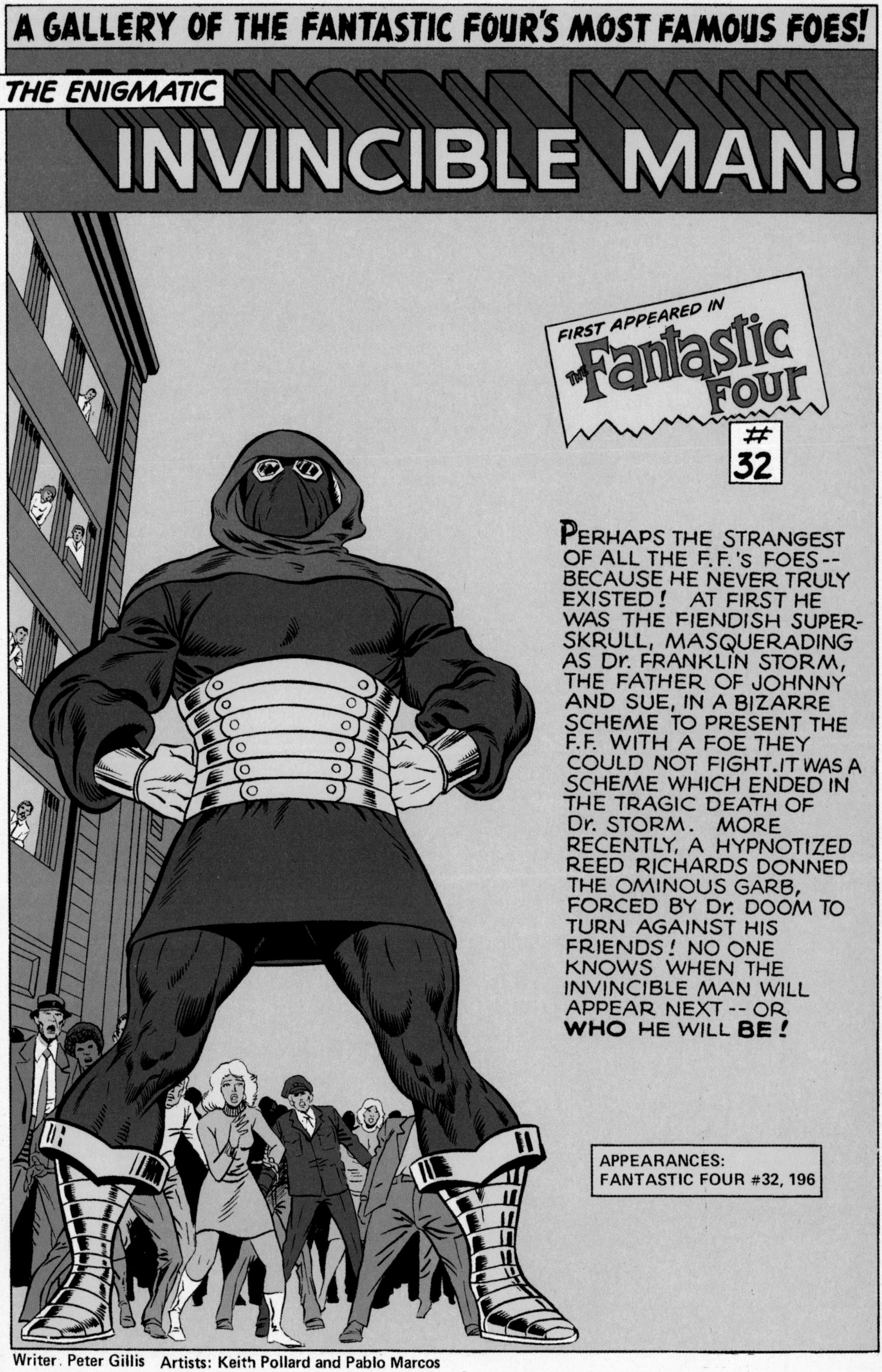
A GALLERY OF THE FANTASTIC FOUR'S MOST FAMOUS FOES!
THE ENIGMATIC
INVINCIBLE MAN!
FIRST APPEARED IN THE Fantastic Four # 32
PERHAPS THE STRANGEST OF ALL THE F.F.'s FOES--BECAUSE HE NEVER TRULY EXISTED! AT FIRST HE WAS THE FIENDISH SUPER-SKRULL, MASQUERADING AS Dr. FRANKLIN STORM, THE FATHER OF JOHNNY AND SUE, IN A BIZARRE SCHEME TO PRESENT THE F.F. WITH A FOE THEY COULD NOT FIGHT. IT WAS A SCHEME WHICH ENDED IN THE TRAGIC DEATH OF Dr. STORM. MORE RECENTLY, A HYPNOTIZED REED RICHARDS DONNED THE OMINOUS GARB, FORCED BY Dr. DOOM TO TURN AGAINST HIS FRIENDS! NO ONE KNOWS WHEN THE INVINCIBLE MAN WILL APPEAR NEXT -- OR WHO HE WILL BE!
APPEARANCES: FANTASTIC FOUR #32, 196

Writer: Peter Gillis   Artists: Keith Pollard and Pablo Marcos

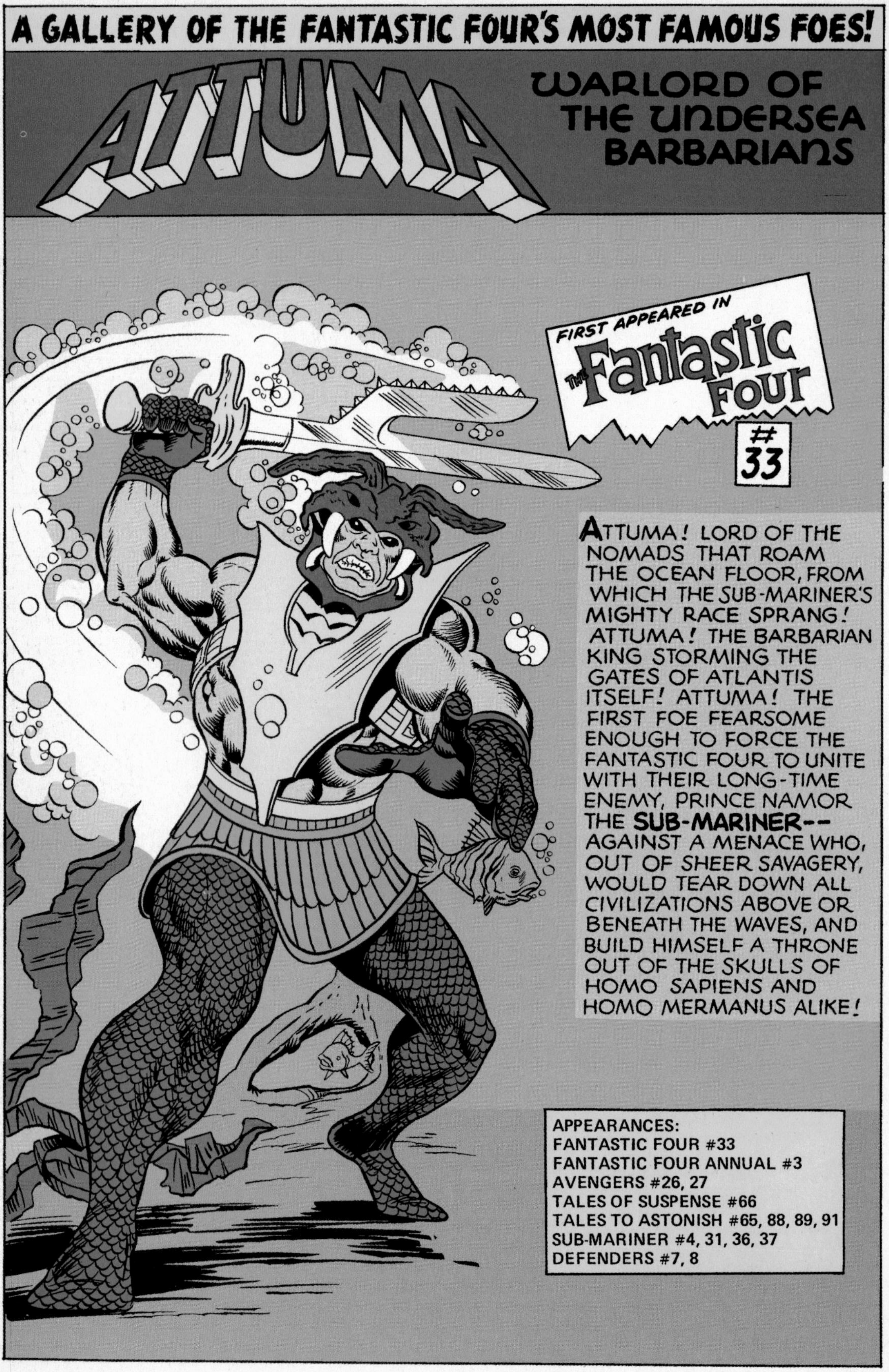
A GALLERY OF THE FANTASTIC FOUR'S MOST FAMOUS FOES!
ATTUMA
WARLORD OF THE UNDERSEA BARBARIANS
FIRST APPEARED IN
THE Fantastic FOUR
33
ATTUMA! LORD OF THE NOMADS THAT ROAM THE OCEAN FLOOR, FROM WHICH THE SUB-MARINER'S MIGHTY RACE SPRANG! ATTUMA! THE BARBARIAN KING STORMING THE GATES OF ATLANTIS ITSELF! ATTUMA! THE FIRST FOE FEARSOME ENOUGH TO FORCE THE FANTASTIC FOUR TO UNITE WITH THEIR LONG-TIME ENEMY, PRINCE NAMOR THE SUB-MARINER-- AGAINST A MENACE WHO, OUT OF SHEER SAVAGERY, WOULD TEAR DOWN ALL CIVILIZATIONS ABOVE OR BENEATH THE WAVES, AND BUILD HIMSELF A THRONE OUT OF THE SKULLS OF HOMO SAPIENS AND HOMO MERMANUS ALIKE!
APPEARANCES:
FANTASTIC FOUR #33
FANTASTIC FOUR ANNUAL #3
AVENGERS #26, 27
TALES OF SUSPENSE #66
TALES TO ASTONISH #65, 88, 89, 91
SUB-MARINER #4, 31, 36, 37
DEFENDERS #7, 8

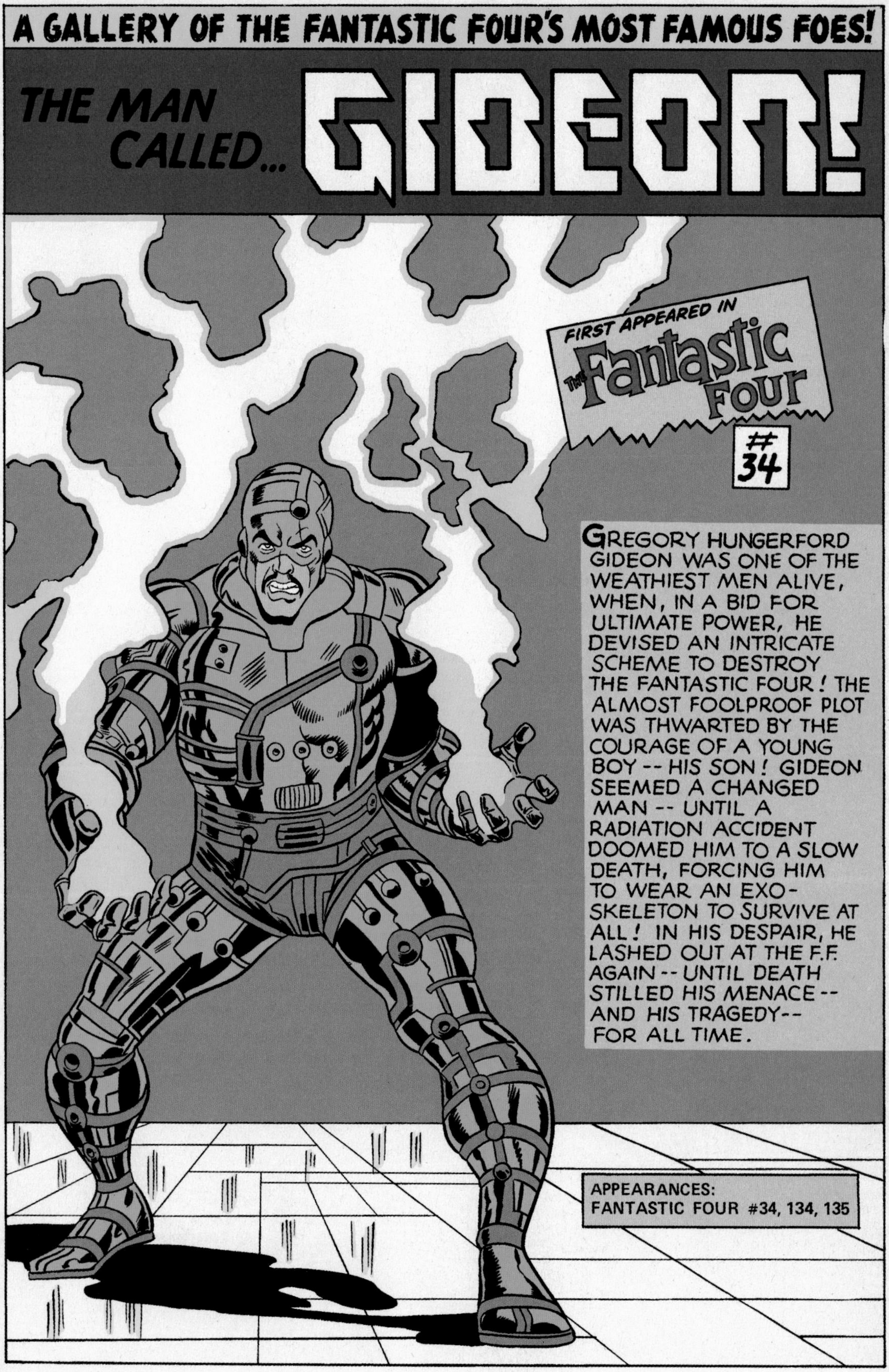
A GALLERY OF THE FANTASTIC FOUR'S MOST FAMOUS FOES!
THE MAN CALLED... GIDEON!
FIRST APPEARED IN THE Fantastic Four #34
GREGORY HUNGERFORD GIDEON WAS ONE OF THE WEATHIEST MEN ALIVE, WHEN, IN A BID FOR ULTIMATE POWER, HE DEVISED AN INTRICATE SCHEME TO DESTROY THE FANTASTIC FOUR! THE ALMOST FOOLPROOF PLOT WAS THWARTED BY THE COURAGE OF A YOUNG BOY -- HIS SON! GIDEON SEEMED A CHANGED MAN -- UNTIL A RADIATION ACCIDENT DOOMED HIM TO A SLOW DEATH, FORCING HIM TO WEAR AN EXO-SKELETON TO SURVIVE AT ALL! IN HIS DESPAIR, HE LASHED OUT AT THE F.F. AGAIN -- UNTIL DEATH STILLED HIS MENACE -- AND HIS TRAGEDY -- FOR ALL TIME.
APPEARANCES: FANTASTIC FOUR #34, 134, 135

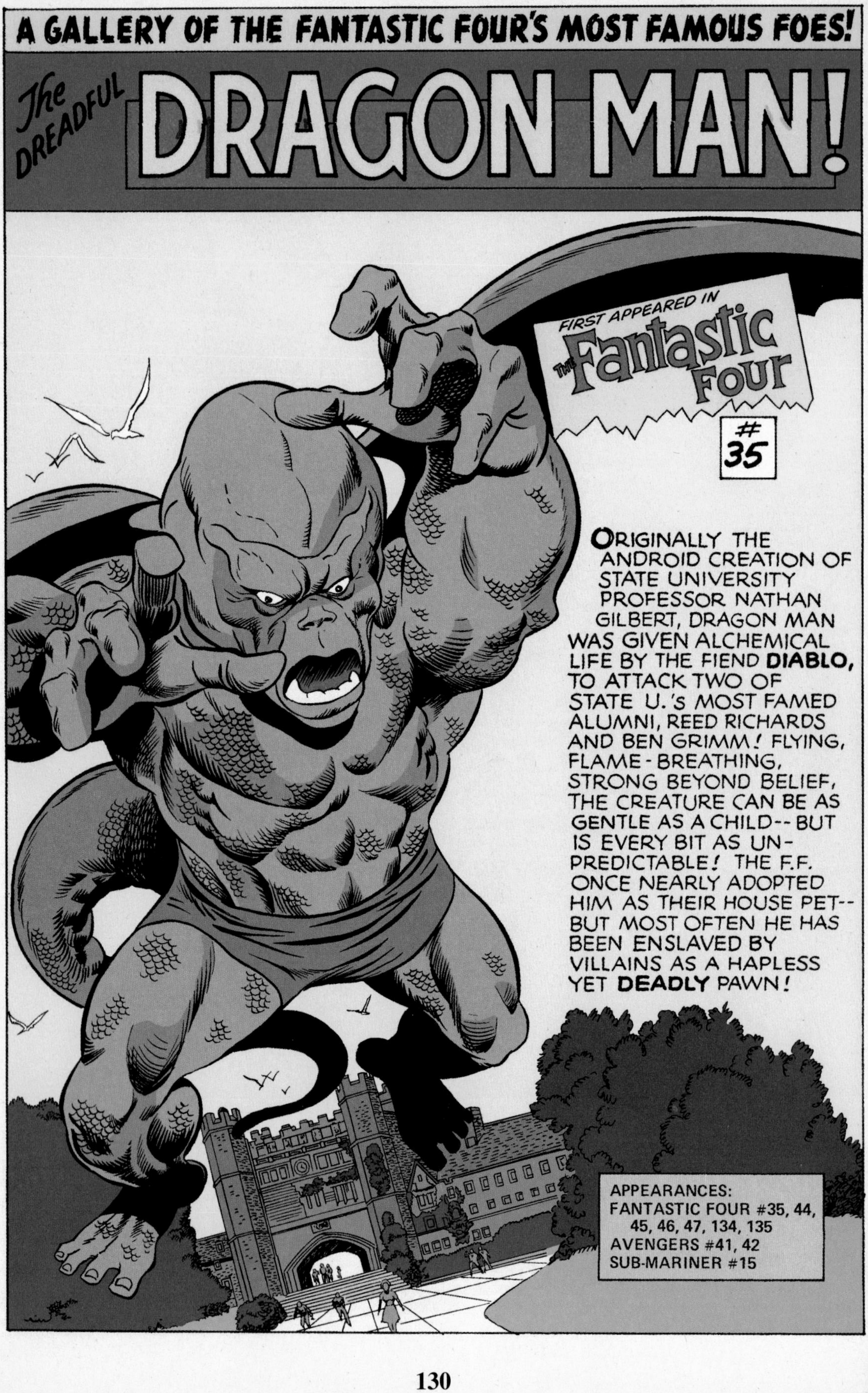
A GALLERY OF THE FANTASTIC FOUR'S MOST FAMOUS FOES!
The DREADFUL DRAGON MAN!
FIRST APPEARED IN THE Fantastic Four #35
ORIGINALLY THE ANDROID CREATION OF STATE UNIVERSITY PROFESSOR NATHAN GILBERT, DRAGON MAN WAS GIVEN ALCHEMICAL LIFE BY THE FIEND DIABLO, TO ATTACK TWO OF STATE U.'s MOST FAMED ALUMNI, REED RICHARDS AND BEN GRIMM! FLYING, FLAME-BREATHING, STRONG BEYOND BELIEF, THE CREATURE CAN BE AS GENTLE AS A CHILD-- BUT IS EVERY BIT AS UN-PREDICTABLE! THE F.F. ONCE NEARLY ADOPTED HIM AS THEIR HOUSE PET-- BUT MOST OFTEN HE HAS BEEN ENSLAVED BY VILLAINS AS A HAPLESS YET DEADLY PAWN!
APPEARANCES: FANTASTIC FOUR #35, 44, 45, 46, 47, 134, 135
AVENGERS #41, 42
SUB-MARINER #15

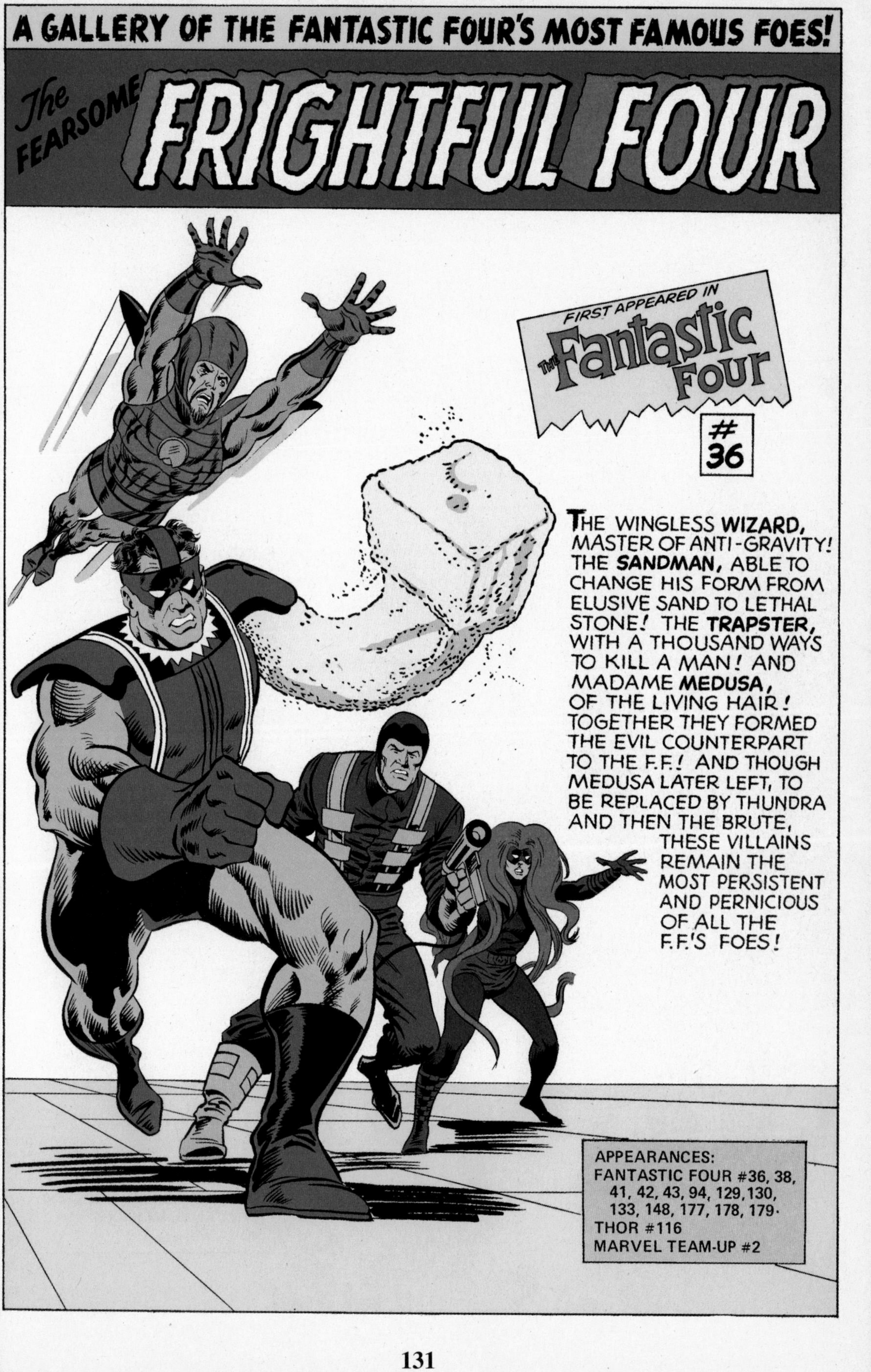
A GALLERY OF THE FANTASTIC FOUR'S MOST FAMOUS FOES!
The FEARSOME FRIGHTFUL FOUR
FIRST APPEARED IN The Fantastic Four #36
THE WINGLESS WIZARD, MASTER OF ANTI-GRAVITY! THE SANDMAN, ABLE TO CHANGE HIS FORM FROM ELUSIVE SAND TO LETHAL STONE! THE TRAPSTER, WITH A THOUSAND WAYS TO KILL A MAN! AND MADAME MEDUSA, OF THE LIVING HAIR! TOGETHER THEY FORMED THE EVIL COUNTERPART TO THE F.F.! AND THOUGH MEDUSA LATER LEFT, TO BE REPLACED BY THUNDRA AND THEN THE BRUTE, THESE VILLAINS REMAIN THE MOST PERSISTENT AND PERNICIOUS OF ALL THE F.F.'S FOES!
APPEARANCES:
FANTASTIC FOUR #36, 38, 41, 42, 43, 94, 129, 130, 133, 148, 177, 178, 179.
THOR #116
MARVEL TEAM-UP #2

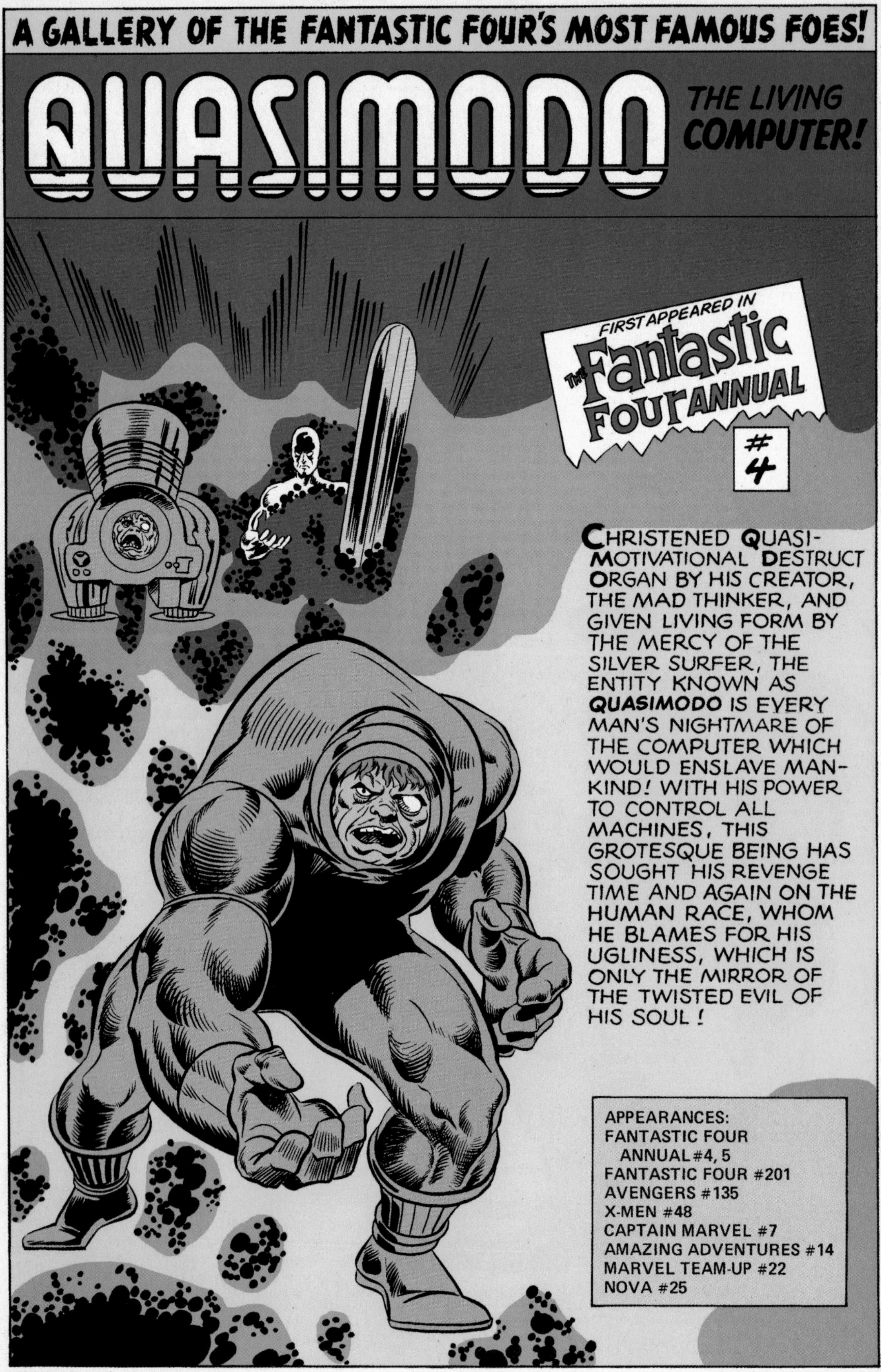
A GALLERY OF THE FANTASTIC FOUR'S MOST FAMOUS FOES!
QUASIMODO
THE LIVING COMPUTER!
FIRST APPEARED IN
The Fantastic Four ANNUAL
#4
CHRISTENED QUASI-MOTIVATIONAL DESTRUCT ORGAN BY HIS CREATOR, THE MAD THINKER, AND GIVEN LIVING FORM BY THE MERCY OF THE SILVER SURFER, THE ENTITY KNOWN AS QUASIMODO IS EVERY MAN'S NIGHTMARE OF THE COMPUTER WHICH WOULD ENSLAVE MAN-KIND! WITH HIS POWER TO CONTROL ALL MACHINES, THIS GROTESQUE BEING HAS SOUGHT HIS REVENGE TIME AND AGAIN ON THE HUMAN RACE, WHOM HE BLAMES FOR HIS UGLINESS, WHICH IS ONLY THE MIRROR OF THE TWISTED EVIL OF HIS SOUL!
APPEARANCES:
FANTASTIC FOUR ANNUAL #4, 5
FANTASTIC FOUR #201
AVENGERS #135
X-MEN #48
CAPTAIN MARVEL #7
AMAZING ADVENTURES #14
MARVEL TEAM-UP #22
NOVA #25

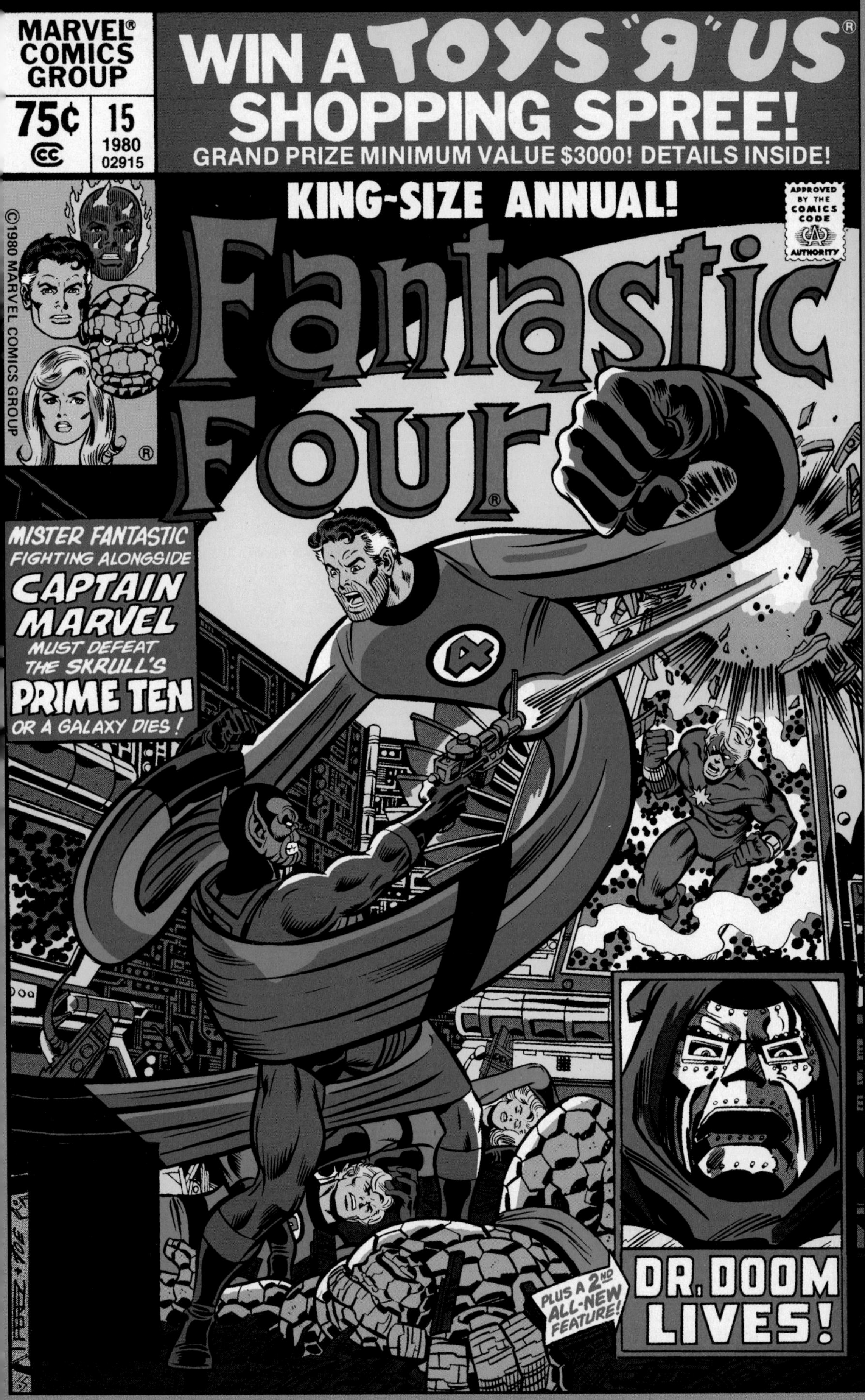

MARVEL® COMICS GROUP
75¢
15
1980
02915
WIN A TOYS "R" US® SHOPPING SPREE!
GRAND PRIZE MINIMUM VALUE $3000! DETAILS INSIDE!
KING-SIZE ANNUAL!
APPROVED BY THE COMICS CODE AUTHORITY
©1980 MARVEL COMICS GROUP
Fantastic Four®
MISTER FANTASTIC FIGHTING ALONGSIDE CAPTAIN MARVEL MUST DEFEAT THE SKRULL'S PRIME TEN OR A GALAXY DIES!
PLUS A 2ND ALL-NEW FEATURE!
DR. DOOM LIVES!

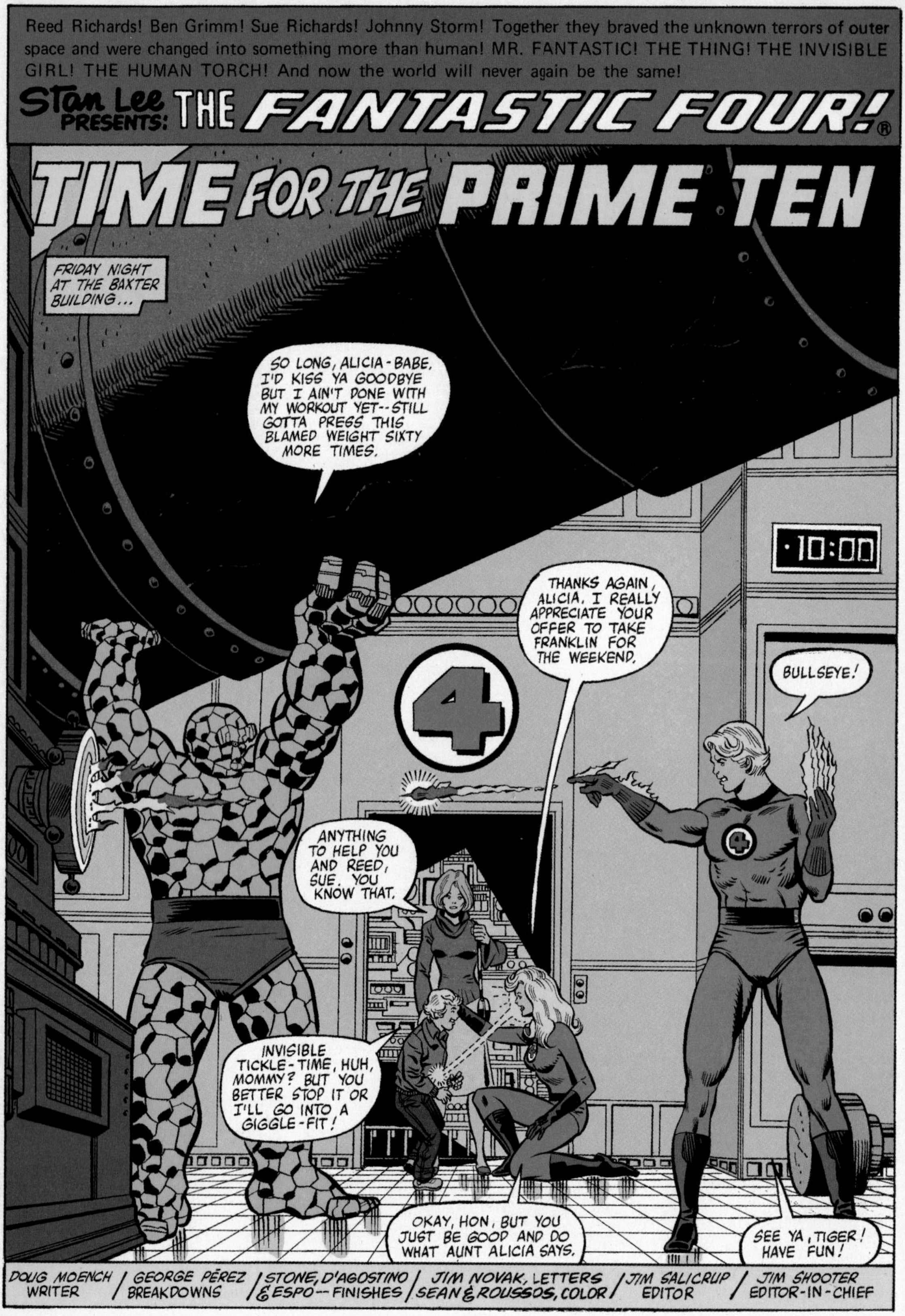

Reed Richards! Ben Grimm! Sue Richards! Johnny Storm! Together they braved the unknown terrors of outer space and were changed into something more than human! MR. FANTASTIC! THE THING! THE INVISIBLE GIRL! THE HUMAN TORCH! And now the world will never again be the same!
Stan Lee PRESENTS: THE FANTASTIC FOUR!
TIME FOR THE PRIME TEN
FRIDAY NIGHT AT THE BAXTER BUILDING...
SO LONG, ALICIA-BABE. I'D KISS YA GOODBYE BUT I AIN'T DONE WITH MY WORKOUT YET--STILL GOTTA PRESS THIS BLAMED WEIGHT SIXTY MORE TIMES.
·10:00
THANKS AGAIN, ALICIA. I REALLY APPRECIATE YOUR OFFER TO TAKE FRANKLIN FOR THE WEEKEND.
BULLSEYE!
ANYTHING TO HELP YOU AND REED, SUE. YOU KNOW THAT.
INVISIBLE TICKLE-TIME, HUH, MOMMY? BUT YOU BETTER STOP IT OR I'LL GO INTO A GIGGLE-FIT!
OKAY, HON, BUT YOU JUST BE GOOD AND DO WHAT AUNT ALICIA SAYS.
SEE YA, TIGER! HAVE FUN!
DOUG MOENCH WRITER / GEORGE PÉREZ BREAKDOWNS / STONE, D'AGOSTINO & ESPO--FINISHES / JIM NOVAK, LETTERS SEAN & ROUSSOS, COLOR / JIM SALICRUP EDITOR / JIM SHOOTER EDITOR-IN-CHIEF

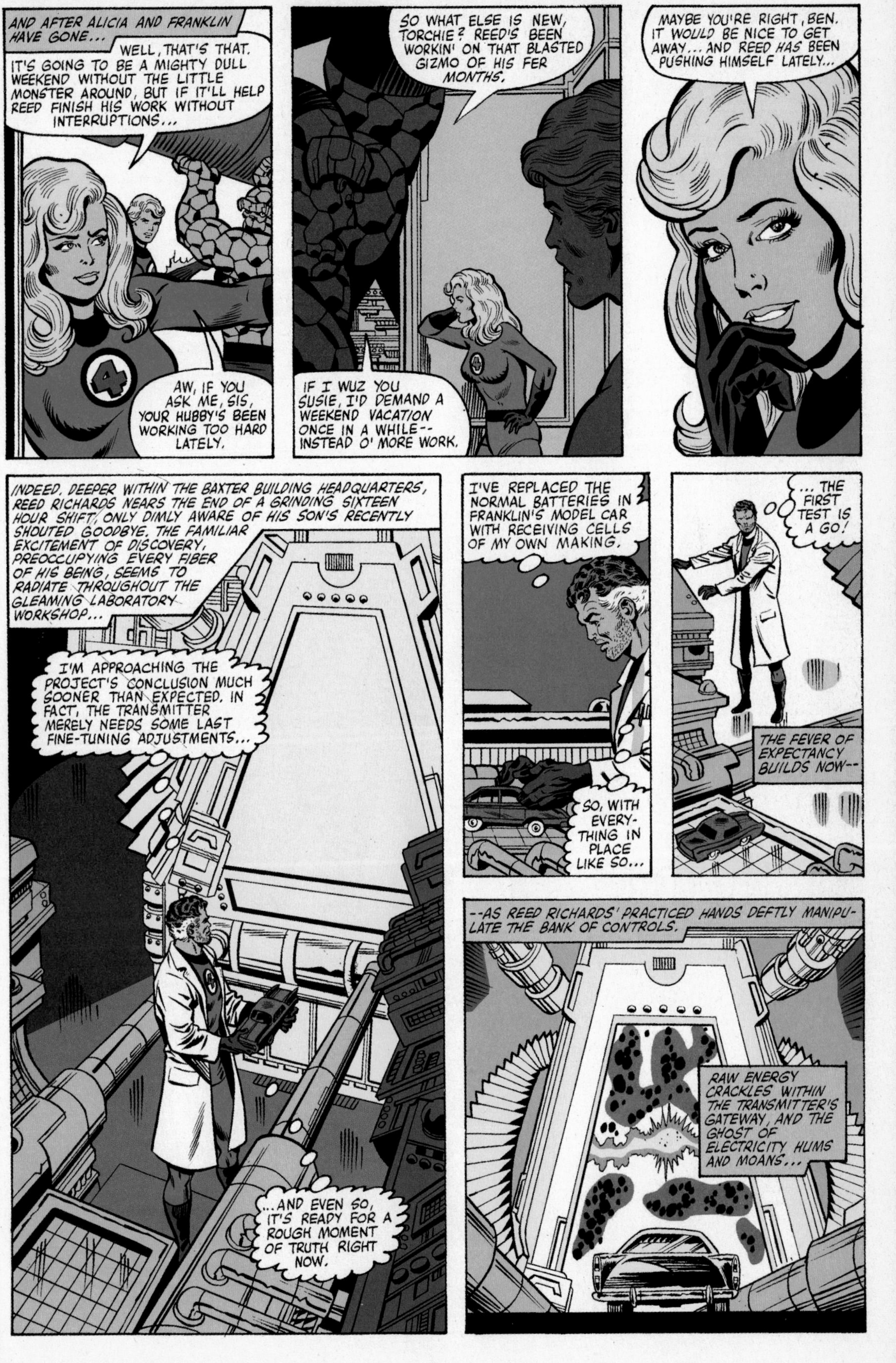
AND AFTER ALICIA AND FRANKLIN HAVE GONE...
WELL, THAT'S THAT. IT'S GOING TO BE A MIGHTY DULL WEEKEND WITHOUT THE LITTLE MONSTER AROUND, BUT IF IT'LL HELP REED FINISH HIS WORK WITHOUT INTERRUPTIONS...
AW, IF YOU ASK ME, SIS, YOUR HUBBY'S BEEN WORKING TOO HARD LATELY.
SO WHAT ELSE IS NEW, TORCHIE? REED'S BEEN WORKIN' ON THAT BLASTED GIZMO OF HIS FER MONTHS.
IF I WUZ YOU SUSIE, I'D DEMAND A WEEKEND VACATION ONCE IN A WHILE-- INSTEAD O' MORE WORK.
MAYBE YOU'RE RIGHT, BEN. IT WOULD BE NICE TO GET AWAY... AND REED HAS BEEN PUSHING HIMSELF LATELY...
INDEED, DEEPER WITHIN THE BAXTER BUILDING HEADQUARTERS, REED RICHARDS NEARS THE END OF A GRINDING SIXTEEN HOUR SHIFT, ONLY DIMLY AWARE OF HIS SON'S RECENTLY SHOUTED GOODBYE. THE FAMILIAR EXCITEMENT OF DISCOVERY, PREOCCUPYING EVERY FIBER OF HIS BEING, SEEMS TO RADIATE THROUGHOUT THE GLEAMING LABORATORY WORKSHOP...
I'M APPROACHING THE PROJECT'S CONCLUSION MUCH SOONER THAN EXPECTED. IN FACT, THE TRANSMITTER MERELY NEEDS SOME LAST FINE-TUNING ADJUSTMENTS...
...AND EVEN SO, IT'S READY FOR A ROUGH MOMENT OF TRUTH RIGHT NOW.
I'VE REPLACED THE NORMAL BATTERIES IN FRANKLIN'S MODEL CAR WITH RECEIVING CELLS OF MY OWN MAKING.
SO, WITH EVERY-THING IN PLACE LIKE SO...
... THE FIRST TEST IS A GO!
THE FEVER OF EXPECTANCY BUILDS NOW--
--AS REED RICHARDS' PRACTICED HANDS DEFTLY MANIPU-LATE THE BANK OF CONTROLS.
RAW ENERGY CRACKLES WITHIN THE TRANSMITTER'S GATEWAY, AND THE GHOST OF ELECTRICITY HUMS AND MOANS...

GOT TO FOCUS THE ENERGY FROM THE GATEWAY TERMINAL, AIM IT AT THE RECEIVING CELLS IN THE CAR, AND ...YES! IT'S TWITCHING...!

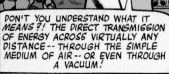

IT MOVED! THE BEAUTIFUL LITTLE HUNK OF PLASTIC MOVED!

I'VE DONE IT! IT WORKS!!

WHAT'S ALL THE BELLOWIN' ABOUT? WHAT WORKS?

MY ENERGY TRANSMITTER, BEN! IT WORKS!

DON'T YOU UNDERSTAND WHAT IT MEANS?! THE DIRECT TRANSMISSION OF ENERGY ACROSS VIRTUALLY ANY DISTANCE -- THROUGH THE SIMPLE MEDIUM OF AIR -- OR EVEN THROUGH A VACUUM!

IT'S EVEN BETTER THAN SATELLITE SOLAR-STATIONS WHICH WOULD BEAM MICROWAVES DOWN TO COLLECTING AND STORING TERMINALS! THE CAR MOVED!

"THE CAR MOVED"?

YES -- WITHOUT BATTERIES! AND MY TRANSMITTER ELIMINATES THE NEED FOR CABLES OR CORDS!

YA DON'T SAY. IT'S ALMOST SPOOKY, STRETCH.

NOT AT ALL! IT'S A GODSEND FOR AN ENERGY-DEPLETED FUTURE!

IT... IT'S WONDERFUL, DARLING! I'M SO HAPPY FOR YOU -- SO PROUD OF WHAT YOU'VE DONE!

YEAH, YA MIGHT EVEN COP THE NOBEL PRIZE, STRETCH.

THE PRIZE IS AN HONOR, CERTAINLY, BUT MORE IMPORTANT THAN THAT, BEN...

I MIGHT NOW RECEIVE THE GRANTS NECESSARY FOR SOME REAL RESEARCH INTO ADVANCED PHYSICS -- FASTER-THAN-LIGHT TRAVEL, PERHAPS -- AS I'VE ALWAYS DREAMED OF --

KLUNK

THAT CAME FROM THE FRONT DOOR!

YEAH -- BUT NONE O' THE ALARMS WENT OFF!

WITH POSSIBLE DANGER KNOCKING AT THE DOOR, REED RICHARDS INSTANTLY BECOMES MR. FANTASTIC, NATURAL LEADER OF THE FABULOUS FOURSOME...

I DON'T KNOW WHO COULD HAVE CIRCUMVENTED OUR SECURITY SYSTEM-- WHAT PAST OR NEW ENEMY--

--BUT WE'VE GOT TO BE PREPARED FOR EVERY CONTINGENCY!

FLAME ON!

WE'RE RIGHT BEHIND YA, STRETCH!

ALL RIGHT, THIS IS IT, EVERYONE SET?

WE'RE READY. JUST OPEN THE DOOR AN' LEMME CLOBBER 'EM.

BUT WHEN THE DOOR IS FLUNG OPEN--

WHAT?! I DON'T BELIEVE IT! YOU-- ?!

HIM-- ?!

UH... HELLO. LONG TIME NO SEE.

IT'S ONLY WILLIE LUMPKIN --OUR OLD MAILMAN-- WIGGLIN' HIS BLAMED EARS, NO LESS!

SUSAN RICHARDS
C/O FANTASTIC FOUR
THE BAXTER BUILDING
35TH FLOOR
NEW YORK, NY 10022

I'VE, UH, BEEN ON A LEAVE OF ABSENCE ...

...BUT WHEN I WENT DOWN TO VISIT MY OLD PALS AT THE POST OFFICE AND NOTICED THIS PACKAGE ADDRESSED TO MRS. RICHARDS--

--I THOUGHT I'D BRING IT OVER SPECIAL MYSELF, JUST LIKE THE OLD DAYS. KINDA AGAINST THE RULES, TECHNICALLY SPEAKING ...

... BUT I DIDN'T THINK YOU'D MIND.

OF COURSE NOT, WILLIE-- WE'VE MISSED YOU. COME ON IN FOR SOME COFFEE.

LISTEN, JOHNNY, I'M WORRIED ABOUT THE ALARM SYSTEM. I MIGHT HAVE INADVERTANTLY SHORTED IT OUT DURING MY EXPERIMENT WITH THE ENERGY TRANSMITTER.

I'M GOING TO CHECK IT OUT. MAKE MY EXCUSES TO WILLIE FOR ME, WILL YOU?

SURE, REED. AFTER ALL, CONSIDERING ALL THE OLD ENEMIES WE'VE GOT, WE CAN'T AFFORD TO BE CAUGHT WITH OUR PANTS DOWN EVEN FOR A SECOND.

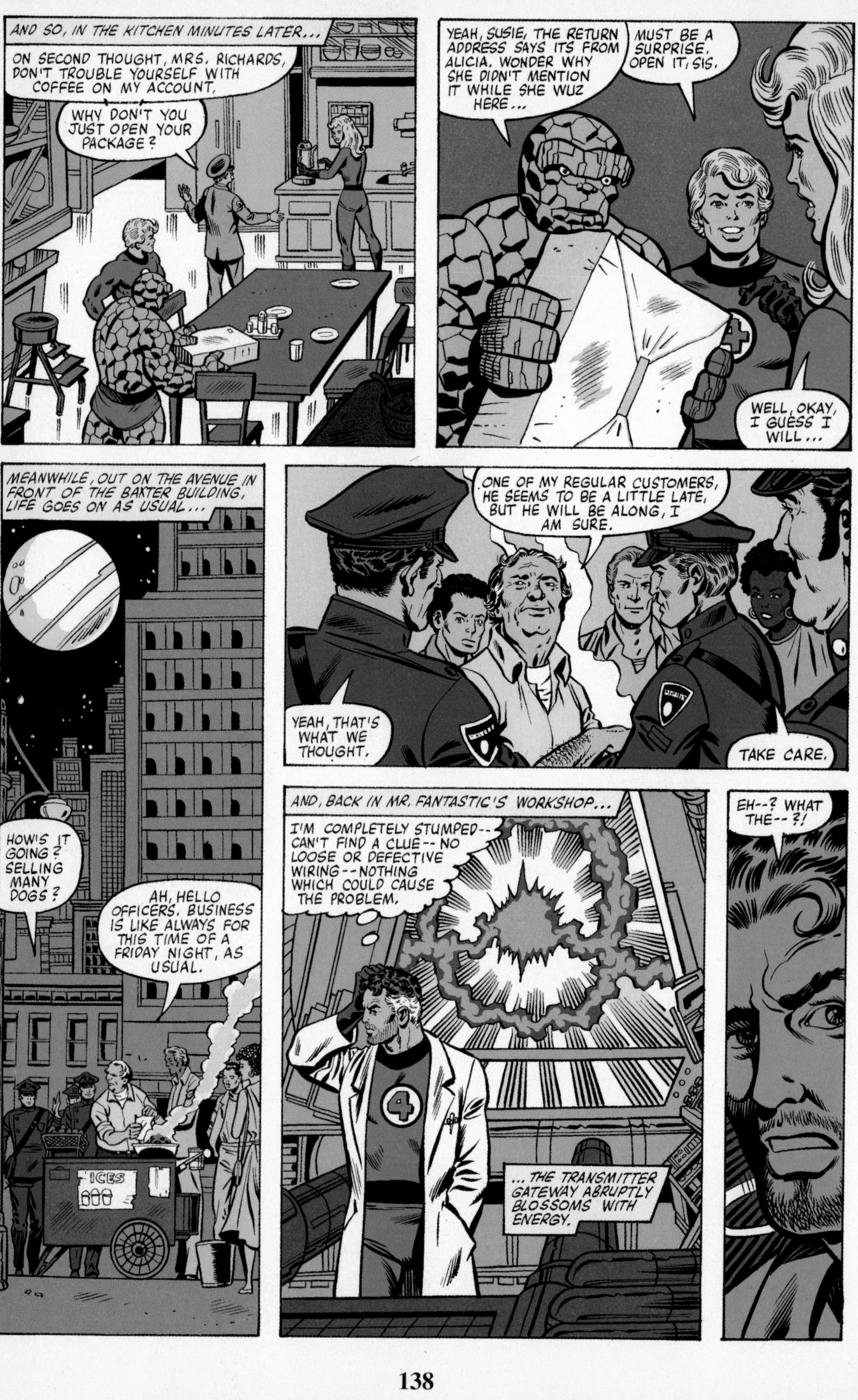
AND SO, IN THE KITCHEN MINUTES LATER...
ON SECOND THOUGHT, MRS. RICHARDS, DON'T TROUBLE YOURSELF WITH COFFEE ON MY ACCOUNT.
WHY DON'T YOU JUST OPEN YOUR PACKAGE?
YEAH, SUSIE, THE RETURN ADDRESS SAYS ITS FROM ALICIA. WONDER WHY SHE DIDN'T MENTION IT WHILE SHE WUZ HERE...
MUST BE A SURPRISE. OPEN IT, SIS.
WELL, OKAY, I GUESS I WILL...
MEANWHILE, OUT ON THE AVENUE IN FRONT OF THE BAXTER BUILDING, LIFE GOES ON AS USUAL...
HOW'S IT GOING? SELLING MANY DOGS?
AH, HELLO OFFICERS. BUSINESS IS LIKE ALWAYS FOR THIS TIME OF A FRIDAY NIGHT, AS USUAL.
ICES
ONE OF MY REGULAR CUSTOMERS, HE SEEMS TO BE A LITTLE LATE, BUT HE WILL BE ALONG, I AM SURE.
YEAH, THAT'S WHAT WE THOUGHT.
TAKE CARE.
AND, BACK IN MR. FANTASTIC'S WORKSHOP...
I'M COMPLETELY STUMPED-- CAN'T FIND A CLUE-- NO LOOSE OR DEFECTIVE WIRING--NOTHING WHICH COULD CAUSE THE PROBLEM.
...THE TRANSMITTER GATEWAY ABRUPTLY BLOSSOMS WITH ENERGY.
EH--? WHAT THE--?!

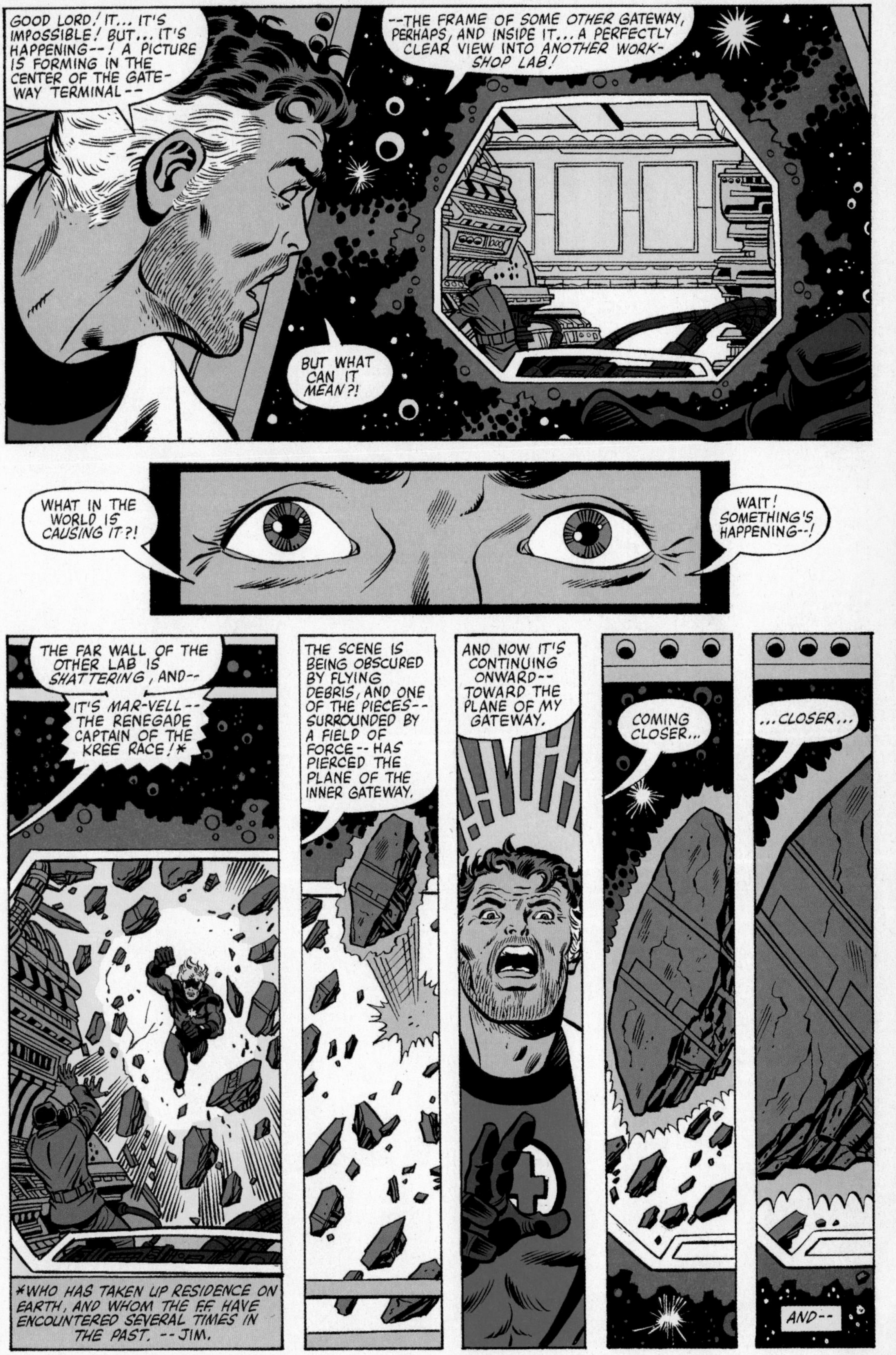
GOOD LORD! IT... IT'S IMPOSSIBLE! BUT... IT'S HAPPENING--! A PICTURE IS FORMING IN THE CENTER OF THE GATEWAY TERMINAL--
--THE FRAME OF SOME OTHER GATEWAY, PERHAPS, AND INSIDE IT... A PERFECTLY CLEAR VIEW INTO ANOTHER WORKSHOP LAB!
BUT WHAT CAN IT MEAN?!
WHAT IN THE WORLD IS CAUSING IT?!
WAIT! SOMETHING'S HAPPENING--!
THE FAR WALL OF THE OTHER LAB IS SHATTERING, AND--
IT'S MAR-VELL--THE RENEGADE CAPTAIN OF THE KREE RACE!*
*WHO HAS TAKEN UP RESIDENCE ON EARTH, AND WHOM THE F.F. HAVE ENCOUNTERED SEVERAL TIMES IN THE PAST. --JIM.
THE SCENE IS BEING OBSCURED BY FLYING DEBRIS, AND ONE OF THE PIECES--SURROUNDED BY A FIELD OF FORCE--HAS PIERCED THE PLANE OF THE INNER GATEWAY.
AND NOW IT'S CONTINUING ONWARD--TOWARD THE PLANE OF MY GATEWAY.
COMING CLOSER...
...CLOSER...
AND--

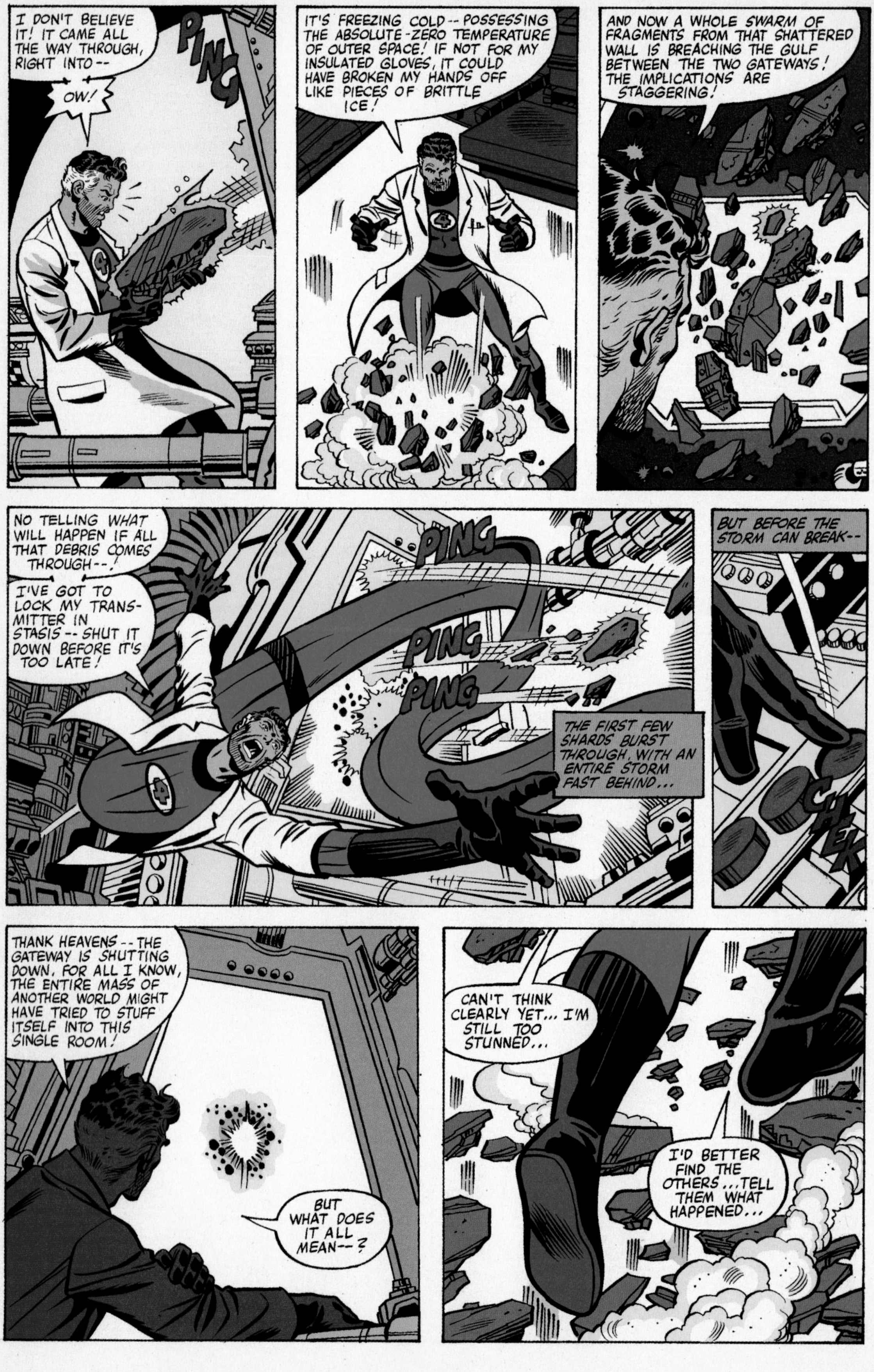

I DON'T BELIEVE IT! IT CAME ALL THE WAY THROUGH, RIGHT INTO --
PING
OW!
IT'S FREEZING COLD -- POSSESSING THE ABSOLUTE-ZERO TEMPERATURE OF OUTER SPACE! IF NOT FOR MY INSULATED GLOVES, IT COULD HAVE BROKEN MY HANDS OFF LIKE PIECES OF BRITTLE ICE!
AND NOW A WHOLE SWARM OF FRAGMENTS FROM THAT SHATTERED WALL IS BREACHING THE GULF BETWEEN THE TWO GATEWAYS! THE IMPLICATIONS ARE STAGGERING!
NO TELLING WHAT WILL HAPPEN IF ALL THAT DEBRIS COMES THROUGH--!
I'VE GOT TO LOCK MY TRANSMITTER IN STASIS -- SHUT IT DOWN BEFORE IT'S TOO LATE!
PING
PING
PING
THE FIRST FEW SHARDS BURST THROUGH, WITH AN ENTIRE STORM FAST BEHIND...
BUT BEFORE THE STORM CAN BREAK--
CHEK
THANK HEAVENS -- THE GATEWAY IS SHUTTING DOWN. FOR ALL I KNOW, THE ENTIRE MASS OF ANOTHER WORLD MIGHT HAVE TRIED TO STUFF ITSELF INTO THIS SINGLE ROOM!
BUT WHAT DOES IT ALL MEAN-- ?
CAN'T THINK CLEARLY YET... I'M STILL TOO STUNNED...
I'D BETTER FIND THE OTHERS... TELL THEM WHAT HAPPENED...

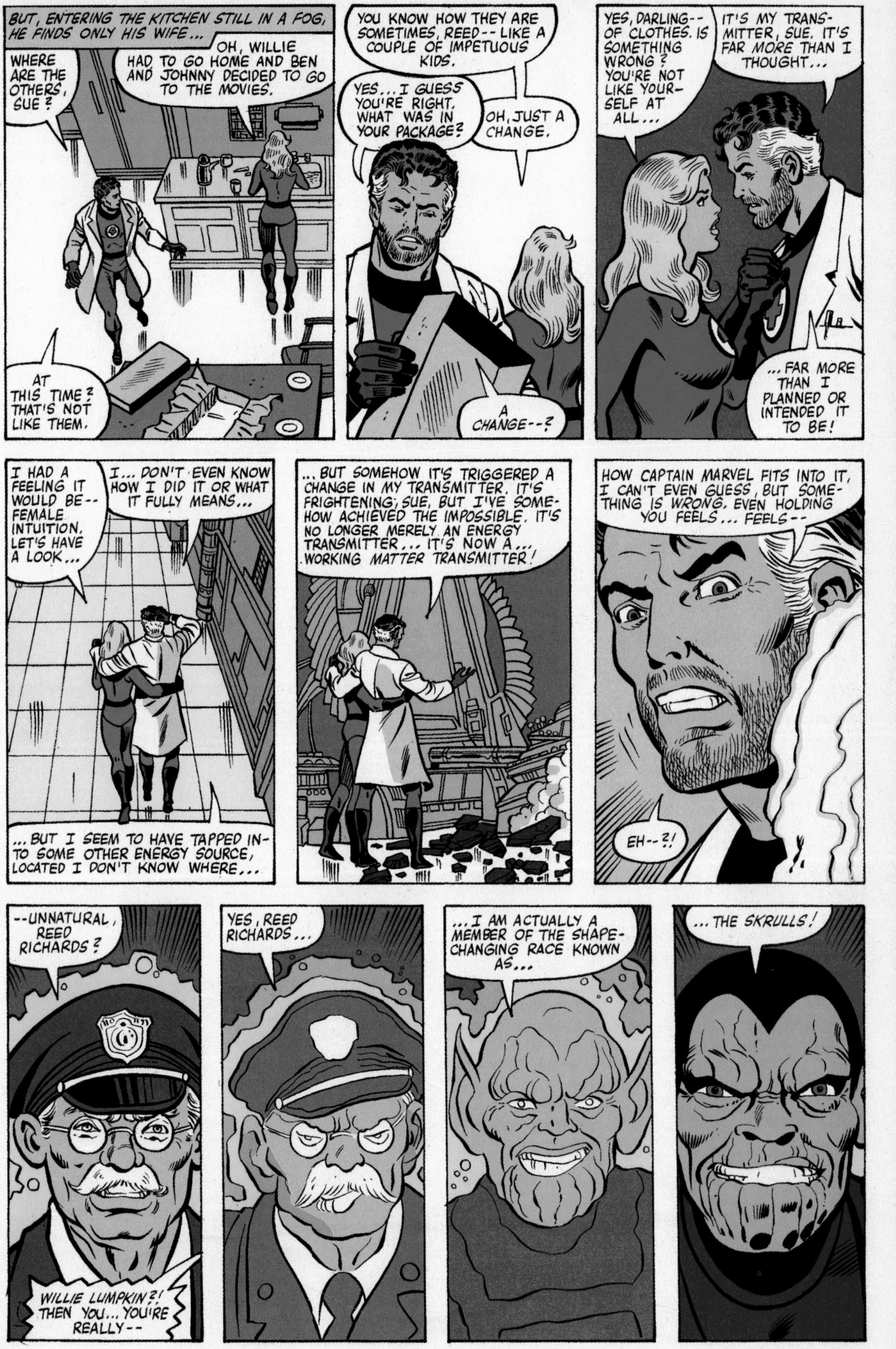
BUT, ENTERING THE KITCHEN STILL IN A FOG, HE FINDS ONLY HIS WIFE...
WHERE ARE THE OTHERS, SUE?
OH, WILLIE HAD TO GO HOME AND BEN AND JOHNNY DECIDED TO GO TO THE MOVIES.
AT THIS TIME? THAT'S NOT LIKE THEM.
YOU KNOW HOW THEY ARE SOMETIMES, REED-- LIKE A COUPLE OF IMPETUOUS KIDS.
YES... I GUESS YOU'RE RIGHT. WHAT WAS IN YOUR PACKAGE?
OH, JUST A CHANGE.
A CHANGE--?
YES, DARLING-- OF CLOTHES. IS SOMETHING WRONG? YOU'RE NOT LIKE YOURSELF AT ALL...
IT'S MY TRANSMITTER, SUE. IT'S FAR MORE THAN I THOUGHT...
...FAR MORE THAN I PLANNED OR INTENDED IT TO BE!
I HAD A FEELING IT WOULD BE-- FEMALE INTUITION. LET'S HAVE A LOOK...
I... DON'T EVEN KNOW HOW I DID IT OR WHAT IT FULLY MEANS...
...BUT I SEEM TO HAVE TAPPED INTO SOME OTHER ENERGY SOURCE, LOCATED I DON'T KNOW WHERE...
...BUT SOMEHOW IT'S TRIGGERED A CHANGE IN MY TRANSMITTER. IT'S FRIGHTENING, SUE, BUT I'VE SOMEHOW ACHIEVED THE IMPOSSIBLE. IT'S NO LONGER MERELY AN ENERGY TRANSMITTER... IT'S NOW A... WORKING MATTER TRANSMITTER!
HOW CAPTAIN MARVEL FITS INTO IT, I CAN'T EVEN GUESS, BUT SOMETHING IS WRONG. EVEN HOLDING YOU FEELS... FEELS--
EH--?!
--UNNATURAL, REED RICHARDS?
WILLIE LUMPKIN?! THEN YOU... YOU'RE REALLY--
YES, REED RICHARDS...
...I AM ACTUALLY A MEMBER OF THE SHAPE-CHANGING RACE KNOWN AS...
...THE SKRULLS!

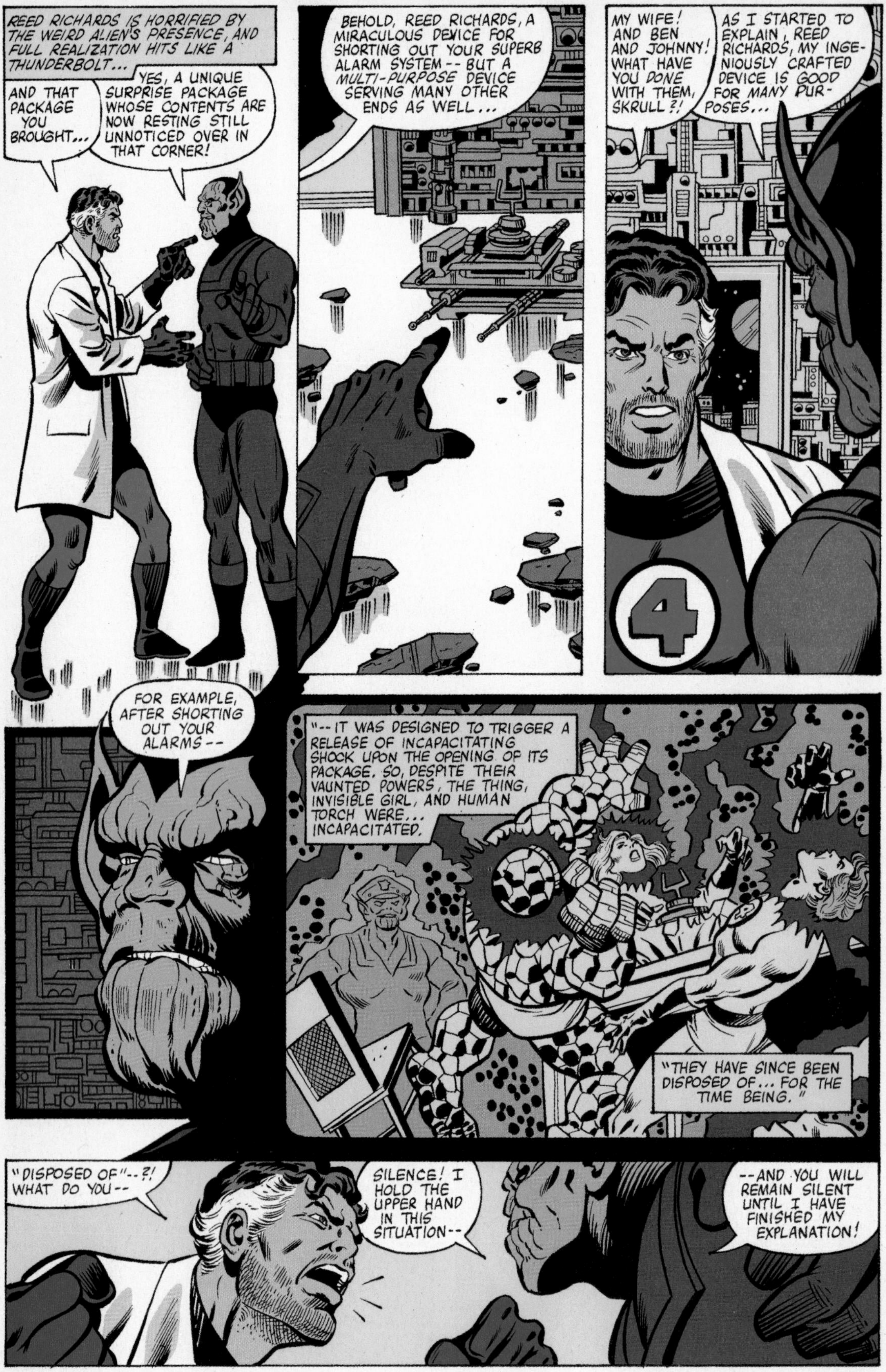
REED RICHARDS IS HORRIFIED BY THE WEIRD ALIEN'S PRESENCE, AND FULL REALIZATION HITS LIKE A THUNDERBOLT...
AND THAT PACKAGE YOU BROUGHT...
YES, A UNIQUE SURPRISE PACKAGE WHOSE CONTENTS ARE NOW RESTING STILL UNNOTICED OVER IN THAT CORNER!
BEHOLD, REED RICHARDS, A MIRACULOUS DEVICE FOR SHORTING OUT YOUR SUPERB ALARM SYSTEM -- BUT A MULTI-PURPOSE DEVICE SERVING MANY OTHER ENDS AS WELL...
MY WIFE! AND BEN AND JOHNNY! WHAT HAVE YOU DONE WITH THEM, SKRULL?!
AS I STARTED TO EXPLAIN, REED RICHARDS, MY INGENIOUSLY CRAFTED DEVICE IS GOOD FOR MANY PURPOSES...
4
FOR EXAMPLE, AFTER SHORTING OUT YOUR ALARMS --
"-- IT WAS DESIGNED TO TRIGGER A RELEASE OF INCAPACITATING SHOCK UPON THE OPENING OF ITS PACKAGE. SO, DESPITE THEIR VAUNTED POWERS, THE THING, INVISIBLE GIRL, AND HUMAN TORCH WERE... INCAPACITATED.
"THEY HAVE SINCE BEEN DISPOSED OF... FOR THE TIME BEING."
"DISPOSED OF"--?! WHAT DO YOU--
SILENCE! I HOLD THE UPPER HAND IN THIS SITUATION--
--AND YOU WILL REMAIN SILENT UNTIL I HAVE FINISHED MY EXPLANATION!

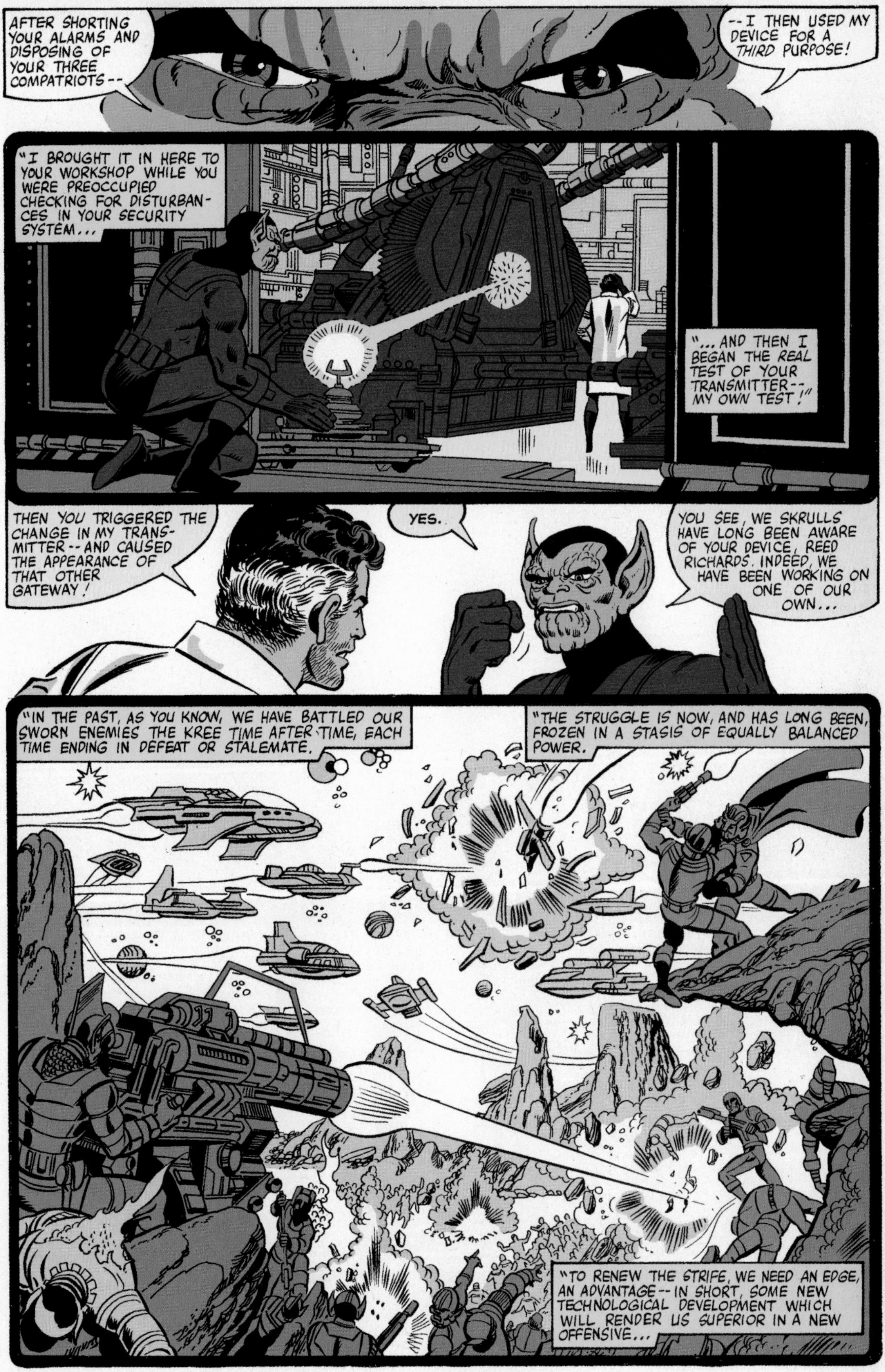
AFTER SHORTING YOUR ALARMS AND DISPOSING OF YOUR THREE COMPATRIOTS--
--I THEN USED MY DEVICE FOR A THIRD PURPOSE!
"I BROUGHT IT IN HERE TO YOUR WORKSHOP WHILE YOU WERE PREOCCUPIED CHECKING FOR DISTURBANCES IN YOUR SECURITY SYSTEM...
"... AND THEN I BEGAN THE REAL TEST OF YOUR TRANSMITTER-- MY OWN TEST!"
THEN YOU TRIGGERED THE CHANGE IN MY TRANSMITTER--AND CAUSED THE APPEARANCE OF THAT OTHER GATEWAY!
YES.
YOU SEE, WE SKRULLS HAVE LONG BEEN AWARE OF YOUR DEVICE, REED RICHARDS. INDEED, WE HAVE BEEN WORKING ON ONE OF OUR OWN...
"IN THE PAST, AS YOU KNOW, WE HAVE BATTLED OUR SWORN ENEMIES THE KREE TIME AFTER TIME, EACH TIME ENDING IN DEFEAT OR STALEMATE.
"THE STRUGGLE IS NOW, AND HAS LONG BEEN, FROZEN IN A STASIS OF EQUALLY BALANCED POWER.
"TO RENEW THE STRIFE, WE NEED AN EDGE, AN ADVANTAGE--IN SHORT, SOME NEW TECHNOLOGICAL DEVELOPMENT WHICH WILL RENDER US SUPERIOR IN A NEW OFFENSIVE...

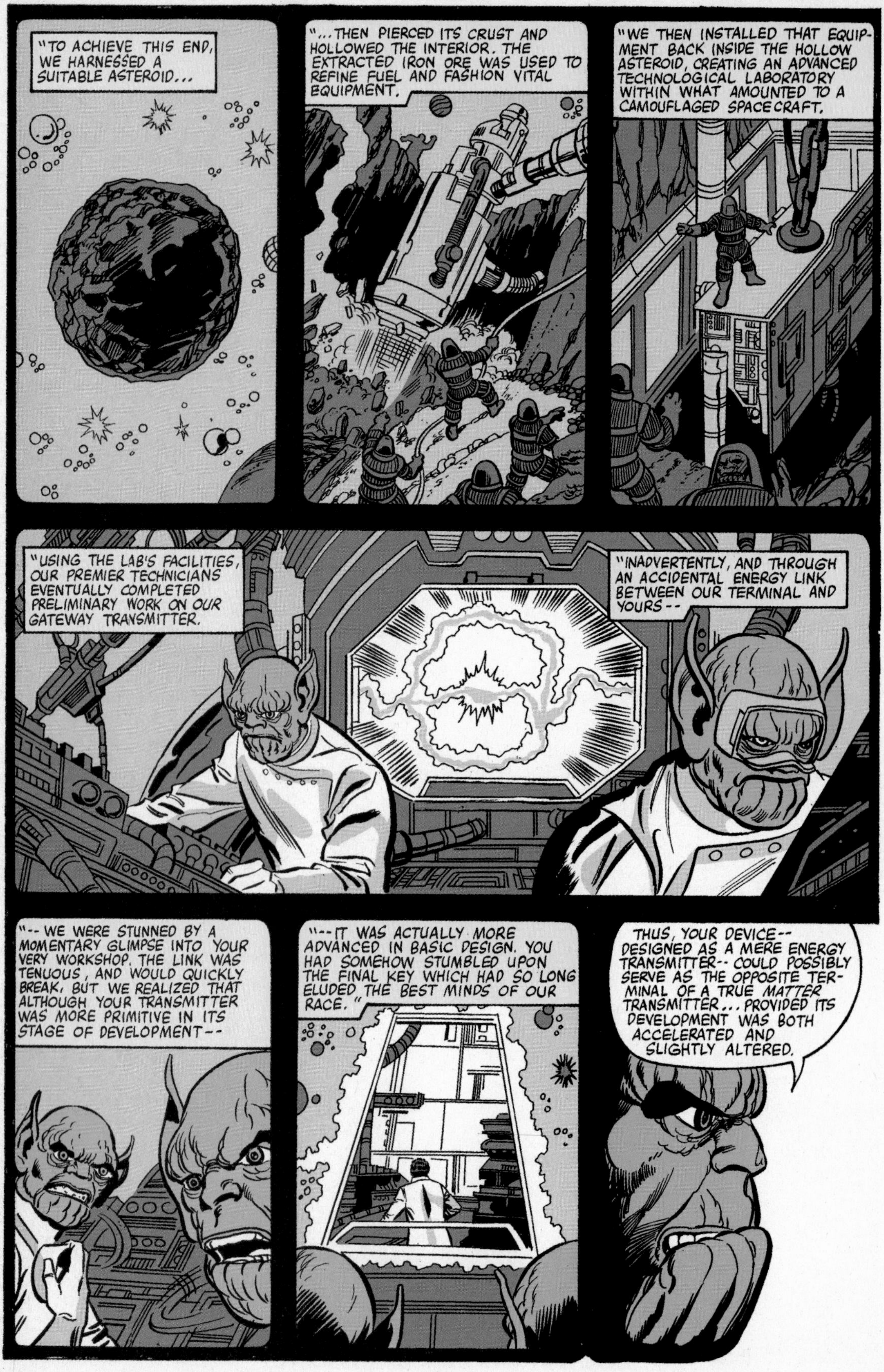
"TO ACHIEVE THIS END, WE HARNESSED A SUITABLE ASTEROID...
"...THEN PIERCED ITS CRUST AND HOLLOWED THE INTERIOR. THE EXTRACTED IRON ORE WAS USED TO REFINE FUEL AND FASHION VITAL EQUIPMENT.
"WE THEN INSTALLED THAT EQUIPMENT BACK INSIDE THE HOLLOW ASTEROID, CREATING AN ADVANCED TECHNOLOGICAL LABORATORY WITHIN WHAT AMOUNTED TO A CAMOUFLAGED SPACECRAFT.
"USING THE LAB'S FACILITIES, OUR PREMIER TECHNICIANS EVENTUALLY COMPLETED PRELIMINARY WORK ON OUR GATEWAY TRANSMITTER.
"INADVERTENTLY, AND THROUGH AN ACCIDENTAL ENERGY LINK BETWEEN OUR TERMINAL AND YOURS--
"--WE WERE STUNNED BY A MOMENTARY GLIMPSE INTO YOUR VERY WORKSHOP. THE LINK WAS TENUOUS, AND WOULD QUICKLY BREAK, BUT WE REALIZED THAT ALTHOUGH YOUR TRANSMITTER WAS MORE PRIMITIVE IN ITS STAGE OF DEVELOPMENT--
"--IT WAS ACTUALLY MORE ADVANCED IN BASIC DESIGN. YOU HAD SOMEHOW STUMBLED UPON THE FINAL KEY WHICH HAD SO LONG ELUDED THE BEST MINDS OF OUR RACE."
THUS, YOUR DEVICE-- DESIGNED AS A MERE ENERGY TRANSMITTER-- COULD POSSIBLY SERVE AS THE OPPOSITE TERMINAL OF A TRUE MATTER TRANSMITTER... PROVIDED ITS DEVELOPMENT WAS BOTH ACCELERATED AND SLIGHTLY ALTERED.

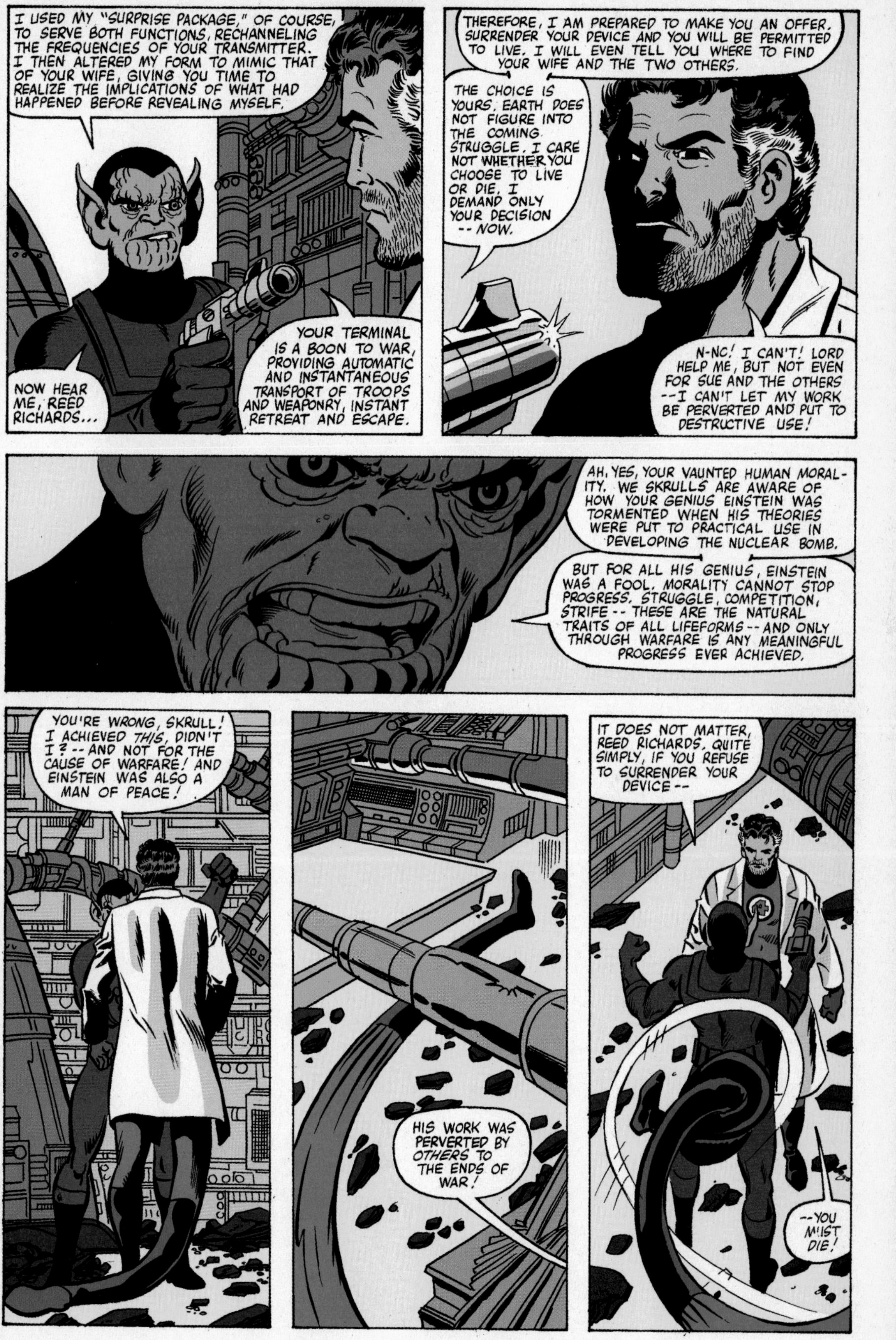
I USED MY "SURPRISE PACKAGE," OF COURSE, TO SERVE BOTH FUNCTIONS, RECHANNELING THE FREQUENCIES OF YOUR TRANSMITTER. I THEN ALTERED MY FORM TO MIMIC THAT OF YOUR WIFE, GIVING YOU TIME TO REALIZE THE IMPLICATIONS OF WHAT HAD HAPPENED BEFORE REVEALING MYSELF.
NOW HEAR ME, REED RICHARDS...
YOUR TERMINAL IS A BOON TO WAR, PROVIDING AUTOMATIC AND INSTANTANEOUS TRANSPORT OF TROOPS AND WEAPONRY, INSTANT RETREAT AND ESCAPE.
THEREFORE, I AM PREPARED TO MAKE YOU AN OFFER. SURRENDER YOUR DEVICE AND YOU WILL BE PERMITTED TO LIVE. I WILL EVEN TELL YOU WHERE TO FIND YOUR WIFE AND THE TWO OTHERS.
THE CHOICE IS YOURS. EARTH DOES NOT FIGURE INTO THE COMING STRUGGLE. I CARE NOT WHETHER YOU CHOOSE TO LIVE OR DIE. I DEMAND ONLY YOUR DECISION -- NOW.
N-NO! I CAN'T! LORD HELP ME, BUT NOT EVEN FOR SUE AND THE OTHERS -- I CAN'T LET MY WORK BE PERVERTED AND PUT TO DESTRUCTIVE USE!
AH, YES, YOUR VAUNTED HUMAN MORALITY. WE SKRULLS ARE AWARE OF HOW YOUR GENIUS EINSTEIN WAS TORMENTED WHEN HIS THEORIES WERE PUT TO PRACTICAL USE IN DEVELOPING THE NUCLEAR BOMB.
BUT FOR ALL HIS GENIUS, EINSTEIN WAS A FOOL. MORALITY CANNOT STOP PROGRESS. STRUGGLE, COMPETITION, STRIFE -- THESE ARE THE NATURAL TRAITS OF ALL LIFEFORMS -- AND ONLY THROUGH WARFARE IS ANY MEANINGFUL PROGRESS EVER ACHIEVED.
YOU'RE WRONG, SKRULL! I ACHIEVED THIS, DIDN'T I? -- AND NOT FOR THE CAUSE OF WARFARE! AND EINSTEIN WAS ALSO A MAN OF PEACE!
HIS WORK WAS PERVERTED BY OTHERS TO THE ENDS OF WAR!
IT DOES NOT MATTER, REED RICHARDS. QUITE SIMPLY, IF YOU REFUSE TO SURRENDER YOUR DEVICE --
-- YOU MUST DIE!

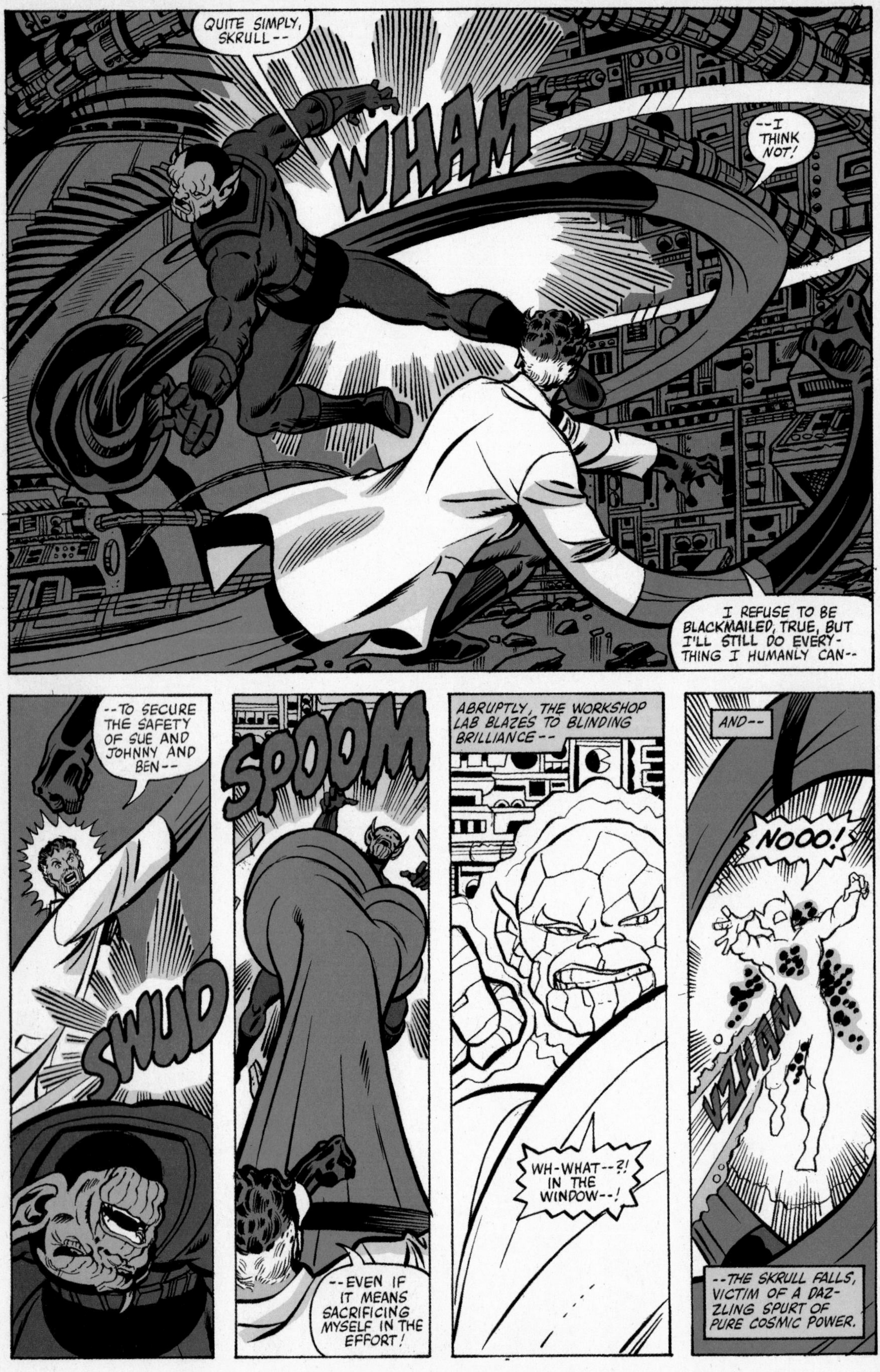
QUITE SIMPLY, SKRULL--
WHAM
--I THINK NOT!
I REFUSE TO BE BLACKMAILED, TRUE, BUT I'LL STILL DO EVERY-THING I HUMANLY CAN--
--TO SECURE THE SAFETY OF SUE AND JOHNNY AND BEN--
SWUD
SPOOM
--EVEN IF IT MEANS SACRIFICING MYSELF IN THE EFFORT!
ABRUPTLY, THE WORKSHOP LAB BLAZES TO BLINDING BRILLIANCE--
WH-WHAT--?! IN THE WINDOW--!
AND--
NOOO!
VZHAM
--THE SKRULL FALLS, VICTIM OF A DAZ-ZLING SPURT OF PURE COSMIC POWER.

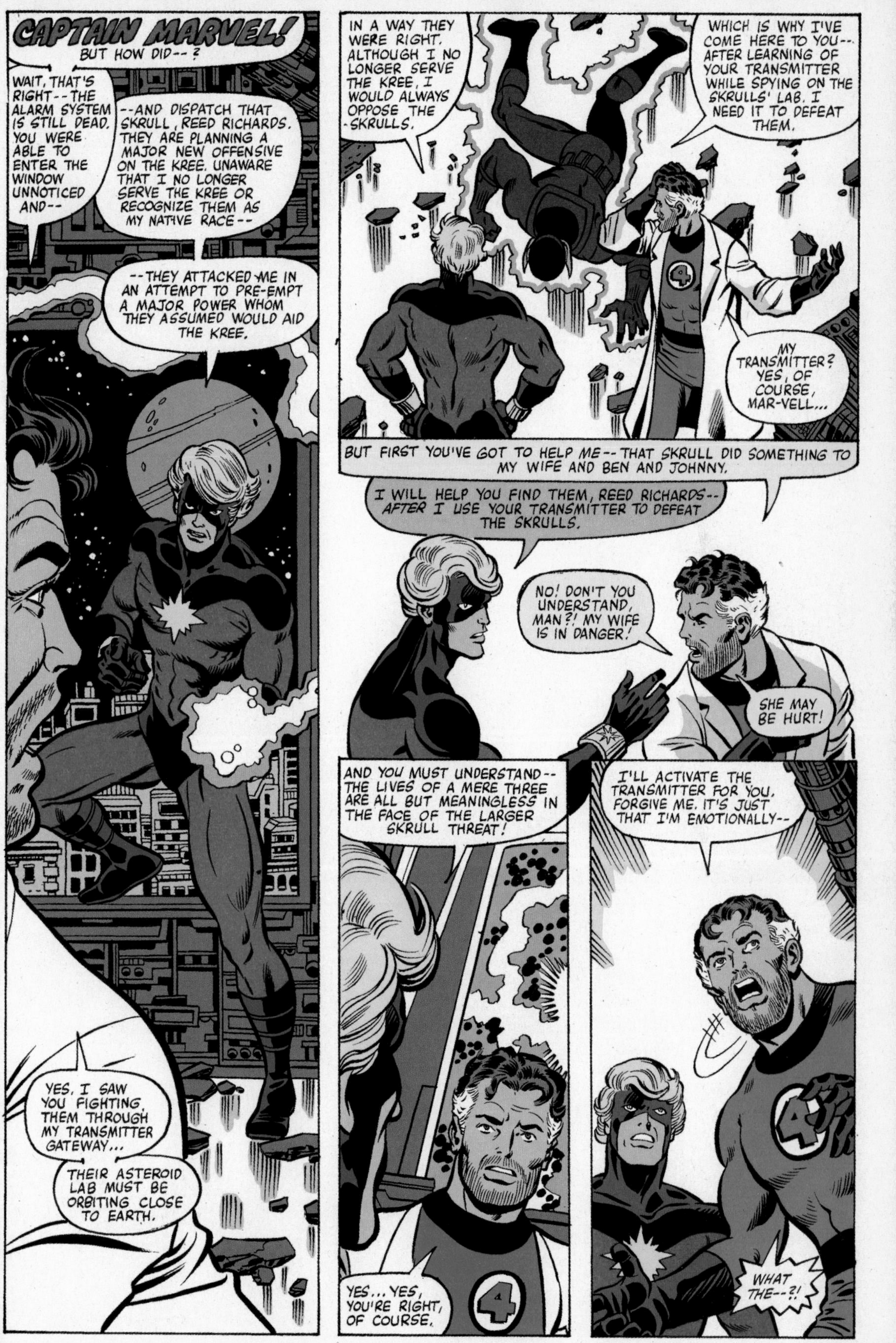
CAPTAIN MARVEL!
BUT HOW DID-- ?
WAIT, THAT'S RIGHT--THE ALARM SYSTEM IS STILL DEAD. YOU WERE ABLE TO ENTER THE WINDOW UNNOTICED AND--
--AND DISPATCH THAT SKRULL, REED RICHARDS. THEY ARE PLANNING A MAJOR NEW OFFENSIVE ON THE KREE, UNAWARE THAT I NO LONGER SERVE THE KREE OR RECOGNIZE THEM AS MY NATIVE RACE--
--THEY ATTACKED ME IN AN ATTEMPT TO PRE-EMPT A MAJOR POWER WHOM THEY ASSUMED WOULD AID THE KREE.
YES, I SAW YOU FIGHTING THEM THROUGH MY TRANSMITTER GATEWAY...
THEIR ASTEROID LAB MUST BE ORBITING CLOSE TO EARTH.
IN A WAY THEY WERE RIGHT. ALTHOUGH I NO LONGER SERVE THE KREE, I WOULD ALWAYS OPPOSE THE SKRULLS.
WHICH IS WHY I'VE COME HERE TO YOU--AFTER LEARNING OF YOUR TRANSMITTER WHILE SPYING ON THE SKRULLS' LAB. I NEED IT TO DEFEAT THEM.
MY TRANSMITTER? YES, OF COURSE, MAR-VELL...
BUT FIRST YOU'VE GOT TO HELP ME--THAT SKRULL DID SOMETHING TO MY WIFE AND BEN AND JOHNNY.
I WILL HELP YOU FIND THEM, REED RICHARDS--AFTER I USE YOUR TRANSMITTER TO DEFEAT THE SKRULLS.
NO! DON'T YOU UNDERSTAND, MAN?! MY WIFE IS IN DANGER!
SHE MAY BE HURT!
AND YOU MUST UNDERSTAND--THE LIVES OF A MERE THREE ARE ALL BUT MEANINGLESS IN THE FACE OF THE LARGER SKRULL THREAT!
YES... YES, YOU'RE RIGHT, OF COURSE.
I'LL ACTIVATE THE TRANSMITTER FOR YOU. FORGIVE ME. IT'S JUST THAT I'M EMOTIONALLY--
WHAT THE--?!

WITHIN THE INNER GATEWAY-- ANOTHER CAPTAIN MARVEL-- STILL IN THE SKRULL ASTEROID LAB!

THEN ONE OF YOU IS AN IMPOSTER-- A SKRULL HIMSELF!

HE IS THE SKRULL, REED RICHARDS-- A SUPER-SKRULL PREPARING TO USE THE GATEWAYS TO COME HERE-- MASQUERADING AS ME TO DECEIVE YOU! DON'T YOU SEE?! THE SKRULLS WANT YOUR DEVICE TOO! YOU'VE GOT TO USE IT ON HIM NOW-- STOP HIM BEFORE HE GETS HERE!

"USE" IT ON HIM? WHAT DO YOU MEAN? HOW--?

INSTEAD OF TRANSMITTING AND REASSEMBLING HIS ATOMS HERE, YOU MUST SCRAMBLE THOSE ATOMS, DISPERSE THEM THROUGH SPACE AND TIME-- NOW! YOU MUST USE THE TRANSMITTER NOW!

YES... VERY WELL... I'LL USE THE TRANSMITTER...

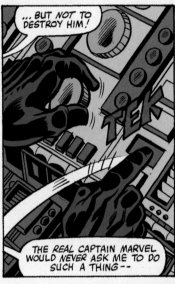

...BUT NOT TO DESTROY HIM!

THE REAL CAPTAIN MARVEL WOULD NEVER ASK ME TO DO SUCH A THING--

--NOT EVEN TO A SKRULL!

NO! WHAT ARE YOU DOING--?!

I'M DOING ALMOST EXACTLY AS YOU REQUESTED, SKRULL--!

I'M USING THE TRANSMITTER-- BUT I'M USING IT TO BRING THE REAL CAPTAIN MARVEL HERE!

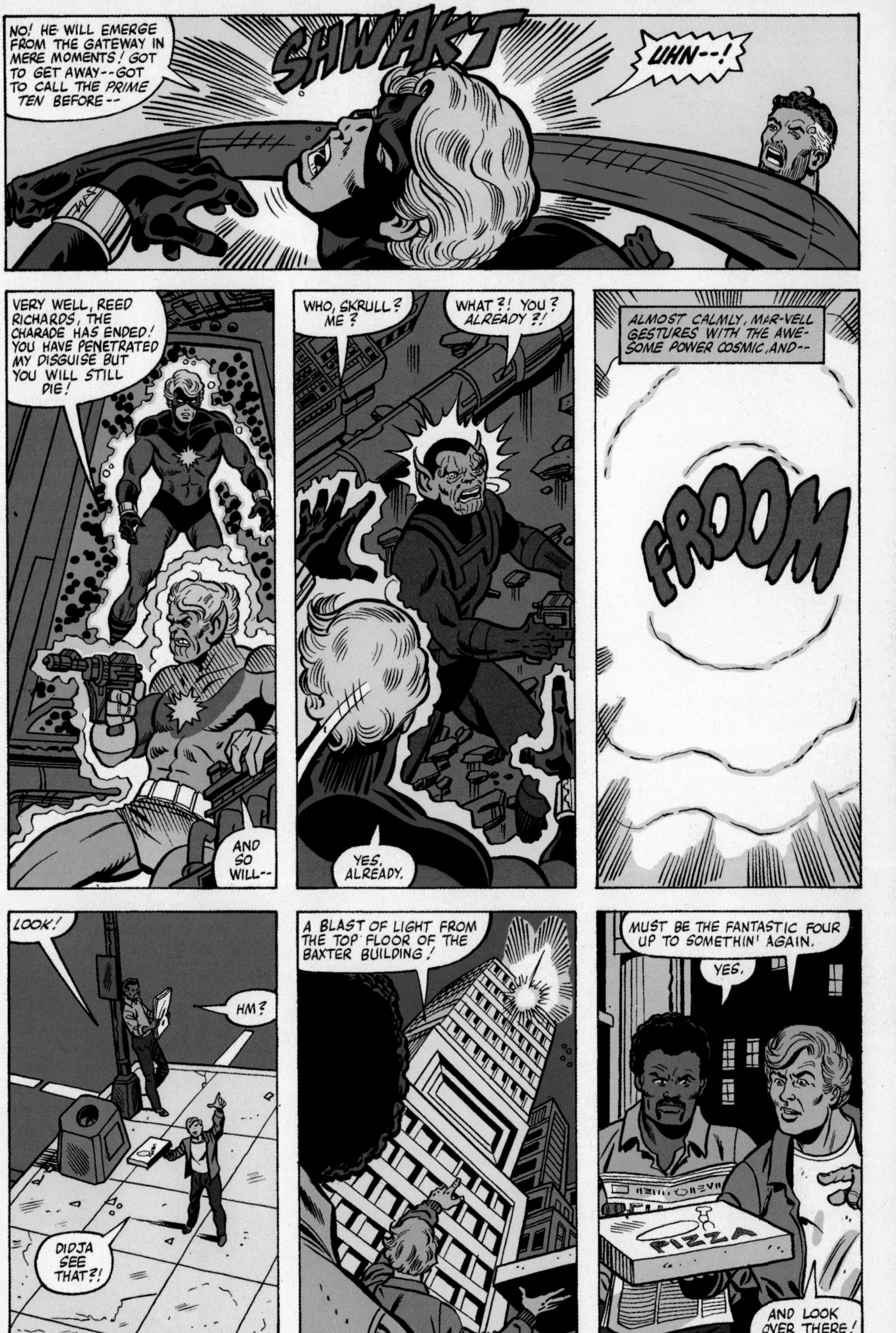
NO! HE WILL EMERGE FROM THE GATEWAY IN MERE MOMENTS! GOT TO GET AWAY--GOT TO CALL THE PRIME TEN BEFORE--
SHWAKT
UHN--!
VERY WELL, REED RICHARDS, THE CHARADE HAS ENDED! YOU HAVE PENETRATED MY DISGUISE BUT YOU WILL STILL DIE!
AND SO WILL--
WHO, SKRULL? ME?
WHAT?! YOU? ALREADY?!
YES, ALREADY.
ALMOST CALMLY, MAR-VELL GESTURES WITH THE AWESOME POWER COSMIC, AND--
FROOM
LOOK!
HM?
DIDJA SEE THAT?!
A BLAST OF LIGHT FROM THE TOP FLOOR OF THE BAXTER BUILDING!
MUST BE THE FANTASTIC FOUR UP TO SOMETHIN' AGAIN.
YES.
PIZZA
AND LOOK OVER THERE!

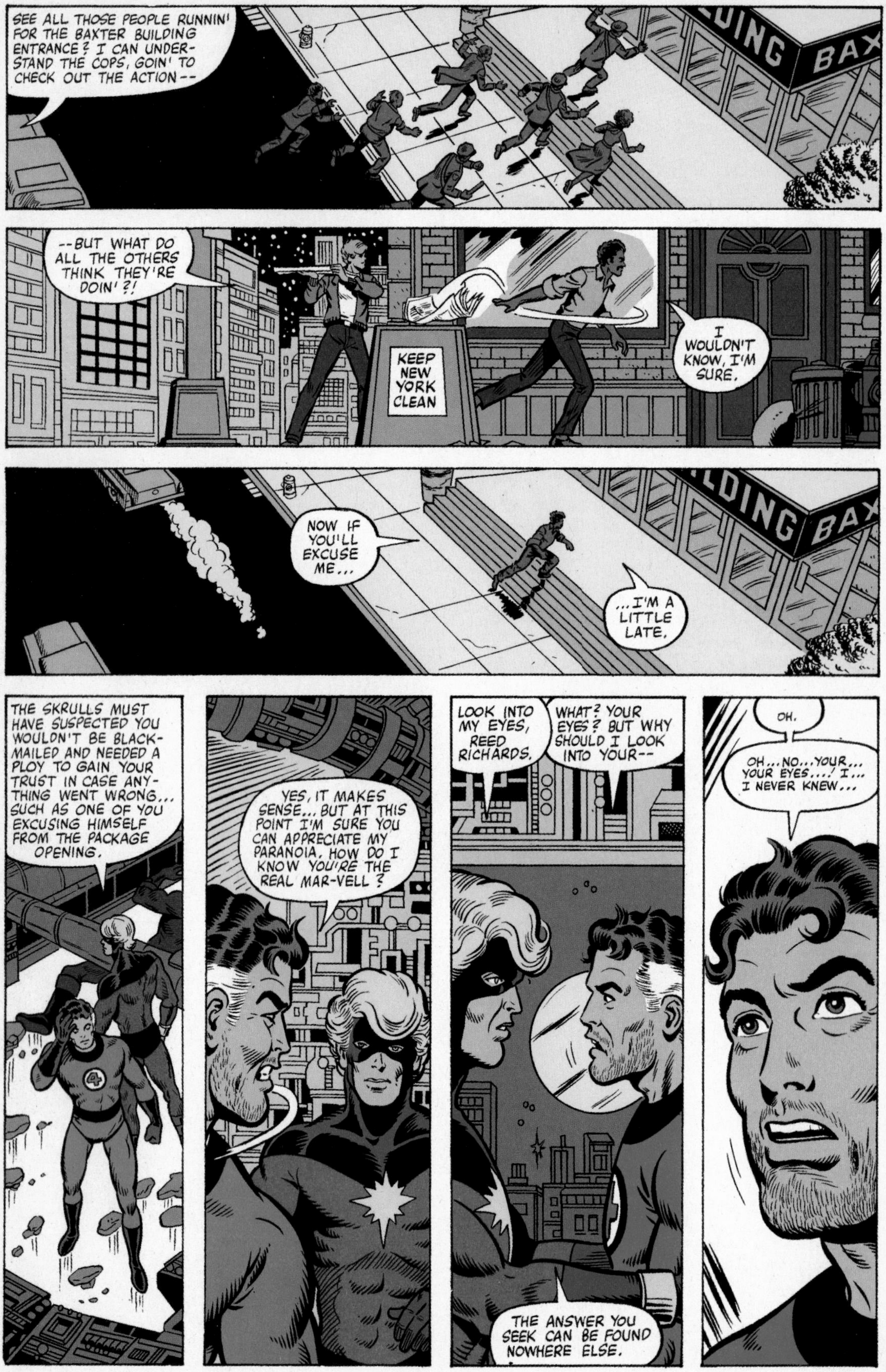
SEE ALL THOSE PEOPLE RUNNIN' FOR THE BAXTER BUILDING ENTRANCE? I CAN UNDERSTAND THE COPS, GOIN' TO CHECK OUT THE ACTION--
--BUT WHAT DO ALL THE OTHERS THINK THEY'RE DOIN'?!
KEEP NEW YORK CLEAN
I WOULDN'T KNOW, I'M SURE.
NOW IF YOU'LL EXCUSE ME...
...I'M A LITTLE LATE.
THE SKRULLS MUST HAVE SUSPECTED YOU WOULDN'T BE BLACKMAILED AND NEEDED A PLOY TO GAIN YOUR TRUST IN CASE ANYTHING WENT WRONG... SUCH AS ONE OF YOU EXCUSING HIMSELF FROM THE PACKAGE OPENING.
YES, IT MAKES SENSE... BUT AT THIS POINT I'M SURE YOU CAN APPRECIATE MY PARANOIA. HOW DO I KNOW YOU'RE THE REAL MAR-VELL?
LOOK INTO MY EYES, REED RICHARDS.
WHAT? YOUR EYES? BUT WHY SHOULD I LOOK INTO YOUR--
THE ANSWER YOU SEEK CAN BE FOUND NOWHERE ELSE.
OH.
OH... NO... YOUR... YOUR EYES...! I... I NEVER KNEW...

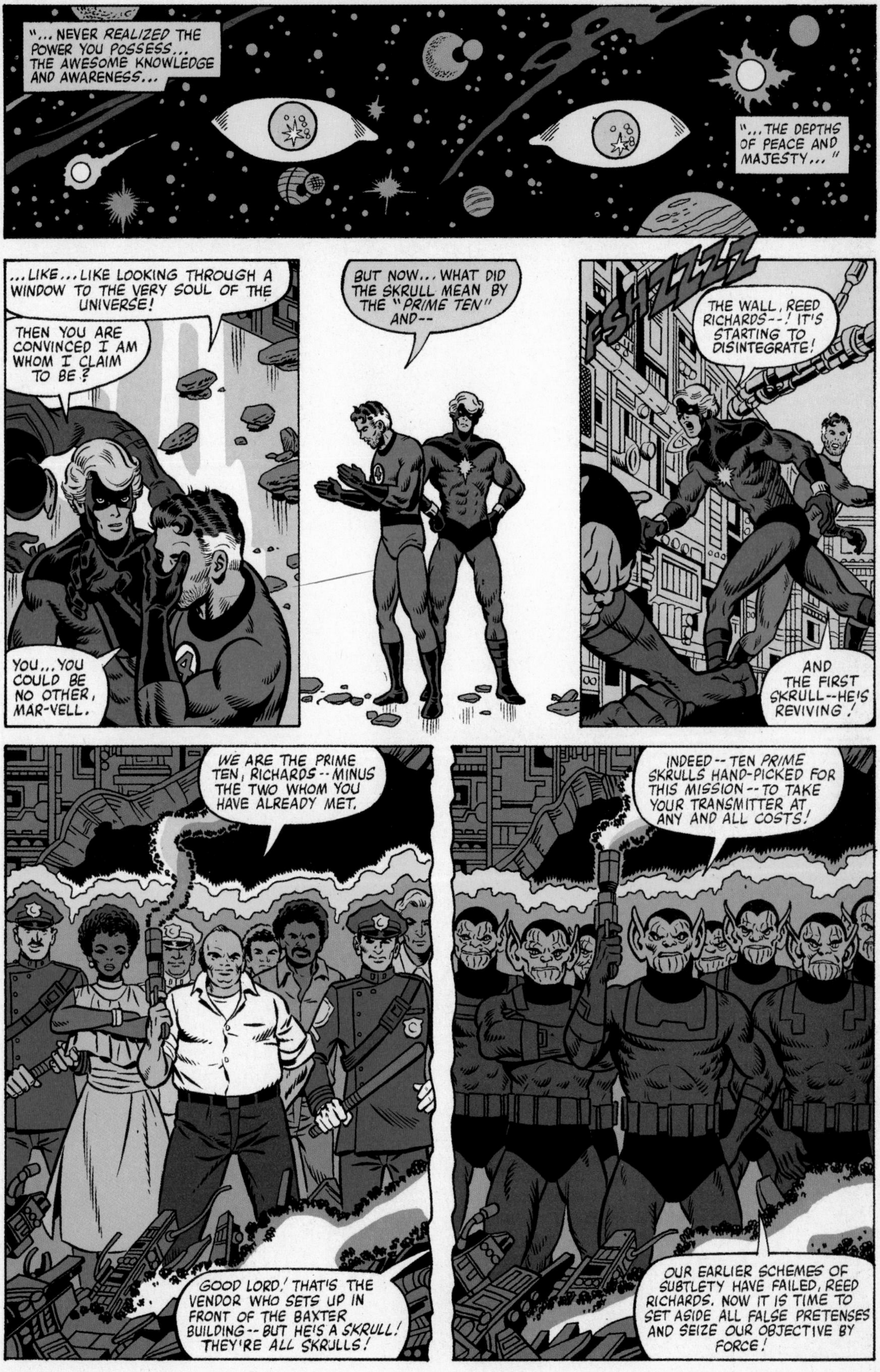
"... NEVER REALIZED THE POWER YOU POSSESS... THE AWESOME KNOWLEDGE AND AWARENESS...
"... THE DEPTHS OF PEACE AND MAJESTY..."
... LIKE... LIKE LOOKING THROUGH A WINDOW TO THE VERY SOUL OF THE UNIVERSE!
THEN YOU ARE CONVINCED I AM WHOM I CLAIM TO BE?
YOU... YOU COULD BE NO OTHER, MAR-VELL.
BUT NOW... WHAT DID THE SKRULL MEAN BY THE "PRIME TEN" AND--
FSHZZZZZ
THE WALL, REED RICHARDS--! IT'S STARTING TO DISINTEGRATE!
AND THE FIRST SKRULL--HE'S REVIVING!
WE ARE THE PRIME TEN, RICHARDS--MINUS THE TWO WHOM YOU HAVE ALREADY MET.
GOOD LORD! THAT'S THE VENDOR WHO SETS UP IN FRONT OF THE BAXTER BUILDING--BUT HE'S A SKRULL! THEY'RE ALL SKRULLS!
INDEED--TEN PRIME SKRULLS HAND-PICKED FOR THIS MISSION--TO TAKE YOUR TRANSMITTER AT ANY AND ALL COSTS!
OUR EARLIER SCHEMES OF SUBTLETY HAVE FAILED, REED RICHARDS. NOW IT IS TIME TO SET ASIDE ALL FALSE PRETENSES AND SEIZE OUR OBJECTIVE BY FORCE!

NOW *BOTH* OF THE *FALLEN SKRULLS* HAVE *REVIVED!*

TAKE THEM-- BUT BEWARE OF THE *KREE* MAR-VELL!

EVEN WITH OUR *COMBINED POWERS,* MAR-VELL, CAN WE HOPE TO DEFEAT *TEN* SKRULLS?

IF WE CAN MANEUVER THEM INTO YOUR *TRANSMITTER* AND SEND THEM BACK TO THEIR *ASTEROID LAB*--

YES, BUT WITH JUST THE *TWO* OF US-- HOW?

IF ONLY THE *OTHERS* WERE HERE TO HELP US FIGHT AS A *TEAM,* THEN IT MIGHT BE A *FAIR FI*--

WE *ARE* HERE, STRETCH!

WHAT?! THAT WAS *BEN'S* VOICE!

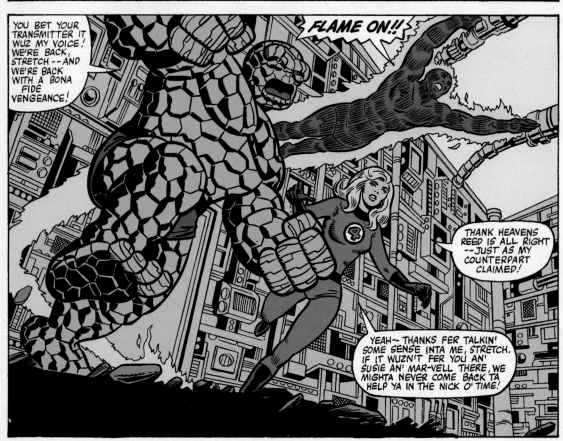

YOU BET YOUR *TRANSMITTER* IT WUZ MY VOICE! WE'RE *BACK,* STRETCH -- AND WE'RE BACK WITH A *BONA FIDE* VENGEANCE!

FLAME ON!!

THANK HEAVENS *REED* IS ALL RIGHT --JUST AS MY *COUNTERPART* CLAIMED!

YEAH-- THANKS FER TALKIN' SOME *SENSE* INTA ME, STRETCH. IF IT WUZN'T FER YOU AN' SUSIE AN' MAR-VELL THERE, WE MIGHTA NEVER COME BACK TA HELP YA IN THE NICK O' TIME!

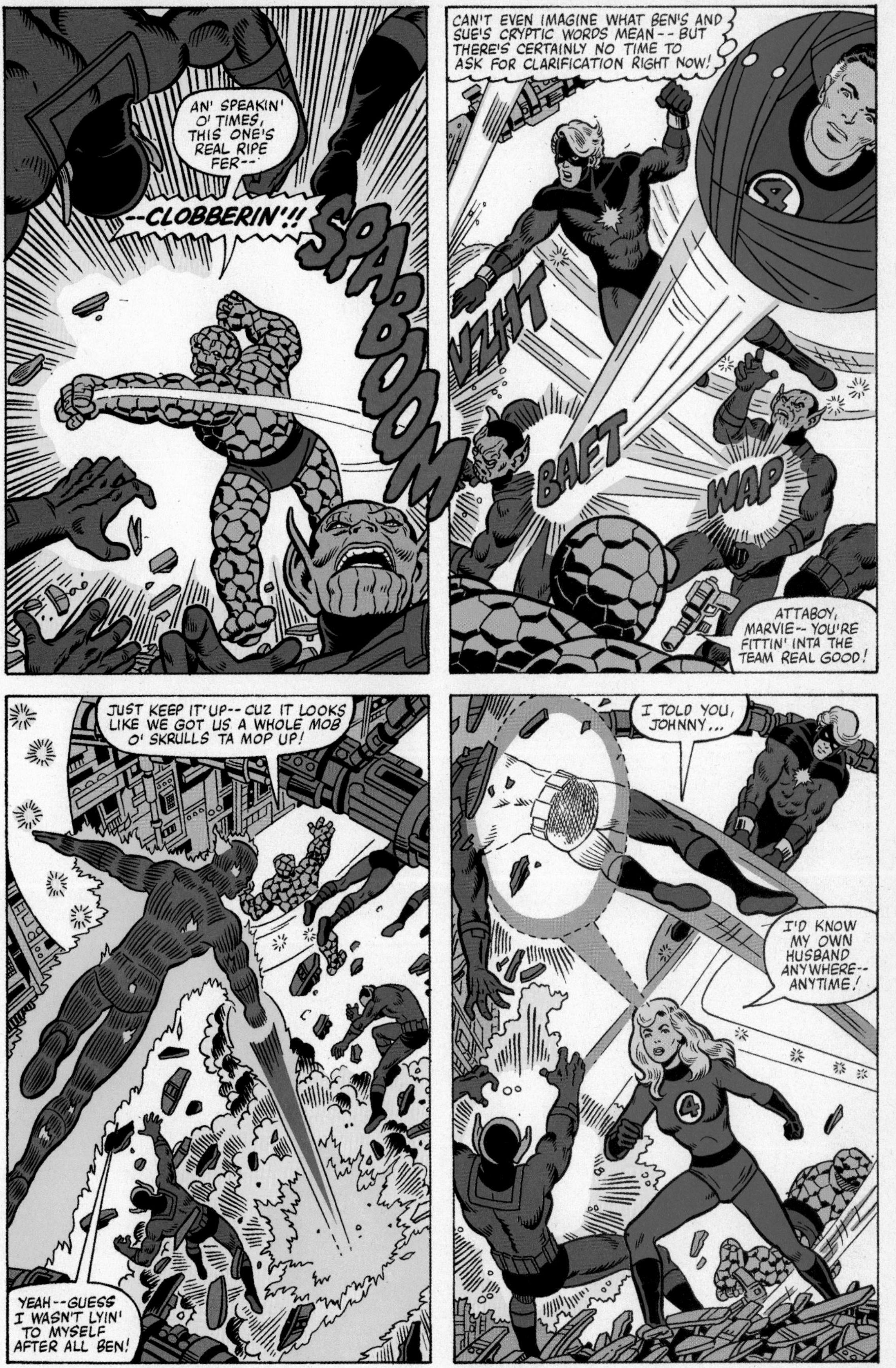
AN' SPEAKIN' O' TIMES, THIS ONE'S REAL RIPE FER--
--CLOBBERIN'!!
SPABOOM
CAN'T EVEN IMAGINE WHAT BEN'S AND SUE'S CRYPTIC WORDS MEAN-- BUT THERE'S CERTAINLY NO TIME TO ASK FOR CLARIFICATION RIGHT NOW!
VZHT
BAFT
WAP
ATTABOY, MARVIE-- YOU'RE FITTIN' INTA THE TEAM REAL GOOD!
JUST KEEP IT UP-- CUZ IT LOOKS LIKE WE GOT US A WHOLE MOB O' SKRULLS TA MOP UP!
YEAH--GUESS I WASN'T LYIN' TO MYSELF AFTER ALL BEN!
I TOLD YOU, JOHNNY...
I'D KNOW MY OWN HUSBAND ANYWHERE-- ANYTIME!

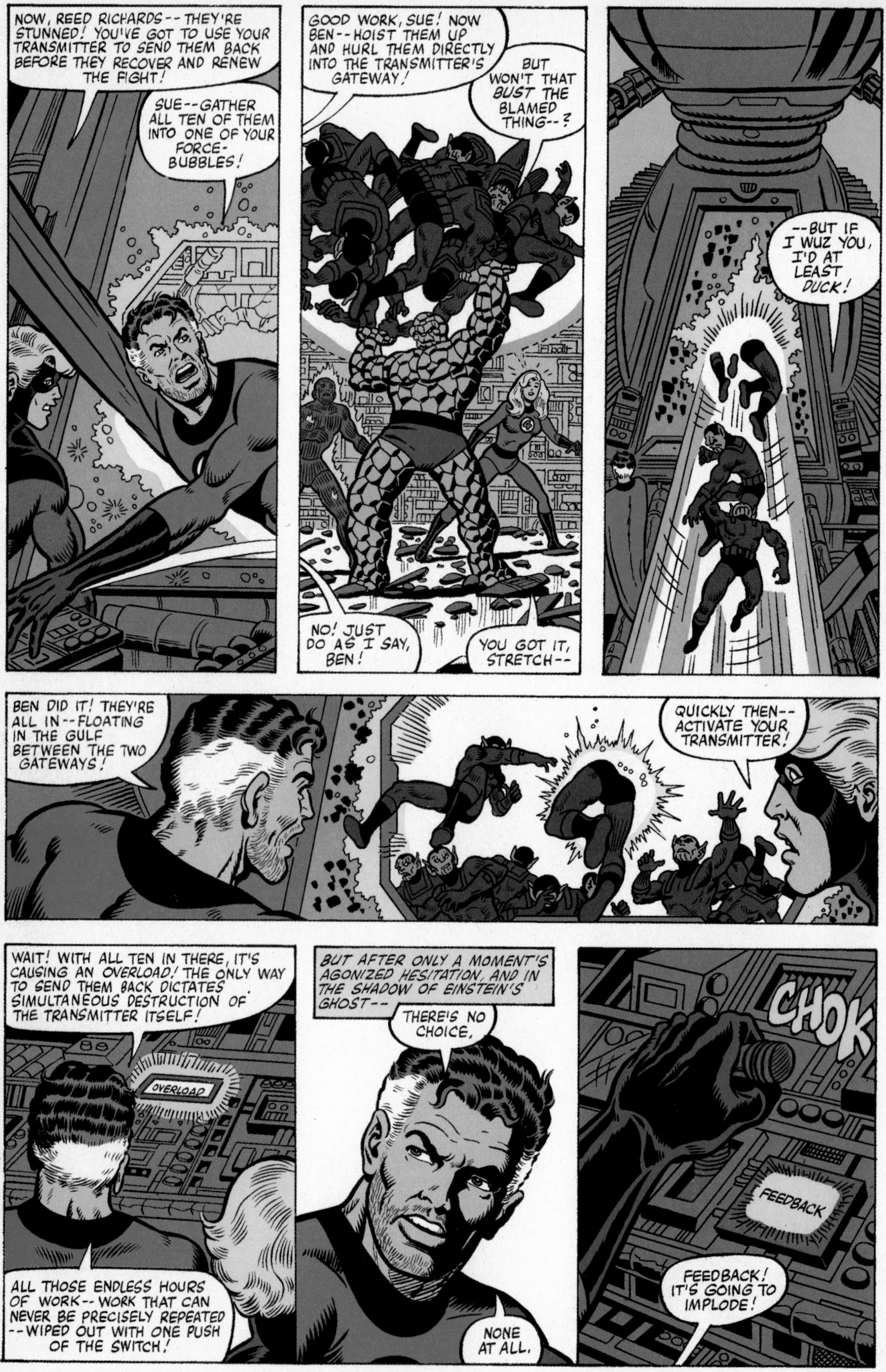
NOW, REED RICHARDS-- THEY'RE STUNNED! YOU'VE GOT TO USE YOUR TRANSMITTER TO SEND THEM BACK BEFORE THEY RECOVER AND RENEW THE FIGHT!
SUE--GATHER ALL TEN OF THEM INTO ONE OF YOUR FORCE-BUBBLES!
GOOD WORK, SUE! NOW BEN--HOIST THEM UP AND HURL THEM DIRECTLY INTO THE TRANSMITTER'S GATEWAY!
BUT WON'T THAT BUST THE BLAMED THING--?
NO! JUST DO AS I SAY, BEN!
YOU GOT IT, STRETCH--
--BUT IF I WUZ YOU, I'D AT LEAST DUCK!
BEN DID IT! THEY'RE ALL IN--FLOATING IN THE GULF BETWEEN THE TWO GATEWAYS!
QUICKLY THEN--ACTIVATE YOUR TRANSMITTER!
WAIT! WITH ALL TEN IN THERE, IT'S CAUSING AN OVERLOAD! THE ONLY WAY TO SEND THEM BACK DICTATES SIMULTANEOUS DESTRUCTION OF THE TRANSMITTER ITSELF!
OVERLOAD
ALL THOSE ENDLESS HOURS OF WORK--WORK THAT CAN NEVER BE PRECISELY REPEATED --WIPED OUT WITH ONE PUSH OF THE SWITCH!
BUT AFTER ONLY A MOMENT'S AGONIZED HESITATION, AND IN THE SHADOW OF EINSTEIN'S GHOST--
THERE'S NO CHOICE.
NONE AT ALL.
CHOK
FEEDBACK
FEEDBACK! IT'S GOING TO IMPLODE!

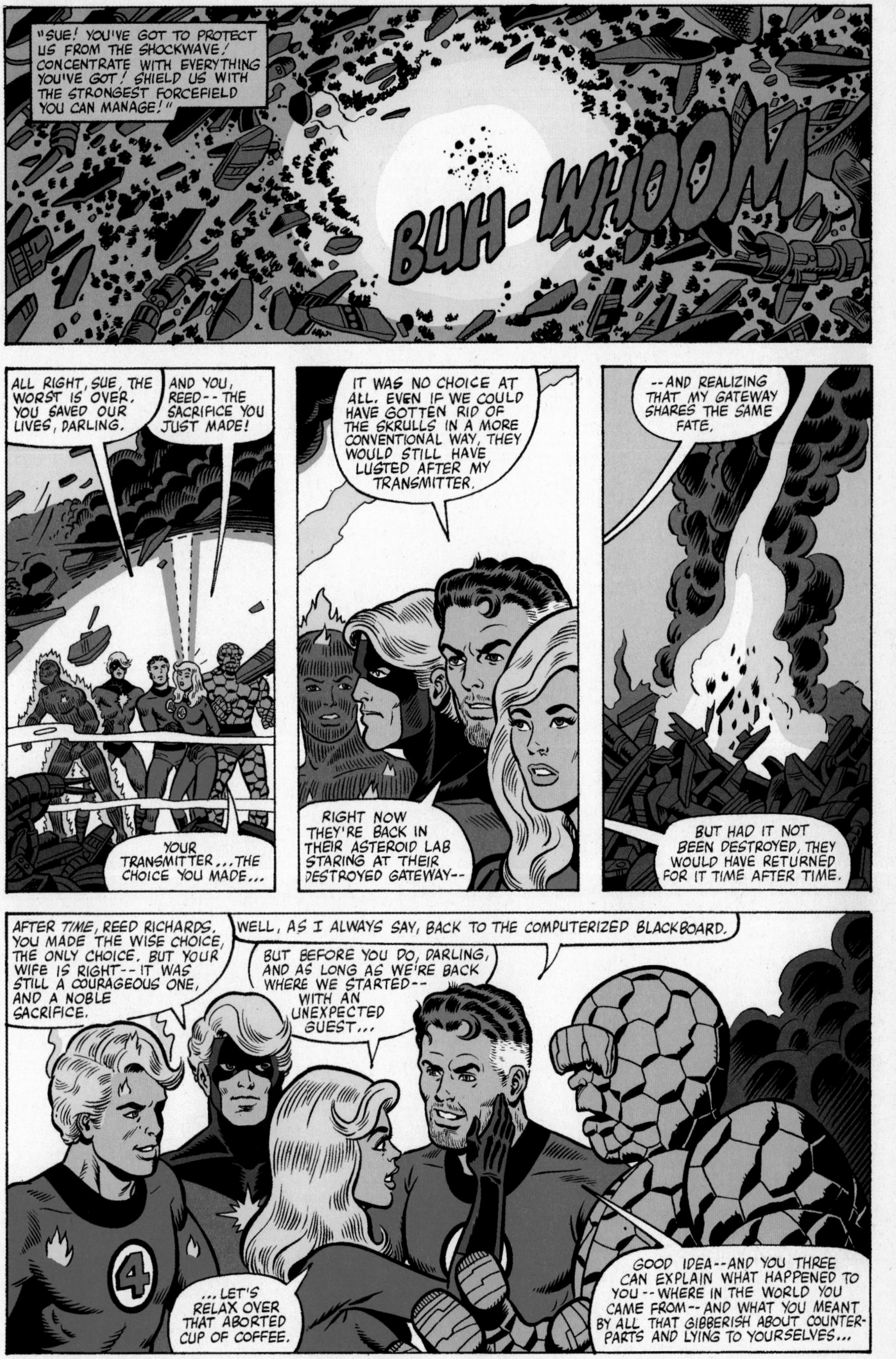
"SUE! YOU'VE GOT TO PROTECT US FROM THE SHOCKWAVE! CONCENTRATE WITH EVERYTHING YOU'VE GOT! SHIELD US WITH THE STRONGEST FORCEFIELD YOU CAN MANAGE!"
BUH-WHOOM
ALL RIGHT, SUE, THE WORST IS OVER. YOU SAVED OUR LIVES, DARLING.
AND YOU, REED-- THE SACRIFICE YOU JUST MADE!
YOUR TRANSMITTER... THE CHOICE YOU MADE...
IT WAS NO CHOICE AT ALL. EVEN IF WE COULD HAVE GOTTEN RID OF THE SKRULLS IN A MORE CONVENTIONAL WAY, THEY WOULD STILL HAVE LUSTED AFTER MY TRANSMITTER.
RIGHT NOW THEY'RE BACK IN THEIR ASTEROID LAB STARING AT THEIR DESTROYED GATEWAY--
--AND REALIZING THAT MY GATEWAY SHARES THE SAME FATE.
BUT HAD IT NOT BEEN DESTROYED, THEY WOULD HAVE RETURNED FOR IT TIME AFTER TIME.
AFTER *TIME*, REED RICHARDS. YOU MADE THE WISE CHOICE, THE ONLY CHOICE. BUT YOUR WIFE IS RIGHT-- IT WAS STILL A COURAGEOUS ONE, AND A NOBLE SACRIFICE.
WELL, AS I ALWAYS SAY, BACK TO THE COMPUTERIZED BLACKBOARD.
BUT BEFORE YOU DO, DARLING, AND AS LONG AS WE'RE BACK WHERE WE STARTED-- WITH AN UNEXPECTED GUEST...
...LET'S RELAX OVER THAT ABORTED CUP OF COFFEE.
GOOD IDEA--AND YOU THREE CAN EXPLAIN WHAT HAPPENED TO YOU--WHERE IN THE WORLD YOU CAME FROM--AND WHAT YOU MEANT BY ALL THAT GIBBERISH ABOUT COUNTER-PARTS AND LYING TO YOURSELVES...

EPILOGUE

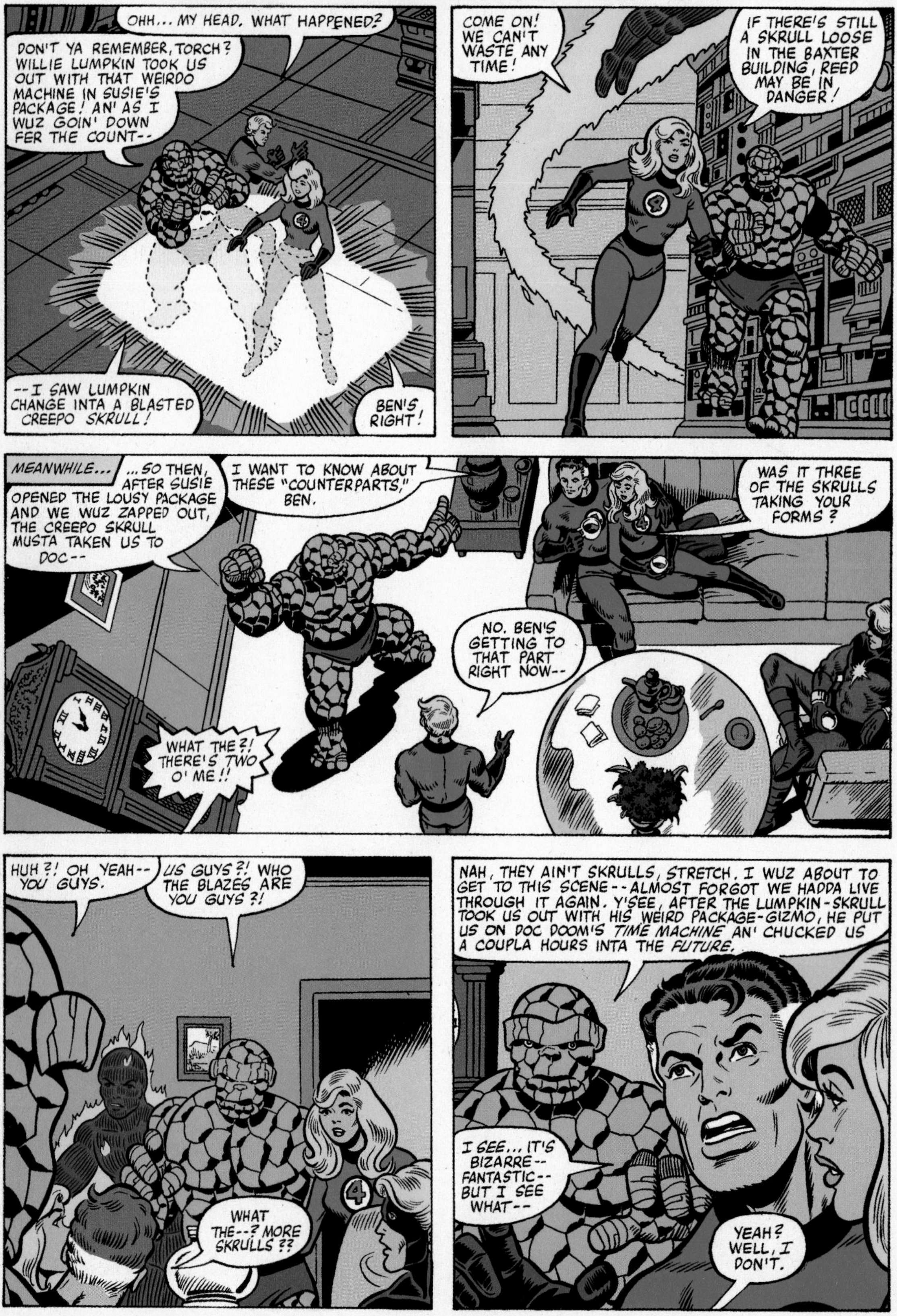

OHH... MY HEAD. WHAT HAPPENED?
DON'T YA REMEMBER, TORCH? WILLIE LUMPKIN TOOK US OUT WITH THAT WEIRDO MACHINE IN SUSIE'S PACKAGE! AN' AS I WUZ GOIN' DOWN FER THE COUNT--
--I SAW LUMPKIN CHANGE INTA A BLASTED CREEPO SKRULL!
BEN'S RIGHT!
COME ON! WE CAN'T WASTE ANY TIME!
IF THERE'S STILL A SKRULL LOOSE IN THE BAXTER BUILDING, REED MAY BE IN DANGER!
MEANWHILE...
...SO THEN, AFTER SUSIE OPENED THE LOUSY PACKAGE AND WE WUZ ZAPPED OUT, THE CREEPO SKRULL MUSTA TAKEN US TO DOC--
I WANT TO KNOW ABOUT THESE "COUNTERPARTS," BEN.
WAS IT THREE OF THE SKRULLS TAKING YOUR FORMS?
NO. BEN'S GETTING TO THAT PART RIGHT NOW--
WHAT THE?! THERE'S TWO O' ME!!
HUH?! OH YEAH--YOU GUYS.
US GUYS?! WHO THE BLAZES ARE YOU GUYS?!
WHAT THE--? MORE SKRULLS??
NAH, THEY AIN'T SKRULLS, STRETCH. I WUZ ABOUT TO GET TO THIS SCENE--ALMOST FORGOT WE HADDA LIVE THROUGH IT AGAIN. Y'SEE, AFTER THE LUMPKIN-SKRULL TOOK US OUT WITH HIS WEIRD PACKAGE-GIZMO, HE PUT US ON DOC DOOM'S TIME MACHINE AN' CHUCKED US A COUPLA HOURS INTA THE FUTURE.
I SEE... IT'S BIZARRE--FANTASTIC--BUT I SEE WHAT--
YEAH? WELL, I DON'T.

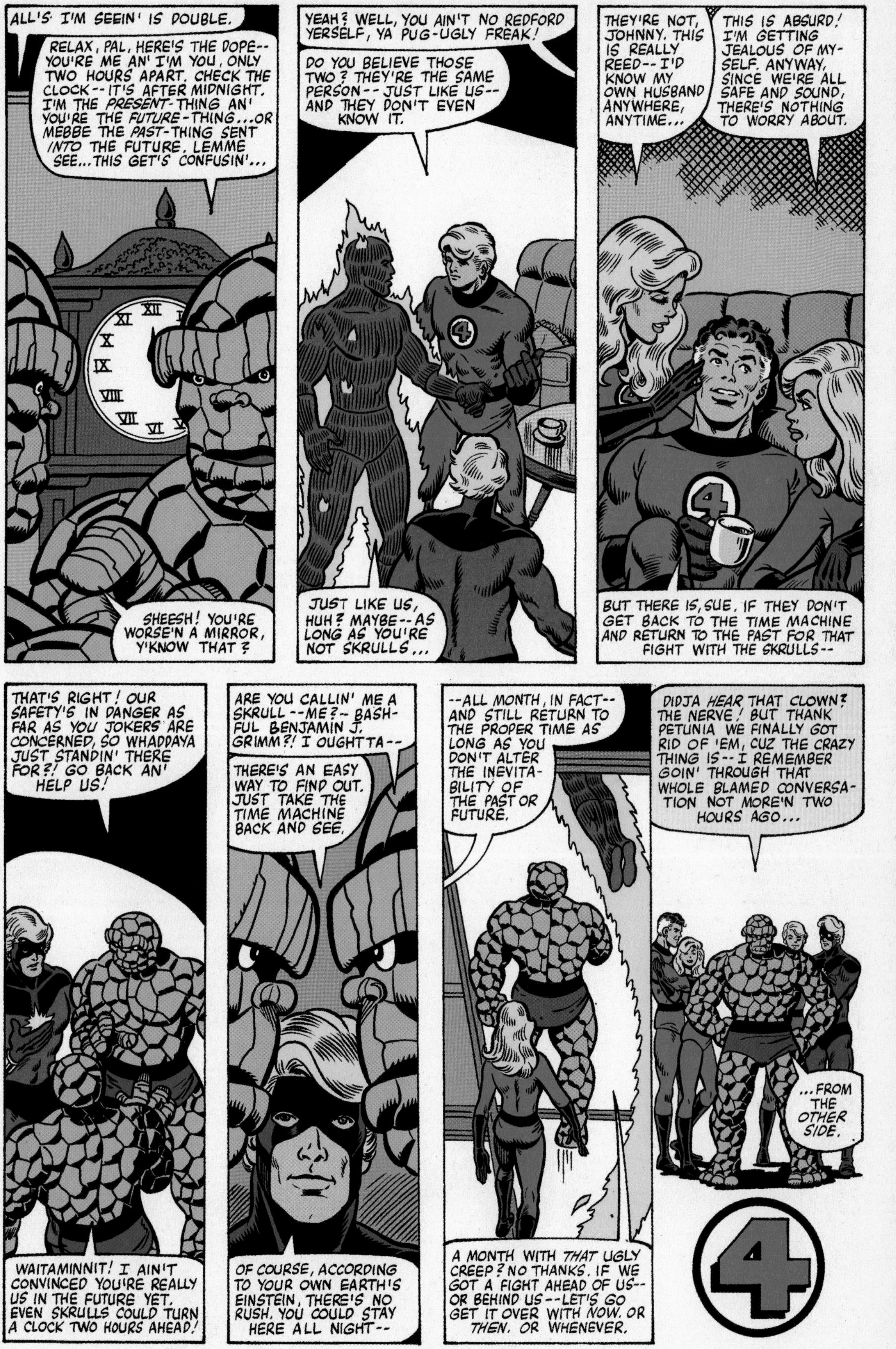
ALL'S I'M SEEIN' IS DOUBLE.
RELAX, PAL, HERE'S THE DOPE-- YOU'RE ME AN' I'M YOU, ONLY TWO HOURS APART. CHECK THE CLOCK--IT'S AFTER MIDNIGHT. I'M THE PRESENT-THING AN' YOU'RE THE FUTURE-THING...OR MEBBE THE PAST-THING SENT INTO THE FUTURE. LEMME SEE...THIS GET'S CONFUSIN'...
SHEESH! YOU'RE WORSE'N A MIRROR, Y'KNOW THAT?
YEAH? WELL, YOU AIN'T NO REDFORD YERSELF, YA PUG-UGLY FREAK!
DO YOU BELIEVE THOSE TWO? THEY'RE THE SAME PERSON--JUST LIKE US--AND THEY DON'T EVEN KNOW IT.
JUST LIKE US, HUH? MAYBE--AS LONG AS YOU'RE NOT SKRULLS...
THEY'RE NOT, JOHNNY. THIS IS REALLY REED--I'D KNOW MY OWN HUSBAND ANYWHERE, ANYTIME...
THIS IS ABSURD! I'M GETTING JEALOUS OF MY-SELF. ANYWAY, SINCE WE'RE ALL SAFE AND SOUND, THERE'S NOTHING TO WORRY ABOUT.
BUT THERE IS, SUE. IF THEY DON'T GET BACK TO THE TIME MACHINE AND RETURN TO THE PAST FOR THAT FIGHT WITH THE SKRULLS--
THAT'S RIGHT! OUR SAFETY'S IN DANGER AS FAR AS YOU JOKERS ARE CONCERNED, SO WHADDAYA JUST STANDIN' THERE FOR?! GO BACK AN' HELP US!
WAITAMINNIT! I AIN'T CONVINCED YOU'RE REALLY US IN THE FUTURE YET. EVEN SKRULLS COULD TURN A CLOCK TWO HOURS AHEAD!
ARE YOU CALLIN' ME A SKRULL--ME?--BASH-FUL BENJAMIN J. GRIMM?! I OUGHTTA--
THERE'S AN EASY WAY TO FIND OUT. JUST TAKE THE TIME MACHINE BACK AND SEE.
OF COURSE, ACCORDING TO YOUR OWN EARTH'S EINSTEIN, THERE'S NO RUSH. YOU COULD STAY HERE ALL NIGHT--
--ALL MONTH, IN FACT--AND STILL RETURN TO THE PROPER TIME AS LONG AS YOU DON'T ALTER THE INEVITA-BILITY OF THE PAST OR FUTURE.
A MONTH WITH THAT UGLY CREEP? NO THANKS. IF WE GOT A FIGHT AHEAD OF US--OR BEHIND US--LET'S GO GET IT OVER WITH NOW. OR THEN. OR WHENEVER.
DIDJA HEAR THAT CLOWN? THE NERVE! BUT THANK PETUNIA WE FINALLY GOT RID OF 'EM, CUZ THE CRAZY THING IS--I REMEMBER GOIN' THROUGH THAT WHOLE BLAMED CONVERSA-TION NOT MORE'N TWO HOURS AGO...
...FROM THE OTHER SIDE.

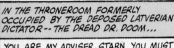

IN THE THRONEROOM FORMERLY OCCUPIED BY THE DEPOSED LATVERIAN DICTATOR -- THE DREAD DR. DOOM...

YOU ARE MY ADVISER, STARN. YOU MUST HELP ME! I AM PLAGUED WITH WORRIES, VEXED BY UNCERTAINTY!

UNCERTAINTY, KING ZORBA?

SINCE MY ELECTION BY THE PEOPLE OF LATVERIA, MATTERS HAVE ONLY GOTTEN WORSE, STARN! I'VE HAD TO MAKE SO MANY HARD DECISIONS -- IT IS FAR MORE DIFFICULT THAN I IMAGINED!

SO IT HAS BEEN WITH EVERY NEW MONARCH IN HISTORY, MY LIEGE. THE AFFAIRS OF--

KEESH

WHAT THE--?!

OUTSIDE, KING ZORBA -- THE SOUNDS OF A MOB!

THE RETURN OF DOCTOR DOOM!
CHAPTER ONE
The POWER of the PEOPLE!

IT IS AS I FEARED, KING ZORBA. THE PEOPLE PROTEST THE SWEEPING CHANGES YOU HAVE INSTITUTED!

BUT THEY ELECTED ME TO MAKE CHANGES -- TO IMPROVE THE QUALITY OF LIFE IN LATVERIA!

NO MORE TAXES!

GIVE US DOOM!

DOOM WAS BETTER!

YOU'VE BETRAYED US, ZORBA! YOUR INCREASED TAXES WILL BREAK THE BACK OF OUR NATION!

A CHILLING NEW CHAPTER IN THE HISTORY OF LATVERIA! CHRONICLED BY:

DOUG MOENCH, WRITER
TOM SUTTON, ARTIST
JIM NOVAK, LETTERER
BEN SEAN, COLORIST
JIM SALICRUP, EDITOR

JIM SHOOTER, EDITOR-IN-CHIEF

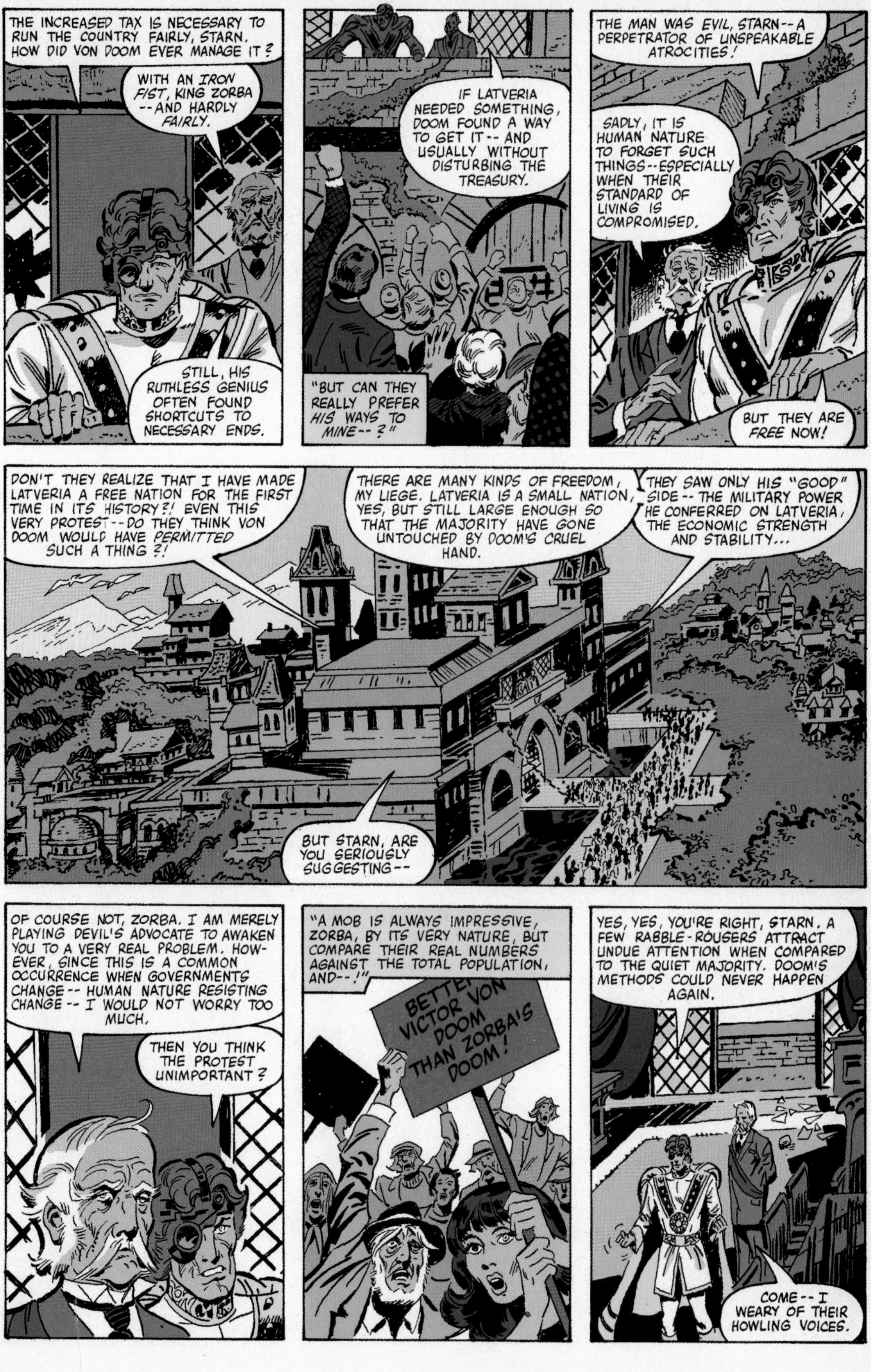
THE INCREASED TAX IS NECESSARY TO RUN THE COUNTRY FAIRLY, STARN. HOW DID VON DOOM EVER MANAGE IT?
WITH AN IRON FIST, KING ZORBA --AND HARDLY FAIRLY.
STILL, HIS RUTHLESS GENIUS OFTEN FOUND SHORTCUTS TO NECESSARY ENDS.
IF LATVERIA NEEDED SOMETHING, DOOM FOUND A WAY TO GET IT -- AND USUALLY WITHOUT DISTURBING THE TREASURY.
"BUT CAN THEY REALLY PREFER HIS WAYS TO MINE-- ?"
THE MAN WAS EVIL, STARN-- A PERPETRATOR OF UNSPEAKABLE ATROCITIES!
SADLY, IT IS HUMAN NATURE TO FORGET SUCH THINGS--ESPECIALLY WHEN THEIR STANDARD OF LIVING IS COMPROMISED.
BUT THEY ARE FREE NOW!
DON'T THEY REALIZE THAT I HAVE MADE LATVERIA A FREE NATION FOR THE FIRST TIME IN ITS HISTORY?! EVEN THIS VERY PROTEST--DO THEY THINK VON DOOM WOULD HAVE PERMITTED SUCH A THING?!
THERE ARE MANY KINDS OF FREEDOM, MY LIEGE. LATVERIA IS A SMALL NATION, YES, BUT STILL LARGE ENOUGH SO THAT THE MAJORITY HAVE GONE UNTOUCHED BY DOOM'S CRUEL HAND.
THEY SAW ONLY HIS "GOOD" SIDE -- THE MILITARY POWER HE CONFERRED ON LATVERIA, THE ECONOMIC STRENGTH AND STABILITY...
BUT STARN, ARE YOU SERIOUSLY SUGGESTING--
OF COURSE NOT, ZORBA. I AM MERELY PLAYING DEVIL'S ADVOCATE TO AWAKEN YOU TO A VERY REAL PROBLEM. HOWEVER, SINCE THIS IS A COMMON OCCURRENCE WHEN GOVERNMENTS CHANGE -- HUMAN NATURE RESISTING CHANGE -- I WOULD NOT WORRY TOO MUCH.
THEN YOU THINK THE PROTEST UNIMPORTANT?
"A MOB IS ALWAYS IMPRESSIVE, ZORBA, BY ITS VERY NATURE, BUT COMPARE THEIR REAL NUMBERS AGAINST THE TOTAL POPULATION, AND--!"
BETTER VICTOR VON DOOM THAN ZORBA'S DOOM!
YES, YES, YOU'RE RIGHT, STARN. A FEW RABBLE-ROUSERS ATTRACT UNDUE ATTENTION WHEN COMPARED TO THE QUIET MAJORITY. DOOM'S METHODS COULD NEVER HAPPEN AGAIN.
COME-- I WEARY OF THEIR HOWLING VOICES.

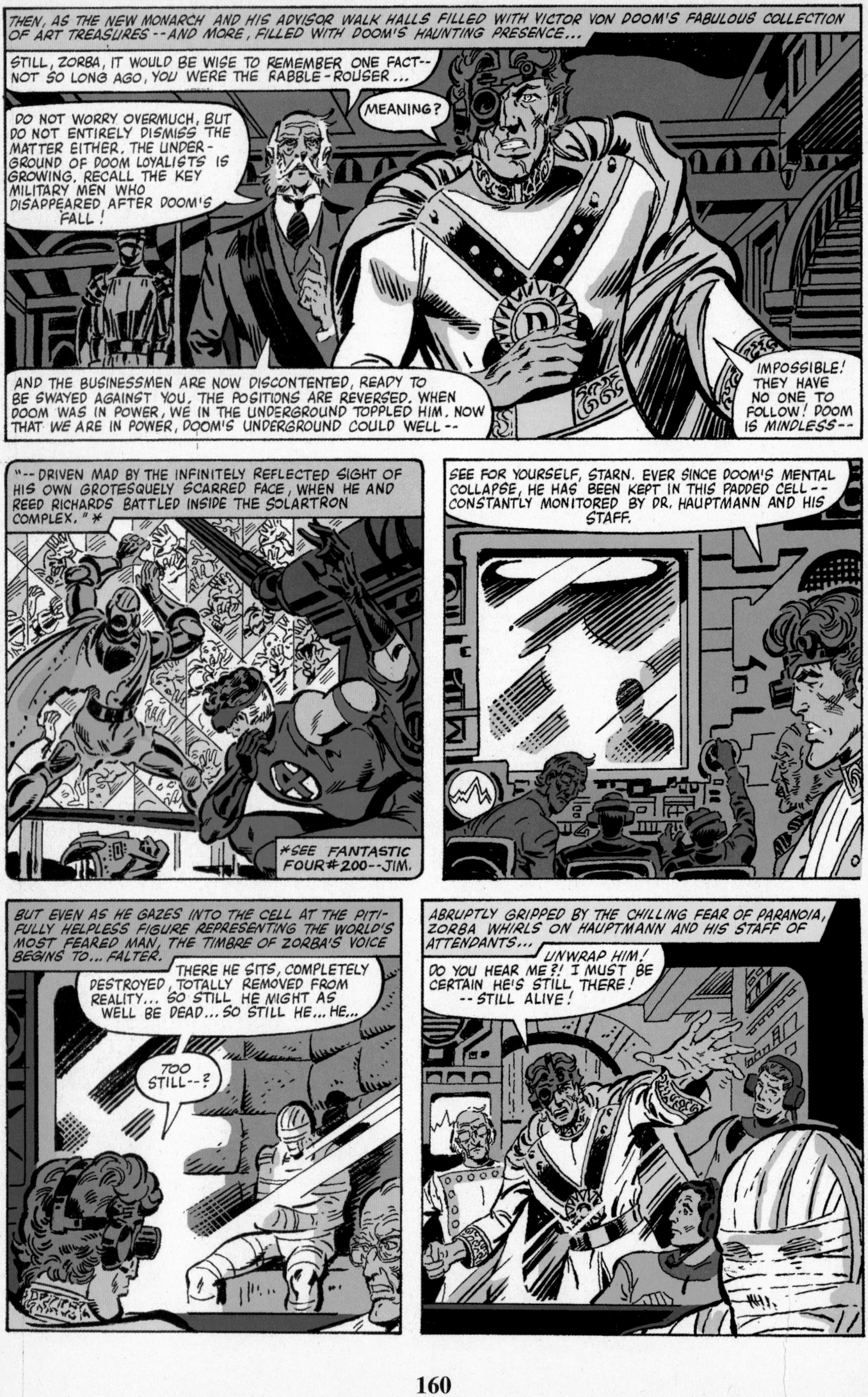
THEN, AS THE NEW MONARCH AND HIS ADVISOR WALK HALLS FILLED WITH VICTOR VON DOOM'S FABULOUS COLLECTION OF ART TREASURES--AND MORE, FILLED WITH DOOM'S HAUNTING PRESENCE...
STILL, ZORBA, IT WOULD BE WISE TO REMEMBER ONE FACT--NOT SO LONG AGO, YOU WERE THE RABBLE-ROUSER...
MEANING?
DO NOT WORRY OVERMUCH, BUT DO NOT ENTIRELY DISMISS THE MATTER EITHER. THE UNDERGROUND OF DOOM LOYALISTS IS GROWING. RECALL THE KEY MILITARY MEN WHO DISAPPEARED AFTER DOOM'S FALL!
AND THE BUSINESSMEN ARE NOW DISCONTENTED, READY TO BE SWAYED AGAINST YOU. THE POSITIONS ARE REVERSED. WHEN DOOM WAS IN POWER, WE IN THE UNDERGROUND TOPPLED HIM. NOW THAT WE ARE IN POWER, DOOM'S UNDERGROUND COULD WELL--
IMPOSSIBLE! THEY HAVE NO ONE TO FOLLOW! DOOM IS MINDLESS--
"--DRIVEN MAD BY THE INFINITELY REFLECTED SIGHT OF HIS OWN GROTESQUELY SCARRED FACE, WHEN HE AND REED RICHARDS BATTLED INSIDE THE SOLARTRON COMPLEX."*
*SEE FANTASTIC FOUR #200--JIM.
SEE FOR YOURSELF, STARN. EVER SINCE DOOM'S MENTAL COLLAPSE, HE HAS BEEN KEPT IN THIS PADDED CELL--CONSTANTLY MONITORED BY DR. HAUPTMANN AND HIS STAFF.
BUT EVEN AS HE GAZES INTO THE CELL AT THE PITIFULLY HELPLESS FIGURE REPRESENTING THE WORLD'S MOST FEARED MAN, THE TIMBRE OF ZORBA'S VOICE BEGINS TO... FALTER.
THERE HE SITS, COMPLETELY DESTROYED, TOTALLY REMOVED FROM REALITY... SO STILL HE MIGHT AS WELL BE DEAD... SO STILL HE... HE...
TOO STILL--?
ABRUPTLY GRIPPED BY THE CHILLING FEAR OF PARANOIA, ZORBA WHIRLS ON HAUPTMANN AND HIS STAFF OF ATTENDANTS...
UNWRAP HIM! DO YOU HEAR ME?! I MUST BE CERTAIN HE'S STILL THERE! --STILL ALIVE!

BUT KING ZORBA, I ASSURE YOU HE IS STILL ALIVE! WE HAVE THE MOST SOPHISTICATED ELECTRONIC EQUIPMENT--

DIDN'T YOU HEAR ME, HAUPTMANN?! UNWRAP HIM AT ONCE!

HURRY! I MUST SEE! I MUST BE SURE!

YES, MY LIEGE, THE BANDAGES WILL BE--

WAIT! HIS FACE--!

IT'S NOT VICTOR VON DOOM AT ALL! IT...IT'S A ROBOT!

WHAT?! THEN GET BACK, YOU FOOLS! IF IT'S ONE OF DOOM'S ROBOTS, IT'S LIABLE TO--

BOOOM

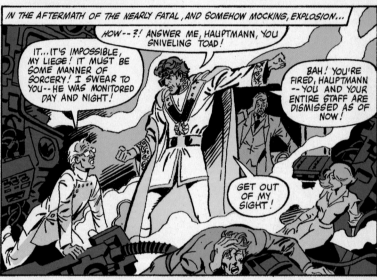

IN THE AFTERMATH OF THE NEARLY FATAL, AND SOMEHOW MOCKING, EXPLOSION...

HOW--?! ANSWER ME, HAUPTMANN, YOU SNIVELING TOAD!

IT...IT'S IMPOSSIBLE, MY LIEGE! IT MUST BE SOME MANNER OF SORCERY! I SWEAR TO YOU--HE WAS MONITORED DAY AND NIGHT!

BAH! YOU'RE FIRED, HAUPTMANN--YOU AND YOUR ENTIRE STAFF ARE DISMISSED AS OF NOW!

GET OUT OF MY SIGHT!

I...I STILL CAN'T BELIEVE IT, STARN. HOW COULD VON DOOM HAVE POSSIBLY ESCAPED--?

HE DIDN'T, ZORBA--HE WAS KIDNAPED! AND THERE IS ONLY ONE WAY TO LEARN HOW AND BY WHOM--WE MUST INFILTRATE THE DOOM LOYALIST UNDER-GROUND, SPY ON THEM AND--

NO! THAT'S JUST WHAT DOOM HIMSELF WOULD HAVE DONE! LATVERIA IS FREE NOW! I WILL NOT AUTHORIZE SPYING ON ANY CITIZEN--NO MATTER WHAT HIS POLITICAL BELIEFS ARE!

AS YOU WISH, MY MONARCH. BUT IN THE MEANTIME, I HOPE AND PRAY THAT VON DOOM REMAINS AS HE WAS... A HARMLESS CREATURE OF SHATTERED MIND AND SPIRIT.

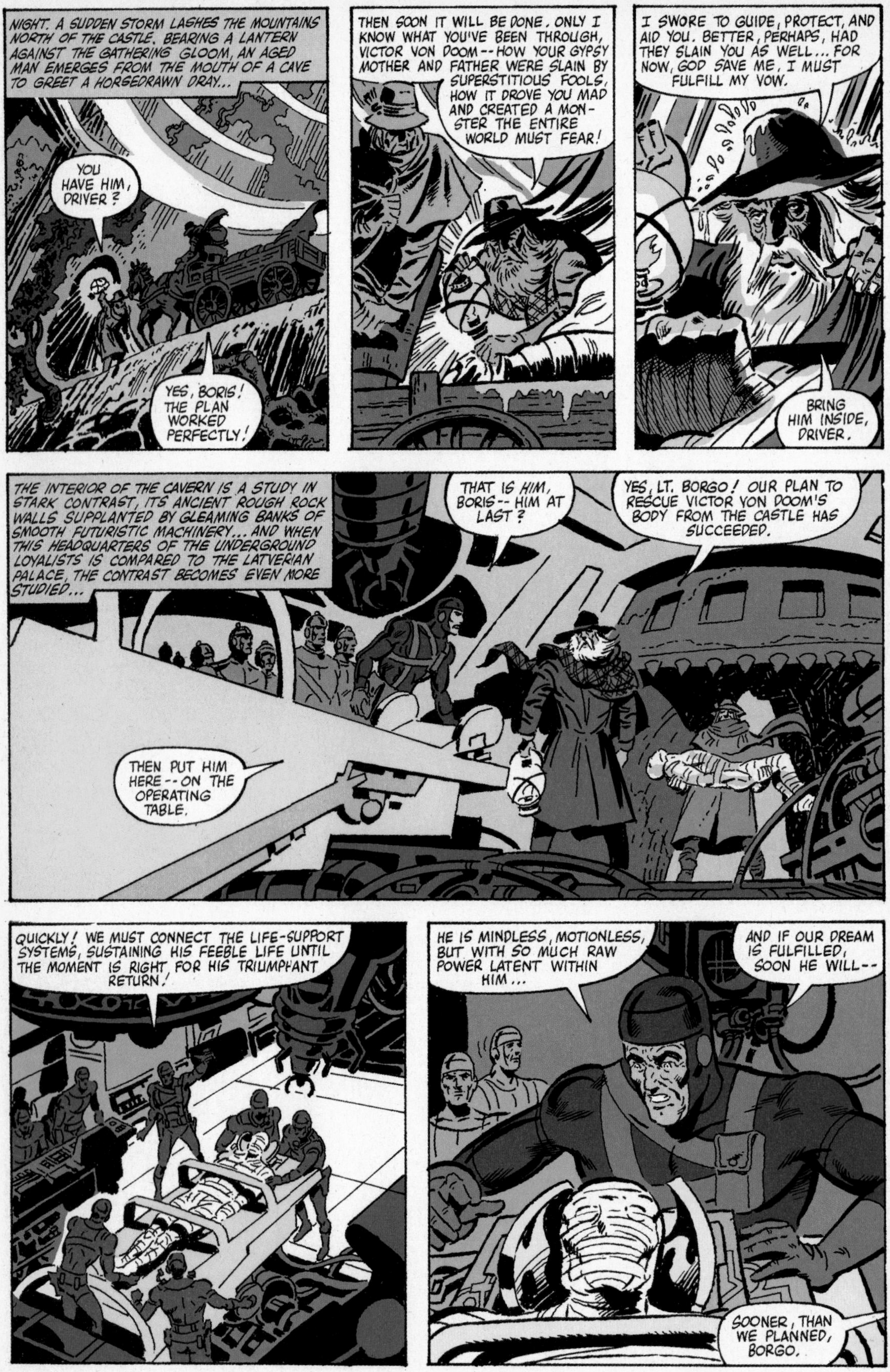
NIGHT. A SUDDEN STORM LASHES THE MOUNTAINS NORTH OF THE CASTLE. BEARING A LANTERN AGAINST THE GATHERING GLOOM, AN AGED MAN EMERGES FROM THE MOUTH OF A CAVE TO GREET A HORSEDRAWN DRAY...
YOU HAVE HIM, DRIVER?
YES, BORIS! THE PLAN WORKED PERFECTLY!
THEN SOON IT WILL BE DONE. ONLY I KNOW WHAT YOU'VE BEEN THROUGH, VICTOR VON DOOM--HOW YOUR GYPSY MOTHER AND FATHER WERE SLAIN BY SUPERSTITIOUS FOOLS, HOW IT DROVE YOU MAD AND CREATED A MONSTER THE ENTIRE WORLD MUST FEAR!
I SWORE TO GUIDE, PROTECT, AND AID YOU. BETTER, PERHAPS, HAD THEY SLAIN YOU AS WELL... FOR NOW, GOD SAVE ME, I MUST FULFILL MY VOW.
BRING HIM INSIDE, DRIVER.
THE INTERIOR OF THE CAVERN IS A STUDY IN STARK CONTRAST, ITS ANCIENT ROUGH ROCK WALLS SUPPLANTED BY GLEAMING BANKS OF SMOOTH FUTURISTIC MACHINERY... AND WHEN THIS HEADQUARTERS OF THE UNDERGROUND LOYALISTS IS COMPARED TO THE LATVERIAN PALACE, THE CONTRAST BECOMES EVEN MORE STUDIED...
THAT IS HIM, BORIS--HIM AT LAST?
YES, LT. BORGO! OUR PLAN TO RESCUE VICTOR VON DOOM'S BODY FROM THE CASTLE HAS SUCCEEDED.
THEN PUT HIM HERE--ON THE OPERATING TABLE.
QUICKLY! WE MUST CONNECT THE LIFE-SUPPORT SYSTEMS, SUSTAINING HIS FEEBLE LIFE UNTIL THE MOMENT IS RIGHT FOR HIS TRIUMPHANT RETURN!
HE IS MINDLESS, MOTIONLESS, BUT WITH SO MUCH RAW POWER LATENT WITHIN HIM...
AND IF OUR DREAM IS FULFILLED, SOON HE WILL--
SOONER, THAN WE PLANNED, BORGO.

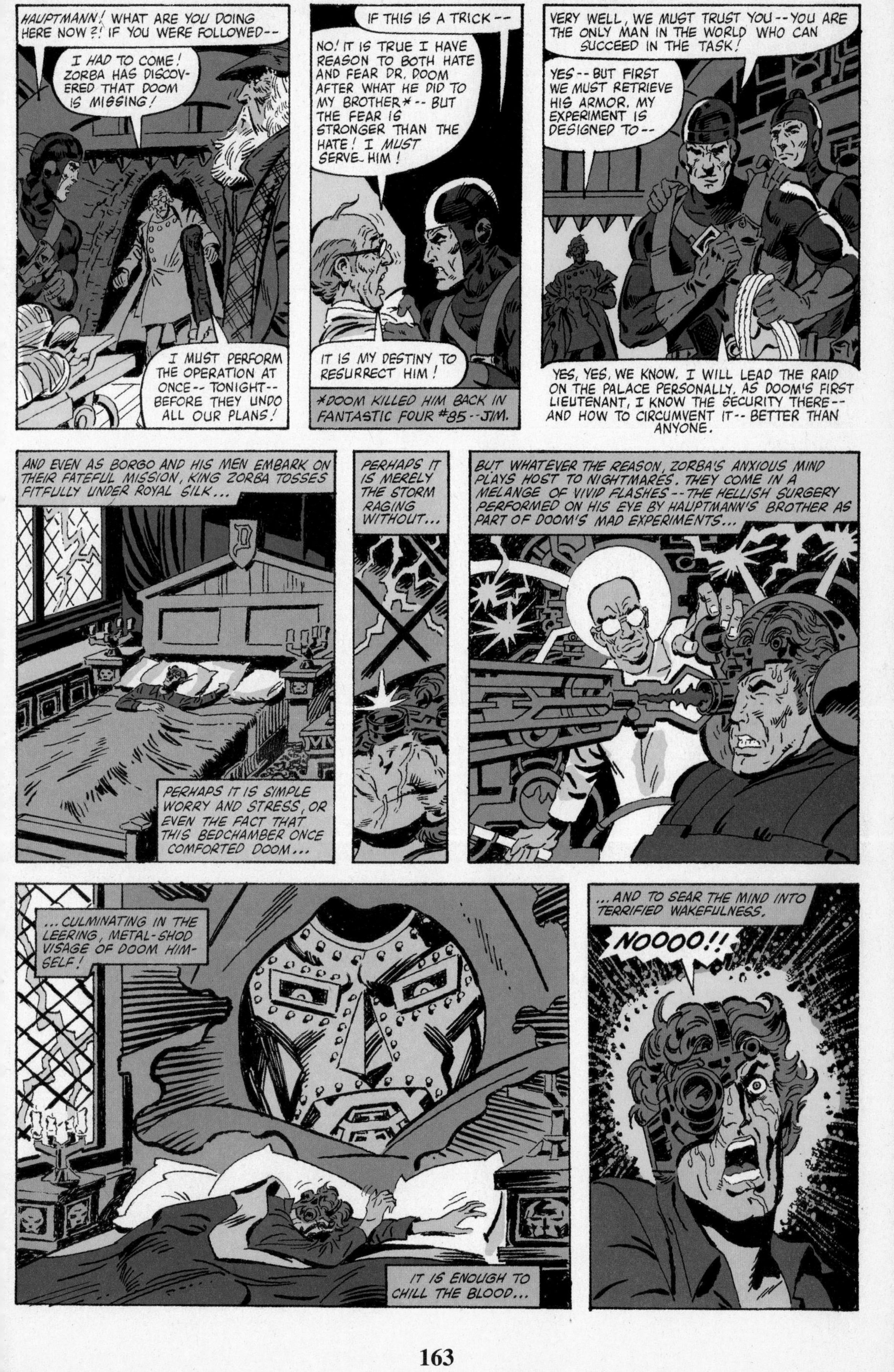
HAUPTMANN! WHAT ARE YOU DOING HERE NOW?! IF YOU WERE FOLLOWED--
I HAD TO COME! ZORBA HAS DISCOVERED THAT DOOM IS MISSING!
I MUST PERFORM THE OPERATION AT ONCE-- TONIGHT-- BEFORE THEY UNDO ALL OUR PLANS!
IF THIS IS A TRICK--
NO! IT IS TRUE I HAVE REASON TO BOTH HATE AND FEAR DR. DOOM AFTER WHAT HE DID TO MY BROTHER*-- BUT THE FEAR IS STRONGER THAN THE HATE! I MUST SERVE HIM!
IT IS MY DESTINY TO RESURRECT HIM!
*DOOM KILLED HIM BACK IN FANTASTIC FOUR #85--JIM.
VERY WELL, WE MUST TRUST YOU--YOU ARE THE ONLY MAN IN THE WORLD WHO CAN SUCCEED IN THE TASK!
YES--BUT FIRST WE MUST RETRIEVE HIS ARMOR. MY EXPERIMENT IS DESIGNED TO--
YES, YES, WE KNOW. I WILL LEAD THE RAID ON THE PALACE PERSONALLY. AS DOOM'S FIRST LIEUTENANT, I KNOW THE SECURITY THERE-- AND HOW TO CIRCUMVENT IT-- BETTER THAN ANYONE.
AND EVEN AS BORGO AND HIS MEN EMBARK ON THEIR FATEFUL MISSION, KING ZORBA TOSSES FITFULLY UNDER ROYAL SILK...
PERHAPS IT IS SIMPLE WORRY AND STRESS, OR EVEN THE FACT THAT THIS BEDCHAMBER ONCE COMFORTED DOOM...
PERHAPS IT IS MERELY THE STORM RAGING WITHOUT...
BUT WHATEVER THE REASON, ZORBA'S ANXIOUS MIND PLAYS HOST TO NIGHTMARES. THEY COME IN A MELANGE OF VIVID FLASHES--THE HELLISH SURGERY PERFORMED ON HIS EYE BY HAUPTMANN'S BROTHER AS PART OF DOOM'S MAD EXPERIMENTS...
...CULMINATING IN THE LEERING, METAL-SHOD VISAGE OF DOOM HIMSELF!
IT IS ENOUGH TO CHILL THE BLOOD...
...AND TO SEAR THE MIND INTO TERRIFIED WAKEFULNESS.
NOOOO!!

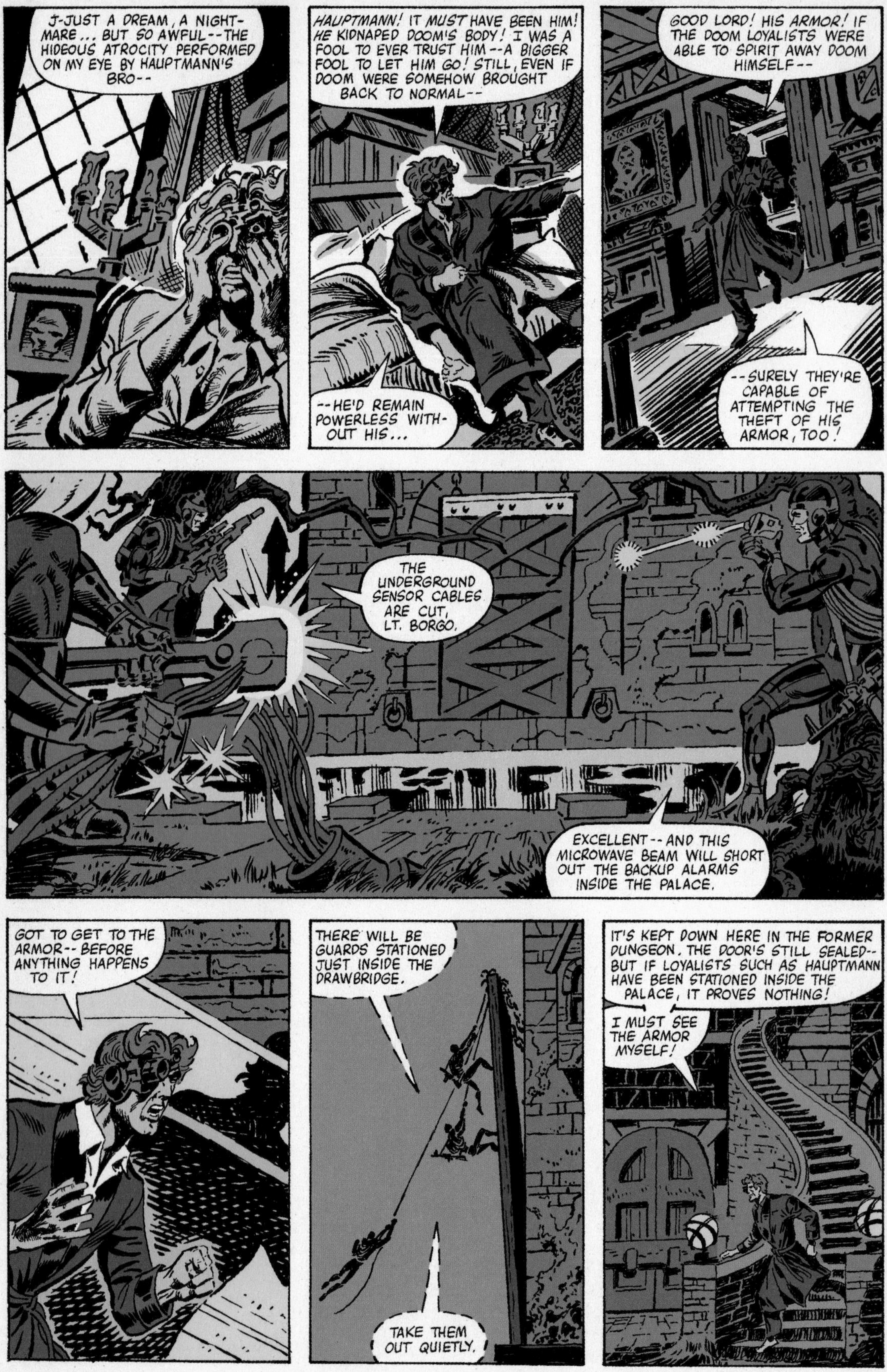
J-JUST A DREAM, A NIGHTMARE... BUT SO AWFUL--THE HIDEOUS ATROCITY PERFORMED ON MY EYE BY HAUPTMANN'S BRO--
HAUPTMANN! IT MUST HAVE BEEN HIM! HE KIDNAPED DOOM'S BODY! I WAS A FOOL TO EVER TRUST HIM--A BIGGER FOOL TO LET HIM GO! STILL, EVEN IF DOOM WERE SOMEHOW BROUGHT BACK TO NORMAL--
--HE'D REMAIN POWERLESS WITHOUT HIS...
GOOD LORD! HIS ARMOR! IF THE DOOM LOYALISTS WERE ABLE TO SPIRIT AWAY DOOM HIMSELF--
--SURELY THEY'RE CAPABLE OF ATTEMPTING THE THEFT OF HIS ARMOR, TOO!
THE UNDERGROUND SENSOR CABLES ARE CUT, LT. BORGO.
EXCELLENT--AND THIS MICROWAVE BEAM WILL SHORT OUT THE BACKUP ALARMS INSIDE THE PALACE.
GOT TO GET TO THE ARMOR--BEFORE ANYTHING HAPPENS TO IT!
THERE WILL BE GUARDS STATIONED JUST INSIDE THE DRAWBRIDGE.
TAKE THEM OUT QUIETLY.
IT'S KEPT DOWN HERE IN THE FORMER DUNGEON. THE DOOR'S STILL SEALED--BUT IF LOYALISTS SUCH AS HAUPTMANN HAVE BEEN STATIONED INSIDE THE PALACE, IT PROVES NOTHING!
I MUST SEE THE ARMOR MYSELF!

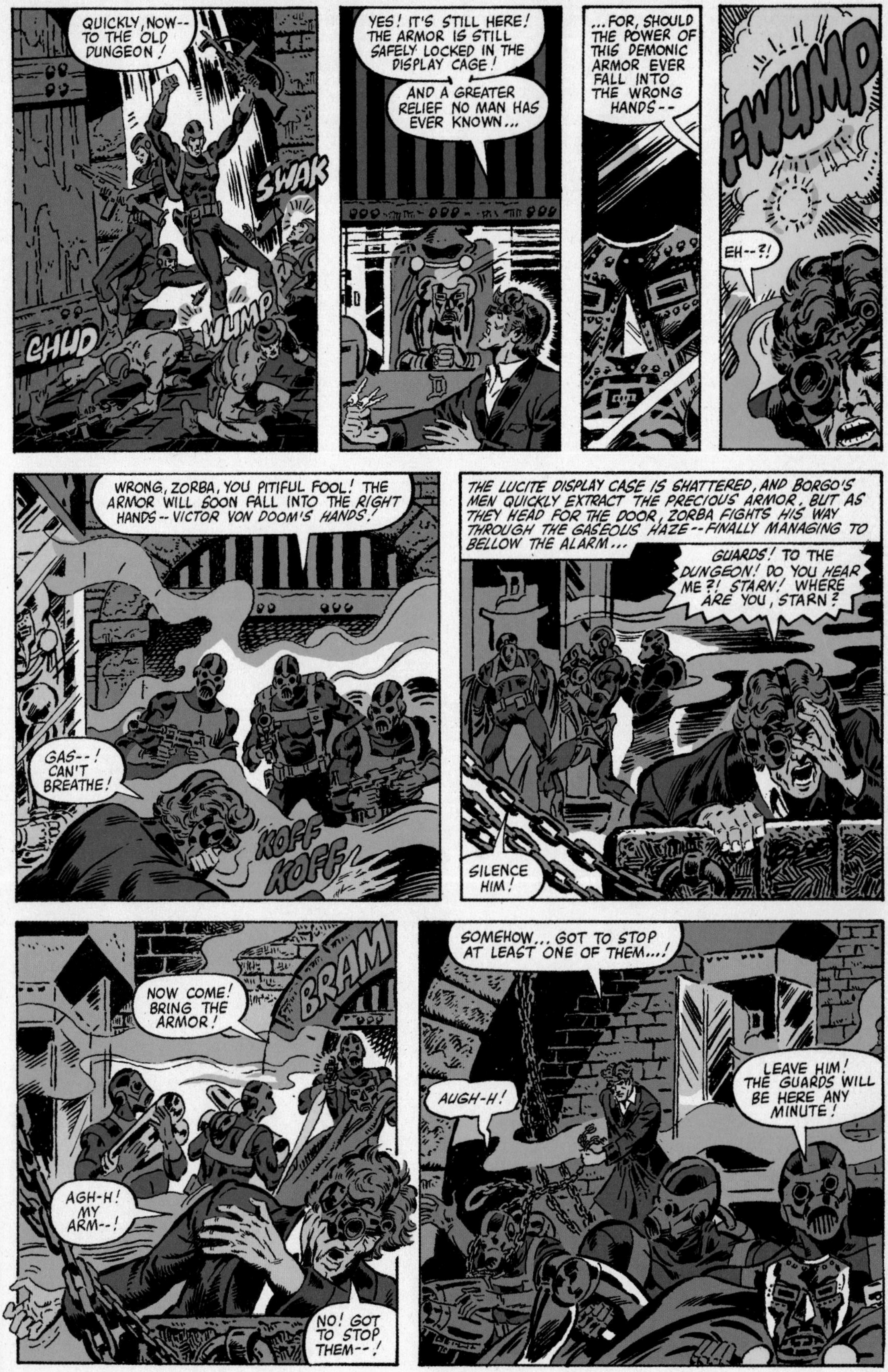
QUICKLY, NOW-- TO THE OLD DUNGEON!
SWAK
CHUD
WUMP
YES! IT'S STILL HERE! THE ARMOR IS STILL SAFELY LOCKED IN THE DISPLAY CAGE!
AND A GREATER RELIEF NO MAN HAS EVER KNOWN...
...FOR, SHOULD THE POWER OF THIS DEMONIC ARMOR EVER FALL INTO THE WRONG HANDS--
FWUMP
EH--?!
WRONG, ZORBA, YOU PITIFUL FOOL! THE ARMOR WILL SOON FALL INTO THE RIGHT HANDS--VICTOR VON DOOM'S HANDS!
GAS--! CAN'T BREATHE!
KOFF KOFF
THE LUCITE DISPLAY CASE IS SHATTERED, AND BORGO'S MEN QUICKLY EXTRACT THE PRECIOUS ARMOR. BUT AS THEY HEAD FOR THE DOOR, ZORBA FIGHTS HIS WAY THROUGH THE GASEOUS HAZE--FINALLY MANAGING TO BELLOW THE ALARM...
GUARDS! TO THE DUNGEON! DO YOU HEAR ME?! STARN! WHERE ARE YOU, STARN?
SILENCE HIM!
BRAM
NOW COME! BRING THE ARMOR!
AGH-H! MY ARM--!
NO! GOT TO STOP THEM--!
SOMEHOW... GOT TO STOP AT LEAST ONE OF THEM...!
AUGH-H!
LEAVE HIM! THE GUARDS WILL BE HERE ANY MINUTE!

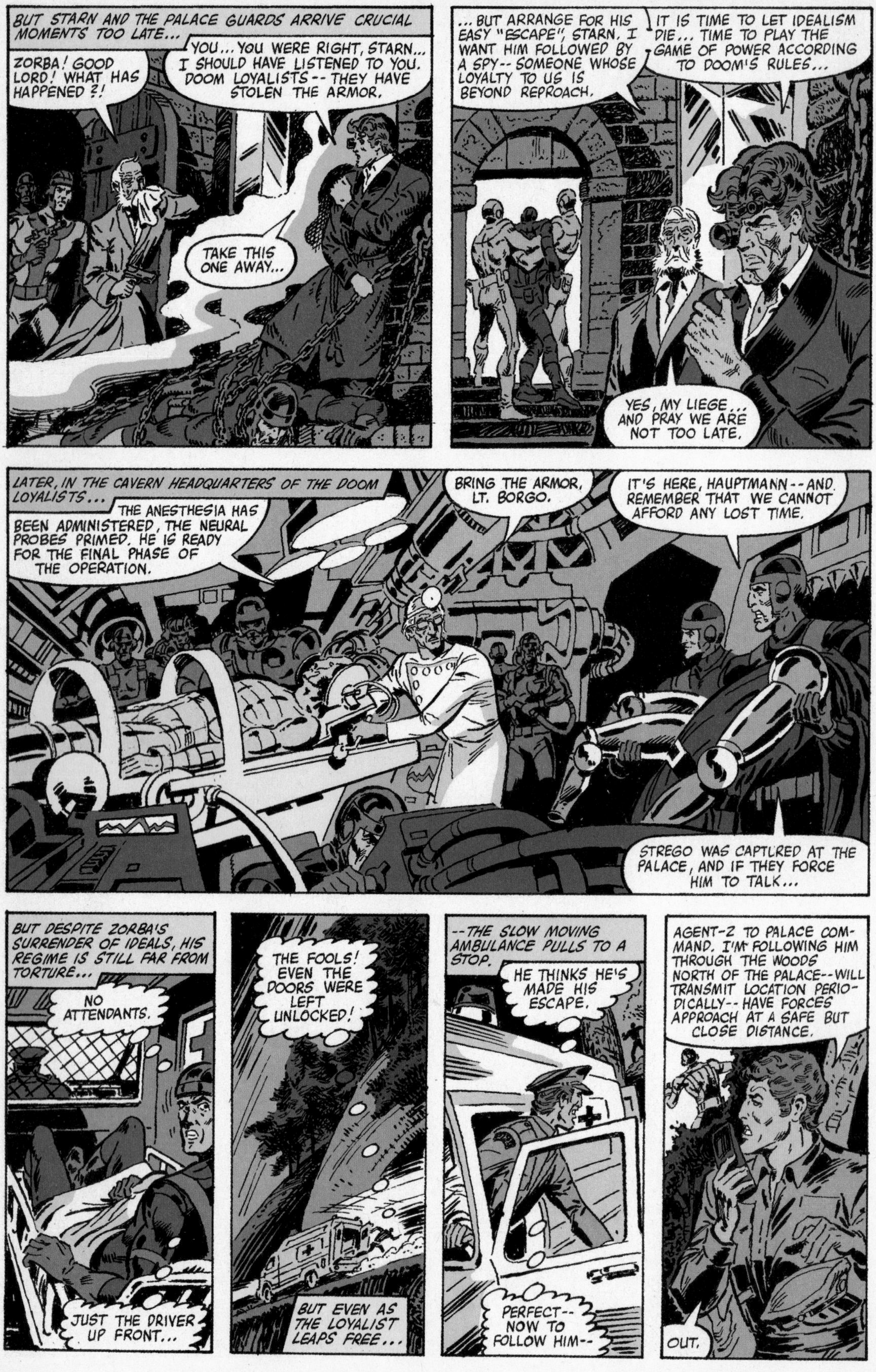
BUT STARN AND THE PALACE GUARDS ARRIVE CRUCIAL MOMENTS TOO LATE...
ZORBA! GOOD LORD! WHAT HAS HAPPENED?!
YOU...YOU WERE RIGHT, STARN... I SHOULD HAVE LISTENED TO YOU. DOOM LOYALISTS--THEY HAVE STOLEN THE ARMOR.
TAKE THIS ONE AWAY...
...BUT ARRANGE FOR HIS EASY "ESCAPE", STARN. I WANT HIM FOLLOWED BY A SPY--SOMEONE WHOSE LOYALTY TO US IS BEYOND REPROACH.
IT IS TIME TO LET IDEALISM DIE... TIME TO PLAY THE GAME OF POWER ACCORDING TO DOOM'S RULES...
YES, MY LIEGE... AND PRAY WE ARE NOT TOO LATE.
LATER, IN THE CAVERN HEADQUARTERS OF THE DOOM LOYALISTS...
THE ANESTHESIA HAS BEEN ADMINISTERED, THE NEURAL PROBES PRIMED. HE IS READY FOR THE FINAL PHASE OF THE OPERATION.
BRING THE ARMOR, LT. BORGO.
IT'S HERE, HAUPTMANN--AND REMEMBER THAT WE CANNOT AFFORD ANY LOST TIME.
STREGO WAS CAPTURED AT THE PALACE, AND IF THEY FORCE HIM TO TALK...
BUT DESPITE ZORBA'S SURRENDER OF IDEALS, HIS REGIME IS STILL FAR FROM TORTURE...
NO ATTENDANTS.
JUST THE DRIVER UP FRONT...
THE FOOLS! EVEN THE DOORS WERE LEFT UNLOCKED!
BUT EVEN AS THE LOYALIST LEAPS FREE...
--THE SLOW MOVING AMBULANCE PULLS TO A STOP.
HE THINKS HE'S MADE HIS ESCAPE.
PERFECT--NOW TO FOLLOW HIM--
AGENT-Z TO PALACE COMMAND. I'M FOLLOWING HIM THROUGH THE WOODS NORTH OF THE PALACE--WILL TRANSMIT LOCATION PERIODICALLY--HAVE FORCES APPROACH AT A SAFE BUT CLOSE DISTANCE.
OUT.

THE BODY IS STILL IMMOBILE, STILL HELPLESS, BUT-- NOW SHEATHED IN THE DREAD ARMOR-- ONE CAN ALMOST FEEL THE LIMITLESS POWER WAITING TO BE AWAKENED...

IF YOU FAIL, HAUPTMANN, I SHALL CRUSH THE VERY LIFE FROM YOUR BONES WITH MY OWN--

THERE IS NO CHANCE OF FAILURE, LT. BORGO. AFTER ALL, DID I NOT LEARN THIS TECHNIQUE FROM DR. DOOM HIMSELF?

ACTIVATE THE GENERATOR.

YES, DR. HAUPTMANN-- ACTIVATING NOW!

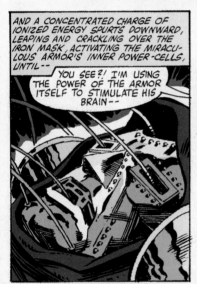

AND A CONCENTRATED CHARGE OF IONIZED ENERGY SPURTS DOWNWARD, LEAPING AND CRACKLING OVER THE IRON MASK, ACTIVATING THE MIRACULOUS ARMOR'S INNER POWER-CELLS, UNTIL--

YOU SEE?! I'M USING THE POWER OF THE ARMOR ITSELF TO STIMULATE HIS BRAIN--

--TO REAWAKEN THE DORMANT LIFE WITHIN HIM! AND IT'S WORKING! HIS IRON FIST IS TREMBLING--!

HE'S ALIVE! THE OPERATION IS A SUCCESS!

OUTSIDE... AGENT-Z TO PALACE COMMAND, WE'VE GOT THEM! HE'S ENTERING A CAVERN IN VICTORUM MOUNTAIN!

BRING YOUR FORCES IN AT ONCE!

WHERE?! WHERE AM I?! WHAT HAS BEEN DONE TO ME?!

YOU... YOU'RE SAFE, MY LIEGE... WITH FRIENDS! I... I HAVE USED THE POWER OF YOUR MASK... YOUR ARMOR... TO BREAK THROUGH THE BARRIER IN YOUR MIND!

HAUPTMANN? YES-- OF COURSE! I REMEMBER NOW-- REED RICHARDS THOUGHT HE COULD DEFEAT ME-- AND ZORBA THOUGHT HE COULD USURP MY THRONE!

BUT THEY WERE WRONG-- ALL WRONG! VICTOR VON DOOM HAS RISEN IN TRIUMPH!

167

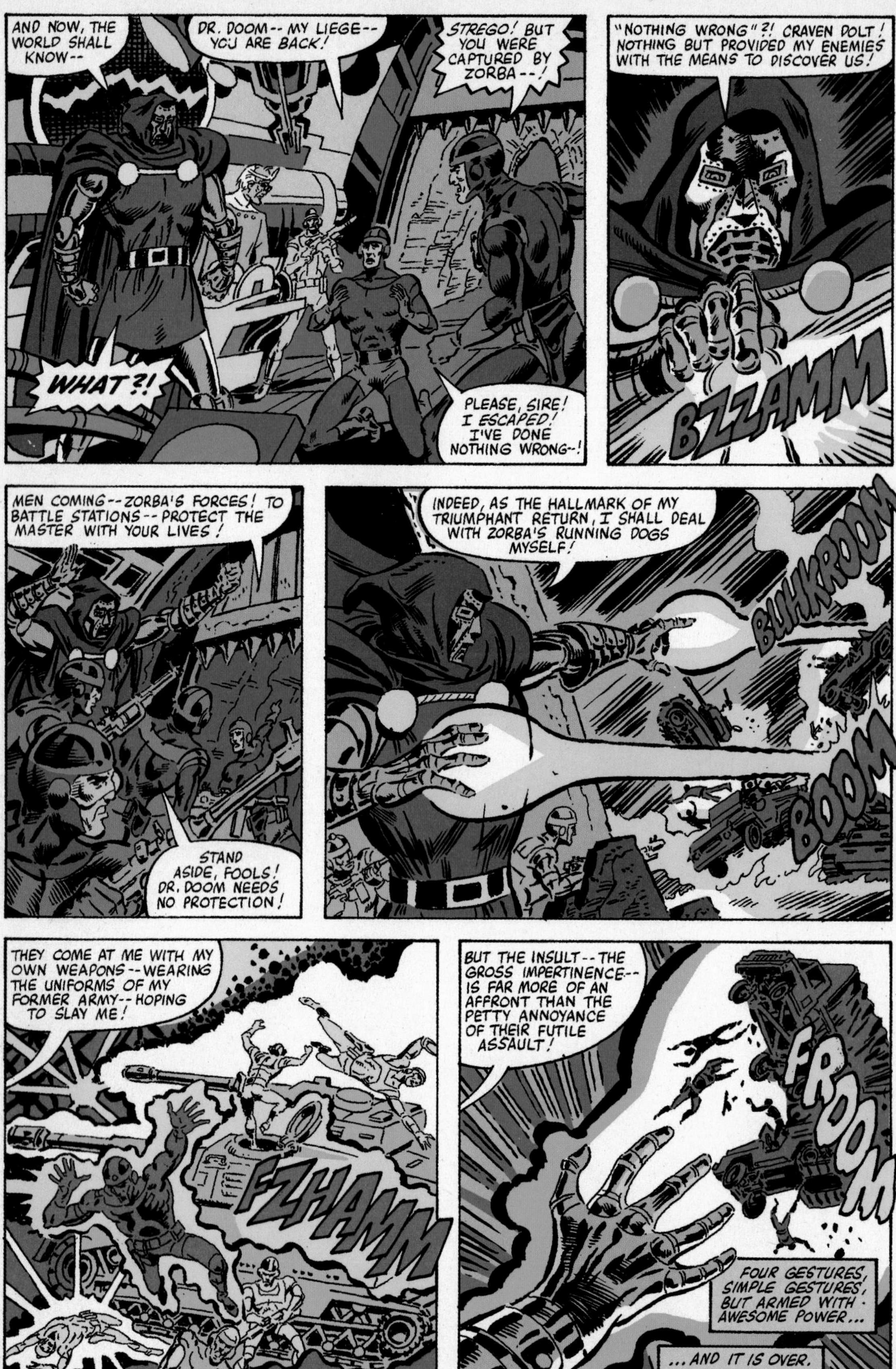
AND NOW, THE WORLD SHALL KNOW--
DR. DOOM-- MY LIEGE-- YOU ARE BACK!
STREGO! BUT YOU WERE CAPTURED BY ZORBA--!
WHAT?!
PLEASE, SIRE! I ESCAPED! I'VE DONE NOTHING WRONG--!
"NOTHING WRONG"?! CRAVEN DOLT! NOTHING BUT PROVIDED MY ENEMIES WITH THE MEANS TO DISCOVER US!
BZZAMM
MEN COMING--ZORBA'S FORCES! TO BATTLE STATIONS--PROTECT THE MASTER WITH YOUR LIVES!
STAND ASIDE, FOOLS! DR. DOOM NEEDS NO PROTECTION!
INDEED, AS THE HALLMARK OF MY TRIUMPHANT RETURN, I SHALL DEAL WITH ZORBA'S RUNNING DOGS MYSELF!
BUHKROOM
BOOM
THEY COME AT ME WITH MY OWN WEAPONS--WEARING THE UNIFORMS OF MY FORMER ARMY--HOPING TO SLAY ME!
FZHAMM
BUT THE INSULT--THE GROSS IMPERTINENCE--IS FAR MORE OF AN AFFRONT THAN THE PETTY ANNOYANCE OF THEIR FUTILE ASSAULT!
FROOM
FOUR GESTURES, SIMPLE GESTURES, BUT ARMED WITH AWESOME POWER...
...AND IT IS OVER.

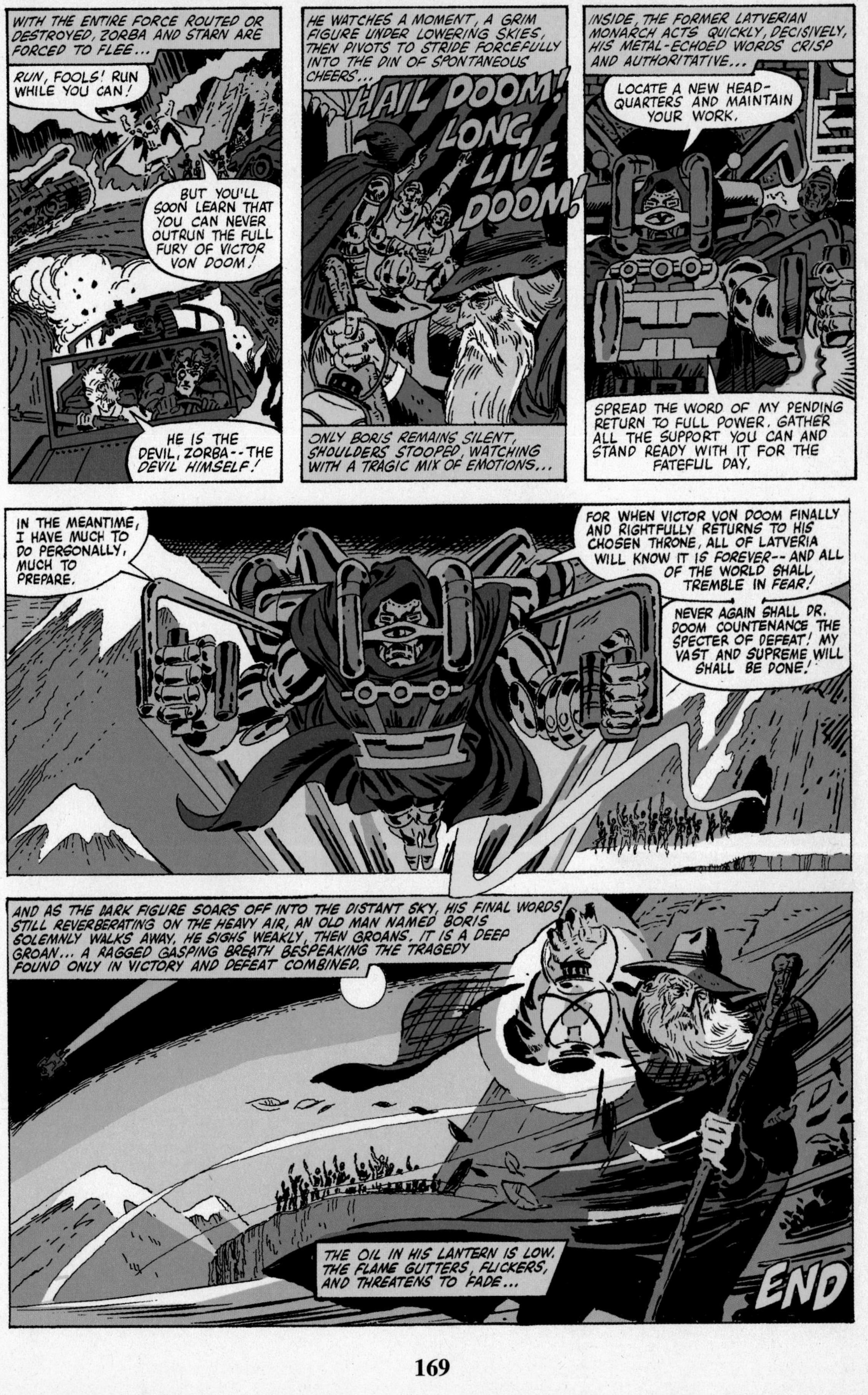

WITH THE ENTIRE FORCE ROUTED OR DESTROYED, ZORBA AND STARN ARE FORCED TO FLEE...
RUN, FOOLS! RUN WHILE YOU CAN!
BUT YOU'LL SOON LEARN THAT YOU CAN NEVER OUTRUN THE FULL FURY OF VICTOR VON DOOM!
HE IS THE DEVIL, ZORBA--THE DEVIL HIMSELF!
HE WATCHES A MOMENT, A GRIM FIGURE UNDER LOWERING SKIES, THEN PIVOTS TO STRIDE FORCEFULLY INTO THE DIN OF SPONTANEOUS CHEERS...
HAIL DOOM! LONG LIVE DOOM!
ONLY BORIS REMAINS SILENT, SHOULDERS STOOPED, WATCHING WITH A TRAGIC MIX OF EMOTIONS...
INSIDE, THE FORMER LATVERIAN MONARCH ACTS QUICKLY, DECISIVELY, HIS METAL-ECHOED WORDS CRISP AND AUTHORITATIVE...
LOCATE A NEW HEAD-QUARTERS AND MAINTAIN YOUR WORK.
SPREAD THE WORD OF MY PENDING RETURN TO FULL POWER. GATHER ALL THE SUPPORT YOU CAN AND STAND READY WITH IT FOR THE FATEFUL DAY.
IN THE MEANTIME, I HAVE MUCH TO DO PERSONALLY, MUCH TO PREPARE.
FOR WHEN VICTOR VON DOOM FINALLY AND RIGHTFULLY RETURNS TO HIS CHOSEN THRONE, ALL OF LATVERIA WILL KNOW IT IS FOREVER--AND ALL OF THE WORLD SHALL TREMBLE IN FEAR!
NEVER AGAIN SHALL DR. DOOM COUNTENANCE THE SPECTER OF DEFEAT! MY VAST AND SUPREME WILL SHALL BE DONE!
AND AS THE DARK FIGURE SOARS OFF INTO THE DISTANT SKY, HIS FINAL WORDS STILL REVERBERATING ON THE HEAVY AIR, AN OLD MAN NAMED BORIS SOLEMNLY WALKS AWAY. HE SIGHS WEAKLY, THEN GROANS. IT IS A DEEP GROAN... A RAGGED GASPING BREATH BESPEAKING THE TRAGEDY FOUND ONLY IN VICTORY AND DEFEAT COMBINED.
THE OIL IN HIS LANTERN IS LOW. THE FLAME GUTTERS, FLICKERS, AND THREATENS TO FADE...
END

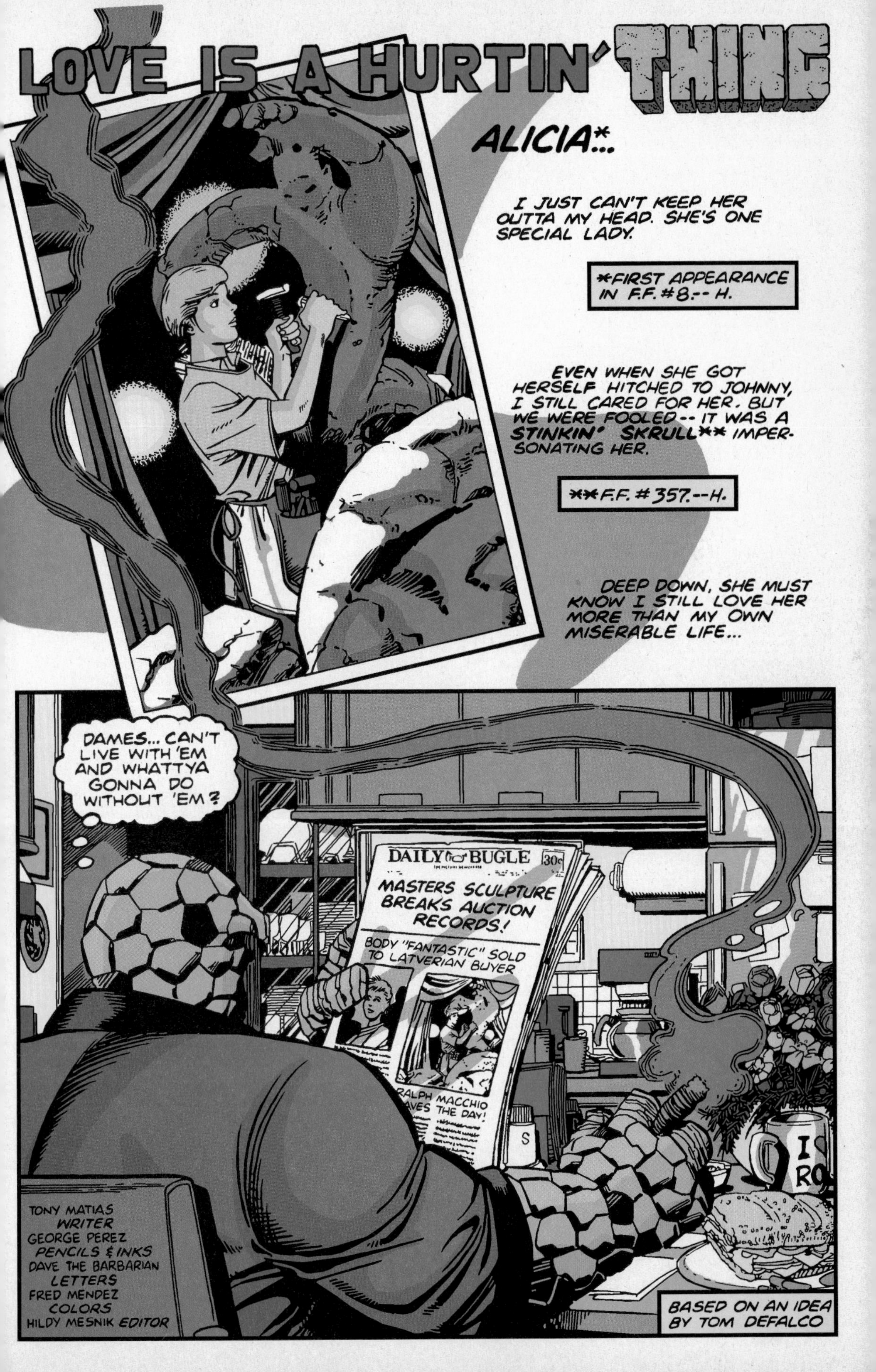

LOVE IS A HURTIN' THING
ALICIA*...
I JUST CAN'T KEEP HER OUTTA MY HEAD. SHE'S ONE SPECIAL LADY.
*FIRST APPEARANCE IN F.F. #8.-- H.
EVEN WHEN SHE GOT HERSELF HITCHED TO JOHNNY, I STILL CARED FOR HER. BUT WE WERE FOOLED -- IT WAS A STINKIN' SKRULL** IMPERSONATING HER.
**F.F. #357.--H.
DEEP DOWN, SHE MUST KNOW I STILL LOVE HER MORE THAN MY OWN MISERABLE LIFE...
DAMES... CAN'T LIVE WITH 'EM AND WHATTYA GONNA DO WITHOUT 'EM?
DAILY BUGLE
30¢
MASTERS SCULPTURE BREAKS AUCTION RECORDS!
BODY "FANTASTIC" SOLD TO LATVERIAN BUYER
RALPH MACCHIO SAVES THE DAY!
TONY MATIAS WRITER
GEORGE PEREZ PENCILS & INKS
DAVE THE BARBARIAN LETTERS
FRED MENDEZ COLORS
HILDY MESNIK EDITOR
BASED ON AN IDEA BY TOM DEFALCO

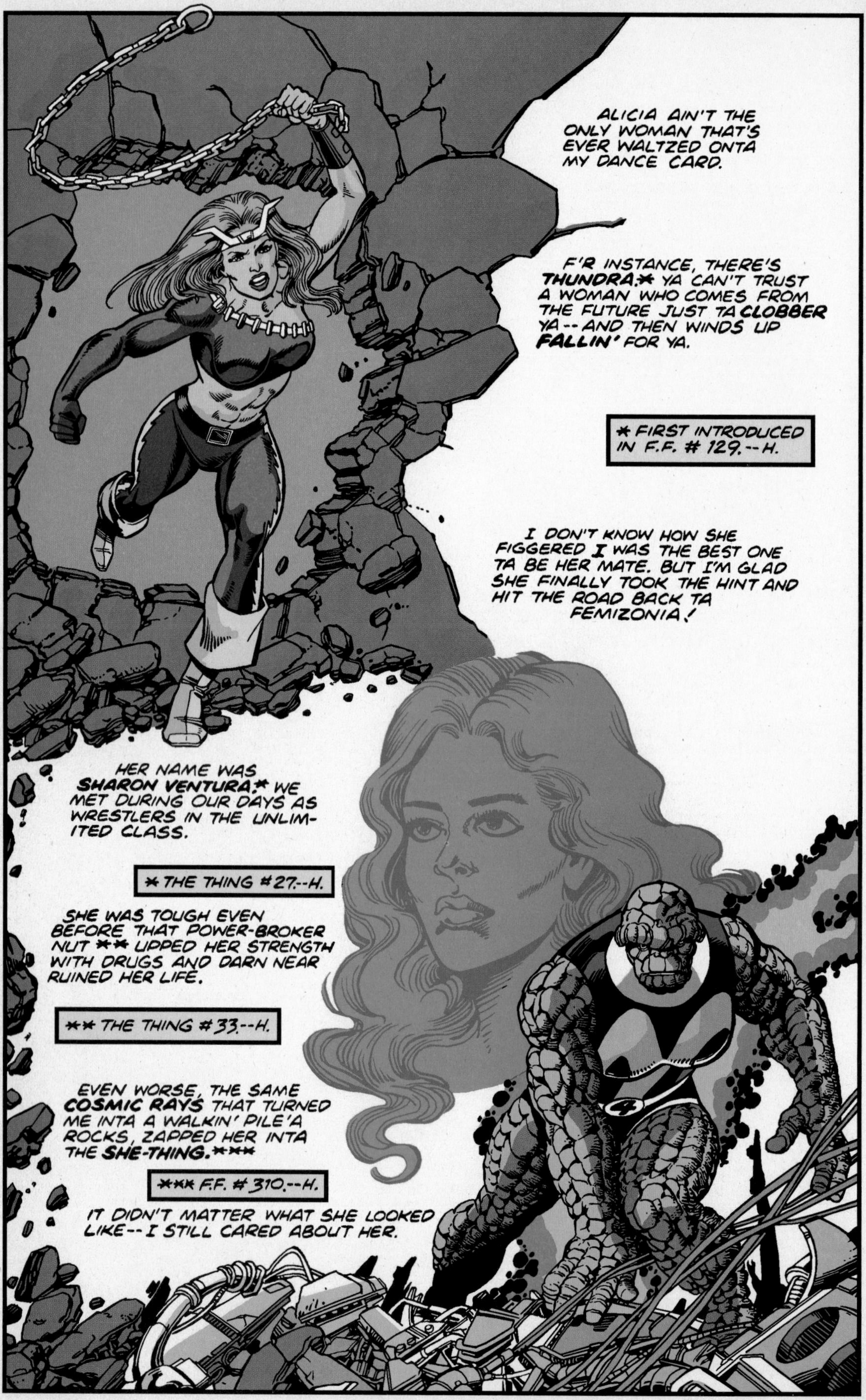
ALICIA AIN'T THE ONLY WOMAN THAT'S EVER WALTZED ONTA MY DANCE CARD.
F'R INSTANCE, THERE'S THUNDRA.* YA CAN'T TRUST A WOMAN WHO COMES FROM THE FUTURE JUST TA CLOBBER YA -- AND THEN WINDS UP FALLIN' FOR YA.
* FIRST INTRODUCED IN F.F. # 129.--H.
I DON'T KNOW HOW SHE FIGGERED I WAS THE BEST ONE TA BE HER MATE. BUT I'M GLAD SHE FINALLY TOOK THE HINT AND HIT THE ROAD BACK TA FEMIZONIA!
HER NAME WAS SHARON VENTURA.* WE MET DURING OUR DAYS AS WRESTLERS IN THE UNLIMITED CLASS.
* THE THING # 27.--H.
SHE WAS TOUGH EVEN BEFORE THAT POWER-BROKER NUT ** UPPED HER STRENGTH WITH DRUGS AND DARN NEAR RUINED HER LIFE.
** THE THING # 33.--H.
EVEN WORSE, THE SAME COSMIC RAYS THAT TURNED ME INTA A WALKIN' PILE'A ROCKS, ZAPPED HER INTA THE SHE-THING.***
*** F.F. # 310.--H.
IT DIDN'T MATTER WHAT SHE LOOKED LIKE-- I STILL CARED ABOUT HER.

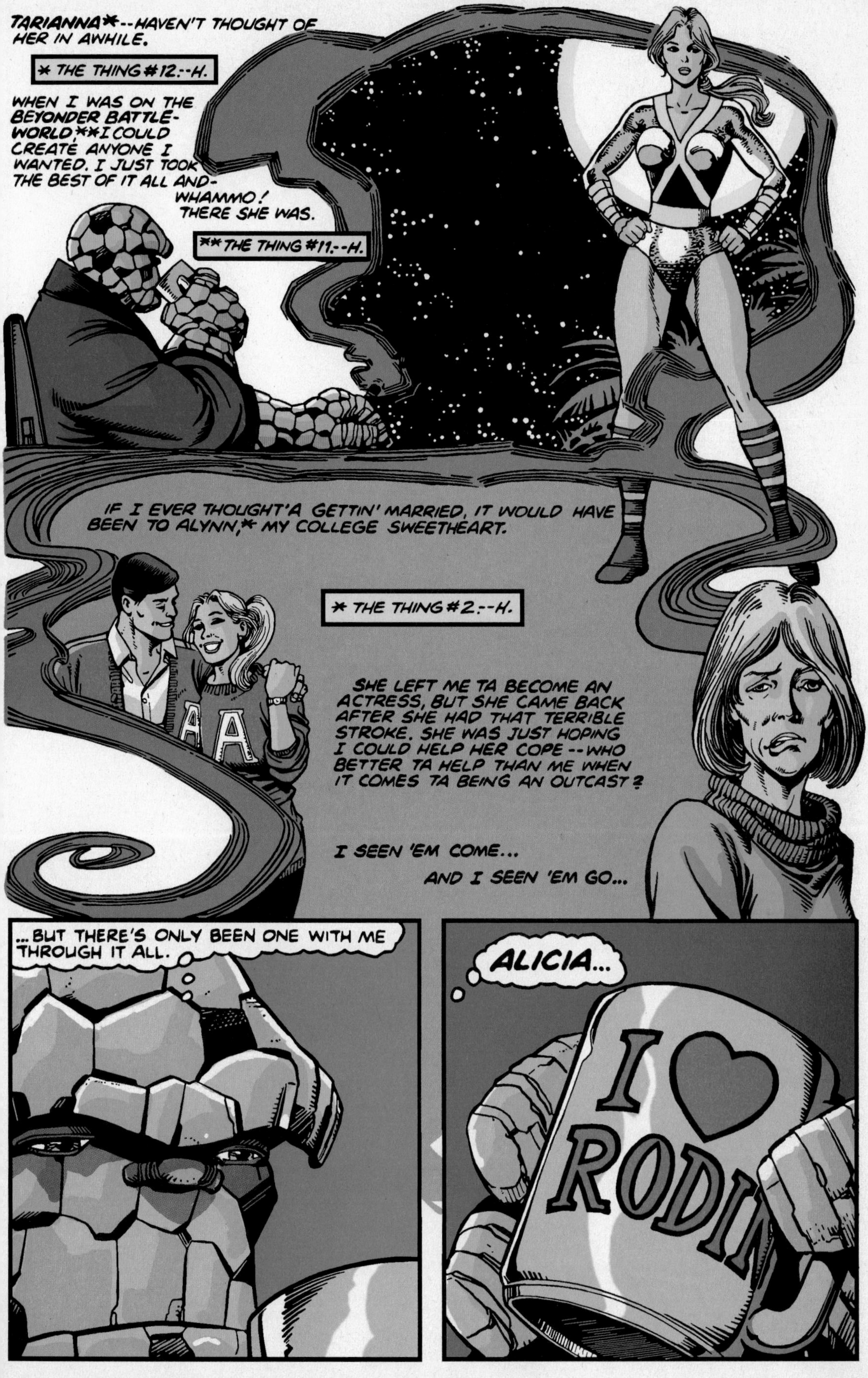
TARIANNA*--HAVEN'T THOUGHT OF HER IN AWHILE.
* THE THING #12.--H.
WHEN I WAS ON THE BEYONDER BATTLE-WORLD,** I COULD CREATE ANYONE I WANTED. I JUST TOOK THE BEST OF IT ALL AND-- WHAMMO! THERE SHE WAS.
** THE THING #11.--H.
IF I EVER THOUGHT'A GETTIN' MARRIED, IT WOULD HAVE BEEN TO ALYNN,* MY COLLEGE SWEETHEART.
* THE THING #2.--H.
SHE LEFT ME TA BECOME AN ACTRESS, BUT SHE CAME BACK AFTER SHE HAD THAT TERRIBLE STROKE. SHE WAS JUST HOPING I COULD HELP HER COPE -- WHO BETTER TA HELP THAN ME WHEN IT COMES TA BEING AN OUTCAST?
I SEEN 'EM COME...
AND I SEEN 'EM GO...
...BUT THERE'S ONLY BEEN ONE WITH ME THROUGH IT ALL.
ALICIA...
I ♥ RODIN

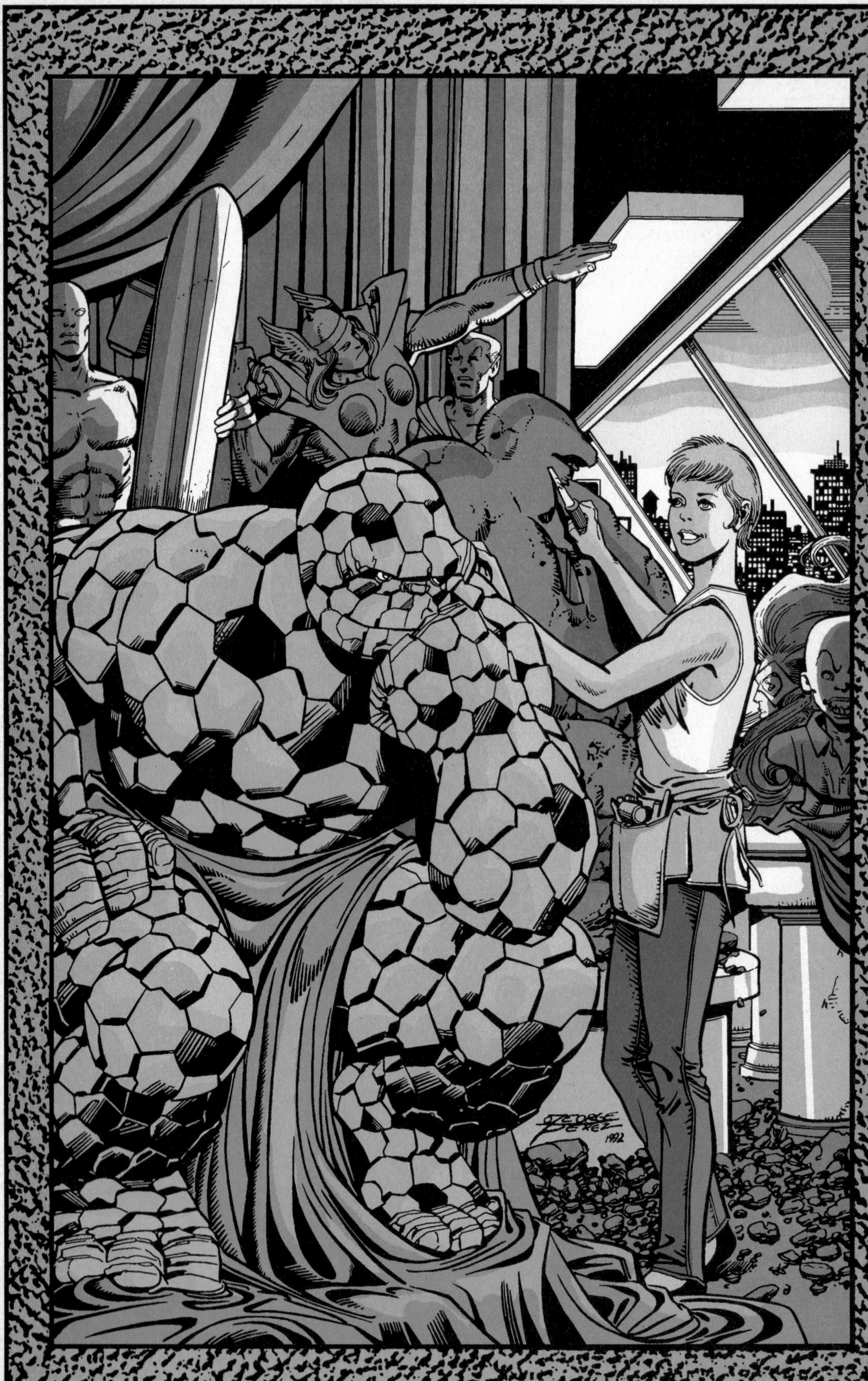
GEORGE PEREZ
1992

Melissa Public Library
Melissa, Texas